# VERDI AND/OR WAGNER

Peter Conrad

OR

AGNER

*Worlds, Two Centuries*

color

son

*On the jacket*: (left) portrait of Verdi, woodcut after a photograph, 1893; (right) portrait of Wagner, engraving by Veit Froer, 1883, after a photograph of *c.* 1871.

*Frontispiece*: (left) Verdi caricatured by 'Ape', published in *Vanity Fair*, London, 15 February 1879; (right) Wagner caricatured by 'Spy', published in *Vanity Fair*, 19 May 1877.

First published in 2011 in hardcover in the United States of America by Thames & Hudson Inc., 500 Fifth Avenue, New York, New York 10110

thamesandhudsonusa.com

Library of Congress Catalog Card Number 2011922634

ISBN 978-0-500-51593-8

Printed and bound in China by Toppan Leefung Printing Ltd

# CONTENTS

# 1 | *Counterparts*

## STAND-OFF IN A GARDEN

This is surely as close as they ever got to each other: they stand, with a buffer zone of lawn between them, in a garden at the edge of Venice beyond the Arsenal, where the floating city begins to trail off into the lagoon. Despite their proximity, each pretends to be alone. A path relegates them to separate patches of grass; one of them hides in the shrubbery, while the other, asserting his right of occupancy, stands on a slope and stares across the water. Their memorials are modest enough, since they are not the kind of men who rear on bronze horses or balance atop columns like conquerors. Reduced to heads, they are set on pedestals that state their names. The one who skulks in the bushes is Giuseppe Verdi. The other – his jaw set at a confrontational angle like a mountain ledge as he scans the horizon for detractors, or perhaps for devotees on pilgrimage to his shrine – is Richard Wagner.

So comparable but so incompatible, they were born in the same year – Wagner on 22 May 1813 in Leipzig, Verdi on 10 October 1813 in Le Roncole near Busseto in the Duchy of Parma. For official purposes Wagner's father was a clerk in the police service, although Richard may have been the son of a Jewish actor called Ludwig Geyer whom his mother, widowed when the boy was six months old, soon married. Verdi's background was less shadowy, though not quite as humble as he liked to claim when calling himself a rough-hewn peasant: his father kept an inn that doubled as a village grocery.

As their busts testify, Verdi and Wagner were both cultural heroes, but of different kinds – a native son attached to the soil versus a wandering exile; a tribune of the people versus a dictatorial aesthete; a man of progress versus an atavistic myth-maker; a spokesman for afflicted humanity versus a creator of gods, giants, dragons, dwarfs and fairies. Like saviours, both composers appeared as if in answer to a prayer. When Verdi's first opera, *Oberto*, was performed at La Scala in November 1839, a critic remarked that the audience's grateful, almost worshipful reaction meant 'We have a Messiah.' A less enthusiastic reviewer in Leipzig in 1845 complained that Wagner was being touted as 'the Messiah of opera'. By the end of their lives they had turned into incarnations of their times, the Zeitgeist made flesh. All of Italy grieved when Verdi died on 27 January 1901, and the government decreed a period of mourning longer than that awarded to a monarch. The Italian parliament devoted a session to eulogizing him, during which one of the deputies justly claimed that Verdi was more than a man of the nineteenth century: he personified the century, which lived in and through him. Wagner, however, did not wait for others to promote him posthumously to the role of legislator for the age. He knew, he said, that his purpose was 'to tell the century all that we have to say to it!'

Despite their affinities, Verdi and Wagner spent the best part of the nineteenth century managing not to meet, and since the early twentieth century they have stood in the Venetian garden at a diplomatic distance, not quite turning their backs on each other but also stubbornly declining to reach an accord. The differences were personal, and the busts, for all their second-hand crudity, hint at that. In his shelter of leaves, Verdi craves anonymity: he despised publicity, shunned high society, and prematurely retreated from the cities where his operas were performed to live like a farmer on his estate at Sant'Agata near Busseto. Across the way, Wagner on his small eminence confronts the world rather than withdrawing from it. He is a candidate for a hero's life, prepared for struggle and intent on prevailing, proud of his isolation. The planes of Wagner's clean-shaven face were already sculptural before anyone attempted to carve them in marble, but Verdi is less sleek and smooth, and his bust gives him the fringe of beard he always wore – another defence, like the encroaching leaves of his impromptu bower, against being seen and evaluated. Wagner has no arms: the brain in that armoured skull can apparently dispense with appendages. Verdi, however, is allowed the use of his right arm, which grips a roll of music paper against his chest. His hand makes a stout, dependable gesture of faith, like an American pledging allegiance to shared verities. One man is portrayed as a frowning mind, the other as a more sensitive being who translates emotions into song as if the heart's affections had been directly transmitted – in crotchets and quavers that stand for spasms and palpitations – to the page he holds.

The pedestal that props up Wagner's self-sufficient head has a squashier interior, a metaphorical recess of punctured flesh and spilt blood. On the plinth, a pelican's scissory beak rends its breast to feed its jostling offspring, which pick at the exposed entrails. Ezra Pound, walking in the gardens near the end of his life, was asked by his minder what the low-relief medallion meant. 'Toujours les tripes,' he said: a vile daily diet of offal. In fact the self-rending bird is a religious icon, traditionally an emblem of Christ's sacrifice for the sake of fallen mankind. Profanely reinterpreted here, it suggests the source on which Wagner drew for his last opera: 'Was ist die Wunde' asks the stricken Amfortas in *Parsifal*, wracked by what he calls a delicious pain, or 'seligsten Genusses Schmerz'. The lesion is music, and it can only be healed by the touch of the spear that tore the gash in his body: the addict's relief is a renewed dose. The icon suggests that Wagner made music by playing upon his overtaxed senses – an experiment in intensification that helped provoke the cardiac emergencies that finally killed him in Venice in 1883. The French poet Catulle Mendès, who visited him in Lucerne in 1869, said that Wagner's small body trembled with excitement from head to toe, like a violin string plucked pizzicato. Verdi by contrast had the tough constitution of a countryman. During the 1840s, when he worked at a maddening pace to keep up with the commissions he received, he suffered repeated psychosomatic upsets, with stress unsettling his stomach and bowels or leaving him with a painful, scratchy throat. His heart, however, lasted him until 1901.

Friedrich Nietzsche thought Wagner 'the most enthusiastic mimomaniac … who ever existed', as hyper-emotional as a gesticulating opera singer. The undemonstrative Verdi had no interest in self-display, and the sentiments inscribed on the unrolling sheet of music held by the figure in the park are national not personal. The page is the chorus 'Va, pensiero' from *Nabucco*, sung by homesick Hebrew slaves in Babylon; in popular mythology, this lament turned into a yearning anthem for oppressed Italy. Wagner's bust portrays him as a self-tormenting egotist, whereas Verdi is shown to be the choirmaster for an entire country. Nor did his bequest to the nation end with his art. The only reason for loving (or hating) Wagner is his music, but Italians continue to honour Verdi's humane generosity as well as his genius. This was a man who built a hospital – which still functions – so that his tenant farmers and their families could receive immediate medical care on his estate; he intervened angrily when he learned that patients were served inferior food and the destitute made to pay for funerals. He also founded the Casa di Riposo in Milan, a rest home for impoverished musicians who had outlived their gifts, and endowed it with his royalties. When he died, Gabriele d'Annunzio tallied the nation's debt to him in an ode, making all Italians Verdi's grateful dependants. He nourished us, d'Annunzio claimed, like bread; his music was as vital as food, containing – as the poem says – all the sweet, rich savour of the earth.

The temperamental opposition between Verdi and Wagner was entrenched by geographical and cultural divisions. Theirs was a world still rooted in locality, suspiciously guarding its borders. When the hero in *Tannhäuser* makes his pilgrimage from Germany to Rome to seek a papal pardon, he travels through Italy with his eyes closed, not wanting to be distracted by the beauty of the landscape. Hedonistic enjoyment is for simple, pagan people; as a German, he prefers the more elevated calling of spiritual pain. Wagner did not share this abstinence, and in later life he fled to Italy during German winters, which is how he came to die in Venice. His son Siegfried even aligned his father's operas with the work of Italian Renaissance painters: *Lohengrin* reminded him of Raphael, *Tristan* of Titian, *Götterdämmerung* of Tintoretto. Verdi likewise ventured beyond his native ground in quest of operatic subjects and on several occasions set plays by Schiller, whose characters – the radical bandits in *I masnadieri*, the Oedipal prince in *Don Carlos* – have the reckless moral insurgency that German romantics admired. But during the Franco-Prussian War of 1870–71 he reverted to an ancient hostility and denounced the modern Germans as Huns, wreckers of civilization. In 1882 he protested against Italy's entry into the Triple Alliance with Germany and Austria-Hungary, insisting that the country's true ally was France.

Critics in the nineteenth century habitually contrasted sensual Italian song with the cerebral German symphony, claiming that Italians used music to express feeling, whereas for Germans it was a mode of thought. True to an inherited prejudice, Verdi pitied Wagner's lack of a lyricism that came naturally to musicians in southern climates, and said that Wagner had chosen a hard road because the easier one was not open to him. On his side of the Alps, Wagner had little regard for Verdi's melodic instinct. At work on *Parsifal*, he warned himself not to be 'led astray by the melodies': tunes were like sirens, beguiling the ear while they softened the brain. In 1863, writing to Mathilde Wesendonck about a concert tour, he sniffed at the musical diet of 'Verdi etc.' on which the Hungarians subsisted, and assumed that this explained their gratitude for his performances of his own music. In 1882 in Venice he heard a snatch of Verdi bellowed on the Grand Canal, probably by a gondolier, and scoffed at the fatuous sentiment of the unidentified aria and its mannered rhythm.

Although Verdi outlived Wagner by seventeen years, his last decades were soured by critical complaints that his own music had become Wagnerian. He reacted as indignantly as if he had been called a traitor. 'Fine result after 35 years of career,' he said in 1875, rejecting claims that he had dwindled into 'an imitator of Wagner!!!' Verdi was accused of abandoning the old Italian model of opera – where the plot was disposed of in recitative while the action intermittently paused for arias that vented ire or lust – and adopting the symphonic continuity of Wagner; now his orchestra challenged the dominion of singers who expected a more subdued, deferential accompaniment. The caricaturist Carl von Stur physically merged the two composers in a sketch published in the Viennese journal *Der Floh* in 1887. Otello, Desdemona and Falstaff look on from a corner while Verdi sails away in Lohengrin's swan-powered dinghy. He has borrowed Wagner's velvet smock and even wears his floppy beret, but bangs a drum and grinds a hurdy-gurdy as a sign that he has not quite managed to live down his bad Italian habits. The supposed change in Verdi's style earned him an admirer he would just as soon have done without. In 1892 the conductor Hans von Bülow – Cosima's first husband, who out of reverence for Wagner had pretended not to notice her adultery – sent him a message of contrition. Bülow explained his earlier hostility to Verdi as the bigotry of an 'ultra-Wagnerian' fanatic, and said how much he admired *Aida* and *Otello*. Unfortunately he addressed 'the last of the five kings of modern Italian music' as 'the Wagner of our dear allies': Verdi was therefore at best an alternative or an equivalent to Wagner, and the alliance between Bismarck's industrialized Germany and backward Italy remained unequal. Verdi replied graciously, absolving Bülow of any sin. But to his publisher Giulio Ricordi he commented, 'He is definitely mad!'

The story of the Venetian busts justifies Verdi's grievance about his relegation to second place. The Wagner memorial arrived first, as if he had prior rights: twenty-five years before dying in the Palazzo Vendramin, he spent the winter of 1858–59 composing the second act of *Tristan und Isolde* in another palace on the Grand Canal. The city suited Wagner because its fluent instability matched his music, and after his death Venice seemed to retain a memento of his music in its swampy, opalescently humid air. In 1902 the French novelist Maurice Barrès described the score of *Tristan* as an exhalation from the lagoon. By then Wagnerism was a cult with adherents in all countries, which is why in 1908 a Berlin stockbroker commissioned the sculptor Fritz Schaper to carve the marble bust for the Giardini Pubblici. At its unveiling, a band wheezed through the processional entry of the Landgraf's guests in *Tannhäuser*, with the invited audience listening in decorous silence. This was followed by the more pompous march across the rainbow bridge that leads Wotan and his royal family into Valhalla at the end of *Das Rheingold*. It had been played during rehearsals at Bayreuth in 1876 when Wagner, treading a gangplank, strode onto the stage of his new theatre. In Venice too the extract marked the apotheosis of the composer; the ironic asides of Loge, who foresees doom for the gods, and the complaints of the Rhinemaidens, whose stolen gold has paid for this plutocratic palace, were of course omitted.

Verdi was bemused by Venice. He made his first visit in 1843 to rehearse *I Lombardi alla prima crocciata*, and in a letter reported that it 'is beautiful, it is a poem, but … I wouldn't live here of my own accord'. Preoccupied throughout his life with planting trees, rearing animals and harvesting crops on his own land, he could not feel at ease in this illusory, ungrounded place. But once Wagner established a posthumous presence in the garden, Verdi's absence became an embarrassment, and within six months Gerolama Bortotti's bust was inaugurated; to mark the occasion, a band played popular tunes from half a dozen operas (not including *La traviata* which, as Verdi gruffly reported, was a 'fiasco' when first performed at La Fenice in 1853). A plaque on the pedestal significantly declares 'A Giuseppe Verdi – Venezia'. Wagner – who depended throughout his career on handouts from kings, merchants and subscribers to his festival at Bayreuth – owed his monument to an individual's devotion and his disbursement of private funds, but Verdi's was the grateful donation of the city, paid for by the Consiglio Comunale. Verdi respected his customers, and even gave them the benefit of the doubt when they disliked his work. Wagner meanwhile composed a 'music of the future' which, he predicted, would only be understood when audiences and performers had acquired new reserves of physical stamina and new capacities for intellectual concentration; in his view art was not a product sold in the market but a gift evangelically handed down, like the Grail in *Lohengrin* or *Parsifal*, to a world that was as yet unready and probably unworthy. The busts measure the gap between Verdi and Wagner, and restate their disagreement about art's purpose and its responsibilities. Is the garden path that separates the two men an uncrossable chasm?

|||||||||||||||||||

I was startled to discover them here, on a desultory evening stroll in Venice a few years ago. I came upon Verdi first; I was going nowhere in particular, and could easily have been wandering in the other direction, which would have favoured Wagner. The surprise derived from finding them together, and from having to think of them sharing the same disputed space.

There are thousands of books on Wagner and there must be a few hundred on Verdi, but I know of only a couple that purport to compare them. In *El Genio en su Entorno*, Carmen de Reparaz tours their working environments – or rather some of them, since the Wagnerian half of her book stays at Triebschen, the villa outside Lucerne where Wagner lived for six years between his expulsion from Munich in 1865 and his move to Bayreuth in 1872. I was excited by the title of Ernö Lendvai's *Verdi and Wagner*, then found when I read it that its real concern is Hungarian folk music and the theoretical system devised by Zoltán Kodály to explain its modal rather than tonal structure; Verdi and Wagner interest Lendvai as unwitting forerunners of Béla Bartók and his 'polymodal chromaticism'. Most of the study is about Verdi's *Falstaff,* and the only Wagnerian passage discussed is the heroine's recriminatory narrative in the first act of *Tristan und Isolde.* An epilogue offers to engineer 'The Meeting of Tristan and Aida on the Deck of the Computer' in diagrams that compare the scampering of the temple dancers in *Aida* with the motif that signifies death in *Tristan und Isolde.* Three pages, which soon diverge into another astronomical and astrological salute to Kodály, are not enough to make the match. With the debatable exceptions of these two books, Verdi and Wagner remain in their mutually antagonistic realms.

During their lifetimes, each kept a wary eye and a disapproving ear on the other. In 1865 Verdi heard the overture to *Tannhäuser* at a concert in Paris and pronounced it 'matto', mad. Wagner was brusquely intolerant when he attended a performance of Verdi's *Requiem* in Vienna in 1875: in her diary Cosima, by now Wagner's wife and slavish amanuensis, noted that there was no point in discussing the piece. Verdi at least pondered Wagner's theories, and in 1870 asked to have copies of his essays sent from Paris. He agreed with Wagner's arguments in favour of a sunken orchestra pit, as at Bayreuth, though for practical not mystical reasons. Rather than wanting a cavity from which sound with no visible source would suffuse the air, Verdi simply thought it absurd that musicians in tailcoats and white ties should be jumbled in the same sightline with the Egyptians, Assyrians or Druids onstage. He told his friend Clarina Maffei not to think of Wagner as 'a fierce beast', a distempered savage, but he was equally concerned to deny him the role of prophet. The idea of an aesthetic religion was anathema to Verdi, which is why in 1893 he likened Wagner's endless melody to the tomb of Mohammed, supposedly suspended between heaven and earth.

In the same mischievous letter Verdi joked that he had advanced beyond the concise, catchy tunes of *Traviata* and *Rigoletto* and now, at the age of eighty, intended to match Wagner's longueurs by composing 'an opera in twelve acts plus a prologue and an overture' that would be 'as long as all nine of Beethoven's symphonies put together'. He was ironically in earnest when boasting of his stamina. He had recovered from the sixteen years of inertia that separated *Aida* in 1871 from *Otello* in 1887, then managed a second revival or resurrection with *Falstaff,* composed between 1889 and 1892. He must have felt, in moments of elation like this, that he could do anything. Wagner, not bothering to be competitive, made casual fun of Verdi. In Venice a few months before his death he amused Cosima by improvising 'something *à la* Verdi and *à la* Chopin' at the piano. They were filling in time before supper; this was culinary music, useful as an aperitif. Such dismiss-als concealed a rankling envy that Wagner never openly expressed. In 1866 he was piqued when the city of Nuremberg chose to entertain Ludwig II of Bavaria, his besotted patron, with a performance of Verdi's *Il trovatore.* Perhaps the slight prompted him to complete *Die Meistersinger von Nürnberg,* which honours the city as the home of a German renaissance; he had already urged the king to make Nuremberg his capital, which gave Wagner reason for feeling proprietorial about the place. In 1880 he had a jealous twinge when brooding about Ludwig's failure to summon him back to Munich. What rankled was a rumour that the king had been amusing himself with private performances of operas by other composers, including *Aida.* In July 1873 Cosima heard an open-air concert of military music in Bayreuth, and was taken aback when the brassy din concluded with Elsa's bridal procession from *Lohengrin.* In the unaccustomed context, Wagner's music resembled 'a captive princess in the vulgar triumphal parade, sad and touching'. Cosima's simile is startling: does it allude to the enslaved Aida, who watches the humbled king of Ethiopia led in triumph through Memphis?

Verdi kept an open mind about Wagner, although he preferred others not to know it. He travelled to Bologna in secret to hear the first Italian perfor-mance of *Lohengrin* in November 1871 at the Teatro Comunale, and was annoyed when he was recognized at the station and applauded in the theatre: was this bash-fulness, or anger that he had shown himself to be weak, incapable of ignoring his rival? During the opera he scribbled comments, mostly unfavourable, on a score. He thought the prelude 'too loud', and groaned at the slowness of the action. The most fundamental difference between his work and Wagner's is indeed a matter of pace, which is almost a sign of their separate metabolic rates. Wagner thought that the defining German tempo was 'the walk, the "andante"'. If a cor-responding generalization were made about an instinctive Italian tempo, it would probably have to be a fleeter-footed 'allegro', which – as Alice Ford in *Falstaff* suggests when she sings about the 'allegria' of the merry wives – is a synonym for happiness. Wagnerian music and drama creep forward with stealthy gradualism, never able to be rid of a past whose burden is carried by those inescapable motifs. Time falters, as in the *Tristan* prelude, or stops altogether, as in the unmetrical opening bars of *Parsifal.* Everything seems to be a repetition of some previous event: in *Der fliegende Holländer* the Dutchman whispers that he has seen Senta's image in a remote, antecedent world, and heard before what she is about to say to him. Characters refuse to respond to the provocations of drama, like Tristan failing to defend himself against Melot, or Isolde failing to go to his aid when he is wounded. Cosima congratulated Nietzsche for understanding the reason for this: tragedy, she said, was about suffering not action. Verdi's operas, by contrast, have an impulsive haste that can be invigorating or alarming, a reminder of how instantaneously our moods and destinies alter. In *La traviata*, Violetta's life changes in a moment when she is introduced to Alfredo, and it changes again with equal suddenness when she meets his censorious father. Planning an adaptation of *King Lear* with the librettist Antonio Somma in 1854, Verdi suggested that the dialogue should be 'very animated', with some high-speed patter by Lear's fool. 'In the theatre,' he said with legislative finality, 'lengthy is synonymous with boring.' Wagner, by contrast, thought of ennui as an almost spiritual state – a symptom of disconnection from the world of irrelevant happenings. His favourite philosopher Arthur Schopenhauer called boredom 'a form of suffering unknown to brutes', making it a by-product of mental pleasures that human beings were uniquely privileged to enjoy. Wagner was gratified to be told in 1881 that Berlin audiences found the *Ring* 'tiring': the tetralogy existed to exhaust them as it worked through a last traversal of the world's weary history.

When Wagner died on 13 February 1883, Verdi was obliged to react to the event. He did so in a brief, enigmatic note to Ricordi next day that manages to seem candid while remaining wary and self-aware. It reads like a small dramatic exercise, as if Verdi were orchestrating emotions that might be attributed to one of his characters, even prescribing emphatic gestures to punctuate the outbursts. He begins with an iterated adjective, which could be the sudden onset of a dramatic recitative: 'Triste. Triste. Triste!' The repetition may be playing with the name of Tristan, twisted into an anagram by the character himself when he uses the alias Tantris. Only in the next line – which is given its own paragraph, to suggest that it follows after a baleful, wrenching pause – does Verdi reveal the reason for his sadness, although Ricordi would have known it from the start: 'Wagner is dead!' The exclamations convey the shock of immediacy, although Verdi adds that he read the news the day before. Can he still be so jolted by the loss of a man he did not know? 'I was, so to speak, terrified!' he recalls, with another exclamatory increase in dynamics to convey the sense of metaphysical dread that the news provoked. The opening line about his sadness establishes a ground bass of numb, muffled distress, but terror seems melodramatically excessive, and Verdi's uncertainty about the appropriate tone voices itself in the qualification 'so to speak'. Because he is dealing in superlatives, the idiom of operatic intensity, he corrects a word and increases its volume by changing 'potente' to 'potentissimo'. Then another gesture mimes a feeling that may, like the protestations of Verdi's characters, be a little hyperbolic: 'Let us not discuss it,' he says, after which he continues the discussion by declaring that 'It is a great individual who has disappeared! A name that leaves the most powerful imprint on the history of art!' Here the note breaks off. Verdi designed it as a semi-public utterance, a formal obituary for a colleague, and despite the punctuated fortissimi he chooses his words with diplomatic deliberateness. The tribute he pays is to Wagner's idiosyncratic personality, to his name; there is no reference to his music, although Verdi makes an Italianate music of his own by trebling the word 'triste'.

Some of what lurks between the lines here was articulated a fortnight later by Verdi's second wife Giuseppina Strepponi in a letter to Cesare Vigna, the Venetian physician to whom *La traviata* was dedicated. Strepponi notes that Verdi, who 'never knew or even met Wagner', is away; his absence entitles her to pronounce her own verdict on 'this great individuality'. Her phrase has a critical edge, suggesting that Wagner was too eccentric for his own good, and in a first draft of the letter she wondered whether he might not have been a candidate for consignment to a lunatic asylum. The aside, which she suppressed, was addressed to Vigna in his professional capacity: he was an alienist, specializing in the treatment of mental patients. Wagner did not, Strepponi says, suffer from 'the little itch of vanity' that we all share but was possessed by 'an incandescent, measureless pride, like Satan or Lucifer', which made him discontented 'even when he was glorified by kings, by his country, and overwhelmed with riches'. She is implicitly making a contrast with Verdi – more contented and less hubristic, though also personally much richer than Wagner. The dichotomy is extreme, as satisfyingly simple as a combat between tempter and redeemer. Like Christ lifting up Mary Magdalene, Verdi did not reproach Strepponi for the irregular life she had led before they met, when during a busy career as an operatic soprano she managed to produce three illegitimate children, with whom she soon lost touch. The benevolence he displayed towards her is present in his music: he pours out melody like balm to heal an afflicted world. Strepponi viewed Wagner as his eternal enemy, a rebel angel who exists to negate God.

As a loyal spouse, Cosima was more than a match for Strepponi. In 1871 she listened as the conductor Hans Richter took Wagner on a 'dreadful musical tour' by arguing the case for the operas of Gounod, Meyerbeer, Bellini, Donizetti, Rossini and Verdi. She felt 'physically sick' at hearing rival composers praised, and took up a volume by Goethe to settle her stomach. Wagner had to silence Richter as he outrageously contended 'that Verdi was no worse than Donizetti'. Some organ fugues by Bach quelled Cosima's dyspepsia and re-established the primacy of German music, but she continued to regard a taste for Verdi as the unforgivable sin. In 1900 Bruno Walter, while conducting Siegfried Wagner's opera *Die Bärenhäuter* in Berlin, was accorded an audience with her. He made polite noises about her son's work, to which she responded with the categorical pronouncement that Siegfried had 'succeeded in writing the finest non-tragic opera since *Die Meistersinger*'. Embarrassed by her 'blasphemous utterance', Walter changed the subject. Later in the conversation he broke a strict rule of Bayreuth etiquette by mentioning Verdi and praising 'the astonishing change and development in his work, from *Ernani* to *Aida* and finally to *Falstaff*'. Cosima snorted 'Development? I can see no difference between *Ernani* and *Falstaff*.' Walter left in disgrace, exposed as a man whose loyalty was not absolute.

Although Verdi and Wagner never entered into debate with each other, the world took them to be rivals, and their supporters formed mutually antagonistic teams to exchange insults. The critic Alberto Gasco remarked that, in Italy during the 1890s, to cheer Brünnhilde was a slight to the memory of Violetta: patriotism gave Verdi's fallen woman from *La traviata* precedence over Wagner's airborne goddess from *Die Walküre*. The Berlin critic Karl Frenzel scanned the audience at the first Bayreuth *Ring* cycle in 1876, then named the musicians who pusillanimously stayed away. Verdi was among those whose 'failure … to appear' seemed prudent in retrospect: if he had turned up – along with Gounod, also absent – the two of them, Frenzel said, 'would have shrivelled, pierced to the core by the sense of their own nothingness'. It galled Verdi when the Parisian reviews of *Don Carlos* in 1867 informed him, as he reported, that he was now 'an almost perfect Wagnerian'; likewise the worst affront a disillusioned cultist could dole out to Wagner was to compare him with Verdi. In 1898 in *The Perfect Wagnerite* George Bernard Shaw criticized the *Ring* for regressing from sternly preachy music drama to Italianate grand opera, from the radical attack on capitalism in *Das Rheingold* to the nihilistic frivolity of the apocalypse at the end of *Götterdämmerung*. The oath of bloodbrotherhood sworn by Siegfried and Gunther reminded Shaw of the showy duets between tenor and baritone in *Ernani* or *Otello*, and the trio of vengeance in which Brünnhilde suborns Gunther and Hagen to kill Siegfried belonged with the merry, murderous plotting in *Un ballo in maschera*.

As if paying retribution, Wagner was posthumously punished when Verdi died in 1901. Plans had been made to give the first Italian staging of the *Ring* in Turin later that year; Ricordi, who happened to own the rights, vetoed the production because the nation was still mourning its Bard. In New York, Wagner got his own back. On the night of Verdi's death, 27 January, the event was solemnly marked during a concert at the Metropolitan Opera when Walter Damrosch conducted the funeral march from *Götterdämmerung* – a tactless choice, but what was the alternative? 'Va, pensiero' from *Nabucco* impersonally allows an entire community to voice its woes; Verdi composed no symphonic music glorifying individuals, and his sole contribution to the Met concert – which included some scraps of Gounod, Leoncavallo's *Pagliacci* prologue, and Elisabeth's greeting to the hall of song from *Tannhäuser* – was the *Rigoletto* quartet, in which the jester's sorrow and his daughter Gilda's distress are plaited together with the amorous conniving of the libertine who has seduced her and the cynical laughter of his latest conquest. The loss of a hero does not bring history to a terminus, as in *Götterdämmerung*. Verdi's quartet is a reminder that tragedy and comedy are obliged to coexist in a muddled, crowded world where some are revelling while others grieve.

The quarrel persisted long into the twentieth century. Parisian modernists like Stravinsky rejected the high-pitched frenzy and hypnotic tedium of Wagner and instead praised Verdi's mellifluousness and buoyancy. In a memoir of musical life under the Third Reich, Wilhelm Furtwängler's secretary Berta Geissmar reflected on the politics of aesthetic taste in Germany and Austria, and remarked that 'the Wagner-Verdi controversy' was bitter. The Nazis requisitioned Wagner, and in 1939 E. M. Forster turned the Wagnerian myth against Germany when he remarked in his essay 'What I Believe' that the bellicose grunting and grumbling of Fafner, the giant who metamorphoses into a dragon between *Das Rheingold* and *Siegfried*, could be heard 'under Europe today'. Opponents signalled their resistance in revivals of Verdi's operas, newly translated to emphasize their liberality and their humanism. Two well-meaning novels by Franz Werfel and Bertita Harding plotted a reconciliation between Verdi and Wagner, a tidy but fanciful act of closure that occurs – where else? – in Venice. Werfel published *Verdi: Roman der Oper* in 1924; an English translation appeared in 1947, two years after Werfel, a Jew born in Prague who had fled from Vienna following the German annexation of Austria, died in Los Angeles. The novel speculates about the composer's mental state during the six lean years between *Aida* and *Otello*, and blames Wagner for his creative blockage. At the end of 1882 Verdi travels to Venice, where Wagner is living. He wants to see this stranger who has caused his work to be derided. Though he carries with him the score of *Tristan und Isolde*, he is wary of opening it. A series of sightings throughout the city turns Verdi's theoretical dislike into hatred; he feels capable, given the opportunity, of killing Wagner. The novel tantalizes us with a fictional alternative to history, as Leo Tolstoy does when he sends Pierre to assassinate Napoleon in *War and Peace*. Would the elimination of Wagner have forestalled Hitler?

The first non-meeting arranged by Werfel occurs at La Fenice, where *La traviata* opened almost thirty years earlier. Now a juvenile symphony by Wagner is being performed in the composer's presence. Verdi does not attend the concert but sees Wagner in the foyer afterwards, surrounded by flattering acolytes. Lurking in a corner, Verdi resents the cult of personality that earns Wagner acclaim for an early, inferior work, and he compares him to Napoleon. The friction between the two men has a sexual frisson in it. Werfel emphasizes Verdi's male uprightness and self-control: smoking a cigar, he enjoys the 'masculine smell of American tobacco'. When his eyes meet Wagner's, he glimpses a 'feminine soul', seductively determined to captivate the world. What Wagner sees is a man immune to his wiles, 'over whom he had no power, a face firmly closed in upon itself and seeking nothing of others'. Yet Verdi feels an erotic magnetism in Wagner's gaze, which sends out 'a cry of recognition, a call across all the differences that divided them – accidents of birth, of race, of thought? – the call "Come!"' Verdi does not respond to the invitation. Next they pass in gondolas on the Grand Canal. Wagner is dozing, which allows Verdi the chance for a closer look, and he rises to his feet in a moment of homicidal rage: he feels creatively dead, 'and that man slumbering there, his unsuspecting enemy, had killed him'. His resentment is atavistic, 'the hate of the Romans against the barbarians of the Dark Ages'. A third foiled meeting follows in the Piazza San Marco during Carnival in early 1883. A band is playing excerpts from *Aida*. The two men accidentally brush against each other and Verdi, in a calmer mood, is about to introduce himself when he hears someone mention *Aida* and thinks he sees a grimace on Wagner's face. He misreads the signals: Wagner is dismissing a rant against Italian opera by one of his sycophants, and has declared *Aida* to be 'true music'.

Finally Verdi goes to hear *La forza del destino* at La Fenice, receives a grateful kiss from a young soprano, and interprets this as life's farewell to him. Later that evening he feels suicidally depressed. Aware of the need to conclude business, he leafs through the score of *Tristan*, and is unmanned by admiration. He resolves to call on Wagner the next day, but when he wakes up he has a seizure, and lies in bed miserably convinced that his rival will outlive him, winning the biological contest. He recovers, regains his psychological equilibrium, and accepts that both he and Wagner have their roles to play in the world. He sets out to pay his courtesy call, having prepared an appeasing speech in which he intends to admit that *Aida* marked the demise of Italian opera. At the Palazzo Vendramin, a weeping porter informs him that Wagner has just died. Verdi goes to a church to meditate on this turn of events, and wonders whether death hesitated between them before deciding to take Wagner. He feels an unholy joy in being spared; he is ashamed of this resurgent delight in life, but it announces his creative renewal. *Otello* and *Falstaff* logically follow.

Werfel leaves the conflict unresolved, although Verdi, satisfying the novelist's political urge to restrain and reprove Germany, emerges as both survivor and victor. Bertita Harding's *Magic Fire*, a fictionalized biography of Wagner published in 1953, tries harder to broker an understanding between the two men. Like her fellow Americans when they put Europe back together again after the war, she cajoles the former combatants to shake hands. As in Werfel's novel, there are three tantalizingly close encounters between Verdi and Wagner. The first is during the winter of 1858–59, when Wagner was working on *Tristan* at the Palazzo Giustiniani in Venice. A barrel organ in the alley grinds out a Verdi medley, and Wagner envies those effortless melodies; it's more likely that he would have slammed the window, after telling the organist to move on. Harding has a servant inform him that Verdi is in town to conduct *Traviata* at La Fenice. Wagner – sent hurtling ahead to the end of his opera by the impatient novelist – completes the 'Liebestod' there and then, and rushes off to buy a standing place in the gallery. That night he feels a twinge during Verdi's ovations, but he leaves the theatre 'humbly'. Is this the only occasion when that adverb has been applied to Wagner?

A corresponding and equally unlikely act of homage by Verdi comes next. In 1882 at Bayreuth he is spotted by Franz Liszt at a performance of *Parsifal*, but disappears before Wagner, besieged by fans, can reach him in the crowd. Wagner sends him an invitation to the concert at La Fenice that marks the fiftieth anniversary of his symphony: this is the setting for their initial near miss in Werfel's novel. Verdi makes the trip to Venice and waits outside the theatre in a gondola, 'too discerningly honourable to push himself forward'. He passes the time by explaining Wagner's music to his gondolier, who prefers *Aida*. Verdi has trouble getting him to appreciate the Ride of the Valkyries, and admits 'one really must be German to understand that'. The birds chirping in the forest in the second act of *Siegfried* are more intelligible, since they recall Saint Francis of Assisi. But national barriers intrude: 'Francesco, he was a saint,' says the gondolier. 'In church I never hear of a Saint Sigifrido!' Verdi gives up his attempt to proselytize, but when Wagner steps into view he shouts 'Riccardo Wagner! Bravo, bravissimo!' It is as difficult to picture as Wagner's sheepishly modest exit from La Fenice after hearing *Traviata*. Then Harding's Verdi chases Wagner through the side canals, bribing the gondolier to row faster so he can catch up with his colleague and congratulate him. Wagner, travelling in a barge with eight oarsmen, gives him the slip.

The comradely rapprochement, as overburdened with expectation as an international summit conference, fails to happen. Even flushed romantic fiction cannot make it happen. A century later, it has still not happened: Verdi and Wagner remain apart, perhaps no longer inimical but still estranged. In the Giardini Pubblici the benches near their busts have been situated so as to prevent you – unless you risk dislocating your neck – from seeing both of them at once.

# Stereophony

We are accustomed to choosing between Wagner and Verdi, for reasons of taste, ideology or nationality, or simply for the pleasure of partisanship. The contrast is that between right and left, black and white, evil and good. W. H. Auden called Wagner 'an absolute shit', a light-fingered scoundrel with the sartorial tastes of a drag queen, while honouring Verdi as both 'a genius and a gentleman', someone he wished he could have known. Seeing the busts in the garden made me realize that they belonged to separate parts of my experience, as if their music addressed different regions of my body and brain.

Looking back, I associate Wagner with periods of post-adolescent gloom I am glad I outgrew. His music encourages the foolhardy acts that German romantics called sublime, which others perform on our behalf: Senta hurling herself into the sea in *Der fliegende Holländer*, Brünnhilde riding into the fire in *Götterdämmerung*. This is the music of a prolonged and deliriously ecstatic death, like that of the hero in *Tristan und Isolde*. Failing that, it is the music of depression. As Tristan lies unconscious on his sickbed, a shepherd surveys the flat, empty sea and pipes a bleak lament that lasts three minutes. The passage is so technically elaborate that two cor anglais players have to join forces in the pit to get through its helplessly repetitive threnody. Ernest Newman called it 'one of the strangest and most poignant [melodies] ever imagined by man' – strange because so primitive, so extraneous to the dramatic situation, and not so much poignant as funereal, overcome near the end by a choking grief. It is a pastoral elegy for a mortified world, and when the orchestra steals back, its cushioning softness is a relief after such raw anguish. For Tristan this is 'die alte Weise', the old tune, which has accompanied him throughout his life from the moment when his dying mother gave birth to him. It is the oldest music of all, mortality made audible, and you need to be strong – which by the third act of this opera few of us are – to survive the experience of listening to it. Wagner's unstable chromatic harmonies worry us into a state of tension because the music is always shifting its ground. Before day dawns at the start of *Götterdämmerung*, we grope through a half-light as the sound billows and deflates, surges forward and then wavers, as if caught between dream and waking. Brass brings the sun up, but Siegfried soon embarks on the river, which heaves, speeds through rapids, then runs dry. We are either fumbling in a mist or tossed on a flood; the music seeks to uproot us, to leave us unbalanced, with our heads spinning. Or it sucks us into a vortex. In 1928 in his novel *Humdrum*, Harold Acton described an audience of socialites listening to *Götterdämmerung* at Covent Garden. They obey 'that drowning-man code of behaviour, that customary allowance of oneself to wallow and to sink, which is the prime rule of Wagnerian etiquette'. The music delivers the dubious bliss of self-extinction.

If Wagner was a drug, then Verdi in my early experience was a tonic. Wagner induced a delicious listlessness, but an excerpt from Verdi could be relied on to activate my sluggish body, even if his characters were hurling insults at one another. The passages I always returned to, in the first recordings I owned, were those in which a whole world seemed to be inflamed by contending energies: the trio in the dark garden in *Don Carlos* with its blurted secrets and raging threats, or the simultaneous voices of conquerors, captives, priests and warriors at the end of the victory parade in *Aida*. Of course there is more than physical arousal in this music; its moral generosity and solicitude took me longer to understand. For Verdi melody was a symptom of affection, and his operas exhibit all the varieties of love, sacred as well as profane, parental as well as connubial. Wagner, by contrast, devised a chromatic formula that with its drooping irresolution and unsatisfiable yearning captures the fatality and compulsiveness of sex: love and death conjoin in the chord that describes infatuation at the start of *Tristan und Isolde.*

In *La traviata* when the courtesan and her newest admirer sing about 'quell'amor ch'è palpito/Dell'universo intero', the words need no translation. The strings in the orchestra throb and so do we, attuned to the lovers by the vibrant air between and around us. Violetta and Alfredo have good reason for claiming that the entire universe is animated by desire, because music – spreading through aural space and turning the crowded theatre or our solitary room into a sensorium – universalizes emotion. Verdi's music pulses, and it can quicken the blood. In *Falstaff* the sodden, dejected old toper scrambles out of the river into which he has been dumped and is reanimated by an orchestral trill, which proves as effective as a fibrillator. Planning their practical joke, the merry wives let loose a tuned fusillade of laughter, a concert of silvery giggling that encourages us to live playfully, keeping pain at bay. Wagner's equivalent is the amusement of the Rhinemaidens when they consign Siegfried to his doom in *Götterdämmerung* – a symptom, he told Cosima, of nature's 'childlike cruelty'. The war whoop of Brünnhilde's 'Hojotoho' in *Die Walküre* expresses the same murderous hilarity, as does the mirthlessly ejaculated laughter with which Kundry in *Parsifal* mocks Christ on his way to Calvary. In Brünnhilde's case the heady jumps between octaves express a divine contempt for cowardly, earthbound humanity, while the plummeting of Kundry's voice follows the character's leap into a pit of damnation and despair. Hysteria in Verdi has a different sound. In his *Macbeth* the heroine's sleepwalking scene ends with a high D flat, a stratospheric note that comes as a last paradoxical demand on a character who is supposed – according to Verdi's own instructions – not to sing but to speak the Shakespearean text in a voice that is broken, hollowed by despair. Although the note itself is cruel, compelling sopranos to fudge it or (in less scrupulous times) to engage a lighter-voiced colleague to sing it for them in the wings, there is an extraordinary mercy to Verdi's notion. The ravaged woman, traumatically condemned to re-enact her crime, finally drifts into a sleep that may, like death, be dreamless. She climbs a musical scale into a clearer, thinner atmosphere where the D flat like a sharpened icicle of sound pierces the flesh and releases the soul.

Tragedy in Wagner is an act of will, provoked by a spiritual pride that we are expected to admire. Brünnhilde refuses to give up the ring in *Götterdämmerung*, even though Waltraute explains the consequences of keeping it. Lohengrin, deciding to retreat to Monsalvat, says 'Ich muss, ich muss!' There is no point in asking why he must: if he didn't go, there would be a happy ending, an intolerably banal prospect. On one occasion, enjoying each other's company, Wagner and Cosima laughed, she reported, 'like Tristan and Isolde'. Then they paused for a guilty inquest: did Tristan and Isolde ever laugh? were they capable of it? Wagner decided that they must have done so sometimes, during their less exalted daylight lives. Verdi had no such misgivings; his characters, unlike Wagner's, would prefer to be happy if they could. His subject is the human comedy – although, because of his lyrical sympathy for the hurts we all suffer, this collision of quarrelsome desires usually has a tragic outcome. Minutes before she collapses in *La traviata*, Violetta subscribes to Alfredo's soothing fantasy about leaving Paris to recuperate. Minutes before Manrico is hauled off to be executed at the end of *Il trovatore*, his supposed mother Azucena fantasizes about taking him back to the safety of the mountains where he can play his lute in peace. Tragedy is not what they choose, as Wagner's characters crave death, but it overtakes them anyway, and to remain alive can be worse than dying: 'E vivo ancor!' groans Luna when Azucena tells him he has killed his brother. Verdi's agnostic *Requiem* ends with the soprano whispering her plea to be freed from death, or at least from the fear of it. The 'Libera me' was the section Verdi volunteered to compose when rallying his colleagues to prepare a collaborative requiem for Rossini, and in selecting it he was responsible for a liturgical innovation. This prayer is no part of the traditional Latin Mass for the dead; Verdi borrowed it from another church service because it gave voice to the fundamental human instinct that underlies all religions and is never entirely appeased by their doctrinal promises. In Wagner, the menace of that inescapable end can be transcended with the help of music: at the climax of their duet, the lovers in *Siegfried* describe their carnal union as a laughing death. The exception to Verdi's pessimism is *Falstaff*. In his last opera, composed when he was an old man, he disarms death, concluding the action with a rollicking fugue that announces continuation, a resilience that will not accept defeat.

More is at issue here than the divergent cultures of Italy and Germany. Verdi and Wagner occupied different metaphysical regions. Verdi wrote what medieval theorists called 'musica humana'. His music listens to the torments of human beings and attempts to harmonize their troubles; it is Verdi, not Wagner, who exemplifies Nietzsche's pronouncement that God died of pity for mankind. His 'Stabat Mater', which he worked on in 1896–97, has the chorus ask for one last time the question that sums up his entire endeavour. 'Quis est homo, qui non fleret?' the singers demand, with a surge of emotional emphasis like a heaved sigh. Who, being human, would not sympathize or empathize? – not only with the grief of Mary at the foot of the Cross but with any fellow creature who is bereaved or betrayed or afflicted. This is why Desdemona in *Otello* follows Shakespeare's willow song with an 'Ave Maria' (a text Verdi first set in 1843 in *I Lombardi* and again on two other occasions in the 1880s, before and after the composition of *Otello*) – not because she believes in divine intervention, but because the words of the prayer, translated into soft, lambent sound like the Logos taking on warm human flesh, calm her agitation and give her courage. Wagner, on the other hand, composed something like what the theorists called 'music mundana', which was anything but mundane: it mapped the harmony of the universe – or, in Wagner's case, its rush towards dissolution. He sought to transfigure reality or else to annihilate it, and his music has origins that seem celestial or perhaps infernal. It drifts down from the sky like light when the prelude to *Lohengrin* describes a saviour's shimmering descent from on high. Conversely, at the start of *Das Rheingold* the music sounds from the deep as an insistent, wavering E flat evokes the welling-up of the river and of life itself. When Klingsor activates his spells in *Parsifal*, it boils and rumbles in some subliminal pit. Whatever its origins, this music no longer vouches for the solidity of cosmic order. Wagner composed the death of the gods and the possible end of the world. If that meant returning music to the silence from which it first emerged, then so be it: in 1878 he wished that, having invented the invisible orchestra by lowering the Bayreuth pit out of sight, he could now create an 'inaudible orchestra'.

Listening to *Götterdämmerung* as he drove through the mountains in California in 1976, the composer John Adams startled himself by saying out loud 'He cares'. It is less easy to decide what Wagner cares about. He cares about sensations, and about emotions so long as they are wildly elemental. Sieglinde in *Die Walküre* tells Siegmund, 'Du bist der Lenz': he is spring, the germinating season that has thrust open the door and toppled resistance. Awoken by Siegfried on the mountaintop, Brünnhilde says that her aroused blood is like a sea or a wildfire. Wagner is less interested in the misadventures and miseries that befall us as human beings. Compare a father's farewell to his daughter in *Rigoletto* and *Die Walküre*. The Verdian scene, which alludes to Lear's inconsolable howling over Cordelia, bravely tries to ease the pain of the situation. The dying Gilda comforts her distraught father, as well as cheering herself up by anticipating a heavenly encounter with the mother she never knew. Yet after her last breath Rigoletto can only bellow about his accursed life: music would be lying if it made the situation bearable. When Wotan kisses the divinity from Brünnhilde and puts her to sleep, the orchestra boils and then blazes around them. They disappear into this maelstrom of sound that, like the magic fire, keeps us from getting close enough to investigate the intimate complexities of the episode. Why does Wotan confess his love, with so many regretful endearments, only after Brünnhilde is safely silent and powerless? Was his anger the cover for an unparental affection, which he overcomes by sacrificing her? Is there a second incestuous relationship in the opera, to supplement the union of the Wälsung twins? The orchestral conflagration, first kindled by Brünnhilde when she begs for the barricade of flame, is at once an incitement and a prohibition: it announces that all of us, whether gods or mortals, are victims of the urges that rage through us and magnetize us towards one another.

From the first, listeners to Wagner's music felt as if they too were experiencing the painfully exquisite rapture of the lovers in *Tristan und Isolde*. Nietzsche said that after hearing *Tristan* 'one fairly floats in bliss and exaltation'. Discussing *Tristan* with a journalist from the *Berliner Tageblatt*, Verdi had recourse to the rhetoric of overwhelmed inarticulacy: 'Before this gigantic work,

I stand in wonder and terror.' An undertone of alarm can be detected since, in the vocabulary of the sublime, terror (which is what Verdi said he felt when he heard of Wagner's death) is close to horror. His remark about the gigantism of *Tristan* is all the more telling because its scale is so intimate, by contrast with the vertiginous scenery of the *Ring*. This after all was Wagner's effort to write a profitable, portable Italianate romantic opera. What Verdi wondered at and was terrified by was the work's tonal audacity and the throat-tearing rigours of the vocal writing. The sublime offered a spectacle of danger and a prospect of death, both physically and psychologically; it could be experienced by facing up to a storm at sea like that in *Der fliegende Holländer* or a conflagration like that at the end of *Götterdämmerung* – or by looking into the score of *Tristan und Isolde*.

Wagner's characters are entranced by music, which sometimes saps their capacity for dramatic action: Senta limply daydreams in her high-backed chair while the other women spin, Tannhäuser slumps before Venus with his head in her lap, Isolde languishes on her couch. Verdi's music gets its impetus from drama. His people only sing if they are driven by some physical need, by either love or hate or – as with Carlo in *La forza del destino*, who is overcome by 'gioia immenso' because he has found a reason to kill his best friend – by both at once. In 1850 Verdi discussed possible subjects with his librettist Francesco Maria Piave, who went on to write the texts for *Stiffelio* and *Rigoletto*. Verdi said he had no preference for genre, and was happy to accept subjects that were 'grandiose' or 'fantastic'. (In fact, though, he seldom bothered with grandeur – except when using the massed forces of grand opera to decry brutal theocratic regimes in *Don Carlos* and *Aida* – and left fantasy to Wagner, whose operas include mermaids and flying horses, a doe that turns out to be a princess and a swan that is actually a bewitched prince.) After professing impartiality, he told Piave what he really wanted: 'the impassioned is the safest'. It was safe because the passions, in Verdi's view, were our biological safeguards, the motive forces of human life and therefore the progenitors of opera.

Bruno Walter reported that the moment he heard the entry of the cellos in the prelude to *Tristan*, 'I was no longer of this world'. This world – the troubled, downcast place where the rest of us have to live – proves more resistant in Verdi's operas, which is why he viewed *Tristan* with incredulity. Suffocating in their sealed tomb, Aida and Radamès fade out of life, but the remorseful Amneris is left behind to utter the last, grave and grieving word. The evangelical pastor in *Stiffelio* belongs to a sect called Assasverian – an invented word that perhaps alludes to the wandering Jew Ahasuerus, who was condemned, like Kundry in *Parsifal*, by his hard-hearted response to Christ on the way to Calvary. Wagner said that his Dutchman was another offshoot of Ahasuerus, but the garbled name is wasted on Stiffelio, whose wanderings are essential to his ministry and who has in any case come home to Salzburg. Though Verdi may have been grumpily anti-social, he had no conception of what it meant to be an existential outcast, expelled not just from polite society like Violetta but from membership of humanity.

Angry railing passion was important to Verdi, but so was compassion, which speaks with a stiller, smaller, more melodious voice. Many of the most eloquent passages in his operas are about amelioration, as one character persuades another to be less hard-hearted. This is the appeal Violetta makes to her abusive lover Alfredo and to his disapproving father. Amelia pleads with the husband who intends to kill her for infidelity in *Un ballo in maschera*. In *Aida* a daughter begs for clemency from the father who psychologically torments her by revoking her birthright. In *Rigoletto* a father first berates the courtiers who have abducted his daughter, then piteously asks them to spare her and to respect his grief; covering their embarrassment with a sardonic joke, they slink shamefacedly away. Verdi understood the art of emotional ingratiation, and could never withhold the clemency for which his characters ask. This benevolence is already apparent in his first opera *Oberto*, where the trios and quartets slow down the action and force people who are intent on revenge to think again about their motives. The result of this stalled self-scrutiny is, for the three surviving characters, a decision to behave differently: the singing cure is more effective than Sigmund Freud's talking cure.

Although it is no longer fashionable to think of art in moralistic terms, I have the feeling that Verdi's music is good for us – that it makes us more tenderly concerned, more forgiving. I don't consider Wagner's music to be bad for us, but others, including his own characters, have reached that conclusion without wanting to deny its irresistible fascination. Elisabeth in *Tannhäuser* in her opening address to the hall of song gives a candid anatomy of the emotions stirred up in her by that art: pleasure but also pain, unnamed feelings and unknown longings. She could be analysing our responses to Wagner, who delights and torments us in equal parts, and provokes yearnings that he tantalizingly declines to satisfy. Hence Elisabeth's ravished, ravaged question, 'Heinrich! Was tatet Ihr mir an?' She asks Tannhäuser what he has done to her; his singing is an assault, threatening her moral security. Charles Baudelaire went further. He rejoiced in the 'knowledge of the diabolical element in man' that he heard in the overture when the plodding chant of the pilgrims is drowned out by the hellish pleasures of the Venusberg. The composer César Franck, more cautious than Baudelaire, scribbled 'poison' on his score of *Tristan und Isolde*, as if marking a bottle with the skull and crossbones. Thomas Mann's stories about Wagnerites warn about the dangers of this music. In one case a performance of *Die Walküre* incites a brother and sister to commit incest; in another *Tristan* proves fatal when a patient in a sanatorium listens to a mere piano transcription of its overheated intensity. Can an opera kill you? Wagner blamed himself for the demise of the tenor Ludwig Schnorr von Carolsfeld, who caught a fever after singing the first performance of *Tristan* in Munich in 1865, fell into a delirium like the hero, and called out the composer's name, as if crying for Isolde, on his deathbed. 'I drove you to the abyss!' Wagner wrote in a diary entry posthumously addressed to the tenor, adding 'I pushed him over.' There were other victims: in 1911 and 1968 the conductors Felix Mottl and Joseph Keilberth collapsed while conducting *Tristan* in Munich and died shortly afterwards. Giuseppe Sinopoli died on the podium in Berlin in 2001 during a performance of *Aida*, but no one attributed his heart attack to the strain of Verdi's music.

This sonic contagion is not the whole truth. Marcel Proust, a devotee of Wagner who imitated in prose his infinitely elastic musical sentences and his recurrent motifs, remarked in a letter that 'The essence of music is to awake in us a mysterious depth of soul … which may … be called religious'. That mystery is closed off in Verdi's operas, where religion is merely a reinforcement of state power: the priests in *Aida*, the Inquisitor in *Don Carlos* and the papal legate who unjustly condemns Gaston in *Jérusalem* are all politicians. Wagner's characters are conscious of sin and crave redemption, and his orchestra – when it raises the drowned bodies of the Dutchman and Senta in a soothed, lightened modulation at the end of *Der fliegende Holländer*, or completes the Mass at the end of *Parsifal* by making a holy spirit audible in the wavy haze of strings, rippling harps and murmuring voices – answers their prayers. A journalistic article written by Wagner in 1841 during his indigent stay in Paris charmingly gives thanks to this power. In fine weather, the writer and a friend attend an outdoor concert. The friend, called R—, deputizes for Wagner himself, and he silences quibbles about faulty intonation in the alfresco performance of Mozart and Beethoven by draining his glass of punch and crying 'Praise be to God, who created the season of spring and the art of music!' Wagner was no more an orthodox believer than Verdi, so it is telling that he equates both God and music with the earth's seasonal renewal. Gurnemanz in the third act of *Parsifal* hails the rite of spring as a benediction, but it is the gentle pressure of the orchestra murmuring beneath his sermon that transcribes the thaw, the new life nudging to the surface, and the grateful tears of those who witness this pagan resurrection.

Emotionally and topographically, Wagner belonged, as he told a patron in 1858, 'on wondrous heights' or 'right down in the depths'. He shuttled between mountain peaks and the bed of a river or a subterranean grotto; Verdi took up residence on the middle ground, our human terrain.

|||||||||||||||||||

The epiphany in Wagner's article occurs, significantly enough, in a public garden, like the one in Venice where the busts stand. In 1882, on the day when he heard the gondolier singing Verdi, he set off with Cosima for the Giardini Pubblici to hear a band play 'something from *Lohengrin*'. A trimmed, tamed garden is an odd setting for his music. Despite the storms and floods and lakes of flame in his operas, it needs to be heard in a closed, almost cloistral space, sealed against distracting reality like the theatre at Bayreuth; in any case, they lost their way at this unfamiliar end of Venice and had to make do with a visit to the Arsenal. A park laid out for leisurely promenading is also too genteel for Verdi, whose music was more at home on city streets or in a rural workplace. In 1845 a barrel organ churned out a medley from his *Giovanna d'Arco* in Milan. Crowds gathering to listen interfered with traffic, so the police declared the music a public nuisance. In 1861 Verdi noted that the peasants treading grapes in the courtyard of his villa sang to mark time. He didn't mention what they sang, but it could have been one of his arias. Despite the incongruity, chunks of both Verdi and Wagner were performed in the Giardini Pubblici during their lifetimes, though surely not on the same programme; to gauge the distance between them, we have to imagine two bands playing in competition.

Sometimes the sounds might converge: the divided strings in the *Lohengrin* prelude could match those in the prelude to *La traviata*, though their meanings differ. Wagner follows the descent of a refined spirit wafting down into our material world, whereas Verdi's orchestra records the pain of a human being whose material existence is fading away, reduced to a breathy wisp of spirit; Wagner's mystical vision could not be further from Verdi's emotional diagnosis of the tubercular Violetta.

Otherwise the excerpts would clash discordantly. To exemplify love in Verdi and Wagner, you would need to have Otello's dying reminiscence of the kiss he gave Desdemona playing in one ear while the heroine's expiring rhapsody from *Tristan und Isolde* poured into the other. Otello sings about an unbearable loss: although he repeats a musical phrase from the earlier love duet, the kiss is no longer mutual and he bestows it on a corpse. Isolde has no such regrets. Wagnerian love is a metaphysical thirst; the music she hears streaming from Tristan's inert body buoys her up and changes her grief to what she calls, in her final gasping words, the highest joy. Otello cannot forgive himself for killing Desdemona, though he makes a touchingly futile attempt to win her back to life by reviving the memory of their happiness. Isolde, lifted aloft by a self-induced exaltation, is telling us that Tristan is better off dead, as she soon hopes to be. Otello distractedly repeats Desdemona's name, separating its syllables and elongating them as if that might bring her back. Isolde's 'Liebestod' reduces Tristan to a meagre generic pronoun, 'er': the individual has been superseded, replaced by her ideal version of him. Perhaps just one of these scenes is about love, which is a victory over the ego. The subject of the other is eroticism, satisfied only when its pleasant pain is snuffed out by unconsciousness.

Or the two bands could compare the pyre on which Manrico imagines his supposed mother Azucena being burned in *Il trovatore* with the funeral pyre of Siegfried in *Götterdämmerung*. Verdi's tenor emits tuned shrieks of distress; he feels the fire searing human flesh, and is sympathetically inflamed by fury. Brünnhilde, after throwing the torch onto the pile of logs, admires the blaze, which will consume a polluted world and incinerate the gods. The fire seems radiant to her, the flames laugh, her high notes express exhilaration. She even expects the horse she rides to share her glee. Here is an example of the 'inhuman feelings' Turgenev found in Wagner, whose characters, he said, were 'not people'. Brünnhilde is a goddess, indifferent to squeamish mortal fears. Manrico, at the same moment of crisis, is pathetically human – not a troubadour or a serenading lover but a panicking son.

After this, the vying bands might try the triumphal march from *Aida* and the overture to *Die Meistersinger*. Verdi's trumpet fanfares and clattering cymbals introduce a celebration of military success that has a harsh, blinding glare, as if a North African sun were refracted from the brass; the march concusses the ground, only to fall apart when the prisoners of war sing their lament. Wagner's mastersingers troop into church or onto the meadow outside the city with swaggering confidence, and the solemnity of the orchestra – which manages to combine a lyrical reverie with the procession's officious tread, and suspends the onward progress to allow the attendant apprentices to break ranks for some juvenile capering – promotes them from artisans and artists to municipal heroes, ancestral defenders of German culture. Verdi's ensemble enables victors and victims to tell their divergent stories; when Wagner's scattered themes come together, the result is a unanimity that is compelling but also perhaps compulsory or conscriptive, since the dissident Walther von Stolzing is not allowed to remain outside this musical freemasonry. The overture's last notes introduce a chorale chanted by the whole community: music is destined to acquire the power of speech, as Wagner argued in his interpretation of Beethoven's Ninth Symphony, and here all the world speaks with one voice.

For a paired encore, the bands might give superimposed performances of the slaves' chorus from *Nabucco* and the ride of the Amazonian warrior maidens from *Die Walküre*. 'Va, pensiero' is so well known that those who hummed along in the Giardini Pubblici may not have noticed that there is more to it than pining for a lost or (in the case of nineteenth-century Italy) uncreated homeland. The slaves sing an edited version of Psalm 137, amending its words to remove a righteous sense of grievance in their desire for revenge on the Babylonians, whose children are to be dashed on the stones of the toppled city. In the psalm, the captives are too downcast to praise Zion when their masters require it, and they dejectedly hang their harps in the willow trees beside the river. Verdi's chorus cannot refuse to 'sing the Lord's songs in a strange land', but perhaps they agree too readily, and succumb too easily to self-pity. The lulling, cradling music, like the spirituals of American slaves, is their communal consolation, and it exemplifies art's duty – in a phrase Verdi applied to Alessandro Manzoni's novel *I promessi sposi* – to be 'a comfort to mankind'. The chorus assuages a metaphysical homesickness: Liszt described poets, by which he also meant musicians, as 'exiles from heaven'. After murmuring their memories of Zion, the slaves suddenly shout a rhetorical question about the abandoned instruments in the trees. Why, they ask, does the seer's golden harp hang there mute and useless? Music can produce a volume of infuriated sound that might serve as a weapon to bludgeon the city's walls. Although 'Va, pensiero' usually earns an encore, the high priest Zaccaria is not impressed by it. He berates its tearful effeminacy, quickens the tempo, and bestirs the slaves with his prophecy of Babylon's fall, describing snakes that will writhe among the skulls and hyenas gnawing corpses. Lyricism is ineffectual; what matters to a leader like Zaccaria is music's capacity to incite the supine mass to action.

Even if we stop before this epilogue, the chorus offers intimations of another function that music performs. After the occupying Austrian and French armies withdrew, Italians had no reason to go on grieving for the 'patria sì bella e perduta!', so in time 'Va, pensiero' came to serve another purpose. More than a lament for the place of our nativity, it perhaps refers with weary resignation to our place of rest. In 1901, when Verdi and Strepponi were transferred from their temporary graves in the Cimitero Monumentale in Milan to a crypt in the Casa di Riposo, Toscanini conducted 'Va, pensiero' at the cemetery. Verdi himself made similar use of the piece in 1867 during a vigil at the deathbed of Antonio Barezzi, one of his earliest supporters and the father of his first wife Margherita. As the story goes, Barezzi directed his eyes towards a piano in the corner of the room.

Verdi, intuiting the weak old man's unexpressed wish, began playing 'Va, pensiero'. Barezzi mumbled his gratitude and quietly died. Like a psychopomp, music had eased his passage across the border.

This reassurance is not matched by Wagner's Ride of the Valkyries, if we imagine it sounding from the other end of the Giardini Pubblici. Its volatility is hard to resist: the trills are like coils compressing an energy that explodes outwards, the whisking of the strings thrashes the air, and the striding rhythm of the brass somehow makes it possible to imagine heavy bodies – horses and their riders – advancing through this turbulent atmosphere without being dragged down by gravity. Here is the kind of bracing meteorological challenge for which romantic poets, facing up to 'the press of the storm' like Robert Browning, eagerly volunteered. Then the battalion of women call to each other with high notes that ricochet across the sky, and join in a fit of laughter as their horses competitively jostle. The hilarity is witchy and malevolent, because we are in a region beyond life, beyond human concerns. The Valkyries are riding home with bodies they have scavenged from the battlefield; the carnage below – the result of feuds between clans, probably stirred up by their father Wotan – allows them to take their pick of valiant cadavers, which will be reactivated to guard the imperilled fortress of Valhalla. One of the warrior maidens carries the remains of Sintolt the Hegeling, another has his sworn foe Wittig the Irming slung over her saddle. There is a moment of shocked bathos when Brünnhilde, having rescued Sieglinde, gallops in with a passenger of the wrong kind. 'Das ist kein Held!' shrieks the affronted Helmwige: instead of a dead man, Brünnhilde has brought back a live, pregnant woman, out of place in this aerial mortuary.

'Va, pensiero' has a pacifying influence. Wagner's version of the afterlife could not be less like Verdi's quiet homecoming. Instead of resurrection, *Die Walküre* imagines ghouls who will go on killing after death, with the Valkyries as hyenas like those that prey on corpses in Zaccaria's vision of fallen Babylon. Perhaps Verdi was too much of a humanist to be able to conceive of the divine or the demonic. Despite his agnosticism, he remarked when Barezzi died that it might be agreeable to believe in a hereafter: then the living man's grief would prove to the dead man how truly he was loved. The fiction of heaven is precious because it permits the perpetuation of our affections.

Love as a need for complementarity and completion, or as a self-negating suicide? A bonfire that potentially purifies the world, or one that sears and singes human flesh? Gods who, like Isis and Osiris in *Aida*, assume credit for events on earth and expect obsequious humans to pay tribute, or a god like Wotan in *Götterdämmerung* who sits waiting expectantly for the moment when human beings will declare him superfluous and allow him to die? Heaven as the blessing of unconsciousness, or as the bloody epilogue to earthly conflicts? My imaginary double concert, each half assaulting a different ear, would induce at best a head-ache, at worst a nervous breakdown.

# 2 | *National Characters*

## NORTH AND SOUTH

In the early nineteenth century, before technology abridged distances, geography set limits to human lives. Each on his own side of the Alps, Wagner and Verdi belonged to countries and cultures with no common ground. Wagner told Nietzsche that being German, more than an accident of birth, was 'a purely metaphysical conception, unique in the history of the world'. For his part, Verdi felt an attachment that was purely physical to what he described, in a letter from Paris, as 'my little patch of sky at home'. It did not matter that the flat, bleak plain around Busseto was a nondescript corner of the dishonoured land he called 'our poor Italy'. He accepted the region as his fate, something he had to live with, like his face. Wagner's homeland was an idea, Verdi's a portion of earth on which he was raised, and on which, when he became a landowner, he grew crops.

Not long before the two composers were born, the French saloniste Anne-Louise-Germaine de Staël invented a 'science of nations' that owed its acute sense of locality to her own experience of migration and exile. Her father, who had served as the finance minister of Louis XVI, was Swiss; she first fled from Paris in 1792 during the Revolution, and after Napoleon again expelled her from the city in 1803 she spent time in Weimar, Berlin and Vienna. A stay in Italy prompted her novel *Corinne, ou l'Italie*, about a female bard who grows up in England but chafes against its social strictures and absconds to Rome. De Staël went on to write a study of German philosophy and literature, and in her account of Zacharias Werner's play about Attila – later the source for Verdi's opera – she implicitly denounced Napoleon's imperial advance across Europe. Like her novel, *De l'Allemagne* challenged the provinces conquered by the emperor to rise up against him; the book's ideal reader, as Wagner later remarked, was 'a Frenchman disgusted with his own civilization'. In 1810 the police destroyed the first edition and harried de Staël into exile once more. She travelled to Scandinavia and Russia, ventured back to Italy after Waterloo in 1815, then returned to Paris where she died in 1817.

Her taxonomy of southern and northern cultures appeared at the beginning of a century in which nations, emerging from the disintegration of Napoleon's empire, began to define themselves as political units of a new kind – not mere administrative entities like states, but families of men whose kinship gave them a collective will. The enlightened eighteenth century assumed that human experience was everywhere the same, so that Samuel Johnson could 'with extensive view/Survey mankind from China to Peru'. De Staël's gaze was less panoramic, and it fixed on idiosyncracy not uniformity. Hence the ambiguous allegiances of Corinne – and in analysing her heroine's dual 'nationality', de Staël coined a word that made character an outgrowth of its native soil.

The countries that intrigued her most were 'two nations out of fashion', Italy and Germany. They were unfashionable because they were set apart from the axis of France and England, which in their different ways defined political and economic modernity. Italy and Germany were recidivist realms – charming because wayward in one case, exciting because wild in the other – which appealed to those who disliked the ideological regimentation of France or the stuffy mercantilism of England. Corinne's poetic improvisations announce her desire to live freely, without rules. She explains that Italians waste no time on politics because there is no fatherland to bother them. They concentrate instead on the joys of the body, and vacillate between an indolence that she calls 'oriental' and a ferocious tumult when their passions are stoked up: that alternation sounds like the biorhythm of Verdi's characters – swooning arias, energetic cabalettas. In another generality that pulls the continent apart, Corinne declares that 'the peoples of the south are inhibited by prose and depict their true feelings only in verse'. Prose, which requires a level head and a rational articulation of ideas, is best left to flat-minded northerners. The Italians in de Staël's novel therefore versify their feelings in a singsong mode of speech that turns into the lilt of cantilena. Soon enough Corinne became an operatic character, singing rhapsodic arias rather than extemporizing poems: in Rossini's *Il viaggio a Reims* the voice of the diva Corinna, unseen offstage like a supernatural portent, swoops and shimmers while a plucked harp makes the air tingle.

Like Italy, Germany was a country without a centre or a capital, where the social spirit, according to de Staël, had little power. Here artists and thinkers lived and worked in solitude, nervously aware of the encroaching forests and the monsters lurking there – the landscape explored by Carl Maria von Weber's *Der Freischütz* (in which Wagner while a schoolboy played the bogey Kaspar) and later by *Siegfried*. Corinne is synonymous with Italy because she is a creature of instinct; the north has a tendency to spiritualism, equally propitious for music. As de Staël said in *De l'Allemagne*, the English rule the seas and the French, thanks to Napoleon, are for the time being in control of the earth, but Germany has its own impalpable territory: its empire is in the air, which condenses into mist, fog, fuzzy obscurity.

These are the same imaginary nations described by the patriotic agitator Giuseppe Mazzini, who thought that their contradictory mentalities or moods were defined by music. Mazzini contrasted a nation of abstruse philosophers with a nation of earthy hedonists. German symphonies, he thought, were about 'God without man', whereas Italian opera – best represented by Rossini – was the province of 'man without God'. The reversible terms warn against the pitfalls of binary thinking, but it is tempting to apply the formula to Verdi and Wagner. Verdi's is a humanized world: the storm in *Rigoletto* moans and shrieks as the chorus gives voice to the wind, and the aural vista of the nocturnal Nile in *Aida* is soon invaded by the mumbling of the priests inside the temple. Strepponi tried in vain to convince him of God's existence by pantheistically raving, as she said in 1872, about 'the marvels of sky, earth, and sea, etc., etc'. He laughed at her unsung aria. Wagner was happier when making music describe a world where man has been consumed or superseded: Siegfried falls silent when he embarks on the surging Rhine, a river that, as de Staël said, was as majestically steady and indefatigable as an epic hero. In Sicily in the spring of 1882, after an excursion to see some wildflowers in bloom, Cosima recorded a comment Wagner made about the indifference of Italians to their own landscape. Anything not human was alien to them; their poetry ignored 'trees budding, blossoming, and fading, deep shadows, dew' – all the delicate, transitory life to which Germans, who lived through more extreme seasonal contrasts, so wistfully responded. A decade earlier, Wagner delightedly recalled the performance of his *Siegfried Idyll* at dawn in his lakeside house in Lucerne. The small band of players was like an indoor forest: the strings, he said, were trees, the woodwinds like birds hiding among the branches. Humanity, in the form of the boisterous Siegfried, was not missed. The possibility of effacing human life altogether occurs to Corinne when she wanders through the ruins of the Colosseum in Rome and watches culture crumble into vegetative nature. She is not downcast by the decay: 'Has the universe,' she asks, 'no other goal than man?' Ultimately Wagner's world belongs neither to men nor to the gods they make in their own image. It is the playground of the elements

– of the wind that blusters through the Steersman's song at the beginning of *Tristan und Isolde*, the fire that blazes from the orchestra at the end of *Die Walküre*, or the water that overwhelms the Gibichung hall at the end of *Götterdämmerung*; it opens out into the starry infinity, awash with oceanic sound, that swallows up the transfigured Isolde.

The novelist Stendhal also mapped a polarized continent in which emotions, like food and wine, changed when you crossed the Alps. He considered love and music to be Mediterranean inventions, at home in the unbridled south. The north was a region of fretful intellect, where composers elaborated mathematical systems rather than giving in to passion. Stendhal said that Italian lovers were eager, jealous, thrillingly quick to draw a dagger; Germans elevated the erotic instinct, regarding it as 'a divine emanation, something mystical'. Verdi and Wagner did not exactly fit the stereotypes – it was the philandering Wagner who behaved like a Latin lover, whereas Verdi was reticent in his dealings with women – but the characters in their operas behave as Stendhal expected southerners and northerners to do. When Alfredo is introduced to Violetta, he says he has been in love with her for a year, but the drama makes their mutual attraction seem instantaneous. His adoration changes in an instant to hatred, then changes back when he learns about Violetta's reason for quitting him. Wagner's characters are not so quick to act on physical urges; what slows them down is their curiosity about the source of that 'emanation', which may be diabolical not divine. They analyse their emotions and even, like Tristan and Isolde, engage in subtle philosophical debate about the self's predicament while making love. Hence Elsa's frustration when she is forbidden to interrogate Lohengrin: Wagnerian love is inquisitive and querulous by nature.

'South of the Alps,' Stendhal told his timid French readers in one of his travel books, 'society is a despot with no prisons'. No code of politesse got in the way of impulse and appetite, and Italian life resembled an opera by Rossini, all chuckling mirth and gesticulating enjoyment. A country that conducted itself according to Verdian principles would probably have displeased Stendhal: no more brio or sparkly *sprezzatura*, too much saturnine passion, too many arguments about political ideas. In a continent opened up by travel and by Napoleon's wars, Stendhal worried that the peninsula might lose its sealed immunity. The Italian language, with its easy abundance of rhymes and its open-throated vowels, was better suited to singing than to speaking, and he hoped that music would be able to defend it against the sterile influence of French rationalism.

A more dangerous cultural menace came from the north. In 1836 in an essay on the philosophy of music, Mazzini looked at romanticism from the point of view of subjugated Italy, and likened the movement's roving exponents to 'the northern invaders at the decay of the Roman Empire'. Earlier barbarians, like the warlord Attila who storms into Italy again in Verdi's opera, had laid waste to a classical civilization; now their modern successors, haunters of Gothic ruins, returned to pick through the debris like Byron's Childe Harold. Or they returned to conquer. In 1870 when the Prussian Kaiser announced his intention to reform the world, Verdi was reminded of 'the old Attila (another such missionary)'. He was not placated when Bismarck promised to spare besieged Paris, whose humiliation prompted Wagner to write his disgraceful lampoon *Eine Kapitulation*. Attila stopped short 'before the capital of the antique world', and in Verdi's opera he is debarred from entering Rome. Verdi did not expect Bismarck to desist, and noted that Paris was already being bombarded. Nor did he forget his grudge against the northern marauder. In 1893, while in Rome for the first local performance of *Falstaff*, he invited the Viennese critic Eduard Hanslick to lunch. Hanslick was Wagner's model for the pedantic marker Beckmesser, first called Veit Hanslich, in *Die Meistersinger*; he disliked Verdi's early operas, and even carped about *Otello*. Verdi, with a mischievous grin, introduced him to the other guests as 'the Bismarck of musical criticism'. Later that year the abiding animosity between south and north caused Verdi a musical problem: when *Falstaff* was taken on a European tour, the French baritone Victor Maurel – who appeared in the first performances, and originally wanted monopoly rights in the title role – refused to appear in Berlin, since he too remembered the Franco-Prussian War.

The suspicion and hostility were mutual. In 1874, almost twenty years before his letter of apology regretting his earlier hostility to Verdi's music, Hans von Bülow happened to be in Milan when Verdi conducted the *Requiem* there. Without attending the concert, Bülow damned Verdi as 'the all-powerful despoiler of Italian taste'. Acclaim for the *Requiem* struck him as 'a triumph … of Latin barbarism', all the more offensive because its composer was now a public dignitary, whom he ridiculed as 'Senator Verdi'. Bülow hoped that German impresarios would keep the offensive piece out of the sonorous fatherland. Verdi blamed this German insolence on the servility of Italians, who were too eager to be impressed by the accomplishments of visiting northerners. Like the Great Wall of China, the Alps separated two cultures, or drew a line between culture and the crudity of untutored nature. Whichever side of the mountain range you lived on, the barbarians were on the other, mustering to attack.

In 1823 in his life of Rossini, Stendhal briefly sketched what he called 'the Wars between Harmony and Melody', allegorical figures whom he imagined at loggerheads like Olympian gods, hurling disparagements across the Alps. To keep the peace, he set them at the greatest possible distance from each other: German music, which valued instrumental harmony above all else, was created in Dresden by Bach, while the more naively melodic Italian school had its origins in Naples, with Scarlatti as the founder. Stendhal explained the difference by treating sounds as tastes. Italian melody was irresistible, like luscious fruit gobbled by a child, whereas German harmony, like sauerkraut, was something you had to learn to like. He found foreign dissonance unpalatable and disparaged *Der Freischütz*, with its goblin-infested woodland and its bumptious rusticity, as a strictly 'Teutonic opera' not fit for export, a specimen of 'the primitive and the barbaric'.

Harmony, despite Stendhal's predilections, eventually won the war. When George Eliot heard three operas by Wagner in Weimar in 1855, she wondered whether their lack of tunes implied that melody was 'only a transitory phase of music'. In art as in nature she expected an orderly evolution, which meant that she and others who found Wagner hard to comprehend must be 'tadpoles unprescient of the future frog', still 'limited to tadpole pleasures'. Was melody merely the shameful craving of a childish taste, or the writhing of an unarticulated blob that had not grown legs? In 1879 Wagner sang the delicately faltering, gracious theme that introduces the last movement of Beethoven's fourth piano sonata and said 'This kind of melody is gone forever – innocent sweetness, it is a lost paradise.' His remark was regretful, but he viewed Eden as a state of mental infancy that we rightly outgrow. Verdi would have argued that melody had a more positive value: song is the speech of the sinews and the arteries, of sensations that bypass words. Verdi's melodies possess a sturdy physical vigour, whereas Wagnerian harmony loosens our hold on a world we want to consider real.

Stendhal hoped for a merger of melody and harmony, and predicted that it would happen in Paris, effectively the capital of Europe. Heinrich Heine, discussing opera in France in 1837, repeated the obligatory contrast between melody and harmony, then nominated a new candidate on the German side. Rossini remained the bubbling font of melody, but Heine thought his arias, like the singers who performed them, were too self-indulgent. Italian tunes, he said, were 'isolated … like their famous bandits'. He was referring to the brigands who hid in the Abruzzi mountains and preyed on travellers from the north, but his comment prepares the way for Verdi's outlaws: Manrico who invisibly laments the troubadour's lonely fate in his nocturnal serenade, Ernani who thrusts his way into a palace to taunt the king. Heine found an alternative to this Italian exhibitionism in the work of a composer who was born in Berlin, adopted an Italian forename, and spent his career composing French grand operas – Giacomo Meyerbeer. The tunes in

Meyerbeer's operas may have been short-breathed, but this demonstrated that melody, as Heine put it, had 'drowned in the stream of harmonious masses, just as the characteristic feelings of single men are lost in the united feeling of a whole race'. Meyerbeer's spectacular scenes drilled choral groups in order to dramatize what Heine called 'the great questions of society': religious warfare in *Les Huguenots*, imperial conquest in *L'Africaine*.

During his impoverished early years in Paris between 1839 and 1842, Wagner wrote an essay that likened Meyerbeer to Napoleon and said that his operas 'destroyed the shackles of national prejudice' by combining 'German solidity and Italian beauty'. Back in Germany in 1843, having received no professional favours from Meyerbeer in exchange for this flattery, he took a different view of the matter. A composer could not be European, so he had to choose between belonging to the German or the French school; 'friend Giacomo', a rootless Jew who fluctuated between Berlin and Paris, had – Wagner claimed in a letter – muddied and diluted both traditions. Now all he heard in Meyerbeer's orchestration of public conflict was a sound like Prussian regiments on the parade ground. The masses in Wagner's own operas are rarely harmonious: they either gang up to threaten an enemy, like the Gibichung horde reacting to an imagined attack in *Götterdämmerung* or the knights in the Wartburg rounding on Tannhäuser, or splinter into squabbling sectarian groups like the riotous mob in *Die Meistersinger*. Verdi's feelings about Meyerbeer were equally mixed. The auto-da-fé in *Don Carlos* is his homage to and his denunciation of grand opera, testing Heine's claim about Meyerbeer's 'harmonious flood' that incorporates 'the joys and sorrows of all mankind'. Here state and church join forces to crush dissent and consign heretics to the flames; the grandiose scene exposes the brutality of a regime that relies on theatrical means – the king's armoured costume, his statuesque pose when the cathedral doors open, the ceremonial execution – to intimidate its subjects.

Mazzini too believed that Meyerbeer was 'the prophet of music with a mission, of music standing immediately below religion', and in 1867 he praised *Les Huguenots* both for its melodies and for the 'harmonic substratum' that supported them. Like Stendhal and Heine, Mazzini was waiting for a 'genius-prophet' or 'high priest' who would resolve a musical dispute and at the same time settle the political and philosophical problems of the age: the promised accord between melody and harmony might balance the competing claims of individual and society, or of Italian sensuality and German mysticism. Italy, as its music revealed, was earthy, brilliantly sunny, often feverish. The German spirit was airier. 'The soul lives,' Mazzini said of the symphonies that were its testimony, 'but lives a life that is not of this earth.... It aspires to the infinite, which is its country', and is 'profoundly religious yet with a religion that has no symbol'. But how could earth and heaven, body and soul, be brought together? The synthesis seemed impossible, tantamount to imagining a compound of Verdi and Wagner.

In 1875 in a letter to his friend Opprandino Arrivabene, Verdi toyed with possible exits from the stalemate. Some young composers wanted to be melodists like Bellini, others to be harmonists like Meyerbeer, while another group followed Wagner and considered themselves to be 'futurists'. Verdi wished that all these schismatic principles could be forgotten, along with the difference between German and Italian schools: 'then perhaps the kingdom of art will begin'. But that kingdom, as his phrase implied, was probably not of this earth. In 1894, replying to Bülow's slavish apology, he said that he was happy for northern and southern artists to go their different ways, and even cited Wagner's opinion that national character should be a source of pride. Despite this agreement to differ, Verdi went on to grumble about the inequality between 'the sons of Bach' and 'we, sons of Palestrina'. Italy once had an indigenous tradition, but it had become 'bastardized, and ruin threatens us'. He blamed no one for the adulteration, though he probably thought it was a result of Wagner's influence.

Wagner in his 1851 essay *Eine Mitteilung an meine Freunde* apologized to his followers for his juvenile flirtation with melody, treating it as a dalliance with female tempters who were seditious because foreign. In *Das Liebesverbot*, performed in Magdeburg in 1836, he said he had 'openly thrown myself into the arms of the modern Italian cantilena', while in *Rienzi* he succumbed to 'the Franco-Italian melismus', an infection spread by the grand operas of Gasparo Spontini. He made his peace with Italy when *Lohengrin* was performed in Bologna in 1871 (with Verdi in attendance incognito). Wagner treated the occasion as a breakthrough in international relations. Writing to the mayor of the city, he described German music drama as a remedy for the follies of Italian opera and a contribution to Italy's political struggles. His letter linked the caprices of Italian prima donnas with the tyrannical whims of the kings and princes who once divided the country between them and whose courts, where musicians were hirelings, had kept 'Italy no less than Germany in a state of impotence and fragmentation'. Like Lohengrin descending from the sky to lead the forces of Brabant against the Hungarians, Wagner saw himself taking charge of the fractious situation – as a liberator, or a conqueror? When Arrigo Boito – at the time a perfervid Wagnerian, later Verdi's librettist and the most loyal of his helpers – wrote to congratulate him on the performance, Wagner replied as if he were presiding over a match between countries, like the alliance of Spain and France that is sealed by a royal betrothal in *Don Carlos*: 'Perhaps a new marriage is necessary between the genius of peoples, and in this case we Germans could not have a happier choice of love than one that would mate the genius of Italy with the genius of Germany. If my poor *Lohengrin* should prove the herald of this ideal wedding, it would truly have performed a wondrous mission of love.'

Verdi, replying to Bülow, hoped at best for coexistence and mutual respect. What Wagner had in mind was a union cemented in bed. But the jubilant wedding march in *Lohengrin* leads to a quarrel in the nuptial chamber, and the knight prematurely divorces his bride and calls off his mission. The brief marriage of north and south, of harmony and melody, ended in divorce.

||||||||||||||||||

In less diplomatic moods, Verdi and Wagner – who lived in a Europe more or less continuously at war along its fault lines between north and south or east and west – exchanged the kind of automatic abuse we still direct at those who annoy us by being different.

They could have had a frank debate about Giuseppe Garibaldi, whose swashbuckling march across Sicily in the spring of 1860 with a thousand followers was applauded by Verdi as the most splendid of operatic finales, accompanied by guns instead of an orchestra. Wagner was incensed when Garibaldi threw himself into the Franco-Prussian War in 1871 and captured eight hundred of the Kaiser's troops. The feat earned him a musical insult: one of Wagner's aristocratic acquaintances referred to Garibaldi as 'the old hurdy-gurdy', churning out drivel, and on his own initiative Wagner fancifully imagined him as the warmongering Druid priest Oroveso in Bellini's opera *Norma*. Then, while living in Sicily in 1882, Wagner traced the route taken by Garibaldi and his redshirts from Marsala to Palermo; he now decided to admire him, which meant appropriating his mystique. Rehearsing the marches he had written for Ludwig II and the Kaiser, he told his Sicilian military band that Garibaldi was coming to the concert. 'If only we had a conductor like that!' the players said. In another comical appropriation, Wagner supplemented the overture to *Der fliegende Holländer* with an impromptu narrative, pretending – as Cosima reported – 'that it depicts Garibaldi's entrance into Sicily, the king's prayer, the retreat of the Neapolitan fleet'. When Garibaldi died later that year, Wagner saluted him as 'a classical figure' and likened him to Timoleon, who defended Greece against Carthage in the third century BC.

In the case of Garibaldi, the argument would have ended in a truce, perhaps even in Wagner's recantation. On most other matters he and Verdi, geographically prejudiced, would have sullenly agreed to differ. 'Imagine: no more

Germans!!' Verdi wrote to Piave in 1848 after Austrian troops were expelled from Venice. 'You know how much I liked them!' During the Franco-Prussian War he denounced the Germans as Goths equipped with the latest military hardware, 'men of intellect but lacking in heart, a strong race but uncivilized', and told the librettist of *Aida*, Antonio Ghislanzoni, that when writing verses for the self-congratulatory triumphal scene he should keep in mind the telegram in which Kaiser Wilhelm attributed Prussia's victory over France to divine providence. Verdi looked fearfully ahead to a time when the German empire would extend its reach to Rome, the Mediterranean and 'the Adriatic, which has already been proclaimed a German sea'. The Spanish characters in *La forza del destino* travel to Italy to help fight an enemy who is not named in the version performed in Milan in 1869. The original *Forza*, performed in St Petersburg in 1862, makes clear that the war in question was Italy's earlier campaign to repel the Austrians in 1744: 'Ecco I tedeschi!' cry the grenadiers as they seize their weapons – here come the Germans. The rabble-rousing Preziosilla even calls the northern horde 'Flagel d'Italia eterno', an eternal scourge like Attila.

Wagner's animosities were less justifiable, and he conducted his vendettas retroactively. In 1882 he maligned the Renaissance, telling Cosima that 'the influence of Latinity spelled the death of everything'. He made amends for the catastrophe by endowing Germany with a cultural revival to challenge Italy's: as he saw it, Hans Sachs and the mastersingers established music as a doughtily bourgeois art in Nuremberg at around the same time that Italian courtiers were presenting the first aristocratic operas in Mantua and Florence. In the present, Wagner's most virulent rage was directed at the French, powdered fops who represented 'the putrefaction of the Renaissance' because they no longer possessed the 'barbaric juices' that animated his own permanently primeval countrymen. Among other crimes, he could not forgive the French for defaming Goethe and Schiller in translation: he loathed Gounod's insipid *Faust* and had misgivings about Rossini's *Guillaume Tell*. Italy scarcely threatened this patrimony, and Wagner took a colonist's smug view of its culture. 'From the Italians', he wrote, 'the German … adopted music … as his own.' At least this balances Verdi's equally dogmatic claim, in his letter to Arrivabene, that melody was always and everywhere Italian, even if Germans wrote the tunes.

Wagner was fond of epigrammatic generalities that glanced across Europe and briskly passed judgment on its incompatible societies. In an essay written in Paris in 1840 he maintained that Italians used music as an aid to love-making, while the French treated it as a social amenity; but Germans – here a more high-minded people, despite the sweaty barbarism he later extolled – esteemed it as both a science and a religion. In 1851 in his tract *Oper und Drama* he returned to the triangular contrast, and put female flesh on his caricatures. He now called music, as represented by Italian opera, a courtesan who sold herself for profit. A lyrical gift like Verdi's, seen from this position, was mere promiscuity. Mazzini too described contemporary music as a 'prostituted woman', put to basely commercial uses but longing to be saved, like Violetta in *La traviata*. The art, he said, was 'holy with anticipation', awaiting the composer who would replace flirty blandishments with the expression of emotional truth; it needed 'the baptism of a mission'. Mazzini, whose musical tastes were old-fashioned, never realized that it was Verdi who had elevated a fallen art as well as a fallen woman.

Wagner went on to call French music a coquette, naughtily cavorting through a cancan. Then, surprisingly, he completed the triad by characterizing German music as a prude, an 'unsexed dame' who filled him with horror. Was he thinking of Mozart's Donna Anna recoiling from Don Giovanni, or of the simpering Agathe in *Der Freischütz*? Whatever he meant, his national responsibility was the opposite of that which Mazzini delegated to Italian composers, who needed to recognize that 'music, like woman, has in it the sacredness of natural purity'. Wagner's task was to warm up a virgin, rather than teaching a loose woman to abandon her flighty, hedonistic ways. Music in opera, he said, must be 'a woman who really loves', who is keen for gratification. His early heroines begin in childish innocence, but kindle and blaze as they sing. Senta in *Der fliegende Holländer* gives herself to a demon lover, and Elsa in *Lohengrin* conjures up a phantasmal wooer; Elisabeth in *Tannhäuser* blesses the sinner who has no use for her chastity. Mazzini saw the Italian composer as a reformer or redeemer. Wagner's task – when confronted by the thin-blooded heroines of German predecessors like Weber – was to be a seducer.

For polemical purposes, Verdi and Wagner stayed true to national values. But both were attracted to what lay across the border, and scouted a wider world that was the market for their wares. Verdi wrote for theatres in St Petersburg and Cairo, and on his first visit to London – after a journey by stagecoach, train and steamboat from Milan to Lucerne, Basle, Strasbourg, Baden-Baden, Bonn, Cologne, Brussels and Paris – he said that, having seen this thronging metropolis, he knew that 'Milan is nothing!' Wagner hoped that *Tristan und Isolde* would be performed in Rio de Janeiro, and when his plans for Bayreuth suffered a setback he thought of transferring his festival to the obligingly empty spaces of the American west. In 1880, after reading an article about New Zealand, he said that the 'ability to colonize' proved the virtue of the Anglo-Saxon race, and wished he were young enough to emigrate.

At Bayreuth in 1876 after the first *Ring*, Wagner told the audience, 'My children, here you have a truly German art.' Saint-Säens, reporting on the same speech, gave it a defensive edge: Wagner, he remembered, said that by common consent there was an Italian art and a French art – and now, thanks to him, Germany had caught up. Yet Wagner was no xenophobe. Hence his fondness for Italy, which to him was synonymous with fantasy, offering a choice of escapes from stark, frigid reality: 'Naples is an intoxication,' he told Cosima in 1880, 'Venice a dream.' When it suited him, Wagner could pretend that he preferred to travel in the opposite direction, and he told his English friend Frederick Praeger that on his return from Paris to Dresden in 1842 he felt like Tannhäuser after he quit the fetid Venusberg and inhaled the crisp, virtuous air of the fatherland. But he brought the pagan south home with him: why else did he muddle the geography of myth by installing Venus and her underground court of sylphs and maenads in a mound near the Wartburg in northern Germany, a chilly latitude ill-suited to the goddess of love? His transgressive imagination had no respect for frontiers. He defended his literary excursions by arguing that the Celtic legends he used as sources for *Tristan* and *Parsifal* had been 'shaped anew' by German adaptations. Despite this quibble, the landscapes of *Parsifal* are southern: the temple was a souvenir of Siena Cathedral, and he wanted Klingsor's gardens to look like those of Palazzo Rufolo in Ravello. On a trip to Palermo in 1910–11, the Russian symbolist Andrey Bely decided that Sicily was Wagner's Monsalvat, where the Grail knights guard their sacred trophy. His evidence was a pun: he equated Sicily with St Cecilia, which made the island the birthplace of music. Bely imagined Klingsor hurling his spear from Calabria and puncturing the earth on Etna, which explained the red river of lava that oozes from the wound. The convulsive island was the body of Amfortas, and the volcano's periodic eruptions liquefied the blood in this geological chalice.

Verdi knew that music had a homely municipal function, which he conscientiously discharged. His operas tour an Italy that is federated rather than unified, a scattering of separate centres, each with its own topographical mystique. In *Attila*, Aquilean refugees settle in a marsh, and Foresto has a prophetic vision of Venice rising phoenix-like from the lagoon. He rallies the chorus to believe in the improbable idea, and their unanimous fervour helps to make it happen. It is not like Valhalla in *Das Rheingold*, which is built overnight by unseen labourers and is entered by way of a rainbow bridge; Venice has a foundation, even if it is only piles poking out of the mudflat. *Simon Boccanegra* extols the maritime breezes of Genoa, where Verdi spent his winters, and takes stock of its busy shipping. In *Les Vêpres siciliennes* the patriot Procida celebrates his repatriation with an aria about Palermo, kissing the ground he is grateful to be once more treading. *Rigoletto*, with its depraved court and its murderous slums, is far from being a postcard for Mantua, though the jester takes care to establish that the hired killer Sparafucile is a foreigner. 'Straniero?' he asks suspiciously; Sparafucile replies that he comes from Burgundy. The exchange reveals much about tribal loyalties in this splintered, factional country.

But Verdi did not confine himself to his native land (or even to the southern fringe of Europe, since in *Ernani*, *Il trovatore* and *La forza del destino* Spain is an overheated extension of Italy – a place of honour-bound vows and vendettas, with mountains where gipsies wander and penitents punish the flesh in caves). His imaginative forays worried the nationalist poet Giuseppe Giusti, who after hearing *Macbeth* cautioned Verdi against 'the exotic charms of foreign liaisons', potentially as dangerous as Wagner's escapade with melody, that alien minx. To adapt a play by Shakespeare, especially one so infused by the foul climate of the north, seemed unpatriotic, and Giusti hoped that in future Verdi would pay closer attention to the political ambitions and emotional needs of his countrymen. In his reply to Giusti's letter, Verdi did some nimble sidestepping and blamed Italian dramatists for not providing him with worthy local subjects. He was unrepentant, and in 1857 in *Aroldo*, the revised version of *Stiffelio*, he changed the pastor travelling through Austria to a Saxon crusader – perhaps a properly medieval version of Byron's modern, irreligious Childe Harold – who returns from Syria to his castle in Kent, and then, when he discovers that his wife has taken a lover during his absence, travels north to Loch Lomond, where the homeopathic agency of the landscape soothes his distress. The local details in Piave's libretto are quaintly inaccurate. Women trudge home after harvesting grain, glad to be out of the scorching sun – not a problem that often troubles agricultural workers in Scotland. Shepherds, emblems of pastoral care and Christian forbearance, lead their flocks back to the fold while playing the *piffero*, Verdi's approximation to the bagpipe. Its oboe-like sound is inimitably Italian: Berlioz evoked the roving bands of *pifferari* in the serenade of the Abruzzian mountain-dweller in his Byronic symphony *Harold en Italie*. Hearing the bell for the Angelus, the opera's unCalvinist Scots join in an 'Ave'. Such solecisms were worth the risk for Verdi, who refused to confine himself to a familiar world. Opera sends its characters to extremes, as Wagner challenged it to do when he said that the theatre should expose 'the whole man, with his lowest and highest passions … in terrifying nakedness'; the travels of Aroldo stretch his range of emotional experience from one end of the earth to another – from Palestine to the Scottish highlands, from war against the infidel in a desert to the forgiveness of infidelity in a setting as bare and calm as the 'vale profound' where William Wordsworth heard the solitary reaper singing about 'old, unhappy, far-off things/And battles long ago'.

Explaining his later distaste for Wagner, Nietzsche contrasted the 'damp north' of mysticism with the 'torrid zone' of southern vitality, represented by the catlike frisking of Bizet's *Carmen*. He called Wotan 'the god of bad weather', and as a remedy for the foggy misery of his regime said that music should be 'Mediterraneanized'. The advice was superfluous, since Wagner had already made the journey south. The imaginative itch went back to *Das Liebesverbot*, completed in 1836, long before his first visit to Italy. He took the story from Shakespeare's *Measure for Measure* but on his own initiative changed the setting from Vienna to sixteenth-century Palermo. The puritanical Friedrich, Wagner's version of Shakespeare's Angelo, is a German regent who imposes the titular ban on love by forbidding the licentious festivities of Carnival. Sicily was under Spanish rule in the sixteenth century; Wagner ignored that detail so as to ridicule German guilt about sex. The new location, he explained, allowed the action to be overtaken by 'the southern heat of the blood' and additionally spiced up by a percussion section containing such unWagnerian instruments as castanets and a tambourine. Shakespeare's Vienna is a stew of commercialized vice, repellent to the Duke who deputes Angelo to clean up the city. Wagner's Sicilians cannot be charged with laxity or lechery; they are simply keen to enjoy themselves before Lenten abstinence begins. Problems impede the progress of Shakespeare's play, where the heroine Isabella first has to bribe a proxy to sleep with Angelo – who despite his primness is sexually infatuated with her – and at the end receives another terse, predatory proposal from the Duke. The plot is less of a hindrance for Wagner's people, who are swept along by the pace of music, which is, as he said in *Eine Mitteilung*, 'the joyous throb of life itself'. No disguised Duke coerces the operatic Isabella, and she is free to give herself to her lover Luzio – a character who in Shakespeare's play is ordered to marry a bawd as a punishment for his sleazy intriguing.

The mob in *Das Liebesverbot* takes no notice of Friedrich's prohibition, and Carnival is a riot that could be the trial run for a revolution. This southern custom of farewelling the flesh, with masks as a theatrical cover for erotic licence, always appealed to Wagner. In Paris in 1841 he wrote a chorus to be sung by Carnival revellers rampaging down from the peak of Montmartre – the city's mound of Venus – to invade the sober, business-like streets below; he was hoping for its inclusion in the vaudeville *La Descente de la Courtille*. It begins with a summons sounded on cowhorns, eerily anticipating Hagen's warmongering call to his vassals in *Götterdämmerung*, and it goes on to deploy a battery of noise-makers – trombones, timpani, cymbals, as well as more of the castanets and tambourines heard in *Das Liebesverbot*. This is the kind of crowd heard in the Paris street by the dying Violetta at the end of *La traviata*, although the rhythm of Verdi's offstage chorus is sprightlier than Wagner's stomping, heavy-footed dance. Verdi's partygoers celebrate with an obscene relish, laughing as they deliver a fatted calf to the butcher and prepare to gorge themselves. It is a mercy that their words are so indistinct: the purpose of music and song – they shout – is to intensify their craziness, and like the drunken Dionysian worshippers in Nietzsche's account of Greek drama they pay mocking compliments to the sacrificial animal, 'Sir della festa'. Tragedy and comedy are happening simultaneously, with single lives ending as the collective life rowdily continues. Violetta deflects her self-pity into concern for the poor, who are still suffering despite the mood of popular gaiety, and sends her maid to make a charitable donation.

At the end of his life, Wagner briefly came to share Verdi's tragicomic understanding of Carnival, a fitful flaring-up of life before Lenten self-denial gives believers a small share in the agony of Christ. In Venice in early February 1883, he insisted on venturing out into the jammed streets on the last night of Carnival. His impulse was not as naturally altruistic as Violetta's; he felt it to be a moral duty, a corrective to his self-absorption, the kind of research that a dramatist should undertake. 'A person who does not try to make close contact with the masses is not worth much!' he told Cosima. He got as far as the Piazza San Marco, but recoiled from the crush: the scene suggested 'a black mass in which patches of flesh colour emerge' – a decadent image of bodies festering, not the happy saturnalia of *Das Liebesverbot*. Heart spasms soon confined him to the Palazzo Vendramin, where he died less than a fortnight later.

The further north Wagner's imagination ventured, the more he yearned for the south. *Der fliegende Holländer* takes place on the icy, storm-lashed Norwegian coast, although an earlier version was set in Scotland. For the romantics, both countries were approximations to Ultima Thule, the last remnant of habitable land on the edge of perpetual darkness. In her book on Germany, de Staël called Scandinavia a border zone, shading into the 'nocturnal universe by which our world is surrounded'. Wagner skirted this extremity of earth during a voyage from Riga to London in 1839; it was in a Norwegian fjord that he heard the shouts of the sailors ricocheting from granite cliffs like the bodiless echo of the Dutchman's dead crew. Yet this opera of Nordic storms – where the orchestra mimics the keening of gales and the whiplash of waves, not the pulse of heated southern blood – pines for meridional warmth. The dozing helmsman on Daland's ship nods off during a song about southern shores and Moorish strands. When he awakes he summons a south wind, gentler than the northern blasts that menaced Wagner in the Baltic, and it carries the battered ship home. *Parsifal* is set on another border, a rift where cultures clash. Wagner situated Klingsor's headquarters 'facing the Arab part of Spain', and he sent Kundry to forage further south when she roams through what she calls Arabia in quest of balsam to soothe Amfortas.

In December 1870 Bismarck and the French statesman Léon Gambetta vied to secure papal support towards the end of the Franco-Prussian War. Wagner told Cosima that he saw two principles in combat – the Latin expectation of happiness on earth, carried over from pagan times and revived by the French Revolution, against a morbid German awareness that the world could not be saved and therefore needed to be controlled. Later he played an extract from the dirge about history and its weary recurrences sung by the Norns at the start of *Götterdämmerung*, and summed up the nihilistic cycle: 'Now it is spring, now winter, now war, now peace, it is all the same.' More than countries or climates, north and south represented for Wagner the symbolic termini of the earth, the outer limits of life itself. Sicily in *Das Liebesverbot* is the paradise of infantile instinct, where the rites of spring are celebrated. Scandinavia, on the other hand, announces the onset of cosmic winter, when that bodily fire dies out; it is the setting for Ragnarök, the Norse apocalypse when the gods will be killed off and all life exterminated by ice. Verdi – who lacked Wagner's mental and physical intrepidity – ventured into that frozen darkness twice, on his trips to Russia in 1861–62 to supervise the staging of *La forza del destino*. Strepponi kept an anxious eye on the temperature, and worried that Verdi was 'facing 24, 26, 28 and more degrees of cold, Réaumur thermometer!' Well rugged up, internally warmed by imported supplies of rice, macaroni and salami, he survived what Strepponi called 'the perpetual sorbets of St Petersburg': the only way for an Italian to comprehend the 'mortal cold' was to imagine eating it as a dessert. Organizing the second of his two trips, necessary because the Sicilian soprano due to sing in *Forza* fell ill, Verdi ensured that he would be back in Italy before the worst of the Russian winter.

One evening in 1873 Wagner had a dispute with the French writer Édouard Schuré about the patriotic incorrectness of drinking French wine. Schuré provocatively asked for a bottle of Bordeaux, and received a stern lecture about what it meant to be German. It meant, Cosima reported, 'to feel a longing which cannot be fulfilled in Latin countries' – the longing, among other things, to be elsewhere. The steady gait of the German 'andante' guaranteed, as Wagner said, that the sturdy walker could 'reach everywhere in time, and manfully make the farthest-lying thing his own'. The walking Wagner had in mind was liable to become a strut. 'We are a warrior nation,' he said in 1870 as he watched celebrations of the victory in Sedan, when the Prussian army took Napoleon III prisoner. With Wagner's approval, Gottfried Sonntag, the bandmaster of the infantry regiment stationed in Bayreuth, adapted Siegfried's themes from the *Ring* in his *Nibelungen-Marsch*, militarizing the hero and multiplying him into a brassy platoon of conquerors. If the typical ambling German stayed on his feet for long enough, he might arrive at the limits of speculation and trespass on infinity, while conquering any countries he passed through along the way. Verdi – in person rootedly Latin not restlessly Teutonic, despite his imaginative excursions to remoter realms – was content with his early-morning tours of inspection around the perimeter of his estate at Sant'Agata.

# OLD GERMANY, YOUNG ITALY

The year after the Franco-Prussian War, Bizet made a remark about Wagner that was not meant to be complimentary. 'The German spirit of the nineteenth century,' he said, 'is embodied in that man.' For Wagner himself, the German spirit was a more problematic notion. Having been born in Leipzig, he was a Saxon not a German; his essay on Meyerbeer complained about the country's 'de-nationalized' or perhaps pre-national condition, which would not be altered by territorial or constitutional changes and could only be overcome by 'artistic patriotism'. Yet neither Bavaria nor Prussia had much use for the allegiance he pledged. Forced to leave Munich by Ludwig II's ministers in 1865, he later looked to Bismarck for patronage and hoped that his *Kaisermarsch*, composed in 1871, would be adopted as an anthem by the new regime. Again disappointed, he complained in 1874 that Germany was a Reich without being a nation.

'In France,' Wagner enviously remarked, 'everyone is a Frenchman'; a German had no such certainty. He blamed this lack of identity on the divided loyalties of the Holy Roman Empire, when the authority of German kings had to be confirmed by the pope. That arrangement still rankled: in *Rienzi* the tribune's first political error is his demand that the ambassadors of Bavaria and Bohemia should accept his terms for electing an emperor. In 1865 in his treatise *Was ist Deutsch?* Wagner speculated that true Germans must have felt homesick when papal commands compelled them to follow their kings into foreign lands, unlike the rabble of 'Franks, Goths, Lombards etc.', who happily settled abroad. Elaborating this historical fantasia, Wagner made a detour to condemn a Verdian character for misunderstanding the German soul. This was Charles V, 'King of Spain and Naples, hereditary Archduke of Austria, elected Romish Kaiser and Sovereign of the German Reich', who in *Don Carlos* has abdicated and taken refuge in a monastery. Charles probably renounced the throne because he was crippled by gout; for Verdi, however, his withdrawal made him an apolitical conscience, and his voice echoes through the cloister to warn that worldly ambitions are futile. Wagner had more interest in Charles during his term as Holy Roman Emperor, when he persecuted the Lutherans and put down rebellions by Protestant princes in Saxony and Hesse, pushing Germany to affirm its deviation from what Wagner called 'the un-German, Romanic State-idea'.

The battle lines had been drawn up in the twelfth century: Wagner's vexation about the Holy Roman Empire and its neglect of German interests revived the ancient feud between the Welfs and the Waiblingen, partisans who respectively supported the interests of the papacy and the monarchy during a quarrel about Lothair II's election as emperor in 855. The Welfs made common cause with the dukes of Saxony and Bavaria; their opponents belonged to the house of Hohenstaufen, and took their name from one of the family's castles at Waiblingen, which in Wagner's mythology doubled as the seat of the Nibelungen. The line of Hohenstaufen emperors included Friedrich I, nicknamed Barbarossa, who held out against papal influence in Germany while making territorial claims in Italy in the twelfth century. De Staël likened nations to grandiose individuals and, for good or ill, Barbarossa came to personify Germany, just as Schiller's William Tell represented Switzerland. Wagner saw Barbarossa as a model of rude valour, and thought of writing a play about him; he was disconcerted when Cosima noticed that the man he so admired had captured the monk Arnold of Brescia, a Ghibelline campaigner against the papacy, and handed him over to be executed for heresy in Rome. In 1848 Wagner called for the return of Barbarossa and the dragon-slayer Siegfried 'to smite mankind's evil, gnawing worm'. Later he thrilled at the sight of the Duke of Meiningen, a military leader who visited Bayreuth in 1876 and took a professional interest in the weapon room near the stage with its collection of swords, shields, helmets and axes; he looked to Wagner 'like Wotan, like Barbarossa … completely heathen'. Like an undying god, the fabled emperor recurs throughout German history. Bismarck was hailed as another of his latter-day descendants, and Hitler inserted himself into the lineage by entitling the 1941 air war on the eastern front Operation Barbarossa. Verdi took a different view of the red-bearded ruffian, who had to be slaughtered not summoned back to life: after Barbarossa terrorizes the Lombard contingent in *La battaglia di Legnano*, he is killed offstage by the Veronese warrior Arrigo.

During the thirteenth century the party names of Welf and Waibling spread to Italy, mutating into Guelfi and Ghibellini. The same conflict between papal and imperial power grumbled on, customized to take advantage of local controversies. Simone Boccanegra, the first doge elected in Genoa, was the candidate of the Ghibelline mob, and in Verdi's opera he accuses his daughter's lover of conspiring with the patrician Guelphs. In *La battaglia di Legnano*, however, it is the Guelphs of the Lombard League who repel Barbarossa while patriotically fighting for the papal cause. The terminology was slippery. One of the synonyms for the Welf party was 'Wälische', defined by Wagner in *Was ist Deutsch?* as 'Romanic, Gaelic' – that is, whatever is alien and therefore inimical. The Landgraf in *Tannhäuser* reminds his guests of their battles to defend the German state against 'dem grimmen Welsen', although when Hans Sachs in *Die Meistersinger* warns his fellow citizens against a 'falscher wälscher Majestät' he has no specific threat in mind and is simply warding off foreign adulteration. Wagner argued that Tannhäuser represented 'the spirit of the whole Ghibelline race for every age', and called the song contest at the Wartburg the ideal image of 'Ghibelline manners'. He had good reason: it was Barbarossa's grandson Friedrich II – nominated as another predecessor by Hitler in a Munich speech, along with Luther and Wagner – who helped revive German poetry by his advocacy of the minnesinger Walther von der Vogelweide, one of the minstrels in *Tannhäuser*. But the binary split is a simplification, since Friedrich II also supported the idea of a national language for Italy and made efforts to unify the peninsula.

In *Rienzi* Wagner looked at the ideological feud from the opposite end of Europe, and showed how reversible its values were. Edward Bulwer-Lytton's novel, on which the opera is based, incriminates the Ghibellines by equipping the Colonnas – a Roman family whose members supplied the Church with popes and cardinals – with a retinue of 'wild German bandits', who slaughter Rienzi's young brother. Wagner's Rienzi refers to that incident in passing but otherwise tactfully ignores it; the opera begins when Adriano detaches himself from the Colonnas to protect Rienzi's sister Irene against the aristocratic hooligans who try to abduct her. A character in the novel, omitted from Wagner's opera, explains why this antique rivalry still mattered. The knight Walter de Montreal comes from Norman stock, and Adriano calls him 'one of the old Gothic scourges'. Montreal justifies the slur by behaving like Bismarck and the Kaiser when, as Verdi saw it, they menaced Paris in 1870: he vows that the pope will not be permitted to return from Avignon and says 'Rome must be mine. The city of a new empire, the conquest of a new Attila!' Earlier in the novel, Montreal favours the intermarriage of cultures, not military force. He prophesies that the decadent south will be restored by 'the irruptions of the North', and expects a new world to be born from a blend of 'the Franc and German races'. He despairs of Italy because its cities are riven by 'two opposing powers, which shall destroy each other', with popular liberty and princely order inconclusively clashing. 'Today,' he says, 'the Guelphs proscribe the Ghibellines – tomorrow, the Ghibellines drive out the Guelphs.' There is one way to end the contest: 'All Italy must become republican or monarchical.' Adrian assumes that traders favour a republic, which will leave them free to make money; Montreal argues for rule by tyrants, because merchants esteem only wealth and ignore the military strength that must defend it. The discussion, supposedly taking place in the fourteenth century, actually refers to the situation five hundred years later. These were choices debated by both Wagner and Verdi, who watched as the republics they hoped for reached a compromise with monarchy.

Although it was Wagner who adapted Bulwer-Lytton's *Rienzi*, Verdi had a more natural claim on the subject: the book is even dedicated to his hero Alessandro Manzoni, the novelist whose memory he honoured in the *Requiem*. In 1871 an American journalist described Verdi himself as 'a true Rienzi, manly to the point of roughness' (although, superimposing stereotypes, the same writer also said that his 'masculine, energetic features' suggested 'a Salvator Rosa bandit chief'). In 1848, six years after Wagner's opera was first performed in Dresden, Verdi did consider making his own version of *Rienzi*, but decided against it when the librettist Salvatore Cammarano complained that the bond between Rienzi and Irene was stronger than her affection for her wooer Adrian: in an Italian opera a sibling was no substitute for a lover. For Wagner, Rienzi's lack of an emotional life was no deterrent. When the operatic Irene chides him about his renunciation of personal happiness, he startles her by saying that he had a bride, whom he adored and by whom he was betrayed. He is referring to a city not a woman. As a tribune, he was mystically married to Rome, like Venetian doges who underwent a ceremonial wedding to the sea; the uprising against him was tantamount to adultery. Rienzi offers Irene the chance of a happy unpolitical life with Adriano, but she rejects her lover and resolves to share her brother's fate as 'die letzte Römerin!', the last Roman. In a heady duet they agree to commit suicide and – joined by Adriano – die together in the burning Capitol. The scenario teasingly anticipates the fiery apocalypse in *Götterdämmerung*; to Verdi it would have looked and sounded like ideological insanity.

When Verdi revised *Simon Boccanegra* in 1881, Boito's new text for the scene in the council chamber included a homage to Bulwer-Lytton's hero. Boccanegra underlines the collapse of his project to federate Italy by referring to the glory and the death of Rienzi, thunderously proclaimed by his adviser Petrarch. Boccanegra and Cola di Rienzi were contemporaries, and both had two separate periods in power (conflated by Verdi and Wagner so as to concentrate the action of their operas). Boccanegra was elected the first doge of Genoa in 1339 and was re-elected in 1356; Rienzi, defeated in his wars against the nobles, was driven out of Rome in 1347 and returned in 1354 with an army led by Montreal's mercenaries. But despite the coincidence, the operatic characters are as different as their creators. Wagner's Rienzi challenges the citizens of Rome to be worthy of the columns and temples that overshadow them. Boccanegra, by contrast, when pleading for peace in the council chamber, looks beyond the city and points to the untroubled landscape that surrounds Genoa: the sunny hills and olive groves, the flowers with their deceptive gaiety, the sparkling sea. Wagner's tribune loves a political idea and a historical pedigree that are embodied in architecture; Verdi's doge would rather do away with politics, which means conflict, and seeks to be healed by a nature that has no history.

Wagner tidied up Rienzi's flaws, presenting him as a revolutionary sabotaged by his unworthy society. Although, like Boccanegra, he wanted to abolish baronial rule and unify the peninsula, he fell out with crucial allies and corruptly treated himself to luxuries and showy ceremonies of self-aggrandizement. Rather than rejoicing in the flames that sear the Capitol as Wagner's hero does, the actual Rienzi fled in disguise. Unfortunately he forgot to remove his gold bracelets and jewelled rings, which did not accessorize well with the grubby gardener's clothes he wore as camouflage; he was recognized and put to death by the mob in 1354. In *Simon Boccanegra* Verdi tells more of the truth about the devious self-interest of his politicians than Wagner was prepared to do. Adorno calls his patrician mentor Boccanegra a model of the morally decorous 'tempo antico', almost an honorary ancient Roman, although Fiesco, whose virtue he praises, is a skulking conspirator protected by an alias. Boccanegra promises his fixer Paolo the hand of an heiress, and bribes her by pardoning her exiled brothers. He then discovers that she is his lost daughter Amelia, and deprives the disgruntled Paolo of his reward.

Despite this grubby exchange of political favours, Verdi managed to dispose of Cammarano's objection to *Rienzi*: Boccanegra's paternal love for Amelia – protective, regretful, heart-breakingly tender when he softly elongates the precious word 'figlia' as she parts from him – deserves and gets finer music than that given to her brash, politically fickle lover Adorno. Verdi may have had another reason for his decision not to proceed with the subject of Rienzi. Italian patriots disliked the mystique of Rome, and believed that a new nation required a new centre: the first capital after Italy's unification was in Turin. Napoleon Bonaparte had co-opted Rome's claim to universality, formerly enforced by the

Church: the Inquisitor in Verdi's *Don Carlos* gruesomely refers to the empire of militant dogma as 'l'univers romain'. Wagner, despite his grievance about the clash between Roman power and Teutonic rights, liked the idea of a city that extended its control across continents, as Albert Speer's Berlin was meant to do during the thousand years of the Third Reich. While reading Edward Gibbon's *Decline and Fall of the Roman Empire* in 1871, he concluded that Rome still offered a model of 'the wisest form of government', no matter which country imperially prevailed, and the characters in his Roman opera live up to the city's monumentality. Rienzi acclaims Irene as his 'Heldenschwester', a sister who possesses an authentic Roman fortitude. She thanks him because, like a god, he recreated her, transforming a weak woman into 'einer Römerin'. Rather than an automatic birthright, Romanness is a qualification that must be earned, and it can easily be withdrawn. When Rienzi frees Irene to marry Adriano, he says 'Kein Rom gibt's mehr, sein denn ein Weib!' – forget about Rome, be a woman. In an opera by Verdi this would be a fond, generous wish; in Wagner it sounds like a demotion, paraphrasing Wotan's sarcasm in *Die Walküre* when he condemns Brünnhilde to dwindle into a woman and a wife, who will sit by the fire at her spinning wheel rather than gallop across the sky. The humbled Valkyrie falls to the ground with a shriek: to be humanized is a fate worse than death.

After *Rienzi*, Wagner changed his mind about the city and its virtues. Extending his case about the inequity within the Holy Roman Empire, he claimed that Germans were creators and inventors, Romans mere imitators and exploiters. Hans Sachs corrects the balance in his final proclamation in *Die Meistersinger*, dispensing with 'das heil'ge röm'sche Reich' and setting up in its place 'die heil'ge deutsche Kunst!' Rome is supplanted by Germany, and both pope and emperor recognize the new authority of the artist. In 1878 Wagner said he suspected that 'Latin antiquity must have an oppressive effect on an Italian', and added that Germans were luckier because 'we have no civilization behind us'. Better, apparently, to be a barbarian than the offspring of an over-cultivated race whose achievements were far in the past.

From Verdi's vantage point, at least during the Franco-Prussian War, the Germans were destroyers. But he was not immune to the unhallowed exhilaration of that destructiveness. Although he recommended de Staël's book on Germany to the librettist Temistocle Solera when they began work on *Attila* in 1845, the opera startlingly alters her account of character. In her synopsis of the play by Zacharias Werner, de Staël quotes a scene in which Attila sees an apparition, a giant whose head touches the clouds and who brandishes a sword at the invading army. This ogre wears an ornate golden temple as his headdress, and grips two keys which Attila surmises that he stole from Wotan, who surely used them to open the doors of Valhalla. It is St Peter, warning Attila to retreat from Rome; abashed, he does so. For de Staël this was the moment at which Christianity cowed the heathen. After Attila's assassination by the Burgundian princess Hildegonde – who in Verdi's opera becomes the Aquilean freedom fighter Odabella – the pope prays for his soul, and grateful believers sing 'Hallelujah'. Verdi's Attila has the vision, but reacts to it differently. He tells his retainer Uldino that the old man in his dream ordered him away from Rome; instead of weakening like Werner's hero, Verdi's Attila summons his Druids, mobilizes his troops, and outfaces the spectre in a swaggering cabaletta. He credits 'gran Wodan' with calling him to glory. Attila's Wodan, who receives thanks from the chorus for the booty he awards them as they loot Aquilea, is a true god of war, not the brooding, detached politician that Wagner presents in the *Ring*; he lives up to the etymological rhapsody on his name in the lectures on heroism that Thomas Carlyle delivered in 1840. Carlyle pointed out that 'the word *Wuodan* … connects itself, according to Grimm, with the Latin *vadere*, with the English *wade* and suchlike' and 'means primarily *Movement*, Source of Movement, Power'. Wodan, like Attila, strides through the world, whereas Wagner's Wotan is reduced to wandering around in it before returning to Valhalla to await extinction. But in Verdi's opera a chorus of maidens and children weaken Attila's resolve by sweetly singing about the 'spirto creator', and when the pope challenges him his nerve fails in a fit of unaccustomed piety. As he bends the knee before what the Christians call 'l'Eterno', Attila quotes the warning from his dream and says 'Qui l'uom s'arretra;/Dinanzi ai numi prostrasi il ré!' – here man must stop his advance, and the king defer to the gods. He repeats the line in a ruminative ensemble, which enables its implications to be considered. The warning anticipates Philip II's surrender to the bigoted Inquisitor in *Don Carlos* when the throne, as the king puts it, bows to the superior power of the altar. The victory of eternity is a defeat for man. Attila loses his power of resistance, blusters feebly at the conspirators, and at last meekly allows Odabella to run him through.

The Romans cannot pretend to be morally superior: the general Ezio, who despises the unfledged juvenile emperor Valentinian, assumes he can negotiate with Attila because they both believe only in power. His offer to give Attila the world so long as he keeps Italy for himself is not patriotic; he is simply grabbing a personal share of the spoils. In Werner's play he and Attila were former colleagues, almost like Wagnerian blood brothers. Ready – as he boasts – for any war, Ezio wants to be remembered and mourned as 'l'ultimo romano', the last of the Romans. This is a more ignoble ambition than Irene's wish to die with Rienzi as 'die letzte Römerin'. She and her brother uphold an impersonal idea of the city and reproach those who have defamed it, whereas Ezio's concern is to ensure that a few Romans will survive to honour and immortalize his name. In 1865 the revolutionary patriot Mazzini advised Italians against Caesarism, a worship of authority as mindless as the gibbering awe of primitive men who collapse before a flash of lightning. 'Attila,' he said, 'would kill the conscience of the human race!' The young Verdi seemed, at least to his detractors, equally savage. Bülow called him 'the Attila of the larynx', comparing the damage his vocal writing did to singers with the Hun's campaign of pillage. Odabella's opening tirade about the valour of Italian women is one example of this brutality: her voice is a trumpet made of brass not flesh, and the aria's slashing scales and searing high notes make it powerfully exciting. No wonder Attila repays her by restoring her sword, since the performance is proof of her mettle.

The Druids in the opera describe the ravished earth and flame-singed sky as Attila's palace, where he will feast on gory human remains. Demolished buildings provide him with an open-air cathedral, and the body and blood consumed at his infidel Mass are not symbolic substitutes for the real thing. Verdi here celebrated the ferocity of the Teutonic gods with a zest and zeal that even Wagner could not outdo. In 1882 Josef Rubinstein played the last scene of *Götterdämmerung* on the piano, and Wagner spontaneously joined in to sing Brünnhilde's war whoop of exultation as she gallops into the flames. Cosima recorded his satisfaction: 'so heathen and Germanic!' The words were synonyms, doubling his pride in the spectacle of suicide and deicide he had imagined. He then recalled the racial theories of Arthur de Gobineau, who lamented the miscegenation that had weakened Aryan supremacy, before reaching a conclusion that was grimly but smugly final. 'The Germanic world,' Wagner said, 'came to an end with this work.' Modern times were too meek and law-abiding to tolerate the return of truly Germanic values.

||||||||||||||||||

The question *Was ist Deutsch?* had many answers. Discussing the prelude to the third act of *Die Meistersinger* in 1874, Wagner told Cosima that the German character was good-humoured, equable, averse to pathos and ecstasy. If that was so, his own high-pitched emotional nature, which lunged between sublime altitudes and pits of pathetic despair, made him an honorary foreigner. In 1905 the American novelist and music critic James Huneker said that the 'sensuous glow and glitter' of Wagner's orchestra seemed more Jewish or Celtic than Teutonic.

Wagner remained a conundrum for Nazi ethnologists, and in 1937 Walther Rauschenberger classified him as Nordic-Dinaric, which made him a mongrel. His will to power and unstinting energy were safely Nordic, but his Dinaric tincture derived from an imaginary sub-group associated by the Nazis with the Adriatic and the Balkans; the racial anthropologist Hans Günther assigned Verdi to the same category. As evidence for his decision, Rauschenberger pointed to Wagner's ripe sensuality and his plush taste in decor. Despite the bogus racial taxonomy, the analysis of his character was plausible enough. Perhaps Nietzsche was right when he outrageously declared that Wagner had no true national characteristics, and simply played at being German with his usual histrionic skill.

On occasion, Wagner admitted that 'German' was merely a word. Even worse, it was an adjective, belonging to a class of words that parasitically cling to more substantial nouns and hazard subjective guesses about qualities and characteristics. 'Deutsch', according to the philologists Wagner consulted, did not refer to a racial group or ethnic stock. It simply meant what was plain, familiar, 'deutlich' or clear, and was supposedly used by people living west of the Rhine and north of the Alps to set themselves apart from the Goths, Franks and Lombards by delineating a kind of character that was stalwart, doughty. Sachs takes that definition for granted in his sermon at the end of *Die Meistersinger*, where the adjectives in the phrase 'was deutsch und echt' are interchangeable: what is German is true, and vice versa. At various times Wagner remarked on the inimitable Germanness of Gurnemanz in *Parsifal* with his 'simple fervour', and of Sachs, whose paternal gravity is 'distinct from the Latin type'. He also commended Wolfram in *Tannhäuser* as 'a truly German character', because he so nobly rises above his 'male feelings' and sings an aria to the evening star instead of confessing his love for Elisabeth; the Italians and the French, Wagner added, possessed too much 'chaleur de coeur' to understand such an upright, brotherly fellow.

What made those early Germans feel at home in one another's company was their language, which Wagner tried to revive when he pastiched the diction of early epics in the *Ring*. In his 1808 addresses to the German nation, the philosopher Johann Gottlieb Fichte suggested that primitive languages were created 'by nature itself, long before any human art begins'. *Das Rheingold* illustrates the theory: the E flat sonogram of Wagner's Rhine leads to the gurgling of the water nymphs, after which human language intrudes with the barked expostulations of Alberich. Purging verbal hybrids and mimicking alliterative verse with its rhymes on initial letters not final syllables, Wagner devised an idiom that would, he hoped, preserve the country's integrity. His 'Urpoesie' tried to retain the link between metrical stress and physical gesture: it gave words a solid rhythmic footing by placing the emphasis on the first letter, which spurs the syllables into action. End rhymes, like those that make Italian so easy to sing, were for Wagner the symptom of a later sophistication, naturally repugnant to rugged, hearty Germans. Rhymes attached to the last syllable of words flutter loosely, he said, like 'ribbons of melody'. The metaphor is good – an end rhyme can indeed be a decorative afterthought, flaunting in the air – but it hardly wins a philological argument. As for alliteration, the patterned letters that the Rhinemaidens form into words when they chant 'Weia! Waga!/Woge, du Welle' are as happily nonsensical as any Italian vocal exercise.

Modern Europeans muddled up Anglo-Saxon and Latinate words, and Wagner thought their composite, deracinated languages 'evil', as he told Cosima in 1873. Fichte likewise wished to expel the word 'Humanität' from the German vocabulary: it was tainted by Romanness, and reminded him that the Roman definition of what it meant to be human was too morally slovenly to suit Germans, whom he advised to refer instead to their 'Menschlichkeit'. This was more than a quibble, because Fichte's veto on the Latinate word denied the idea of a common humanity; the approved German equivalent, alarmingly close to the concept of manliness, does not make the same inclusive appeal to members of our species who speak different languages. Wagner too defined nationhood linguistically, and wished that Bismarck would legislate against neologisms by imposing fines on newspapers that used imported jargon. Verdi, less apologetic about culture's interference with nature, knew that a national language was likely to be the product of art, a bonus of literature: it was Manzoni who, in the successive revisions of his novel *I promessi sposi*, developed an idiom based on the dialect of Tuscany that gradually became the Italian norm. Verdi was happy to see language uprooting itself and adapting to new human needs. His *Quattro pezzi sacri*, composed in 1896–97, consist of three settings of Latin texts and one piece in the vernacular, 'Laudi alla Vergine Maria', which uses verses from Dante's *Paradiso*. To do without Latin is to dispense with priestly intercession; any woman called Maria is a possible replica of the Virgin, and the poem praises virtues that are mundane, almost ordinary – kindness, charity or approachability (like that of Desdemona interceding for Cassio in *Otello*). The warm glow of the unaccompanied female voices makes Maria the perfection of human nature, divine only by association.

Verdi hoped that song, which is language raised to its highest power, would help to cement community. In *La battaglia di Legnano* the men of Como mistrust their Milanese neighbours and want to placate Barbarossa. Rolando chides them by appealing to a shared tongue, 'il numero sonante/dell'Italico linguaggio'.

Adhesion depends on something stronger than speech: those resonant numbers must be musical. All the same, Como stays outside the vocal ensemble, which is enough to disprove Fichte's thesis about the primal racial bond of language. But music can embolden Verdi's characters to perform actions from which the rest of us might shrink. When Arrigo in *La battaglia di Legnano* enters the underground vault to join the cadre of knights who have sworn to die, the trombones, trumpets, bassoons and timpani induct him into this secret society and enforce his promise. Pledges like this were not merely an operatic fiction. In 1831 Mazzini devised an oath for prospective members of his political organization, Young Italy; instead of propounding shared ideas, the vow made an appeal to emotional empathy, as if the adherents were joining voices in a Verdian ensemble rather than signing up to a doctrinal manifesto. Those who wanted to belong to Mazzini's band had to pledge fidelity by the blush that reddened their brows when they stood beside the citizens of lands freer than their own, and by 'the tears of Italian mothers for their sons dead on the scaffold, in prison, or in exile'. The ceremony concluded with a deadly proviso. 'This do I swear,' the recruits had to say, 'invoking upon my head the wrath of God, the abhorrence of man, and the infamy of the perjurer, if I ever betray the whole or a part of this oath.' The sentence is as solemn as Verdi's rumbling brass when Monterone curses Rigoletto or Boccanegra makes Paolo repeat the curse in the council chamber. Such maledictions not only ostracize the person who is accursed but revoke his humanity. By laughing at another man's distress, Rigoletto loses the right to be pitied, and when Paolo curses himself he forfeits both the will to live and the right to life. A bond of commonality has been ruptured; music grants us admission to that collective existence, but can also expel us from it. Hence the clattering dismissals sounded by bass drum and gong when the weapons of the disgraced Gaston are shattered by the executioner's mace in *Jérusalem*. Percussion is a blow, moral as much as physical: the knight is humbled, after which the unaccommodated man will be put to death. Verdi's orchestra, inheriting an authority that no longer belongs to the Church, wields the power of excommunication. Compared with this, the banishment of Telramund in *Lohengrin* is a legal formality, which he insolently ignores.

In an essay written in Paris in 1840, Wagner traced music in Germany back to its imagined origins, and proposed a humdrum, prosaic source for the art, in keeping with what he saw, on this occasion, as the modest demeanour and domestic virtue of his countrymen. Catholic pomp, he argued, had no place in Germany. Good Germans made do with plainer Protestant devotions, and their musical impulse expressed itself in 'a simple chorale sung by the whole congregation and accompanied by an organ'. In *Die Meistersinger* the vigorous strides of the overture lead into the full-voiced chorale sung inside the church, constructing what the 1840 essay calls a 'magnificent edifice' out of resonant air. 'German vocal music flourished in the churches,' Wagner wrote; 'opera was left to the Italians.' But even an opera as chauvinistic as *Die Meistersinger* had to compromise with profane Italian habits by allowing the church to be used as a setting for flirtation, argument and vocal display, and as soon as the worshippers file out the furniture is rearranged in the nave for the audition that follows.

The Parisian essay suggests another 'exclusively German heritage' that the country's music draws on: this is 'the people's love of song', evinced by chorales and folk tunes. Italian opera begins when a single individual expresses an emotion too intense to be merely spoken. The god of song, in Monteverdi's *Orfeo*, is praised for his vocal splendour, made even more radiant by the strumming of his lyre. He gladly exhibits his virtuosity to entertain the shepherds; the opera, however, truly starts when he responds to the news of Euridice's death with a descant on the two simple, heartbroken notes of his exclamation, 'Ohime'. The understated word itself cannot convey his shock and grief, which is why music has to take over. In Wagner's musical genealogy, the art has a social source, and a more general utility. Where are the people when they are singing? Presumably in their houses: Wagner insisted that Germans disliked communicating their joy in music to 'the masses' or to 'a pleasure-seeking salon-audience', and preferred to indulge it in the company of 'an intimate circle'. Though they lacked that 'one chief organ which we find in the throats of happy Italians', they compensated by organizing string quartets or teaming up in four-part songs. Instrumental music, Wagner argued, is best appreciated as an outgrowth of 'German family life'. The *Siegfried Idyll*, first performed on the narrow staircase at Triebschen, proved the point. And what would the people who loved song have been doing while they sang? If not in church, they were probably working; music, more than a cheery pastime, helps them to coordinate their efforts. Senta's companions in *Der Fliegende Holländer* sing as they spin, and she is rebuked for neglecting her wheel and humming her own introverted tune; the bossy Mary, keeping time, is responsible for the productivity of her charges. Sachs in *Die Meistersinger* hammers leather, singing as he cobbles a shoe. The Norns in *Götterdämmerung* plait the rope that symbolically interweaves human fates, and their shared recitation of the world's history sets the steady, implacable pace for this cosmic chore.

Homely situations like these ground the art. The pulsation of the opening primal chord in *Das Rheingold* embeds German music in nature; later comes the rhythmic clatter of the Nibelungen slaves or the industrial anthem bellowed by Siegfried as he forges his sword. This din is a symbol of culture or manufacture, an almost mechanized noise that disrupts the original harmony. Verdi's operas contain no such scenes of musical labour. The gypsies in *Il trovatore* make their living as tinkers and they pound their anvils like Alberich's subterranean serfs, but the uproar is festive, not the joyless battery overheard in *Das Rheingold.* As they work, Verdi's gypsies sing about the drink that keeps up their strength and the women who fill their earthen cups; they might belong, like Corrado's pirates in *Il corsaro* or Ernani's bandits, to a criminal gang whose work is wickedly playful, and their delight in what they are doing sets them apart from Wagner's demoralized toilers. The Saracen song performed by Eboli in *Don Carlos* fits Wagner's description of non-German music as 'empty titillation', aristocratic folderol – though this is no criticism, since Eboli herself knows it. Everything about the episode is self-conscious, as if the drama onstage had suddenly turned into a flamboyant opera. Outside the monastery of San Yuste, a place devoted to stark meditation on last things, she performs a song about seduction in a Muslim court. The page is ordered to tune the mandolin, attendants volunteer to join in by saying 'Chantons!', and Eboli augments the story with wordless Moorish melismas and literal arabesques of beguiling sound.

When Elisabeth enters, she remarks that she heard people singing, 'libres de souci'. She is singing too, but that hardly counts because she is depressed, homesick for France. In the torrid southern setting of Estremadura, she assumes that music must be a reflex of enjoyment and freedom from care; like the critic Hanslick deploring the lack of 'healthy, ruddy-cheeked melody' in *Otello*, Eboli suspiciously speculates about the queen's sadness, which has been transplanted from further north. In 1887 in an interview with Gino Monaldi, Verdi restated his belief that 'an Italian must write as an Italian, a German as a German'. He agreed that music was universal, but insisted that the men who composed it were formed by their countries and could not change their natures. Things, however, were no longer so simple: what music suits a character like Elisabeth, who is born in France, lives in Spain, and has German emotions – like her namesake in *Tannhäuser* she possesses a masochistic sense of duty – that were given to her by Schiller? While nations were struggling to define themselves, music helped to establish their identity; by the end of the century, to Verdi's consternation, opera had outgrown nationality.

|||||||||||||||||||

If the occasion was right, Wagner could identify with other nations. He used countries as he used women: they were a means of stimulating music. In 1836, stirred by his experience of carousing with refugees in Leipzig and Königsberg, he composed the overture *Polonia*, which dramatized the uprising against Russia five years earlier. Stabbing, crushing interventions blatantly recall the violence of the oppressors, and a melody suggesting the Dutchman's appeal for absolution extends sympathy to the victims. Drum rolls and cavalcades then take over. The next year Wagner composed a louder, more puffed-up overture on *Rule Britannia*. The nautical ditty about ruling the waves – taken from Thomas Arne's eighteenth-century masque about King Alfred, Britain's mythical equivalent of Siegfried or Barbarossa – had to be inflated to suit a world in which empires were global. Arne's navigable state sounds buoyant and bouncy, but Wagner told Cosima that he had pictured 'a great ship' – weightier, probably ironclad and bristling with guns. The imaginary vessel could not have been German: in 1880 Wagner remarked that the country would never become a world power because it lacked access to the sea. Instead, he added, Germany could 'spread culture by colonization' – or was culture an excuse for colonization? In his *Rule Britannia* sombre, conspiratorial undertones and blaring brass alter the quotation from Arne. Power in the eighteenth century implied nimbleness, exhibited by the decorative scales in Arne's song; in the nineteenth century it involved rolling out the big battalions, either military or musical. Wagner sent the score to a promoter in London, who declined to perform it. The British preferred to believe that they had gained their empire absent-mindedly, with no such dogged Prussian forethought.

Verdi acknowledged music's new internationalism in his *Inno delle nazioni*, composed in 1862 for the International Exhibition in London. The text by Boito describes the Crystal Palace as a secular temple showing off the miracles of industrial genius, brought from distant shores by busy fleets of ships – an earthly heaven stocked with commodities that minimize labour rather than saving souls. The tenor soloist cries 'Spettacolo sublime!' as he surveys the cooperation between nations that once were foes. But, like Otello and Desdemona in a duet that should be about their love for each other, he is eager to recall the clash of swords and the storming of chariots. His single moment of true Verdian sensitivity comes when he recalls the elegiac tears shed by the victims of imperial warfare. Music and drama are excited by conflict, indifferent to the goddess of peace and the new god of technology. With its massive stamping tread, the opening 'Gloria' anticipates the clangour of the triumphal march in *Aida* a decade later; capitalism and militarism go hand in hand, expropriating raw materials and opening up markets. Although the *Inno* included 'God Save the Queen' to compliment Britain on its liberal tradition and the 'Marseillaise' to thank France for supporting Italian liberation, the modulations from one anthem to the next are joltingly awkward. Only when the tenor soloist gets to his homeland does he take flight, wafted by an airier orchestration as he addresses 'Italia, o patria mia'. He remains monoglot, singing his country's praises in Italian while the chorus trudges through 'God Save the Queen' in English: why not, if Italian – as Stendhal and the romantics believed – is the native tongue of music?

A sense of obligation made Verdi accept the commission. Wagner, needier financially, was also more ambitious to be recognized as a musical laureate. In 1864 he composed his *Huldigungsmarsch* as a homage for the nineteenth birthday of Ludwig II. The dedication seems incidental; with its atmosphere of chivalric adventuring, it is more a portrait of Wagner's early heroes than of the young king – though there may be no difference, since Ludwig modelled himself on the messianic swan knight Lohengrin. In 1865 Wagner attached the march to the *Tannhäuser* prelude, which was played by an unseen military band at a concert for Ludwig in the Residenz in Munich. Thanks to a convenient E flat the link was musically seamless, but it must have sounded psychologically odd: was the sybaritic hero another version of the self-indulgent king? Wagner's *Kaisermarsch*, composed for the imperial coronation of Wilhelm I in 1871, flattered the Hohenzollern dynasty, with a demotic chorus chanting tributes to the Kaiser and the band intoning a Lutheran chorale as a reminder that in war God automatically sides with the winners. George Bernard Shaw at first decried the *Kaisermarsch* as 'a bit of Verdified Wagner', then decided that the offence lay in its ideological backsliding not its musical banality. The 'exiled communist artist-philosopher' who wrote the text for the *Ring* was now, to Shaw's regret, a narrow-minded jingoist. However, he underestimated Wagner's undogmatic opportunism: following Verdi's example with the *Inno*, he considered sending his march to London to be performed at that year's sequel to the Great Exhibition, and was even willing to customize it for this new market by replacing 'Ein' feste Burg' with the British national anthem.

Wagner then thought better of the idea, and at Christmas revised the bombastic piece for private use. The choral verses – which compared the Kaiser to a flowering oak, and cheered the banners waved by his armies as they stamped through France – were rewritten so his children could sing them to Cosima, 'unserer Mama'. The march described its original dedicatee as the embodiment of 'Siege-Fried', an oxymoronic and uniquely German compound of military victory and peace. The version for domestic use changed this to praise of 'unserem Fidi', little Siegfried Wagner, who was two years old at the time. The composer's first son, like all infants, was an absolute monarch; he had an additional right to imperial superlatives because he ensured the future of the dynasty. For Wagner, patriotism began at home.

# Conquerors

To their contemporaries, Verdi and Wagner were candidates for the highest rank in what Carlyle called his '*Hero*archy'. But they were heroes of a kind unknown before the decade in which they were born, obscure provincials who – like the protagonists of the novels written during their lifetimes by Stendhal, Balzac and Dickens – brashly advanced to the city, impatient for success and ready to shake their fists at the world. These arrivistes could not be explained by reference to family or inherited advantages. When Wagner's stepfather Geyer died in 1821, his mother told him 'He wanted to make something of you', but Wagner had little use for such benevolence and soon broke with his remaining family, never returning to Leipzig. Verdi employed his parents as caretakers at Sant'Agata before he and Strepponi moved there from Busseto, but he was enraged when he heard that his father claimed to have rights over the property and advised the local notary that 'Carlo Verdi and Giuseppe Verdi must remain two distinct and separate persons'. He even begrudged his mother access to a chicken run they had once shared, and insisted that the eggs should be brought directly from the farm to his house in town. In 1851 he legally severed his ties with them, offended by their disapproval of his alliance with Strepponi.

Being self-made, both men – according to their personal myths – were self-taught. Verdi enjoyed pretending to be musically ignorant, and when a critic alleged that Leonora's plea for peace in *La forza del destino* quoted Schubert's 'Ave Maria', he declared plagiarism to be impossible since there was no library in his house. He was being disingenuous, at least about the library: at Sant'Agata he had a collection of scores extending from Palestrina to Brahms, with the chamber music of Mozart, Haydn and Beethoven close at hand beside his bed. Wagner claimed that he had got by with what he called an 'arbitrary self-education'. He copied the scores of composers he admired, which had the additional benefit of helping him to acquire the 'graceful handwriting' – as sinuously elegant as a creeper – that was, as he said in *Mein Leben*, 'so much admired'.

Because they came out of nowhere and lacked the proper introductions, both were criticized for uncouthness. Eugène Delacroix gave Verdi the abusive nickname Merdi, and told George Sand he was a scoundrel, not 'a priest of the living God'. In 1847 Théophile Gautier winced at the sonic crassness of *Jérusalem*, which Delacroix called 'nothing but noise!' The composer Otto Nicolai – who rejected the libretto for *Nabucco* because it consisted of 'unending raging, blood-letting, reviling, striking and murdering' – thought Verdi's music 'degrading', and assumed he was either an ass or a lunatic. In New York the lawyer and diarist George Templeton Strong sniffed at him as the equivalent of a tabloid hack who dealt only in 'italics, large capitals, dashes, and interjection marks'. Wagner was worse than vulgar: affronted auditors found his music psychologically distressing. When César Cui heard the *Lohengrin* prelude in St Petersburg in 1864, he complained that 'the endless unhealthy screeching of the violins is unbearable'. The French composer Daniel Auber said that listening to Wagner's scores was like 'reading, without pausing to take breath, a book that has no commas or full stops'. He then sighed with relief: 'How dreadful it would be if that were music!' Verdi sounded like an exclamatory lout, while Wagner seemed to be an illiterate who had not learned the polite rudiments of his art. In 1859 in Offenbach's skit *Le Musicien de l'avenir*, he self-importantly announces a future in which music will do without notes, harmony and scales. Mozart, Gluck and Weber, unimpressed, eject him from their temple.

In his 1836 *Confession d'un enfant du siècle* Alfred de Musset, three years younger than Verdi and Wagner, defined the interregnum of opportunity that made such upstarts possible. Like Musset himself, the composers took advantage of a crevice between old and new worlds; children of chaos, scornful of the past and avid for a future that had not yet arrived, they were – as Musset said of his own generation – 'sons of the Empire and grandsons of the Revolution'. The empire and the revolution in question were both French, and the model for these ambitious nonentities was Napoleon Bonaparte, the Corsican artillery officer who subdued a continent and awarded himself a crown. A battle fought at Leipzig in October 1813, a few months after Wagner's birth in the city, liberated the German states from Napoleonic rule, but Parma remained a department of his empire, so Verdi began life as a French citizen. In April 1814 Napoleon abdicated and was exiled to Elba. The century's malaise, as Musset defined it, derived from its uncertainty about what would come next – power for the common man, or restoration of the monarchy 'destroyed and parodied' by Napoleon?

Demilitarized, the arc of Napoleonic achievement served as a new model for an artist's life. Stendhal's study of Rossini began by announcing 'Napoleon is dead; but a new conqueror has already shown himself to this world'. This was Rossini, whose operas – according to Stendhal – had spread his fame across Europe and from Moscow to Calcutta. But in 1829, exhausted at the age of only thirty-seven, Rossini retired from opera, leaving the field open for others. Since Wagner regarded his own music as the predestined end of the art's evolution, he enlisted the epicurean humourist as a precursor. On a visit to Rossini's salon in Paris in 1860 he tried to persuade the old man that he too had written the music of the future in *Guillaume Tell*, freeing melody from predictable rhymes and obligatory cadences. Rossini's response was sly. He gasped at Wagner's 'radical revolution', and when hailed as one of its proponents joked that he might resume his career: 'And then … let the ancien régime beware!' It was a Napoleonic challenge, hollowly uttered in jest. Rossini no longer composed; instead, as he told Wagner, he was busy decomposing. In November 1868 when Rossini died, Verdi thought only of paying tribute, not of assuming an inheritance, and organized a consortium of colleagues to work on a *Messa per Rossini*. This Requiem was never performed, thanks to a spurious quarrel Verdi picked with the conductor Angelo Mariani, formerly a prized colleague and loyal friend. The pretext was the inadequacy of the chorus, although the true cause was probably Mariani's engagement to the soprano Teresa Stolz, with whom Verdi himself was infatuated. While pretending to be a simple bucolic fellow, Verdi had a deft talent for intrigue, and his manoeuvrings succeeded in detaching Stolz from his colleague. In the short term Mariani retaliated by switching his allegiance to Wagner: he conducted the *Lohengrin* that Verdi heard – or overheard, lurking in the back of a box at the Teatro Comunale – in Bologna.

As Stendhal's fanfare for Rossini suggests, careers like those of Verdi and Wagner called for political guile, even militaristic ruthlessness. After perusing a score by Verdi, Rossini once remarked that the composer must be an artillery colonel, and a Hamburg reviewer in 1850 said that *Lohengrin* was an 'infernal din' from which only an onstage cannonade was missing. In June 1880 Wagner was writing an essay on religion and art, while simultaneously fretting about *Parsifal*. He fumbled as he searched for the way ahead, then after overcoming his blockages reported to Cosima 'I know now how to do it, as Napoleon said to Venice.' He was referring to Napoleon's vow to humble the city, which held out against him longer than the rest of northern Italy; it was natural for Wagner to liken the disentangling of intellectual or aesthetic knots to the prosecution of warfare. The city that he and Verdi both felt obliged to conquer was Paris – or rather they aimed to storm the citadel of the Opéra. Wagner saw this as an armed undertaking, 'a frontal attack on Paris' as he put it in 1846. But the premiere of *Tannhaüser* there in March 1861 was wrecked by the roués of the Jockey Club, who took offence because the saucy Venusberg ballet had been inserted in the first act, before they made their late arrival; the siege of Paris during the Franco-Prussian War a decade later was, in Wagner's view, a justified reprisal for the mockery he suffered at the Paris premiere. Although Verdi's experience with *Don Carlos* at the Opéra in 1867 was far from disastrous, he was frustrated by the management's demands for officious grandeur and courtly pomp onstage. Otherwise he achieved a Napoleonic universality without needing to declare war. His music prevailed on his behalf, and he claimed in 1862 that wherever you went – to the Indies, or the African interior – you were likely to hear snatches of *Il trovatore*.

Stendhal's flourish was more than fatuous hyperbole: opera kept the Napoleonic will alive. Before Rossini, Italian music had, in Stendhal's opinion, been inglorious, unvaliant – insipidly sweet, but with no power to arouse the passions. As he noted in his novel *La Chartreuse de Parme*, Napoleon's expulsion of the Austrians from Italy in 1796 put an end to 'the old ideas' and to old, timorous codes of conduct; as if encouraged by Rossini's propulsive orchestral crescendi and his vocal pyrotechnics, Italians began to behave heroically, which for Stendhal meant operatically. It became fashionable for people like Fabrice in *La Chartreuse de Parme* to love their country with a wild ardour and to look for flashy opportunities to serve it. Balzac praised Fabrice for demonstrating that 'feeling is equivalent to talent. To feel is the rival of to understand, as to act is the opposite of to think.' Stendhal thought of his own art musically, and likened the novel to a bow that played on the reader's soul. Opera multiplied the number of strings and bows, and added extra forces – winds that breathe with us, percussion that thuds like a beating heart – to orchestrate emotions; in a world where Napoleon's death in 1821 allowed kings to creep back to their thrones and countenanced a return to business as usual, it became the province of adventure and risk. The only actions that matter in opera are gratuitous acts, recklessly and often mindlessly magnificent. Carlo in *I masnadieri* kills Amelia to protect her from the knowledge that she loves a bandit, then insists on being led to the gallows. Siegmund in *Die Walküre*, offered immortality by Brünnhilde, says he would rather die fighting and threatens to prove his sincerity by killing Sieglinde, whom he loves. Elisabeth in *Tannhäuser* defends the man who has shamed and betrayed her and offers her body to the swords of the knights when they close in on him. Gilda in *Rigoletto* chooses to die to save the life of her rapist.

The emphasis on heroic energy was timely. Mazzini disliked the melodies of Bellini for political reasons: their languor suited heroines who walked in their sleep like Amina in *La sonnambula* or worshipped the moon like the Druid priestess in *Norma*, but they were not fit for a time of engagement and struggle, which is why he called Bellini 'emasculate, rather than vigorous and fertile'. Virility came to be the special gift of Verdi's impetuous heroes. At the gaming table in a Parisian salon, Alfredo in *La traviata* sings with the same ferocity as Radamès preparing for battle against the Ethiopian army. Verdi – who was thrilled by Garibaldi's Sicilian campaign in 1860, which began with a rule-breaking uphill bayonet charge – thought at first that politics could be conducted with the same theatrical daring. He later came to understand that politics and opera did not go together, which is why at the end of his life he tried to dissuade his younger colleague Giordano from putting Napoleon into an opera. He could imagine the emperor delivering a dramatic recitative, but not striding to the footlights to sing a romance with his hand on his heart. No general would let down his guard in that way; no politician would permit music to interfere with his calculations of advantage.

Franz Werfel described Verdi as a contradictory amalgam of Garibaldi and Cavour, the two heroes of the Italian revolt. Verdi admired Garibaldi's derring-do and promptly rounded up a hundred rifles when one of his lieutenants sent a request for guns to be distributed to the National Guard. But the rabble-rousing manner of the itinerant agitator – his costume of red shirt, neckerchief and sombrero was borrowed from the tattered army of peasants he fought with in South America – had more in common with Verdi's heroes than with the man himself. The buttoned-down composer was closer to Cavour, the professional politician who founded the newspaper *Il Risorgimento*, became prime minister of Piedmont-Sardinia, and wore himself out managing the administrative and diplomatic snares of unification; he whispered 'Italy is made' as he died in 1861, although he had only succeeded in amalgamating Piedmont and Lombardy, leaving Venetia and Rome to join the union later. Verdi's early operatic protagonists are Garibaldian buccaneers, outside the law like Ernani, Corrado in *Il corsaro*, or Carlo in *I masnadieri*. Their successors, like Cavour, are cramped by the pragmatic frustrations of politics. Boccanegra gives up the piratical open sea for the claustrophobia of the council chamber; Don Carlos must sacrifice personal happiness for the sake of his father Philip II's foreign policy; and Radamès exchanges military prowess for tactical negotiation when he proposes freeing the Ethiopian prisoners he has taken. Verdi's own part-time political career was a civic chore that he undertook reluctantly, as he told the mayor of Busseto when his fellow citizens nominated him as their representative to the assembly in Parma. Bored during parliamentary debates, he scribbled a fugue to amuse himself and to express his wish that he could make a fugitive's getaway from the proceedings. Wagner, who never held office, dismissed the deals, treaties and compromises that make politics the art of the possible. Wotan entrammels himself by agreeing to uphold covenants he knows to be hypocritical; in *Die Walküre* he expects Siegmund to extricate him by acting with an instinctive, merciless liberty which he, as a god, has had to forswear. The symbol of this aggression is a sword, and Wotan later provokes Siegfried to use it against his own staff, which is carved with the runes that memorialize precedent. Yet Wagner was no anarchist: how could he have succeeded in facing down opposition and raising funds for his theatre if he had not been a crafty operator, closer to Cavour than to Garibaldi?

Julien Sorel in Stendhal's *Le Rouge et le Noir* idolizes the obscure junior officer who 'conquered the entire world with his sword', and hides a portrait of Napoleon under his mattress. 'To arms!' he cries as he goes into battle against a society that resents his ambition and thwarts his erotic appetite. Julien is a diminished, latter-day Napoleon whose first act of war is to send a letter, but this gives him a new 'sense of his own power', which he celebrates by going to hear his friend Géronimo sing at the Opéra. The occasion is galvanic: 'Never had music exalted him to such heights. He was godlike.' Wagner's Parisian essay on music in the open air mentions the *Eroica* symphony and speculates about Beethoven's attraction to 'the spectacle of a young demi-god, Bonaparte, destroying the world in order to raise a new one upon its ruins'. At this stage Wagner had no misgivings about the necessity of destruction, or the delight it afforded to the 'fiery genius' of Beethoven. During his time in Königsberg in the late 1830s, he planned to compose an overture about the rise and fall of Napoleon, which would be performed as part of a trilogy with *Polonia* and *Rule Britannia*. He wanted to signal the moment of the hero's greatest triumph with the stroke of a gong. But he doubted, he told Cosima much later, that such a noise was permissible in music, so he gave up the idea. The gong was uneuphonious, a symptom of untuned reality. In any case Schopenhauer, to whose philosophy the politically disenchanted Wagner turned during the late 1850s, persuaded him that renouncing the world mattered more than conquering it.

In 1880, early in his work on *Otello*, Verdi made a final attempt to salvage the idea of heroism. He proposed an epilogue to the second last scene of the opera, in which Otello disgraces himself by striking Desdemona in front of the delegation from Venice. Verdi imagined Cypriot citizens rushing in with the news that the Turks have repaired their fleet and are on the attack, which would allow Otello to recover his composure and gather his troops for another victory. Boito persuaded him to leave the toppled general grovelling on the floor, taunted by Iago. Otello goes on to kill Desdemona and then, when his error is exposed, stabs himself in remorse; as he does so, the critic George Martin has suggested, he paraphrases the poetic obituary for Napoleon written by Manzoni in 1821, 'Il Cinque Maggio'. Manzoni's poem begins by bluntly stating 'Ei fu', he died. Dying, Napoleon – who vauntingly declared that all he owned in the world was 'la gloire et la célébrité' – is neither general nor emperor, and his resplendent titles contract into a pronoun that could refer to any mortal man who has worn out his body. When Otello cries 'Oh! Gloria! Otello fu', he treats himself to the proper name that Manzoni omits, in a last effort to repair his mystique; at the same time he detaches himself from it, as if the tarnished aura belongs to another person, someone who is already defunct. 'Gloria' swells into a puffed-up cloud of sound, though 'fu' is gasped or at best merely uttered, since Otello has run out of the afflatus or inflated confidence that sustained him. His truncated, miserably retrospective verb 'fu' corresponds to the unmusical gong stroke that disrupted Wagner's plans for his Napoleonic overture. Proud for once to be composing the music of the future, Verdi pointed out that, when Otello groans 'morta, morta, morta' over the body of Desdemona, he utters 'sounds that have almost no tonality!' Music's limits were marked for Wagner by clattering noise not tempered tone, for Verdi by a word that is spoken not sung. Either way, the hero's progress had come to an abrupt, discordant halt.

|||||||||||||||||||

In 1852 Mazzini looked back on a failed attempt to renovate human history and concluded that 'after having embodied its idea in a Declaration of the Rights of Man … the French Revolution was only capable of ending in one man – Napoleon'. Mazzini despised egotism as 'a violation of fraternity', and castigated Italians for chasing material happiness and neglecting more altruistic concerns. He detected a symptom of this hedonism in the music enjoyed by 'an idle, sensual and corrupt generation' that regarded the artist as 'a mere improvisatore', hired to rescue society from its besetting boredom. He was thinking of the comic operas composed by Rossini, whose effervescent nonsense was an antidote to his ennui. In Mazzini's view, Rossini 'sacrificed the god to the idol', which made him, like Verdi's Nabucco, a worshipper of graven, gilded fetishes; with his elaborate ensembles, he constructed Babel towers of tongue-twisting patter. Mazzini would probably have been sourly amused by the fact that Rossini's comic opera *Il viaggio a Reims* celebrated the Bourbon Restoration. It was staged in Paris in 1825 during the festivities to honour the coronation of Charles X, although – in an anticlimax typical of Rossini's happy futility – its eager royalists never get to Rheims because there is a shortage of horses to draw their carriages.

Like Julien Sorel using the Opéra as a moral and spiritual gymnasium, Mazzini called for protests 'in the streets, the theatres, in every place of meeting' against Italy's invaders. 'Suppose,' he said, 'that enthusiasm was once more held to be sacred.' Verdi – whose music Mazzini scarcely knew and did not much like – acted on that supposition, but in the process showed it to be impractical. Some of his protagonists are apolitical dilettanti, like the would-be Polish king in *Un giorno di regno* or Riccardo in *Un ballo in maschera*; the only enthusiast for an idea is the Marquis of Posa in *Don Carlos*, who converts the moody, introverted Infante to the cause of Flemish independence. But before Carlos can leave to liberate Spain's colony, the Inquisition intercedes, and – rather than dying in one of his father's prisons, which was the fate of the historical Carlos – he is whisked away to the politically ineffectual refuge of a monastery. Radamès negotiates a humanitarian concession from his fellow Egyptians towards their Ethiopian captives but his partiality for Aida ultimately destroys him, and as he gives up his sword he wails about dishonour in a wrenching minor key.

Musset blamed Goethe and Byron, 'whose genius was second only to that of Napoleon', for infecting his generation with a malady symptomatic of the century. The two writers made anguish a vocation, irresistible to young men whose energies were not directed into political action: Goethe's contribution was the suicidal poet Werther, while Byron created the misanthropic sorcerer Manfred – the hero of a cantata by Schumann and a symphony by Tchaikovsky – who, as Musset said, 'hung over the abyss, as if oblivion were the solution to the hideous enigma which enveloped him'. Mazzini too criticized Byron's narcissism, which made his involvement in the Greek campaign to win independence from Turkey in 1823–24 more an experiment in heroic derring-do than a committed crusade; he described Byron's heroes as 'the funeral hymn, the death-song, the epitaph of the aristocratic idea'. Those three dolefully terminal phrases can be applied to the characters Verdi took from Byron. Jacopo in *I due Foscari* is a lost leader, enfeebled by his own emotional sensitivity, who dies of homesickness when exiled from Venice, and Corrado in *Il corsaro* neglects his obligation to make raids on the Turks, devotes himself instead to freeing a nubile slave from the Pasha's harem, and jumps to his death from a cliff as a self-imposed punishment for his lapses.

In 1862, five years after the publication of Musset's *Confession*, the first version of *La forza del destino* was performed in St Petersburg. At the end Alvaro, deranged by grief and guilt, stands on a mountain peak as thunder cracks and lightning slices the sky. Rebuffing the friars who tell him to repent, he identifies himself as hell's envoy, orders heaven to exterminate the vile human race, and invites the earth to split open so he can return to the inferno. He then leaps into the ravine. When Verdi revised the opera for La Scala in 1869 he amended the hero's fate: now Alvaro is forced to his knees by the Padre Guardiano and persuaded to accept forgiveness and remain alive. The two endings, though only a few years apart, come from different phases in the moral history of what Musset called 'an impious century'. An apocalyptic bang gives way to a whimper of submission, and rage is replaced by resigned quiet, just as Musset at the end of the *Confession* abandons his libertine conduct and asks Christ's pardon. Has Alvaro become wiser, or simply lost the will to go on railing against God?

As the decades passed, Wagner confronted the same political and philosophical crises. Pondering the conclusion of what became *Götterdämmerung*, he found he needed to redefine the capacities of the hero – or, more importantly, of the heroine – and to redraw the boundary that separated heaven from earth, gods from men. Brünnhilde, brooding over the corpse of Siegfried, laments the loss of her wisdom. But as Wagner rewrote the text for the ending between 1848 and 1856, she acquired a new understanding of what has happened to her. In his earliest draft the revolutionary process completes itself. Brünnhilde sermonizes about the curse of a mercenary society, which she cleanses by returning the gold to the Rhinemaidens. Wagner had been persuaded by the Russian anarchist Mikhail Bakunin, whom he met in Dresden, that humanity's salvation depended on the destruction of property rights, so Brünnhilde also cancels the servitude of the proletarian Nibelungen. With her business done, she rides onto the funeral pyre; when the smoke clears she can be seen on horseback in the sky, leading Siegfried towards Valhalla where Wotan awaits them. A year or two later, having been convinced by Ludwig Feuerbach's argument that religion was a man-made folly, Wagner decided that humanity should be freed from the oppression of the gods and gave Brünnhilde extra verses declaring that these immortal beings had vanished like a breath. Then, after reading Schopenhauer, he changed her from a freethinker into a mystic: the 1856 Brünnhilde, calling herself 'she who is now wise', uses her suicide to demonstrate that she has quit the home of desire and delusion and opened the gates of eternal becoming. In lines later cancelled by Wagner because the music made them redundant, she announces her relief at having been spared the humiliating, drearily repetitive penalty of rebirth.

To Verdi, a renunciation like this could only mean a living death, expiation eked out into a life sentence. When he revised *Don Carlos* in 1882–83 for La Scala in Milan he worried about the status of the meddling monk who is supposedly Emperor Charles V, symbolically defunct because he had staged his own funeral, attended it in disguise, and retired to the cloister to pray beside his own empty tomb. Verdi was irritated by the indeterminacy of this figure, 'half ghost and half man': death and life for him were opposites, not stages on a Wagnerian continuum. Alvaro's most wrenching line in the final trio of *La forza del destino* is his complaint when Leonora, bound for what she calls the promised land, refuses to allow him to die with her: 'Tu mi condanni a vivere,' he cries – you condemn me to go on living. It is not an option that any of Wagner's characters would consider for a moment. The St Petersburg Alvaro raves about the world's end, but in *Götterdämmerung* we watch it happening as the river floods and the flames from the pyre lick at the tinder of Wotan's aerial fortress.

# 'Oh, you nineteenth century!'

Awaiting execution, Stendhal's Julien Sorel blames the times for his predicament. He has been condemned for murdering a mistress but he is content to die because, with the Bourbon monarchy restored, society has closed its doors to talented, thrusting Napoleonic rebels like himself. 'Oh, you nineteenth century!' he sighs; in 1830, the best is already past. The century first encouraged hopes, then betrayed them as it declined from romanticism to realism – from the blissful, hopeful dawn recalled by Wordsworth in his poem about the French Revolution to the 'iron time' and 'wintry clime' deplored by Matthew Arnold in an elegy for Wordsworth written in 1850. The world in 1789 seemed on the verge of a millennial renewal; before long it was clear that little had changed. In 1852 the courtesan in Alexandre Dumas' play *La Dame aux camélias*, the source for *La traviata*, defines the mood of the middle-aged century and in doing so pronounces her own death sentence. Her lover's father has delivered a harangue about law, piety, respectability and prosperity, which ends by declaring that her beauty, the only asset she possesses, is perishable. 'Oh!' she says, crushed, 'reality!' Verdi and Wagner both experienced this disillusionment, though Wagner of course was less tolerant of reality, less likely to capitulate to realism.

As Musset said, the century began with the heady memory of revolution and the experience of its failure. At its midpoint, in 1848, another spate of revolutions occurred throughout Europe. Verdi was in Paris, from where he followed the news of Lombardy's revolt against Austria. Mazzini asked him to contribute to the campaign by setting to music Goffredo Mameli's battle hymn 'Suona la tromba'. Verdi hoped that it would be sung as the cannons were fired, but by the time he completed his task the decisive battles had been fought and lost.

Count Radetzky, who led the victorious Austrian army, enjoyed a musical apotheosis when he returned to Vienna: Johann Strauss I composed a march in his honour, to which Radetzsky's officers added bouts of synchronized applause and the rhythmic stomping of their military boots. Dismayed by the Italian defeat, Verdi threatened to give up composing and donate his music paper as wadding for cartridges, although Strepponi, practical as ever, pointed out that 'quavers and semiquavers are ineffective against rifle- and cannon-shot'. He was reduced to bewailing 'a pitiful, puny age', after which he sniffed the air for signs of 'a new revolution' that would overturn the French Republic.

In Dresden, where he held an appointment as conductor of the orchestra at the Saxon court from 1842 to 1849, Wagner was more directly involved in the local disturbances. He made speeches, wrote manifestos, and lectured his colleague Eduard Devrient about abolishing private property and establishing 'the law of love'. Gossip alleged that his radicalism was mere pique, incited by the management's refusal to buy him extra clarinets for *Tannhäuser*. Certainly Wagner's most urgent concern was theatrical politics: the uprising of May 1849 gave him a chance to reshape the kingdom's musical institutions. He thought that the theatre should take precedence in this emancipation because it was the arena of human freedom, and he insisted that admission should be unpaid, not tainted by profiteering. It remained a nobly fanciful theory.

For Verdi, revolution meant an insurrection to reclaim terrain from a foreign power. Wagner's agenda was less specific. He was probably the author of an exalted aria in prose published by the radical *Volksblätter* in April 1849, in which the goddess Revolution stormily vows that she will 'annihilate what exists'. The German word she uses is 'vernichte', a favourite term of Wagner's (and one that he bequeathed to Hitler, who repeatedly threatened that he would reduce those who opposed him to nothing). The Dutchman, longing for an end to his traumatic existence, describes the day of wrath as 'der Vernichtungschlag', the annihilating blow, and hopes that he will sink into the void and be consumed by 'ew'ge Vernichtung'. For Wagner, revolution was a shrill and flaring energy like Shelley's west wind, impossible to restrain or direct. He told his friend Friedrich Pecht that he liked Dresden best when the place was loud with the clangour of alarm bells. He throve, Pecht said, on 'violent excitement', and valued the uprising because it made life dangerous. Wagner was fond of Carlyle's description of the French Revolution as 'spontaneous combustion', a 'universal burning-up'. Hence Brünnhilde's act of arson, torching a society 'sunk' – in Carlyle's words, quoted by Wagner in an 1872 preface to his revolutionary tracts – 'into torpor, abeyance and dry-rot'.

The outcome in Dresden was different. Prussian reinforcements restored the status quo; a warrant for Wagner's arrest was issued, and in May 1849 he fled the city with Bakunin and travelled to exile in Switzerland. From there he announced a new ambition in a letter to Liszt: now he intended 'to commit acts of artistic terrorism'. As so often, he was merely vaunting; it was Verdi, for all his moderate conduct and pragmatic caution, who actually wrote about terrorists. In *I masnadieri*, first performed in 1847, Carlo Moor whimsically sets fire to Prague, while his brother Francesco sneers at law and conscience and demonstrates his amoral freedom by attempting to frighten his aged father to death. This is behaviour more outlandish and foully inhumane than anything to be found in Wagner, whose blasphemers – Tannhäuser, Ortrud or Kundry – are satisfied with transgressions that break no bones. Carlyle, writing about the play by Schiller that was Verdi's source, called Franz von Moor 'a villain of theory': his outrages are experiments in freethinking, testing possibility in a world weakened by religion. Despite this excursion into extremism, Verdi was better suited to villains whose motives are untheoretical, like the coldly lustful Duke of Mantua in *Rigoletto* or Macbeth, who kills for political advantage, not because he relishes the idea of murdering a kinsman.

Wagner had a theory ready to explain art's revolutionary role but, like Verdi's battle hymn, it lagged behind the events that demonstrated its irrelevance. He wrote his essay *Die Kunst und die Revolution* soon after his arrival in Zurich; in analysing conditions in classical Greece it conducted an inquest into more recent disappointments. 'The downfall of tragedy', as Wagner called it, foreshadowed the baffled, obstructed rise of opera. In Athens an entire community combined its resources in 'the great united work', which required the cooperation of all the separate arts. Opera too was a composite product, a rite of consolidation for society. Tragedy addressed itself to a single city or nation; his own art would 'embrace the spirit of a free mankind, delivered from every shackle of hampering nationality'. The workers of the world could unite – to modify the language of Marx and Engels in their *Communist Manifesto*, written the year before – by attending the opera. Wagner knew that the prophecy was unlikely to be fulfilled: in Greece as in Germany 'the spirit of community split itself along a thousand lines of egotistical cleavage'. *Rienzi*, staged in Dresden seven years before the attempted revolution, acknowledges the likely response to such idealism. The tribune summons Romans to be free and great, but they remain embroiled in their habitual wrangling. Verdi was better prepared for disappointment. As he told Cammarano in 1849, he was so 'afraid of being called a Utopian' that he didn't even dare to think that there might be such a thing as a perfect opera, with both words and music written, on the Wagnerian model, by the same person. In art and life he was a pessimist, prepared for treachery, aware that self-interest governed human actions; his unending struggle with duplicitous impresarios, unreliable librettists and capricious singers was his political education. In his letter from Paris about the revolt in Lombardy he concluded that nowadays 'nothing great happens – not even great crimes'. It was the lament of an involuntary realist, obliged – as Henry James said about George Eliot's *Middlemarch* – to make tragedy out of 'unpaid butcher's bills'.

In 1830 Mazzini elaborated an aesthetic creed that resembles Wagner's theory of revolutionary art. He called for a newly ample, populous kind of drama, in which soliloquizing individuals like the tragic heroes of Shakespeare were to be replaced by crowds of common men. The progenitor of this 'drama of humanity' was Schiller, who in *Wallensteins Lager* shows the army of the imperial commander during the Thirty Years War to be a rabble of disgruntled peasants, obstreperous trumpeters and quarrelsome dragoons, with flirtatious canteen women, hectoring monks and Bohemian fiddlers along for the ride. Schiller's hangers-on include a Capuchin friar with an addiction to puns, who – when Verdi used the play as a source for the squabbling scenes in the camp in *La forza del destino* – became the uncharitable and nastily inquisitive Melitone. The friar's wordplay derides Wallenstein, whom he turns into a stone wall and a stain on all; after likening him to Ahab, Herod and Holofernes, the friar ends by identifying the chieftain with Nebuchadnezzar, Verdi's blasphemous Nabucco. The great man, as seen by Schiller's verbally licentious comedian, is a laughable monster. Melitone is less seditious: he grumbles about a woman's intrusion when Leonora arrives at the monastery and contends that Alvaro is the devil in person, but makes no such assault on heroism.

Mazzini wanted the democratized drama to serve as a reformatory for mankind. In 1848 he issued a summons to the young men of Italy: 'Create! To create a people!' Their exertions, he promised, would enrol them in 'a moral priesthood among the peoples of Europe'. Mazzini expected music to propagate this faith, and not only by providing trumpet volleys for cavalry charges; its solemn purpose – as he announced in his *Filosofia della musica* in 1836 – was to 'speak to all humanity in a single voice'. That voice was collective, and presumably it would speak in a kind of Esperanto, since Mazzini, like Wagner, wanted to bypass nationality.

Mazzini's chosen example of the chorus as the 'born interpreter of the voice of the people' came from Dante, who in his *Paradiso* recalled the downtrodden citizens of Palermo in 1282 crying 'Mora! Mora!' to the occupying French army. Here, Mazzini argued, was 'the omnipotence of a general and spontaneous impulse', as an isolated attack on a Frenchman who impertinently frisked a Sicilian woman spread into a general slaughter that left two thousand French soldiers dead. The massacre, which began outside a church as the bell tolled for Vespers, was used by Verdi in 1855 as the subject of *Les Vêpres siciliennes*. He did not, however, treat it as the concerted expression of popular feeling. The countdown to mass murder in the last act begins with private lyrical dreams of happiness, indulged by characters craving exemption from the political strife. Hélène, the sister of an Austrian duke, arrives for her wedding to Henri, a Sicilian patriot who has inconveniently discovered that he is the son of the hated French governor Guy de Montfort. She sings a skipping bolero, showering her friends with coloratura like confetti; Henri responds with a melody that mimics the fluttering of the late afternoon breeze. The patriotic agitator Procida warns them about the bell's signal to the rebels and advises them to flee, but – like so many operatic characters at moments of emergency – they are delayed by music, which suspends the hastier tempo of drama. They sing an indecisive trio, during which the men turn on Hélène when she changes her mind about the wedding: opera remains the province of competitive individuals, who raise their voices at each other rather than calmly sorting out a misunderstanding. The bell sounds, the massacre takes place in the last ninety seconds before the curtain falls, and the libretto does not even specify which characters are killed. For Mazzini, the slaughter was the cumulative outcome of 'a sudden inspiration, a record of glory, the memory of past or the sense of present outrage'; in *Les Vêpres siciliennes* it is a muddled, scrambling anticlimax.

The voice of the people had to be choral. Once soloists made themselves heard, unity and unison fell apart. Perhaps opera itself stood in the way of the human brotherhood that was Mazzini's aim. 'Every act of egotism is a violation of fraternity,' Mazzini said in his critique of Byronic individualism. His disapproving rule applies even to brothers in arms like those in *La battaglia di Legnano*, the opera that stoked up the patriotism of 1848. Rolando, leader of the Milanese soldiers, insists that his wife Lida and their child cannot soothe his grief for his comrade Arrigo's reported death. The chorus chides Lida for her equally selfish preoccupation with mourning, which keeps her from taking part in a military festivity; she is kept alive only by the thought that 'madre son io', and her son is her contribution to the state, needing to be nurtured. But Arrigo turns out not to be dead after all, and happens to be in love with Lida. Rolando surprises them together and punishes Arrigo by locking him in a tower, which will shame him by keeping him out of the battle against Barbarossa. Arrigo jumps into the moat, hurries off to catch up with the army, kills the Germanic chieftain, and dies insisting that his sacrifice vouches for the innocence of his affection for Lida. Both men violate the fraternity of the Lombard League, but there would be no drama without their disagreement.

The unregeneracy of the individual, raising his or her voice above the crowd, had constitutional implications for the new world that was emerging from these national struggles. In a letter from Paris in 1848 Verdi hoped that popular anger would carry the day in Lombardy: 'God forbid that we should rely on our kings,' he added. He was equally wary of Anglo-French intervention, which would leave Italy with 'still another prince'. In 1861, preparing for Verdi's visit to St Petersburg to stage *La forza del destino*, the local impresario made a tense joke about his political reputation and his skill at professional bargaining. So far all conditions had been met, he reported; he only hoped that Verdi would not make a last-minute stipulation that the Czar should abdicate. At home, events confounded Verdi's republican principles. Italy's liberation in 1861 was brokered by the House of Savoy with some outside help from Napoleon III, just as the unification of Germany in 1871 was engineered by Bismarck, the chancellor whose concern was less for the nation and the liberty of its citizens than for advancing Prussia's interests. The conflagration set off by the goddess in Wagner's anonymous tract blazed up only briefly; the guerrilla warfare recommended by Mazzini was also ineffective. Verdi, deferring to the judgment of Cavour, came to accept the impracticality of a republic. By then, to make matters more confusing, he was himself an honorary monarch: a patriotic slogan used his surname as an acronym for Vittorio Emanuele Re d'Italia, and when *Aida* was performed in Milan in 1872 he was presented with an appropriate emblem of office, a gem-encrusted sceptre made of gold and ivory. The rod was ornamental and metaphorical, but Liszt claimed such privileges in earnest for Wagner, who had, he said, the right to 'reign and govern as legitimate monarch' at Bayreuth. Despite the radical principles of the composers, opera remained the anachronistic paradise of the self-crowned ego, a domain ruled by what Mazzini called 'the I as king, despotic and solitary', as brazenly self-glorifying as the high B flats sung by Radamès or Otello.

Wagner resolved the conundrum by relying on a tortuous paradox. In June 1848 he made a speech to the Vaterlandsverein, a republican club in Dresden, in which he attempted to resolve the problem that continued to perplex Verdi in the following decade: how could revolutionary endeavours be reconciled with kingship? His operas had already worried about this. Rienzi refuses a crown, and says that the state needs no head since power belongs to the people. The text for *Lohengrin*, already prepared when Wagner made the speech, more anxiously fudges the prospect of a republic. Before his marriage Lohengrin rejects a dukedom and says he wishes to be known as 'Schützer von Brabant', Brabant's protector. Wagner took the title from Oliver Cromwell, who after the execution of Charles I – detested by Wagner because he wore a long black wig – assumed the role of Lord Protector. In Dresden there was no chance of regicide; instead Wagner amazed his fellow republicans by proposing that, after the king declared Saxony free, executive power should be retained by the House of Wettin and handed on to subsequent generations by right of primogeniture. Breaking down the word 'monarch' into its component parts, Wagner reached the same conclusion as Mazzini in his comment on the ego: it meant the rule of one, the dictatorship of a monad, and was therefore a lie, an anachronism and, worst of all, a 'foreign and unGerman notion'. But Wagner secured a reprieve for the institution by performing some dialectical sleight of hand: while 'monarchism' should be discarded, the concept of 'kinghood' could be preserved, so long as the sole ruler recognized that he was the servant of all the people. Wagner disposed of the contradiction with a slippery pun and some tripping alliteration, typical of the atavistic philology that drove his quest for the national roots embedded in words. 'Fürst' meant 'prince', and signalled that the royal heir must be first – but the word also ordained that he should be first of the folk, the freest of the free. A little less tendentiously, Italians also played with words to solemnize Vittorio Emanuele's new national function. Making use of a language full of synonyms and an etymology that links Latin and the Vulgate, they called him 'Padre della Patria', which gave the compound of states a biological parent and made all Italians siblings.

For Wagner, revolution was a state of spiritual inflammation, more religious than political. The anonymous prose poem in the *Volksblätter* spoke of a 'supernatural force' overturning the world, and hailed the 'ever-rejuvenating mother of mankind' as the source of this upheaval. Political reform mattered less than a divine advent: like Siegmund or Siegfried slicing through Wotan's treaties and contracts, Wagner ridiculed the scratchy nibs of bureaucrats whose fussy documents upheld a 'paper world-order'. The promised outcome was the heaven-shaking cry of millions who, transfigured by enthusiasm, would announce '*I am a man!*' and swarm across the world to spread the doctrine of happiness and create 'the man-become-god'. This eschatological ferocity was incomprehensible to Verdi, who never expected men – as Wagner said to his Dresden comrade Theodor Uhlig in 1850 – to graduate to holiness. When Strepponi paid tribute to the incarnated saviour, she emphasized God's decision to humble himself,not man's ascent to the sky. In 1876, after a year of mistrust and ill will caused by

Verdi's obsession with Teresa Stolz, she sent a Christmas letter to her rival, who was away in Russia. 'The Man-God appears to redeem humanity,' she wrote, 'and to teach by his example the greatest of virtues – that of not only forgiving offences, but of loving the offender.' Strepponi agreed to forgive or at least to forget because we are all imperfect, with sins that need to be remitted. Such magnanimity usually requires the moral support of music; even so, when Eboli in *Don Carlos* admits her adultery with King Philip, Elisabeth coldly compels her to choose between banishment and a nunnery. Verdi's idealists may talk about creating a heaven on earth, but they are never free from petty faults. Posa in *Don Carlos* is a devious politician, a keeper of secrets who is perhaps too proud of his confidential relationship with the king. Why does he disarm Carlos, rather than backing up his challenge to the tyrant who is burning heretics and freedom fighters?

W. H. Auden once asserted that 'the golden age of opera … coincided with the golden age of liberal humanism' and described the high C as evidence of an 'unquestioning belief in freedom and progress': the note, when delivered without cracking, is proof of human perfectibility. That may have been true for enthusiasts like the heroes of Stendhal, roused to compete with the flashy bravura of Rossini's tenors. But Verdi, so dutiful and disciplined, did question freedom, had even graver doubts about progress, and would surely not have insisted on a perilously exposed C as a political credential. His gloom in 1848 derived from a long memory of the empires that had risen and fallen on his native soil; in Italy it is impossible to escape from history, or ignore the detritus it has left behind. Wagnerian revolution encountered no such obstacles, even though the uprising in Dresden also failed, because ultimately it involved an assault on the gods, not a quarrel with the bogeys ridiculed in the *Volksblätter* article: elegant courtiers, haggling stockbrokers, Klemens von Metternich and his security services. Wagner considered Prometheus to be the original liberator, and the design of his tetralogy revived and extended the tragic trilogy in which Aeschylus dramatized the martyrdom of the Titan who stole fire from the hearth of Zeus. Shelley wrote an epilogue to Aeschylus in *Prometheus Unbound* – a 'lyrical drama', or an opera without music in which lyrical rapture unbinds and loosens the closure of drama – and the *Ring* followed its example. Wagner admired Shelley, and said in 1852 that a merger between him and his friend Byron would have produced a single and glorious human being, at once an invincible revolutionary and a supreme artist. The philosophical poet combined with the libertine, the prophet grafted onto the chivalrous crusader: it is a terrifying prospect, although it suggests the range of roles that Wagner saw himself playing. The same mythical heritage was invoked by Mazzini, who applied the Promethean myth to present circumstances by telling a colleague that 'We have snatched a spark from the eternal god and placed ourselves between him and the people.' He remembered not only the Titan's atheistic bravado but his fatherly benevolence: Prometheus used the stolen fire to infuse a divine spark in the creatures he had sculpted from the mud of the riverbank, teaching them to reason and shielding them from the disdain of Zeus. Verdi brought the mythical hero down to earth by saluting Cavour as 'the Prometheus of our nation' before their meeting in 1859: polite flattery surely – which Cavour reciprocated by describing Verdi as 'the famous composer … author of *Il trovatore*, *Traviata*, etc.' and 'a European celebrity' – not evidence of metaphysical zeal.

Mazzini remembered that Prometheus fostered humanity, just as Verdi saw him as the maker of a nation not of individual human beings; the agenda of Wagnerian revolution was less humane. Interviewed by Antoine Goléa in 1966, Wagner's grandson Wieland equated Siegfried with Prometheus, 'the first man who rebelled against the gods and gave men their independence, for which he was punished'. But the Greek martyr has nothing in common with the Germanic ruffian. In *Siegfried* the hero's defiance of Wotan when he shoves him aside is mere hooliganism, and apart from Mime, who has helped raise him and whom he negligently slaughters, there are no men for him to protect and educate. Nor is he unrighteously punished, except for a breach of trust he does not know he is committing when he pimps for Gunther in *Götterdämmerung*. Wieland on another occasion likened Brünnhilde to Prometheus, though again there is no true analogy between them. The fire stolen by Prometheus enabled his rudimentary creatures to cook their meat, keep out the cold, and brighten the darkness. Brünnhilde does not purloin a prized asset from the gods; instead she cremates them. In 1850 Wagner told Uhlig that he had a single prerequisite for revolution: it must begin by burning down Paris. He expected a 'fire-bath', called for strong nerves, and said that the only survivors – like Siegfried who ignores the timid self-preservative instinct and strides through a barricade of flames to reach Brünnhilde – would be those who were strong because they had experienced 'the most fearful terror'. It sounds like an initiation rite, a dark and painfully narrow passage through which candidates must travel before they are admitted to the chamber of revelation.

Wagner went on to disparage the expectation of 'gradual progress'. Instead he demanded immediate gratification, to be achieved by violence: 'our redeemer will annihilate at a terrific pace all that stands in our way'. He so speeded up the revolutionary cycle that redemption and annihilation were no longer consecutive stages of a process that had to work itself out over decades (after which, as in France, there would probably be a restoration of the old order). Conversely, liberty and terror overlapped or fused. The goddess Revolution in the *Volksblätter* article describes herself as 'ever-rejuvenating, ever-creating life', like the pulsing chord that causes the river to well up in *Das Rheingold*. Then – after offering to comfort the oppressed, shatter their chains, and rescue the world from the choking embrace of death – she gives a different account of her revolutionary mission: 'All that exists must pass away, that is the eternal law of nature, the rule of life, and I, the eternal destroyer, have come to fulfill the law.' She paraphrases Erda, the earth goddess and oracle who emerges from a crevice in the rocks in *Das Rheingold* to warn Wotan that the power of the gods is threatened. 'Alles was ist, endet,' Erda announces – exactly the sentiment of Wagner's personified Revolution, although the earth mother is no political philosopher. Having first identified herself as the source, the self-renewing fountain of life, the goddess now presides over a vista of metaphysical desolation that coincides with Charles Darwin's account of the earth as a storeyed boneyard, a fertile mortuary. Verdi was a pessimist because he could find no solace for the brevity of existence, and when he was criticized for the peremptory pile-up of corpses at the end of *Il trovatore*, he pointed out that 'everything in life is death! What else is there?' Wagner, however, concentrated on the succession of worlds, not the ephemeral transit of single human lives. The spectacle did not depress him; he knew, as Darwin put it in 1859 in *The Origin of Species*, that there was grandeur in this view of the cyclical way that nature worked, killing and recreating.

As the nineteenth century aged, revolutionary zeal succumbed to entropic despair. Musset's quest for political certainty and spiritual truth was sabotaged by his realization that 'the earth is dying'. He assumed, having pondered the second law of thermodynamics, that it would die of cold; it might also be incinerated, or submerged by a tidal wave. Those catastrophic options are placed on show at the end of *Götterdämmerung*, with the orchestra insisting that either way the result will be salutary. A similar day of geological judgment is audible in Verdi's *Requiem*. In her prayer to be freed from fear, the soprano imagines the day of wrath when heaven and earth will move. The words she recites give precedence to heaven ('quando coeli movendi sunt et terra') because the schism that the Latin text dreads occurs in the sky, but at the end of the phrase her voice swoops suddenly upwards on 'et terra', turning an afterthought into a quaking climax. What alarms her is to feel the ground moving beneath her feet, as if she were responding to contemporary geology and its discoveries about the infirmity of our ancient, crumbling earth. The chorus voices 'et terra' in a tender, elongated pianissimo that makes it more than an afterthought: that this is our only habitat. Meanwhile a cosmic thunderstorm rumbles through the orchestra, generated not by the wrath of a vindictive, legalistic God but by his retreat from the world. After the last soft repetition of 'Libera me', sound falters and is stifled by empty, unreverberant space; the ebbing rhythm suggests the muffled roar as the 'Sea of Faith' retreats in Matthew Arnold's poem 'Dover Beach'.

*Götterdämmerung* concludes with the world purged by fire and water. The orchestra remembers the motif first sung by Sieglinde in *Die Walküre* when she is told of her pregnancy, a swelling melody usually said to signify redemption through love – but who is left to be redeemed, and in what way are these disasters loving? The last voice heard in Wagner's opera is that of Hagen, dragged under-water to his death as he scrambles to snatch the discarded ring. The *Requiem* ends with a survivor not a victim, and the soprano repeats her plea to be freed from the fear of death because she wants to continue living.

|||||||||||||||||||

Those who lived through the nineteenth century saw it as a single extended lifespan, or as one long day in which Wordsworth's dawn led by stages to Wagner's twilight. At the beginning of the century, romanticism invented the mystique of childhood and challenged the imagination to·retain or recover an innocent, infantile vision. By dying young, poets like Byron or Goethe's Werther escaped the downhill slide into mediocre, middle-aged prose. But Wagner had a life of regulation length, and Verdi lived much longer: they both had to experi-ence the full cycle of changes.

At first it seemed possible that universal justice, as Wordsworth said in 1805, might transmute the earth into what in his poem 'The French Revolution' he calls 'the bowers of paradise'. Wagner shared that hope, then outgrew it. In 1848, toying with the idea of a drama about Achilles, he announced that 'Man is the completion of god. The eternal gods are the elements for the begetting of man.' But the new man remained unbegotten: Siegfried does not deserve the obituary lavished on him by the orchestra. Revising the text of Brünnhilde's immolation, Wagner recognized that the gods too were no longer eternal. Nor was the earth. The faltering prelude to the last act of *Parsifal* evoked, as he told Cosima, an exhausted planet. As the century ended, Wagner himself was blamed for its implosion. Diagnosing the sinister appeal of his music, Nietzsche asked 'What is it in our age that Wagner expresses?' His answer was 'brutality and the most delicate weakness, which exist side by side', or 'that thirst for emotion which arises from fatigue'. Nietzsche here exactly defined decadence, which mixes bestial coarseness and effete refinement; Aubrey Beardsley exemplified that union of opposites in an ink drawing made in 1896 that gives Alberich the over-ripe face of Oscar Wilde.

In 1892 the social critic Max Nordau published a tract about the fin de siècle entitled *Entartung*, meaning 'degeneration'. The word had a Wagnerian pedigree. Taunted by a sailor at the beginning of the opera, Isolde reacts with a scalding attack on the cowardly Tristan and his 'entartet Geschlecht', the decayed race to which he belongs, and Rienzi twice rails at the treacherous Roman mob, calling it 'entartete'. Nordau's rant identified all the stigmata of degeneracy in the character of Wagner, who suffered – according to this bilious diagnosis – from persecution mania and megalomania, and had the handwriting of a graphomaniac; he also punned like a burbling idiot, and possessed the sexual ethics of a tomcat. When Nordau likened the mood of the times to 'the impotent despair of a sick man … dying by inches in the midst of an eternally living nature blooming insolently forever', he might have been describing Amfortas in *Parsifal*, who nurses his venereal wound while the spring meadow derides him by sending up shoots through the frozen ground. Wagner's music catered, Nordau decided, to 'the hysteria of the age', and was responsible – along with the nervous excitement stirred up by Germany's imperial wars – for deranging an entire nation. Thomas Mann studied a casualty of this epochal decline in his novel *Buddenbrooks*, published in 1901. A mercantile dynasty in Lübeck loses its wealth because its vigour bleeds away; young Hanno, the last of the line, admits that he belongs to 'a degenerate family'. The infection dates from his youthful trip to hear *Lohengrin*, which leaves him at the mercy of 'secret thrills and shudders, sudden fervent sobs, and a rapture of insatiable ecstasy', unfit for the workaday world. Officially the boy dies of typhus, though it is Wagner who weakens him and lowers his defences against infection.

In 1918 Oswald Spengler, taking stock of a ruined civilization, detected in Wagner the onset of the West's decline. The 'bitter conclusion' he drew from Wagner's 'abstract music' was that 'all is irretrievably over with the arts of form of the West. The crisis of the nineteenth century was the death-struggle'. The years after Wagner's death in 1883 were those in which the century seemed to run out of stamina, lapsing into what Nietzsche called 'nervous hypersensitiveness'. In an interview Verdi described himself and Wagner as 'aged carcasses' and advised young composers to ignore them both. After the premiere of *Otello* in 1887 he told a group of journalists that all he wanted was 'Rest, absolute rest'. But there was no lapse into inanition of the sort that Brünnhilde expects at the end of *Götterdämmerung* when – tenderly, regretfully, but also imperiously – she sings her elegy for Wotan and for the idea of godhead, 'Ruhe, ruhe, du Gott!' Verdi was soon active again, and *Falstaff* followed in 1893. His creative renewal almost made up for the prostration of an era sapped of strength, as Nietzsche and Nordau believed, by the unbearably exquisite delights of Wagner. Tristan or Amfortas on their sickbeds represented the age's debility; Verdi offered a prescription for recovery. After the first performance of *Falstaff* at La Scala, Boito said that he relied on the opera to restore the health of ailing Italy. Could it also cure the rest of a continent weakened by Wagnerism?

Music, as Boito put it in 1894, was a means of Mediterraneanizing the human spirit. In the short term, he hoped that *Falstaff* would banish the 'ultramontane fog' that had drifted across the Alps. This was his joke about *Der fliegende Holländer*, distilled from Baltic downpours and North Sea gales, which was being performed at La Scala in alternation with Verdi's sunny comedy. Like seasonal gods, the antagonistic spirits of morose, rheumy winter and verdant spring, Wagner and Verdi battled for control of the world.

# 3 | *Maestro, Meister, Muses*

## LESSONS OF THE MASTERS

During the lifetimes of Verdi and Wagner the public image of the artist changed. In an industrial economy, creative workers had to behave professionally, presenting themselves to the world as masters of a trade. Verdi was known to those who dealt with him as 'Maestro' – the only title he answered to, since he refused to be made a Marquis, returned the diploma that conferred on him the meaningless rank of Commendatore, and was a year late for his swearing-in as Senator in 1875. Mastery, however, was relative. When Verdi took up hunting and found that his aim was poor, he grumbled that he needed a newfangled gun that would double his chances of success by combining powder in one barrel with cartridges in the other. 'Good hunters shoot straight even with mediocre guns,' he told the music critic Léon Escudier, 'but a Maestro di Musica needs a weapon that shoots straight by itself.' With Cosima enforcing the protocol, Wagner for his part disappeared behind his elective rank and was deferentially referred to – with mystified awe, not mere respect – as the 'Meister'.

The honorific title may seem an affectation, but composers had only too recently been servants – of a religious community, like Bach in Leipzig, of a single domineering ecclesiastical employer, like Mozart at the court of the archbishop in Salzburg, of an aristocratic patron, like Haydn at the Esterházy court. Romanticism in principle freed artists from catering to the whims of employers. Berlioz established a new code of artistic conduct in his *Symphonie fantastique*, which disconnects the dreamer from society and replaces the demands of external authorities with the whimsical orders issued by phantasmal muses or obsessive fantasies. Liszt, as he told George Sand in 1837, refused to truckle to 'great lords' who treated musicians like jugglers or performing dogs. Instead he exhibited his skill to paying customers in recitals he called 'monologues pianis-tiques'. As touring virtuosi, he and the violinist Paganini free-associated on their instruments, obedient only to personal caprice. By the end of the century, the work of liberating the artist had been done. During the 1890s Richard Strauss adopted the persona of a prankster teasing the bourgeoisie in his symphonic poem *Till Eulenspiegels Lustige Streiche*, and in *Ein Heldenleben* he noisily portrayed himself as a hero, comparable – as he said with his usual cheek – to Caesar or Napoleon: artistic accomplishments are here celebrated as if they were military victories, with the hero bludgeoning a pack of critical detractors on a metaphorical battle-field. In his *Sinfonia Domestica*, first performed in 1904, Strauss aggrandized the daily round of his household, including his baby son's bath-time. Hans Richter, one of Wagner's preferred conductors, remarked that 'all the cataclysms of the downfall of the gods in burning Valhalla' made less noise than young Bubi splash-ing in his tub.

Neither Verdi nor Wagner could afford such jocular megalomania. As an altar boy, Verdi once suffered a more abusively physical version of the indigni-ties Mozart endured during his employment by Prince-Archbishop Hieronymus Colloredo in Salzburg. Entranced by the sound of the organ during Mass, the young Verdi forgot to hand up the cruets, and was shoved aside by the tetchy priest. He fell, hit his head, and fainted. But unlike Mozart, he was able to retali-ate. Whenever he told the story, he said that he had wished for lightning to strike the priest, which a few years later it fortuitously did; the curse, as his operas demonstrate, was an effective means of vigilante justice. Unlike Strauss, whose father was a horn player much esteemed by Wagner, Verdi had no sense of entitlement to a career or even to rudimentary training, which meant that his status as Maestro was hard-won. In 1831 his father asked a charitable foundation in Busseto to award his son a scholarship, and accompanied the request with an abject petition to the Duchess of Parma, Napoleon's widow. The next year Verdi applied for admission to the Imperial and Royal Conservatory in Milan, which now bears his name. He was denied a place, and he never forgot the setback. Antonio Barezzi offered to subsidize his studies, and in 1835 Verdi returned to Busseto as local Maestro di Musica, sharing duties with a church organist. He resigned in 1838, and departed for Milan with his first wife Margherita to make his fortune. His advance was eased by social favours: two Milanese coun-tesses, Clarina Maffei and Emilia Morosini, welcomed him to their salons and became permanent friends. The bear – as Strepponi later called him, at a time when he could get away with being gruff and solitary in his private wilderness at Sant'Agata – clumsily attempted to play the lapdog, and in a letter written to

Morosini in 1842 Verdi called her charming four times before announcing a ban on the obsequious adjective with a brusque 'fermata'. Professional success made him conspicuous, though he liked shedding rank and reputation to pass as an innocuous citizen. In 1853, planning a trip to Naples with Strepponi, he warned his friend Cesare de Sanctis that he wished to be treated as Signor Giuseppe Verdi not Maestro, and particularly wanted not to have to go to the opera. This self-division became a habit. In 1858 Strepponi informed Escudier that Verdi was making a private visit to Paris to dispose of the house he had occupied during rehearsals for *Les Vêpres siciliennes*. 'The Maestro,' she specified, 'remains in Italy.'

Although Wagner was later seen as the symbol of artistic autonomy – a godlike creator, whose notion of the *Gesamtkunstwerk*, the total or compound work of art, absolved him from having to collaborate with librettists, and who built a theatre in which to stage festivals of his own operas – he remained for most of his life a musician of an almost eighteenth-century kind, dependent on the patronage of a merchant like Otto Wesendonck or a king like Ludwig II. He served as a functionary at the Saxon court, where he supplied music for the unveiling of a monument to a previous king in 1843; earlier, during his appointment as theatre director in Riga in 1835, he composed a hymn to celebrate the accession to the throne of Tsar Nicholas I. But he was a courtier with aspirations to supplant the monarch. In 1865, while enjoying the patronage of Ludwig II, he fantasized about setting up a household 'like Versailles under Louis XIV', with flunkeys catering to his every whim.

Despite his rebellious nature, Wagner's time at court taught him the fawning manner cultivated by those who count on the approbation of autocrats. He deployed it with slippery skill in his letters to Ludwig II, combining flattery with flirtation. Pierre Boulez once likened this correspondence to the official communiqués, at once cravenly submissive and puffed up with pomp, exchanged by the Pope and the Holy Roman Emperor. But Wagner abased himself because it served his interest and he maintained his self-respect by acting like an ingrate, just as he took Wesendonck's money while simultaneously making free with his wife. The bond between Wagner and Ludwig was not exactly political, which would have made it a competitive trial of strength (although Wagner did venture to give Ludwig advice about affairs of state: the composer Peter Cornelius likened him to the Marquis of Posa, who presses his liberal opinions on Philip II in Schiller's *Don Carlos*). Each man depended on the other, in whom he saw an inversion of himself, at once desirable and detestable. To extort what he needed, Wagner lavished simpering endearments on the enthroned boy. 'I fly to him as a lover,' he said in 1864. He behaved as if he were a royal catamite, and while waiting to be summoned to the king's presence he studied his portrait, wondering whether he might be able to steel himself 'to renounce the "eternal feminine" completely' for his sake. Would self-prostitution be the price of Ludwig's support? Later he told Hans von Bülow that he regarded the king as a predestined consort and helpmate, marvelling that 'a queen had to give birth to this son for *me*'. When he offered *Tristan* to Ludwig, Wagner presented it as the fruition of their relationship, 'born in pain such as no mother ever suffered for her child'. Despite this anguished delivery, his music restored the proper balance of power: it turned the king into an exhausted female whose only hope of articulacy lay in gasping Wagner's own words. After he heard the opera, Ludwig responded by quoting the last cries uttered by Isolde before she sings her faint, expiring F sharp: 'To drown … sink down – unconscious – highest bliss. – *Divine* work!' For Wagner, mastery had a sexually sinister component. He trafficked in dominance, though sometimes, as with Ludwig, he found an illicit excitement in reversing roles.

Mastery meant the mastering of technical skills, which had to be acquired before the aspiring artist could be admitted to a profession. They were learned during apprenticeship to a master, then passed on to a pupil from the next generation. Studying in Milan in 1832, Verdi was sentenced, as he contrapuntally said, to write 'canons and fugues, fugues and canons of all kinds'. He hated pedantry on principle, and would have had little sympathy with Wagner's more academic view of Bach fugues as 'a vanished species', the relic of a pure Platonic world of form and number into which man had not yet messily intruded. But, as he admitted to Escudier, on occasion 'musical form can be just right'. He therefore wrote a fugal battle to conclude *Macbeth* and ended *Falstaff* with a fugal praise of human folly, finding a dramatic logic in the scholarly drill: in the one case the collision of themes and counter-themes represents the clash of Scottish and English armies; in the other the punctilious coordination of voices assembles the characters in a row as if lined up to submit to a last, unexpectedly lenient judgment handed down by their creator. The results incidentally disprove Wagner's claim that in Bach's fugues 'chaos is turned into harmony', since both the battle in *Macbeth* and the chortling finale of *Falstaff* tolerate a vigorous, rollicking chaos.

The student to whom Verdi transmitted the training he had received was Emanuele Muzio, who referred to him as 'Signor Maestro' or – since he was the only beneficiary of Verdi's tuition – as 'my Maestro'. Muzio repaid Verdi by running errands, and later accompanied him abroad as an assistant, before setting up independently as a conductor and vocal coach. He died in 1890, after reiterating his devotion in a final letter and setting aside funds to train a young man from Busseto so that 'the good example given by Maestro Verdi' could be extended into the future. Verdi was bereft: he had lost a friend, not a factotum.

Wagner needed helpers – especially conductors like Bülow or Hermann Levi – but they had to be executors of his will, ready to sacrifice themselves to him. His misgivings about the contract between paternalistic master and filial pupil are evident in the way Sachs treats his apprentice David in *Die Meistersinger*. The lad is as fulsome as Muzio in his gratitude for what Sachs has taught him, yet he is treated as a household butt, kicked, slapped, belted and boxed on the ear by his short-tempered master. Was this casual abuse Wagner's notion of tuition? The son Cosima finally presented to him in 1869, after giving birth to a pair of dynastically useless daughters, was to be an extension of Wagner, the superintendent of his legacy. Siegfried Wagner was begotten for a purpose, just as Wotan designed Siegmund and Siegfried as his surrogates. In March 1882 Wagner became infuriated by his son's talent for drawing Italian scenery and architecture: would the boy turn out to be a renegade, forgetting his responsibility to prolong a musical heritage and applying for membership of the wrong guild? Wagner knew that to breed the next generation is to relegate yourself to the past, so he had mixed feelings about possessing an heir, let alone a pupil to whom he was expected to act as a foster parent. He tried to make the best of this when discussing Wotan, 'my jovial self-annihilating god'. Writing to Ludwig II in 1864 as he prepared to compose the showdown between Wotan and Siegfried near Brünnhilde's rock, he said 'I want – in order to live eternally – to let myself be destroyed by my Siegfried! O beautiful death! … If I am Wotan, I have succeeded through Siegfried.' He was reconciled to this biological defeat because he assumed that 'Wotan lives on in Siegfried as the artist lives on in his work of art.' Genetically, the father also lives on in his son, although for Wagner that was a second best. The problem did not arise for Verdi, who had no surviving children.

Wagner did not think of himself as a craftsman or a guild member, and felt no responsibility to those who might want to carry on his work: his achievements were unrepeatable, and his music – as he saw it – at once predicted and preempted the future. But he did have his own subtle interpretation of what it meant to be a 'Meister'. In his duet with Walther before the try-out of the prize song, Sachs tells his protégé to produce a 'Meisterlied', a mastersong, which is not simply what others might call a masterpiece. It is, Sachs reveals, the result of self-mastery. Music seems to be as freshly juvenile as birdsong in spring; the young are instinctive singers, but they seldom sustain that glad ebullience through the later seasons of life. The true master can still sing in middle age or elderly winter, without the benefit of youthful impulse. Rules are a compensation for the inevitable desiccation of the sappy emotional source; they preserve feeling, like a musical score whose markings compress sensations that will be released into the air when someone sings the notes. Verdi wanted music to invade the singer's body and propel it through space. As he told Ricordi, the interpreters he favoured seemed to have the devil on their backs, and even a comic character like Alice in *Falstaff* needed an element of witchery, like Ortrud invoking her pagan gods or Kundry propelled into action by Klingsor. 'She must be full of the devil,' Verdi said of Alice. '*She stirs the brew.*' Sachs's lecture elaborates a more sombre account of music as emotion recollected, tranquilly encoded by composition, then reactivated by the performer. As when Sachs the widower gently rebuffs Eva, the artist renounces life; he contents himself with a mournful substitute, a souvenir of loss like the horn, sword and ring that Lohengrin hands to Elsa before his departure. Verdi – who explained his decision to abandon his career after the deaths of his first wife and their children by saying that he could find no consolation in art – would have had no patience with this elegiac, retrospective attitude.

In 1862 Wagner grimly joked that he had given up any hope of seeing his operas staged, and was planning 'to disappear from the face of the earth and continue only to work on my artistic projects in secret like some departed spirit'. His characters already seem to be inhabiting this afterlife. They sing as if remembering, dredging up dreams like Senta when she hums the ballad or Sieglinde when she tells Siegmund that she believes she heard his voice as a child. Walther's mastersong is a reverie that goes back to the beginning of creation, when he saw Eva in an Eden that is also Parnassus; his improvised development of the fantasy convinces Sachs – who suddenly anticipates the Freudian reading of art – that all poetry is the interpretation of dreams. The first of the poems by Mathilde Wesendonck that Wagner set to music was calculated to appeal to his nostalgia for the source of music, buried within us like our recollections of infancy. 'In der Kindheit frühen Tagen/Hört' ich oft von Engeln sagen,' muses the singer: in early childhood, she often heard tell of angels (and in those days it was possible to believe in them). When Verdi's characters relive an infantile past, they do so in sorrowful duets that recover a lost relationship. Gilda asks Rigoletto about a mother she cannot remember, and Amelia, prompted by Boccanegra, recites the story that identifies her as his daughter. Less fondly, Azucena in *Il trovatore* recalls and grieves over her accidental slaughter of her baby, and Amonasro torments his daughter Aida by conjuring up the spectre of her mother, her skeletal arms pointing in accusation. A whole family is reconstituted for a few moments, before the painfully inevitable recognition that the dead cannot be enticed back to life. Wagner's people undertake more solitary journeys into the past, since what they are seeking is not a child or a parent who was taken from them but an ideal image, an imaginary playmate, the self's other half: Mathilde's angel, Senta's demon, Sieglinde's twin.

The song's rehearsal in *Die Meistersinger* lays bare the sad reality of such fantastical retrievals, and also uncovers some of art's secrets. Sachs has mastered his own emotions, but he incites emotion in Walther by urging him on from one verse of the song to the next, and is content – as he pointedly takes up paper, pen and ink – to transcribe and edit the young man's effusions. We see and hear the collaboration between the two parties to any artistic enterprise, the man who suffers (or in this case ecstatically dreams) and the mind that gives form to the raw, unruly feeling. Sachs might be the ageing composer, with Walther as the younger self whose experience he recalls. Their partnership brings together the two sides of Wagner's creative being, to which he allocated sexes: male words, female music. As so often in his strangely hermaphroditic aesthetics, the result is a child. Sachs tells Walther that if he succeeds in composing an after-song it will be a slim, self-sufficient creature, able to stand alone, giving its parents good reason to be proud. The progenitors he refers to happen to be a pair of men, with Eva smiling from the sidelines as a stepmother. Once again Wagner was treating art biologically; the habit prompted him to view his actual children – Isolde, Eva and Siegfried – as characters he had created, not individuals with a need and a right to break free from their maker. Isolde was born on the day that the cuckolded Bülow began rehearsing *Tristan,* and Wagner liked to say that Siegfried was born on the day he completed *Siegfried* (although the disobliging boy in fact arrived a week before the end of his work on the opera). Walther is less malleable than Wagner's own offspring. When Sachs coaxes him to advance to the third section of the song, he impatiently says 'Genug der Wort'!' Enough of words, or of the marital fusion of words and music: he craves satisfaction in reality, not art.

Sachs is Wagner's deftly deceptive self-portrait. Like Wotan when he appears in *Siegfried* as the Wanderer, he is a god in disguise, living incognito among the mortals whose affairs he manages. But whereas Wotan dwindles in *Götterdämmerung* into an offstage spectator of a history he cannot change, Sachs is honoured by the entire community when he arrives on the meadow outside Nuremberg for the festival of song. The chorus, which began the opera by singing the praises of John the Baptist and the Saviour he announced, now salutes Sachs as an aesthetic redeemer. He declares himself unworthy, and in doing so lets slip Wagner's regret at never receiving such unanimous adulation. Hugo Wolf felt a 'religious awe' when he first saw Wagner, Nietzsche regarded him as 'my Jupiter', and Judith Gautier told Cosima – later her rival for Wagner's affection – that she felt she had looked on the face of God. But his music remained an esoteric cult, not a religion, appealing exclusively to followers who, like George Bernard Shaw, identified themselves as Wagnerites.

When the Bayreuth theatre opened in 1876, the audience included the German kaiser, the Bavarian king, the Brazilian emperor and what Tchaikovsky called 'the musical representatives of all civilized nations'. There was no room for the demotic public that sings Sachs's praises; the commoners waited outside to watch the notables arrive. Verdi – a bard acclaimed by an entire nation, not merely by the populace of a single city like 'Nürnbergs teurem Sachs!' – attained the laureate status denied to Wagner, and he reacted to the hero worship of his compatriots with a reticence or embarrassment truer than Sachs's modest demurral. Pressed into serving in the first Italian parliament, Verdi guaranteed that he would perform the role wretchedly, because he was 'only occasionally eloquent'. Nevertheless, according to the journalist Giuseppe Depanis, his countrymen regarded him as their 'guardian deity', more a godfather than the unapproachably lofty God who intimidated Wolf, and they were keen to repay him for his patriarchal protection. As early as 1847, when *Macbeth* was performed in Florence, a group of devotees unharnessed the horses from Verdi's carriage and hauled it back to his hotel themselves. In 1868 he stayed away from the opening of the Teatro Verdi in Busseto; he was present in the form of a bust, which had wreaths sent by several Italian cities laid beneath it as a tribute, and the town's population was granted a holiday as if the date marked some sacred anniversary. In 1887 in Genoa he was given a congratulatory album containing thirty thousand signatures, gathered from all over the country. In 1893 when his train stopped in Turin on the way back from Paris, travellers, porters, policemen, and workers of every kind – people who may never have been inside an opera house, though they would probably all have recognized snatches of the most popular Verdi arias – clustered around his wagon-lit. Those wearing hats reverently removed them. Unlike Sachs's boisterous Nuremberg congregation with its shouts of 'Heil! Heil!', the crowd remained silent, and cheered only when the train began to move away.

It is hard to picture railway workers downing tools to gaze at Wagner in gratitude. True, he was surprised and gratified in 1859 when a customs inspector at the Gare du Nord in Paris whistled a snatch of *Tannhäuser* to him; a little anticlimactically, the man turned out to be a fellow musician, who had translated the opera's libretto into French.

||||||||||||||||||

John Keats thought that a poet ought to be 'the most unpoetical of any thing in existence'. Verdi – sober in demeanour and in the anonymously formal clothes he favoured, diligently workmanlike in his habits – put the rule into practice. In 1860, with no new opera in prospect, he announced to Escudier that instead of composing he was planting cabbages and beans. He did not think those were inferior activities; if anything they were a relief from the labour of what he called manufacturing notes. In 1880 he told his friend Opprandino Arrivabene that he passed his days trudging round his fields: 'a very prosaic life,' he admitted, but healthy. Strepponi made the same point, admonishing her friend Corticelli not to accuse her 'of being prosaic!' because she busied herself with domestic tasks. She and Verdi lived unoperatically – although, as she told Corticelli, as much poetry could be found in modest homely routines as in the delirium she experienced onstage during her career as a singer.

Verdi was happy to be a public success, which meant that his music returned profits, but he despised publicity, which wasted money by paying for popularity and required him to advertise his own existence. He identified such exhibitionism with Wagner, and – alluding to the puffery that preceded the Bologna production of *Lohengrin* – said that he hated being 'lohengrinata', or Lohengrinized. Prodding the conductor Angelo Mariani in a letter over the commemorative requiem for Rossini in 1869, he argued that the project was noble because selfless, and complained that Italians bestirred themselves only if their vanity was tweaked and their names 'proclaimed in the theatres and dragged through the streets'. This inward-turning revulsion recalls the way one of Verdi's most guarded, emotionally indirect characters reacts to the jubila-tion of his followers. Boccanegra strides on, boasting that his name is on every tongue and hoping that this will speed his marriage to Maria. Minutes later, when he is elected doge, the triumph is worthless because he knows that Maria is dead; he ignores the cacophony of bells and drums and the shouts of supporters who cannot know what misery he conceals from public view. Celebrities thrive on recognition by strangers, but Verdi preferred not to be noticed. In 1888 a man called Rocchi sent him a book he had written, and wrote later complaining that Verdi had not acknowledged it. Now Verdi responded, though not in the way that Rocchi might have hoped. 'Why do you,' he asked, 'who do not know me, send me one of your works?' The previous year he refused to travel to Rome when *Otello* was performed there, and wondered why he should be expected to attend. 'To put myself on display? To gather applause?' His 'sense of personal dignity,' he said, would be compromised if he assumed a false face for public consumption, or acted the role of national treasure. Singers were exhibitionists by nature; the composer or dramatist should be an absent god, as innocuous as Shakespeare.

In 1899 Verdi irritably denied reports that he was preparing his memoirs. 'I don't approve of this writing about one's own life!' he told Italo Pizzi. He left such ostentation to Wagner, who at the behest of Ludwig II began to dictate his self-exculpating and self-glorifying *Mein Leben* to Cosima in 1865. After Wagner's death Cosima recalled copies of the autobiography – including those owned by Ludwig II – and destroyed most of them, though not because she had second thoughts about the enterprise. Alive, he shared himself with the world, or at least with the friends who, as he said in his foreword, felt a 'pure sympathy' with him and were therefore licensed to read the book. Dead, his personal life belonged only to his widow.

Although Verdi valued discretion, he had no tolerance for the conspiratorial confidences and stern embargoes by which the Wagners tantalized and disciplined their cliquey entourage. In 1852 he wrote a prickly but coldly reasoned letter rebuking Antonio Barezzi, his benefactor and father-in-law, who had relayed local gossip about his cohabitation with Strepponi. Without mentioning her by name, Verdi shielded his companion from criticism by spelling out her financial independence and her entitlement to respect. He defied intrusive speculation – 'who knows what our relations are?' – and though he denied having anything to hide, he demanded that his privacy should be left unmolested. 'I am a man who can defend himself,' he growled, and threatened to move elsewhere, turning his back on Busseto (even, as he characteristically added, if that meant selling his property at a loss) rather than responding to censorious tattle. He added that he resented the offence to his honour. This is the word that Falstaff disparages in his opera, reducing it and the chivalric affectations it stands for to a puff of air, as empty as its open vowels. Verdi's letter weighs the word down by appealing to the meanings it ought to have: propriety, correctness, the assumption of honesty. Obliquely accusing Barezzi, he snarled at a community whose disapproval menaced his freedom of action and declared that 'my whole being rebels against conforming to other people'.

But Verdi the nonconformist also took refuge in uniformity, signalled by the unchanging, impersonal costume he wore throughout the decades. He even donned metaphorical armour when facing up to hostile audiences, as he told Clarina Maffei in 1884: 'ready to be shot' but immune to pain, he could then enjoy the fight. There are tortuous contradictions here, as an easily wounded man announces that he cannot be hurt and puts his trust in a thick skin, a bristling hedge of beard, and the insulation of a private estate. Perhaps Verdi's understanding of his own motives explains the angry flourish with which he concluded his letter to Mariani about the requiem. Italians, he said, will work happily enough if they are recognized and praised for doing so, 'but when our personalities have to disappear behind an idea ... then we withdraw under the cloak of our egotistical indifference, which is the scourge and ruin of our country'. Verdi wore that cloak himself, although it misrepresented him: he was neither egotistical nor indifferent, but reticence was better than self-dramatization, which he despised.

Opera relies on the intensification of feeling, as Wagner told Mathilde Wesendonck in 1859, so it suited his own physical constitution. Wagner oscillated between 'states of extreme tension', and the purpose of his art was to show those clashing moods in violent conflict. He despised phlegmatic people, whom he compared with the icy crust that hardens over the earth's igneous innards and gives a false impression of solidity; he likened himself to a volcano, liable to vomit forth what is within. In Italy in 1880 he rapped on his children's bedroom door and impersonated a thunderstorm, combining in himself the effects generated by the rumbling orchestra and shrilling chorus in the last act of *Rigoletto*. Verdi might have agreed about the dramaturgy of passion, and he repeatedly asked his librettists to provide him with 'varying moods', as he did when discussing an operatic adaptation of *King Lear* with Antonio Somma in the 1850s: the bastard Edmund had to have opportunities at different points in his aria for expressing irony, contempt and rage. Verdi even referred to these clashes of emotion or character as 'the variety my mad brain needs'. The madness, however, was mere whimsy, because he was making a rationally calculated aesthetic demand; otherwise he masked and muffled his emotions. He was moved by a personal tribute sent to him in 1893 by Ricordi, but restrained himself. 'With a white beard,' he replied, 'the eyes must be kept dry.' Compliments from the French music critic Camille Bellaigue in 1894 elicited no blush because, Verdi said, at his age his skin was coppery, so any rush of blood would be invisible. He was gently taciturn when sending condolences to another friend later that year, explaining that 'words dissolve, sweeten, and destroy feelings!'

When he dictated some autobiographical reminiscences to Ricordi in 1879, Verdi revised the chronology of his early life to emphasize a self-mastery that he shared, unexpectedly, with Wagner's Sachs. As he recalled, he lost his son in April 1840, his daughter a few days later. The third coffin, containing his first wife Margherita, was carried out of his house in June. Then, alone and in anguish, he 'was compelled to write an entire comic opera'. The chronicle ends with his understated announcement that '*Un giorno di regno* was not successful'.

In fact the three deaths were spaced out over a period of almost two years, and the sequence was not quite as he remembered it: the girl died in August 1838, the boy in October 1839, Margherita in June 1840, and the ill-fated comedy received its single performance four months later. Even at a distance of so many years, Verdi could not have forgotten the true timeline; by altering it he underlined the sense of duty that bound him to fulfil professional obligations, and the irony of having to churn out a comedy while recovering from a triple tragedy. The more grievous his feelings were, the more he kept them to himself. He attended Cavour's funeral in 1861 'in full mourning', although – as he told Ricordi, almost apologizing for the conventional display – 'a deeper mourning harrowed my heart'. Shakespeare's Hamlet makes the same comment about the 'inky cloak' he wears after his father's death; for Verdi, operatic song, like the prince's soliloquies in the play, gives vent to what people are unable or afraid to say. Sometimes this relief is denied to his characters. The most emotionally powerful moment in *La traviata*, all the more upsetting because it is so brief and so drastically simple in its musical means, comes when Violetta scribbles a letter to tell Alfredo she is leaving him. We don't hear or see what she is writing; the clarinet gives a desolate paraphrase. Alfredo bustles in to embrace her, and she has to simulate happiness before making a tormented plea for his love. Then, unable to suppress her agitation, she rushes out.

Explaining *Tristan* to Mathilde Wesendonck, Wagner said that he stimulated the music within himself by exacerbating those 'heightened moods'. He then waited for the upsurge of sensation to overwhelm 'the self-interested powers of self-preservation' and expunge 'the delusive madness of personality', explaining that 'it is only in such a state of raving madness that I am totally at home'. He made the same point to Cosima while at work on the self-scourging lament of Amfortas in *Parsifal* in 1878: 'I sit there, look at your picture, shriek, rave, yes, I'm insane when I'm composing.' Even Verdi's most overwrought characters seldom feel this way; Verdi himself never did. In 1847 he wrote to Giuseppina Appiani from Paris complaining about the vexatious librettists, impresarios and music editors who were pestering him. 'Isn't it enough to drive you mad?' he asked, and added that he had no intention of losing his wits.

For Wagner, composition was a performance not a task. He prepared himself by dressing in costumes that he designed – silk or satin undergarments, soft velvet robes, a floppy cap like those worn by Rembrandt in his self-portraits. He abhorred cotton, which felt like barbed wire against his skin, and found linen equally penitential. The fabrics he favoured made him newly aware of the body whose gushing blood, tingling nerves and panting breath were a kind of internal music. Literally fetishistic, his garments had a latent magic or sensual sorcery in their textures and tones. A Viennese milliner was commissioned to make him a puffed, flounced housecoat with ruched pockets and eiderdown quilting; it resembled a snug, padded bed – exactly right for its purpose, as Wagner while composing hovered between wakefulness and dreamy fantasy. His cobbler was astonished by the quantities of fur and wadding that had to be crammed into Wagner's boots to soften his tread. He shared his preening vanity with Rienzi, who in the opera greets the peace envoys dressed in robes that are 'phantastiche und pomphalte', fantastical and pompous. Rienzi was dressing for the role of tribune, and he knew that power – which is impalpable, a mere potential – had to be given material form, made into a personal adornment. There was a conscious sacrilege in Rienzi's choices, since his vestments of white silk trimmed in gold appropriated the papal dress code; his attire announced the church's subordination to the state, just as Wagner's showy wardrobe – the satin trousers admired (or at least remarked on) by Queen Victoria after a command performance, or the yellow damask dressing gown, red cravat, and cloak of black velvet lined with pink satin he wore while conducting rehearsals at Bayreuth – declared to the world that an artist had assumed the ostentatious badges of rank sported by popes or secular potentates. At the same time, one item in the ensemble semaphored subversion. Wagner's soft, slouched felt beret was notoriously fashionable among German revolutionaries, and when he visited London in 1855 he was persuaded to forsake it in favour of a more respectable top hat.

Contemporaries emphasized the flamboyant palette of his clothes: a green housecoat lined with purple satin, or – in the French impresario Léon Carvalho's recollection of a meeting in 1859 – 'a blue jacket with red frogging and a yellow smoking cap trimmed with green torsades' which were replaced, after Wagner worked up a sweat playing a section of *Tannhaüser*, by a yellow jacket with blue highlights and 'a red bonnet decorated with yellow braid'. His wardrobe, like his music, was chromatic. He hated uniforms, which he said were 'the reason everyone thinks alike', and would not have understood why Verdi, whether at the opera or on his farm, wore clothes more suitable for a prosperous businessman. In 1886, during a discussion of costume designs for *Otello*, Boito noted that Verdi negligently mixed the fashions of two different periods. He still wore a cape that was stylish thirty years before, but combined this with more up-to-date high-collared shirts. The amalgam illustrated how quickly styles altered at the behest of designers; it also demonstrated what little attention Verdi paid to such trifles. He dressed neutrally, hoping to be overlooked in a crowd, and one of the most endearing photographs of him as an old man shows him in that antique cape and a top hat in the street outside La Scala. He is reading the newspaper as he walks, withdrawn from his surroundings and safe – or so he thought – in his anonymity.

Rienzi scandalized Catholics by taking a bath in the porphyry sarcophagus used by Pope Sylvester to cure Emperor Constantine's leprosy. Wagner's ablutions were less blasphemous but equally elaborate. At Triebschen he poured ambergris and other scented oils into his tub, then continued to inhale them through the floorboards when he went upstairs to work. His cave of making thus became a scented grotto. The study in his Bayreuth villa was carpeted and wall-papered in red, with cosy corners, pouffes and small sofas like clouds flushed by the sunset. A home, to serve his purposes, had to be a humid hothouse. In his diary he admitted that 'I can … live only in a sort of cloud. Being solely a man of art, I can only lead an artificial life … like a tropical flower in a conservatory'. Pampering was necessary for an artist who liked to describe himself as an expect-ant mother writhing through a protracted delivery and predicted, while working on *Parsifal* in 1877, that his 'accouchement' would probably last for the next three years.

The obstetric image, absurd as it seems, was accurate: Wagner's charac-ters emerged from inside him. During his work on *Das Rheingold* he told Liszt that he felt like a silkworm spinning a cocoon from its own entrails. Experimenting with Buddhism in 1863 as he sketched a drama to be called *Die Sieger*, he explained that 'one must be and become everything oneself: that is how I create my art!' He may have believed that he possessed the serene self-abnegation of the Buddha, though in becoming everything or everyone he was multiplying frac-tions of the self, not cancelling it out. In another letter to Mathilde, he referred to 'my old friend Brünnhilde', and said that he fancied leaping onto the pyre with her so that he could be reborn from the flames as a Christian, properly qualified to compose *Parsifal*. In Mainz in 1862 he gave a reading of the *Meistersinger* text in which he was a jabbering one-man parliament. As the composer Wendelin Weissheimer remembered, in the scene where the masters quarrel they were 'so clearly distinguished that we already thought we could hear a proper ensem-ble'. The choirmaster Heinrich Porges, watching Wagner coach the singers at Bayreuth in 1876, likened him to the slippery Proteus, able to 'transform himself into all possible shapes'. Édouard Schuré saw successive mementoes of his heroes and villains – the hunted paranoia of the Flying Dutchman and the erotic com-pulsiveness of Tannhäuser, along with Hagen's menace and Alberich's spitting rage – flicker across his moody face, like images in a magic lantern show. The Tarnhelm, the cap that renders its wearer invisible, is Wagner's symbol for the dramatist's power of self-transformation. Samuel Taylor Coleridge found this empathetic, versatile spirit in Shakespeare, and Verdi shared it. But in Wagner it is not the result of neutrality and forbearance; instead it acts out the doctrine of metempsychosis, in which, as he told Mathilde Wesendonck in 1860, he fervently believed. The theory, formulated by Pythagoras, held that a soul could migrate between bodies, which to Wagner meant that 'the various individual existences' would eventually 'come together in a meaningful way outside time'. Pythagoras surely did not expect the soul to inhabit many bodies simultaneously, or to vault from one to another as nimbly as Wagner did.

If Wagner's characters are self-divided, it is because they are acting out the divisions within his own unstable nature. Is Tannhäuser a poet who wants to start a revolution, or a voluptuary purveying forbidden delights? The drama allows Wagner to ask the question about himself. After the orchestral Bacchanale, Venus sneers at Tannhäuser's effort to make music thoughtful, to give it a conscience by attaching words to it. 'Welch ein Sang!' she says – what a song! The sheep bells and shepherd's pipe that introduce the world outside the Venusberg are a reminder that music has a different, more humdrum function in the daylight. The same debate about Wagner's purposes and motives spills over into *Die Meistersinger*. While Walther insists that the theme of his song is 'heilig', Kothner condemns it as 'weltlich'. Is music sacred or profane, a bequest from elsewhere or a social resource? Should it aspire to some higher world, as Walther does when singing of Eden and Parnassus, or is it the lava of irrationality, a scalding river that travels underground or inside us?

Sachs's inquest on the madness of the nocturnal affray in his 'Wahn' monologue might be psychoanalysing the agitation of the orchestra that accompanies him, as he imagines men digging into their own flesh and deriving pleasure from the pain they experience. Even sleep offers no respite from this instinctual uproar, because the insanity runs amok there and renews itself in dreams. He concludes that 'der alte Wahn', the ancient madness, is inescapable and incurable, but recognizes its creative benefit: nothing – certainly not art – can happen without it. The orchestra lightens, first in a passage of tentative, tremulous flashes that could be the sun's earliest rays restoring nature to life, then in a confident full-throated surge of melody as Sachs announces midsummer's day. But darkness, with its confused violence and erotic skirmishing, is not forgotten. Perhaps music, supposed to be a gift of Apollo the sun god, actually guides us through the night, like the evening star to which Wolfram sings his aria in *Tannhäuser*. The official motto of the art is expounded in Haydn's *Die Schöpfung* when tonality emerges from indistinct chaos and God declares 'Es werde Licht!' That creative miracle is inverted by Wagner. As Isolde quenches a torch to summon Tristan to join her in the dark garden, she cries 'Es werde Nacht,' with a wickedly exciting upward modulation that tightens Wagner's compulsive hold on us.

During the song contests at the Wartburg and on the Nuremberg meadow, Tannhäuser and Walther take dictation from fantasy or attempt to find words and notes to match a dream. Verdian entertainers do not wait for the spirit to move them. They are workers, lacking the self-conceit of Wagner's artists; like Violetta, they trade in pleasure and are paid to be amusing. In 1837 Liszt described the musician as a prostitute, obliged to repress intimate feelings and instead show off to earn applause and money. *Rigoletto* takes this degrading economy for granted. Sparafucile explains the use to which he puts his sister Maddalena: she dances by the roadside, beguiling his victims and leading them home to be killed. Jesting is Rigoletto's job, but this comic occupation is for him a tragic martyrdom, since he must allow his deformity to be mocked. After the abduction of Gilda, his distracted vocalizing reduces music to its rudiments in his reiterated 'La ra, la ra, la ra' – a scale he cannot mount, because the notes lead him downwards (although the meagre syllables are Verdi's gift to a great singer, who can make them as voluble and subtly suggestive as Shakespearean words). All the same, Rigoletto's grief does not prohibit him from employing theatrical craft to get his way with the courtiers, who know where his daughter is hidden. When his fury fails to move them, he turns to entreaty, like Maddalena who sheds wheedling tears to convince Sparafucile to spare the Duke. 'Ebben, piango,' he decides: now he will cry, which he can do on cue. Like the dethroned Lear, he is unsure whether to command or beg; Verdi here has Rigoletto combine the roles of the hectoring patriarch and the plaintive, abused fool who is Lear's attack dog and also his nagging conscience.

Writing to Ricordi in 1873, Verdi first said that speculation about his intentions annoyed him, then fatalistically shrugged, as if he were Rigoletto without the hump: 'people are right to treat us like this … we who wear out our brains to be their buffoons, and to amuse them'. The play by Victor Hugo that was Verdi's source is called *Le Roi s'amuse*. Verdi's letter adapted the title to the circumstances of his own century: the artist is no longer beholden to a capricious royal patron, but has to amuse a public that is faceless, ignorant, prejudiced and always right. The hero of his next opera, *Il trovatore*, is another put-upon, undervalued artist, so marginal that in two crucial scenes he is heard rather than seen. Manrico the itinerant minstrel plucks his lute offstage to serenade Leonora, and later laments his imminent death from inside the prison tower while the monks, also unseen, sing a 'Miserere'. In her biographical novel about Wagner, Bertita Harding describes Tannhäuser and his fellow Minnesingers as if they were Germanic versions of Manrico, happy-go-lucky bards who 'engaged in lute playing and ballad composing when not drawn into chivalric duels or jousts'. True, Leonora first sees Manrico at a tournament, and he reappears for a sword fight with Luna, but he lacks the swashbuckling gallantry that Harding attributes to the singers at the Wartburg. Like Rigoletto or Violetta or like the young Verdi, Manrico is driven by harsher necessities, and lives more precariously. Liszt, travelling across Europe to play recitals, wearily likened himself to a 'useless clown' or 'ill-fated troubadour', a woebegone colleague of Rigoletto and Manrico.

In Edward Bulwer-Lytton's *Rienzi*, Montreal and Adrian listen to a lay sung by Adeline to the accompaniment of her lute. Montreal – who might be reflecting on the persistence of Italian opera in the mid-nineteenth century – says that 'the race of Troubadours is dead, but the minstrelsy survives the minstrel!' He goes on to disparage the 'fantastic and tortured strains' in which Italian balladeers do their wooing, and Adrian in reply might be defending opera against a foreigner's thin-blooded incomprehension: 'in Italy,' he says, 'common language is exaggeration', so the protestations of the troubadours are realistic enough. A competition ensues between the sad Provençal song of Montreal's 'nightbird' and the Petrarchan lyricism of Italy, to which Adrian remains faithful. The umpire is Adeline, who presides over the contest like Elisabeth or Eva. It is a measure of Verdi's more energetic and impassioned sense of drama that Leonora, in the trio at the beginning of *Il trovatore*, should attempt to arbitrate a duel between the two rowdy brothers who have rival claims on her, rather than sitting in judgment on their prowess as singers. The prize goes to the most determined lover or to the better swordsman, not – as in *Tannhäuser* or *Die Meistersinger* – to the sweetest vocalist.

Manrico belongs neither at court nor among his adoptive family of gypsies, but perhaps he is fortunate to roam through the mountains and sing, when it pleases him, under the windows of highborn maidens. The alternative was the life of a professional musician which, as Verdi complained, began as ill-paid drudgery and developed into an unceasing struggle with piratical colleagues. Grumbling about the vexations of his professional life in his 1873 letter to Ricordi, he said that he and his fellow musicians were 'stupid gypsies', rootless and liable to be harassed by their more settled betters. A Romany troupe performs at Flora's party in *La traviata*, telling fortunes and peddling astrological lore; they claim to predict the future, but it takes no great power of divination to find omens of infidelity in the palm of d'Obigny, Flora's current protector. Entertainments like this reminded Verdi of his own professional shame. An earlier letter to Ricordi, in which he brooded about the failure of *Un giorno di regno* and the more recent fiasco of *Simon Boccanegra*, returned to the analogy: 'We poor gypsies, charlatans, or whatever you want to call us, are unhappily forced to sell our hard work, our thoughts, our dreams for gold.' Did the expenditure of three lire give people the right to hiss him? The pleasure of execration came cheap; for his part, he only asked to be spared from having to look grateful when the same inconsistent public applauded him. Success around the world, he admitted, made up for denigration at home. 'That balances the accounts,' he said: in his dealings with his customers, he kept a credit and debit ledger open.

By composing fewer operas for higher fees, Verdi turned himself from a bullied employee into a manufacturer who stimulated demand by stinting supply. In 1874, writing again to Ricordi, he denied possessing the soul of a business-man – which is why, he said, he didn't write an opera a year after *La traviata* and amass a fortune three times greater than the one he actually accumulated – but refused to let the Neapolitan impresario Antonio Musella treat him as 'a workman, a day labourer, who turns his wares over to the publishing house to be exploited'. Wagner thought of his art as a vocation, a sanctified calling. Although Verdi admitted to possessing 'artistic aims', proven by his painstaking work on the operas between *Un ballo in maschera* in 1858 and *Aida* in 1871, he preferred to consider music as a career. As early as 1845 he began buying up land in Busseto, and told his friend Giuseppe Demaldè that he hoped to fulfill his contracts to write six operas during the next three years and then say farewell. Vegetating had to be postponed, but that made him all the more determined to pension himself off after *Aida*. In 1874, when Clarina Maffei told him that it was his duty to go on compos-ing, he reminded her of his contractual deal with the public. He had written the operas as required; audiences had booed or cheered as they saw fit. Both sides had upheld their part of the bargain, so the business relationship could be terminated. Keen to be relieved of responsibility, Verdi not long before this reimbursed a dissatisfied customer. A tone-deaf buffoon called Prospero Bertani went to hear *Aida* in Parma, considered it a waste of time, and wrote asking for his money back. Verdi sent a refund for the admission price and travel expenses, but balked at paying for Bertani's dinner. He demanded a signed receipt, and attached a note asking Bertani to promise that he would 'undertake no trip to hear any of the Maestro's new operas in the future'. It was a slyly vindictive manoeuvre: Verdi paid out 27 lire and 80 centesimi, but by authorizing Ricordi to publicize the affair he ensured that Bertani – who was ridiculed, threatened, and compelled to go into hiding inside his house – would be the ultimate loser.

Now, as he told Clarina Maffei, returning to the commercial metaphor in a cursory review of his life's work, 'the *accounts are balanced*'. It was a summation

– luckily premature – like that of Anthony Trollope, who ended his *Autobiography* with a tally of the takings from his novels. Ten years later Verdi tried to excuse himself from continuing work on *Otello* by reminding Boito of his 'many *years of service*'. He never gave up thinking of himself as indentured to a public that might now, he suspected, have no further use for him. Mastery was a flattering illusion, since power actually belonged to those who paid to hear his music.

## Getting and Spending

In the industrious nineteenth century, art acquired an extra value from the effort that went into it or the time it took to be completed. John Ruskin was morally affronted when Whistler bragged that his atmospheric nocturnes were painted on the run, in sessions lasting less than an hour. Wagner pretended to share this dilettantism, and while composing *Parsifal* he said 'What comes pouring out of one's soul can't be described as work'. In fact he and Verdi worked equally hard. Verdi claimed that he spent the 1840s toiling like a galley slave; Wagner, whose metaphors were never so menial, made the more exalted boast that his daily occupation was a cosmic labour, bringing a new world to birth.

Verdi specialized in rapid turnover. In the first half of his career he raced from one deadline to the next, sometimes, as he claimed, working from eight in the morning until midnight with only a cup of coffee to sustain him. Between 1839 and 1859 he composed twenty-three operas (if *Jérusalem* and *Aroldo*, the revised versions of *I Lombardi* and *Stiffelio*, are counted as separate works). James Huneker – who shared the decadent enthusiasm for Wagner, which he explored in a book of stories called *Melomaniacs*, published in 1902 – deplored this productivity, and said that Verdi turned out operas 'as indefatigably as incubators chickens'. With tightened nostrils, Huneker added that his music smelled rankly of the soil. In Verdi's homeland, this might not have counted as a slur. In September 1887 *Otello* was performed in Parma as part of the Concorso Regionale Agricolo Industriale, which gave Verdi's music roots in the rich land of his native district, among the fruit and vegetables, cows, horses, ducks and chickens that spilled down the side of the poster advertising the harvest festival. Because the industrialization of agriculture had begun, with Verdi as a pioneer in the use of labour-saving aids, the poster listed his opera among a roster of manufactured marvels: agrarian machines, electrical illuminations, and a gadget that spat out fireworks. In addition, bicycle races showed off society's new pursuit of speed. Huneker would probably have sniffed axle grease as well as the slimy effluent of the Sant'Agata poultry.

Until he slowed down in the 1860s, Verdi capitalized on his success by keeping up with orders from the market. Wagner was longer-sighted and more single-minded, implacable in his concentration on a goal that kept receding into the distance. He began sketching the drama that became *Götterdämmerung* in 1848, and over the next four years unravelled the story backwards until he arrived at *Das Rheingold*. It then took him twenty years to write the music, with a hiatus in the middle of *Siegfried* so that he could – almost parenthetically – compose *Tristan* and *Die Meistersinger*. After this he needed a further two years to build the theatre at Bayreuth in which the *Ring* was first performed in 1876.

Wagner worked to please himself rather than to satisfy impresarios, so he saw no end to his endeavours. If you are self-employed or driven by what Cosima called a 'divinely daemonic power', retirement – the idea cherished by Verdi, who had so many misgivings about twice resuming his career when Boito tempted him with *Otello* and *Falstaff* – is not an option. In 1864, after passing his half century, Wagner projected himself a decade into the future and in a letter to Bülow pretended to look back on the accomplishments of the next ten years: *Tristan* in 1865, the *Ring* in 1867–68, then *Die Sieger* and *Parsifal*, after which he planned to permit himself a 'final *beautiful death*' in 1873. At the age of sixty, having outlived this prediction, he adjusted the chronology and outlined an agenda for two more decades. *Parsifal*, he told Cosima, was to be ready in time for his seventieth birthday, then *Die Sieger* would keep him busy until his eightieth. As early as 1853 Strepponi chided Verdi for continuing to work 'like a nigger' when all their worldly needs were taken care of. She advised him to relax and spend his money, rather than labouring and saving only to gratify 'those who in the sad word *Death!* see the moment of their infamous wishes come true, in the wicked word *Inheritance!*' The Latin commandment she paraphrases is 'carpe diem', which dismisses any idea of eternity; she believed in enjoying the moment, whereas Wagner was expecting immortality. Cosima therefore urged him ahead and tried to procure an infusion of stamina for him through prayers that nagged or blackmailed the deity. 'God will hear me,' she vowed, 'and I want, mean to force him to it.' Wagner's body failed him in 1883, but there was never a point at which he felt, as Verdi did from early middle age onwards, that he had done enough.

In 1946, when the opera-loving novelist James M. Cain promoted an American Authors' Authority to regulate copyright, he appealed to his more other-worldly colleagues by citing the example of Verdi, 'the first businessman in the history of music'. Verdi was certainly vigilant about raking in his rightful profits. He haggled with publishers, queried exchange rates when gold and silver napoleons were converted into lire, and in 1875 scrutinized a lifetime's accounts to prove that he had been short-changed by Ricordi's bookkeepers, gaining himself an indemnity of fifty thousand lire. Later that year he left a wallet containing the same amount – a fabulous sum – in Teresa Stolz's hotel room. He thought he had been robbed, and there was an embarrassing public fuss before he realized his error. He was widely criticized for his ostentation in carrying around an absurd quantity of cash, but he could equally well have been accused of unworldly negligence: a truly acquisitive man would have kept it locked up, and certainly would never have lost track of it, even if visiting a mistress. Strepponi chided him for being motivated by love of money, but she was not exactly right. What he loved was work, and he appreciated money as the gauge of its worth, established – since music has no inherent exchange value and cannot be bartered – in an open market. He understood the invidious relationship between culture and the true wealth of nations, and in 1891 said he wished that Italy had more agriculturalists and fewer musicians, lawyers and doctors. It may have been wrong to dismiss medicine as a luxury, but a cull of lawyers was an excellent idea; by then Verdi's operas counted as a staple product like Parma's cheese, ham and violets, so his very existence made other composers superfluous.

As early as 1846 in a letter to Emilia Morosini he joked about the prospect of becoming a millionaire, relished the 'lovely, full-sounding word', and remarked 'how empty, in comparison, are words like "fame", "glory", "talent", etc.!' This is not quite what Wagner meant when he told Mathilde Wesendonck in 1860 'I must be *rich*'. Verdi intended to earn the money; Wagner expected to be given it, and whenever that happened he frittered it away rather than making it breed. 'I must be able to sacrifice thousands upon thousands in total disregard for the consequences,' he explained to Mathilde, because money had to buy him 'space, time and goodwill'. Verdi took a more professional view of his finances, and had a healthy respect for avarice in others. Commissioning Mariani to buy him some magnolia plants and transport them to Sant'Agata, he explained – in a flourish of complimentary banter – that he now viewed his colleague not only as a musician but as 'a capitalist, a speculator and a usurer', and therefore expected him to charge a 'broker's fee ... and similar thieveries'. Though he condoned profiteering, he condemned extravagance, and in 1861 he tried to dissuade the council in Busseto from wasting money on the pocket-sized opera house that was to be named in his honour. The town did not need it and could not afford it, he said: neither argument would have made sense to Wagner while he was building his own theatre in Bayreuth.

In *Falstaff* Ford bestows a purse on the fat knight, who is being bribed to woo Alice. 'Spendetele!' Ford cries, and a tinkling triangle showers the air with invisible coinage. The idea might have appealed to Wagner. Like Puccini's bohemians he waited for handouts, which to Cosima's dismay he disbursed on luxuries – snuff, furry boots, frothy underclothes, carpets, upholstery in the Pompadour style. 'What is life,' he once demanded, 'without a lambrequin?' For those who can live without one, or even without knowing what one is, a lambrequin is a piece of drapery that hangs from above a door or a mantelpiece: the Wagners were decorating their Bayreuth villa when he asked the rhetorical question. He was generous to others as well, extending his largesse to all the creatures he encountered. During his London visit in 1855 he made a habit of starting the day by feeding the ducks in Regent's Park. Nothing but fresh rolls ordered from a French baker would do; he referred to the routine as 'banqueting'. Fairy gold had less attraction for Verdi, which is why the metallic flurry that accompanies Ford's gift sounds so tinselly, a scintillation that beguiles us for only a few seconds. Falstaff is better served by the glass of wine that revives him after his dunking in the river. Food and drink have substance, and make life possible; money is an abstraction that cannot nourish us. Perusing his bill at the Garter, Falstaff has trouble understanding why two categories of things, goods and coins, should be equated. Who decides that a chicken is worth a shilling, or that thirty bottles of sherry cost two pounds? His puzzlement is both genuine and justified. In 1894 Verdi made a shrewdly Falstaffian joke about the whimsicality of market forces when he heard that the takings from *Falstaff* in Genoa were unexpectedly poor. His corpulent hero, he noted, was reduced 'not paunch-wise but price-wise'. Verdi suggested that the score must be to blame, and proposed that the impresario let people in for free and then charge them for beer. By this time he knew that his music was priceless, but in a monetary economy that did not necessarily make it more valuable than a barrel of beer.

Despite his hard work and his harrying of those who owed him money, Verdi saw through the mercenariness of his society. Alexandre Dumas fils in *La Dame aux camélias* takes stock of an emotional economy where tears are a currency that must not be wasted and should only be shed for relatives, who have made an investment in being properly mourned when disposing of their property. Every transaction in Dumas' novel has a price, with characters always calculating an advantage to themselves. Marguérite's rural idyll with Armand is unwittingly subsidized by another of her admirers, who happens to be renting the cottage she shares with her latest beau. Verdi's Violetta is more selfless: when Germont suggests that she has bankrupted his son Alfredo, she presents the receipts for the belongings she has pawned to pay for the house and its upkeep. Her last act has an almost Falstaffian improvidence. Dying in poverty, she tells her maid to take whatever money they have left and give it to the poor. When she collapses, the doctor clasps her pulse and announces her death in a phrase that condemns our obsession with money as the stuff of life. 'È spenta!' he says: she is spent. The jingling contents of Ford's purse are irrelevant, because what we are expending as we live is breath, not money.

Wagner repudiated the commercial system in which Verdi operated, and tried to imagine a world rid of mercantilism. Hence the quixotic gesture of Pogner in *Die Meistersinger*, who offers his daughter as a prize at the song contest to prove that tradesmen in Nuremberg do not think exclusively of acquisition. Those who accumulate money or hoard treasure want revenge for the disappointments of existence: the Rhinegold is Alberich's compensation for the lack of love. Verdi, rather than abolishing private property as Wagner prompted Brünnhilde to do in his early versions of the immolation, understood that money is mulch, needing to be spread around. In his will he gave his fortune away, making bequests to the poor of Sant'Agata, to almshouses and hospitals in Genoa, and above all to the Casa di Riposo, which he called his grandest work and to which he left a cache of bonds and the income from his copyright, along with his grand piano and spinet. He took to heart Strepponi's point about their lack of children: the human family, as she implied, is an institution devoted to the orderly transmission of real estate and associated financial benefits. Maria Carrara, a second cousin, inherited his property at Sant'Agata and was enjoined to maintain it in its present condition and to look after the fields beyond the garden – but less as a monument to her benefactor than because we all exist to be custodians of the portion of earth allotted to us.

In flippant or impudent moods Wagner compared himself to Robin Hood, thriving outside the law like one of the bandits in Verdi's early operas. His reputation for reneging on debts was not undeserved, but there was a principle behind it. He refused to think of himself as a peasant raising crops or a worker manufacturing goods to sell, as Verdi did; those were occupations too sturdily adult for a man with an infantile streak, who believed that the world owed him a living. Wagner had no shame about this regressive trait, and in 1849 he described himself to Liszt as a 'spoiled child' who often bleated 'like a calf for the stable and for the udder of its life-giving mother'. That teat dispensed money not milk, as he made clear by complaining that he still needed help, despite Liszt's previous magnanimity. It was not the means of subsistence that he asked for. When Liszt chided him, he admitted to being a spendthrift but said that 'when you see the second act of *Tristan* you'll admit that I need a lot of money'. The statement is

Verdi and Wagner in the Giardini Pubblici, Venice

Verdi by Giovanni Boldini, 1886

Wagner photographed by Franz Hanfstaengl, 1871

Verdi's mistreatment by a priest during his childhood service as an altar-boy: anonymous cartoons
illustrating a handwritten extract from the early biography by Anton Giulio Barrili

'Frou–frou Wagner' by F. Grätz,
published in *Der Floh*, 1877

Verdi as 'the Latin (*wälsche*) Wagner' by
Carl von Struh, published in *Der Floh*, 1887

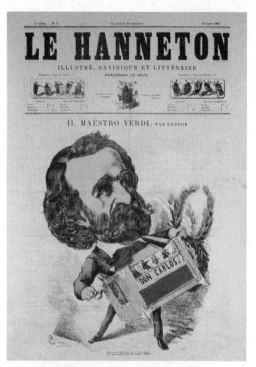

Verdi the hurdy-gurdy man, 1867

Verdi outside La Scala

Wagner caricatured by E. B. Kietz in 1840–41

Giuseppina Strepponi's bedroom at Sant'Agata, with her bust

*La Muse (Richard Wagner)* by Henri Fantin-Latour, 1862

Wagner with Cosima in Vienna in 1872, photographed by
Fritz Luckhardt

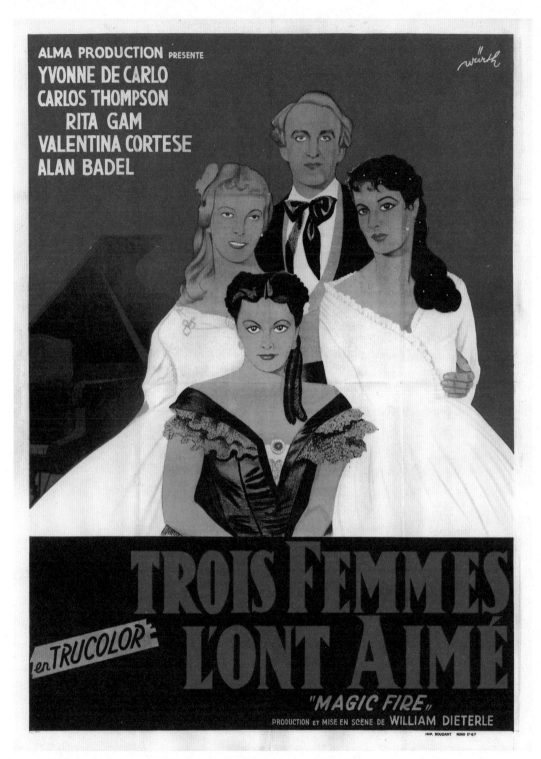

Poster for the French release of the biopic *Magic Fire*, with Alan Badel as Wagner, Rita Gam (left) as Cosima, Valentina Cortese (right) as Mathilde, and Yvonne De Carlo (bottom) as Minna

Verdi presents the plebiscite to King Vittorio
Emanuele II in 1859, from *Illustrazione italiana*

Verdi, caricatured by Delfico,
with Napoleon III in 1867

# Siegfried=Wagner hebt den „Schatz" der Nibelungen.

Da lieg auch du — dunkler Wurm!
Den gleißenden Hort heb' ich hurtig.

Wagner as Siegfried posing with the Nibelungen treasure after he has
killed off his dragon-like critics: caricature by C. V. Grimm, 1879

Wahnfried, with the bust of Ludwig II and the sgraffito by Robert Krausse

The family outside the salon at Wahnfried, photographed by Adolph von Gross – on the top step, Blandine, Heinrich von Stein (Siegfried's tutor), Cosima, Richard, Paul von Joukowsky; below, Isolde, Daniela, Eva, Siegfried, with the dogs Marke and Russ

Wagner in the salon at Wahnfried with Cosima, Liszt and Hans von Wolzogen,
painted by W. Beckmann in 1882

Verdi at Sant'Agata

Santa'Agata from the road, watercolour by Leopoldo Metlicovitz, 1892

Verdi with Boito at Sant'Agata, engraving by Ettore Ximenes
from *Illustrazione italiana*, 1887

Verdi in Russia, 1861 or 1862

Verdi in Paris, photographed by
André Adolphe Disderi during the 1850s

gloriously illogical: Did he need to be rich to compose that music? Or did he mean that he deserved to be enriched as a reward for having composed it? Writing again to Liszt in 1857 about his interrupted work on the *Ring*, he reported that he had led Siegfried into a forest and left him there, 'with heartfelt tears'. He was crying for himself not his hero, since the hiatus had been forced on him by a tight-fisted world. With drier eyes, he added that he intended to keep Siegfried under lock and key, 'as one buried alive.… No one shall see anything of him, as I had to shut him out from myself'. This is how babies do their bargaining, with tantrums as leverage. The fairy-tale context is significant: Wagner plays the wicked uncle who strands the innocent stripling in the woods and may even kill him off, as Mime plans to do in *Siegfried*, if the ransom is not paid.

A few years earlier Wagner told his sister Luise that he had undertaken his most recent water cure so that, with his health restored, he would have the strength to break free from the source of all his torments, which was his art. The clinical experiment failed, as he was quick to point out: his life remained forfeit to his music. Verdi too periodically suspended his career. He first quit after the failure in 1840 of *Un giorno di regno*, and the impresario Bartolomeo Merelli had to beg him to reconsider; in 1860 the tenor Enrico Tamberlick heard rumours of retirement and pleaded with him to resume work; in 1877, writing from Sant'Agata, Verdi told Arrivabene that his piano was definitively nailed shut, which left him free to concentrate on his new occupation as a bricklayer. He was asserting the worker's right to rest, the creator's need for recreation. He did not make others feel responsible for his temporary downing of tools, or expect to wheedle better terms for reopening the shop, like Wagner when he told Liszt that his cerebral nerves were so frayed that he had given up reading, writing and all intellectual life.

Verdi tabulated the sums he had earned in the hope of reaching the fabled total of a million. Wagner, by contrast, despised and disbelieved in money, while at the same time demanding inordinate supplies of it. He understood that it was a recent and spurious invention, a means of multiplying profits that had little reality except on balance sheets, and he was acidly amused when the new German empire minted a coin 'so authentically German that it did not correspond to any other coin from any other nation', useless in trade but 'very profitable for bankers'. With contrivances like this, capitalism had almost magically conjured up wealth by robbing the world of value: faith was replaced by what accountants call credit, a flimsy insurance – as Wagner's behaviour towards his own creditors demonstrated – against treachery and loss. 'Here is money,' Wagner wrote with a sneer to his first wife Minna Planer in 1850, almost like Alfredo in *La traviata* hurling his gains from the gaming table at Violetta. Wagner's money came from his admirer Jessie Laussot, currently his mistress, but in his view that laundered it: rather than being 'extorted from the scurvy masses', it had been delicately pressed into his hand 'by a noble heart which rejoiced in my works'.

Wagner preferred his transactions to be governed by the ceremonious conventions of a gift economy. Patrons donated funds; in return he gave them an opera. 'Money! Money! – How and from whom doesn't matter,' he told Liszt in 1858. The bartering practised by Verdi was beneath Wagner's dignity, so there was seldom any agreement about his end of the bargain. '*Tristan*,' he assured Liszt, 'will repay it all.' The characters in his operas apply this custom to their most intimate dealings. Daland offers Senta to the Dutchman after seeing the pearls and bracelets in his treasure chest. Siegmund calls his sword the 'Brautgabe', or bridal gift, with which he wins Sieglinde. A generation later, Siegfried presents Brünnhilde with a ring and – since there is no question of convertibility, like that between German coins and those of other currencies – receives her horse in exchange. Copyright, which Verdi battled to retain, was nonchalantly surrendered by Wagner. In 1859 he drafted a contract granting Otto Wesendonck and his heirs 'all fees and profits in perpetuity' that might accrue from the *Ring*; in the short term he was to receive six thousand francs for each of the four instalments. It was hardly a commercial arrangement, because Wesendonck paid money for nothing, or placed a bet on a distant, spurious future: Wagner obtained ready cash, while it remained to be seen whether the tetralogy would ever be completed, staged or published.

The *Ring* is, among many other things, a parable about art's uneasy coexistence with money. The giant Fasolt sneers that the gods rule because they are beautiful, but that beauty has to be paid for: their immortal sheen depends on the diet of golden apples brought to them by the goddess Freia. The dwarves, as Mime tells Wotan, want gold with which to adorn their women, which confirms Leo Tolstoy's conclusion in his 1897 essay *What is Art?* that nature intends aesthetic allure as a mere procreative aid, not an emblem of some eternal virtue or verity. Out of circulation on the riverbed, the Rhinegold is a subaqueous sun, worshipped but not owned by the nymphs who guard it. When Alberich has that gold reshaped into the ring, he invents the notion of art, a commodity we don't need but are prepared to pay for at a premium. At the same time he sets in motion a development that leads to the devising of coinage and finally to the replacement of solid metal by paper money, a flimsy and fictitious substitute for goods we can hold or consume or in some way use to support life. Wagner likened the ring to a stock-exchange portfolio, inscribed with promises that exploit our credulity. His own motifs – the musical doodles that stand for the gold or for Wotan's fortress – seemed to collude in this defrauding of reality; an article in *Punch* cleverly described Wagner's music of the future as a species of 'promissory notes', requiring us to invest in the idea of a time to come when his innovations might become intelligible. In 1852 he wrote to Uhlig asserting his need as an artist to be lapped in 'luxurious comfort'. He signed the letter 'Your Nibelung Prince Alberich': the venal gnome, to be worthy of Wagner's identification with him, received a sudden transfusion of royal blood.

Wagner was aware of his transgressions, which were theological as much as financial. 'Art is a great crime,' he once said. Reflecting on his pronouncement – made at a moment of guilty self-reproach after the sudden death of Schnorr von Carolsfeld – Cosima added that 'those can be accounted happy who, like animals, know nothing of [art]'. Lowlier creatures, like the pets and farm animals that Verdi and Strepponi kept at Sant'Agata, could be left to their gambolling and grazing. The aim, for Wagner, was not to make money and purchase contentment. Art carried with it a god's morose, lofty knowledge. It gave him the satisfaction of feeling that he had transcended the triviality of ordinary life, exposed the deceits on which society was founded, and helped to bring about the purgative, enlightening end of the world.

|||||||||||||||||||

Verdi and Wagner, aware of the connection between aesthetics and economics, were both thrilled and terrified by London, the headquarters of industrial capitalism. Here they found evidence of what productivity or creativity cost those who set the human body to compete with the mechanized workhorses of engineering.

In 1847 when Verdi arrived to stage *I masnadieri* at Covent Garden, he reacted to the metropolis with an awe that the wonders of nature failed to arouse in him. 'What chaos in London! What confusion!' he wrote enthusiastically to Barezzi, challenging him – as the rhetoric of the sublime always does – to imagine the inconceivable by picturing two million people tightly clustered together. 'It isn't a city, it is a world,' Verdi said. London mapped infinitude, as proof of which he pointed out that it was necessary to change horses three times in travelling across town. He gaped at the marvels of industrial locomotion: 'steam engines, steamboats flying along'. Above all he was impressed by the noise: 'People shouting, the poor weeping … everybody howling like the damned'. He made it sound like a novel by Dickens, with a crowd of characters jabbering and gesticulating simultaneously. His opera 'did not make a furore', but he was not surprised. Would the altitudinous soprano Jenny Lind have been audible above the mechanized uproar?

In 1877, sailing up the thickly masted Thames in a steamer through a dense forest of belching chimneys, Wagner thought that he was in Nibelheim, a smoggy underworld of sweated labour. London, he said, was 'Alberich's dream come true'. The dream was that of 'world dominion', achieved by Britain's mercantile empire, but it was also Wagner's dream, since he hoped to universalize his aesthetic gospel. He had come to London to raise funds for Bayreuth by conducting excerpts from the *Ring* in concert. As the American critic Paul Rosenfeld argued in 1920, this was a stridently industrial music that proclaimed 'the victory of man over the energies of fire and sea and earth, the lordship of creation, the suddenly begotten railways and shipping and mines, the cataclysm of wealth and comfort'. Steamboats, smoky trains, tingling telegraph wires and what Rosenfeld called 'the whole sinister glittering faëry of gain' seemed to 'tread and soar and sound and blare and swell' to a Wagnerian rhythm; his 'resonant gold' was 'the age's cry of material triumph'. In London, Wagner encountered characters and locations he had imagined in *Das Rheingold.* Gog and Magog, the Guildhall's protective giants, were Fafner and Fasolt. At the Bank of England he recognized Wotan's fortified Valhalla, and he covetously handled the wads of cancelled banknotes shown to him at the Royal Mint. Verdi, in a revealingly different reaction, stood amid affluent splendour looking from the Bank of England towards the docks and confessed to 'feeling very small'. Wagner's ego was equal to the magnitude of the place, though the pieces of paper withdrawn from circulation reminded him that its riches were a hoax. Craftier than Wagner, Verdi told Giuseppina Appiani that he wished he could stay for a couple of years and carry off 'a bag of these *most holy* pounds!' Wagner did some accounting at the end of the visit and, after the deduction of expenses, found he had made a profit of seven hundred dollars – more than he expected, but not enough to appease his Bayreuth creditors.

Cosima attended a service in Westminster Abbey, at the end of which the organist played Elisabeth's prayer from *Tannhäuser*. As the congregation dispersed, she imagined a moribund angel hovering above the crowd of 'silent and unheeding' Londoners. The cacophonous streets, which so stunned Verdi, were subdued by this overheard music. Driving with Richard in a hansom cab through the murk of South Kensington, she registered an inimitably Wagnerian view of the weather. As well as evoking dank, smutty Nibelheim, the damp air worked a sorcery that looked like a demonstration of Schopenhauer's metaphysics, pondered by Tristan and Isolde in their love duet. Mansions loomed out of nowhere, then vanished into the viscous whiteness. The scene looked spectral to Cosima: 'it is precisely here, in this centre of the utmost activity, that I feel most closely aware of the ideality of things and the dreamlike quality of life'. Bertolt Brecht, attacking the way Wagner befuddled the brain, said that his art 'creates fog'. He was using a metaphor, but London, as Wagner and Cosima attested, vouched for its literal truth. Verdi took a less ethereal view of the city's climate. He worried about his lungs and, as he said, soon began to worship the Italian sun he had forsaken; he was a southerner who could never feel at home here.

The smoke, choking dust and stench of coal were a menace, reminding Verdi of the self-expenditure that had taxed his health during a decade of unstinting work. He had suffered a series of breakdowns, which were treated by quacks who prescribed bloodletting and doses of spa waters. His throat plagued him; there were episodes of anorexia, rheumatism, gastritis and a report of consumption. To keep up with the demands on him, Verdi said he needed 'a stomach of bronze': this was the organ that he relied on, the solid basis of his health and sanity. Decades later, when discussing with Boito the likelihood of his being able to complete *Otello*, he left the final decision to his digestive system, declaring 'It's all a matter of the stomach'. In 1845 stomach troubles had caused him to delay a trip to Naples for the staging of *Alzira*. Although he sent medical certificates pronouncing him unfit to travel, the management of the opera house suspected him of malingering and pressed him to make the journey after swallowing a tincture of absinthe. He sometimes thought of impresarios and even audiences as his mortal enemies, intent on killing him to extort their due. When the revised *Don Carlo* was performed at La Scala in 1884, he dismissed the adulation he received and told Arrivabene that his famished public was baying for blood and ordering him 'Work yourself to death if need be, but thrill us once more'. Hence his Rossinian refrain during his years of inactivity between 1872 and 1885, when he defended himself by announcing 'I no longer compose': he had saved his life at the cost of his art.

'We artists are never allowed to be sick,' Verdi complained during the tiff about the postponement of *Alzira*. Half a century later, when the world had been infected by what Thomas Mann called the 'noble malady' of Wagnerism, sickness was almost a professional prerequisite for artists. By then Verdi had taken to asserting, as he did in 1898, that he had the vigour of 'the most robust worker in the fields'; to signal his determination to remain alive, he subscribed to a periodical for the next year. He emphasized the soundness of his 'nervous system', which he said had 'grown stronger with the years'. After a disagreement about *Otello* in 1889, he advised Ricordi to remember 'the inflexible man that I am' and regretted that he had not allowed himself a temperamental explosion – but just as his tears were rationed, so were his fits of displeasure, out of concern for the stability he cultivated. In 1867 Strepponi referred to Verdi's 'character of iron': despite his earlier denial that he was made of this heaviest and most unyielding of industrial metals, she believed that his rigidity got him through the dreary, frozen winters in Sant'Agata. Wagner, however, told Cosima in 1877 that the clue to his character was his softness, which he covered up by his rages and his vehement attacks on those who crossed him. Uninsulated, without Verdi's tough supplementary skins, he could be goaded to paranoid terror by the weather. In Sicily in 1881 he decided that he was 'ill-disposed towards the air here', whose hot panting gusts made him feel 'as if a policeman were grabbing hold of him'.

Far from taking pride in a strengthened nervous system, Wagner used his nerves like twitching filaments or exploratory tentacles, as a way of communicating with the world and registering its atmosphere, both emotional and meteorological. In his dying agony Tristan describes the neural pathways along which music travels as he tracks the potion from his heart to his brain. A fatuous aristocrat in Oscar Wilde's *A Woman of No Importance* must be thinking of Wagner when she says 'Music makes one feel so romantic – at least it always gets on one's nerves'; her wiser friend comments 'It's the same thing, nowadays.' Wagner believed, plausibly enough, that he was a human being of a new and rarefied kind, effectively an invalid. In 1864 he justified his demand for dainty food, caressing clothes and over-padded furniture by telling his friend Eliza Wille 'I am a different kind of organism, my nerves are hypersensitive, I must have beauty, splendour and light!' It may seem a ridiculously petulant remark, but later commentaries on the psychological make-up of artists – influenced by the example of Wagner – saw this kind of overwrought organism as standard equipment for modern men, who as the critic Hermann Bahr argued in 1891 belonged to a race of 'new human beings'. Bahr had a succinct definition of their novelty: 'They are nerves,' he said, and their discharges of nervous energy, like Wagner's fits or seizures, were 'the release of the modern'. Nietzsche called Wagner 'une névrose', and that assessment, made by another precociously modern man who succumbed to manias of his own, is clinically accurate. It explains Wagner's exactitude in scenes where characters suffer from nerves that are jangled or keyed up to a pitch of hysteria: the drowsy confusion of Sieglinde when she hears Hunding threaten Siegmund in *Die Walküre*, the gibbering distress of Mime in his forest den in *Siegfried* as the half-light breeds phantoms. At the end of *Götterdämmerung* the insomniac Gutrune wanders through the Gibichung hall, unable to quieten her anxieties. Her restlessness has little dramatic point, but Wagner, who described his bed as a 'vexation machine' and was seldom able to sleep through the night, is touchingly sympathetic. Verdi's characters are impelled by passion, and when they sing you hear the blood surge through their veins and the intoxicating release of adrenalin. But with the exception of Don Carlos and Otello, their nerves are not troubled by contradictions that are psychologically intolerable and physically unsustainable.

All living things need to warm themselves in the sun, which is why Verdi came to dislike overcast London. The light Wagner called for in his letter to Eliza Wille was more indirect, iridescently dappled and kaleidoscopic; he shrank from the glare that stuns Brünnhilde when she reawakens and greets the sun at the end of *Siegfried*. At the Palazzo Vendramin he worked in what he called a blue grotto, with suffused light that made him feel he was underwater. The light that both aroused and soothed him had to be refracted through a subtle, distorting prism. Singing an excerpt from *Tristan*, he said that it had 'a colour all its own, it is mauve, a sort of lilac'. Pink – fleshlier than stark, blank white, appropriate for blankets and for baby clothes – was his favourite shade, and in Sicily in 1880 he rejoiced in a room upholstered in that colour, which prompted one of his sillier generalizations. This, he informed Cosima, was why he railed against modern civilization, because it had forgotten how to produce that particular pink. She placed a swatch of the fabric between the pages of her diary for future reference. In his correspondence with the milliner who ran up his housecoats, he was pernickety about variants. 'Do not confuse No 2, the dark pink, with the earlier violet pink,' he warned her.

Verdi told Boito that he worked best when he could 'command my physique': the body was his servant, and it was expected to obey him. Wagner's art deranged the senses, and he surrendered to their free-associating bedlam. Baudelaire, after hearing him conduct the prelude to *Lohengrin* in 1860, said that the music conveyed 'the vertiginous imaginings of the opium smoker'. Proust, as hypochondriac as Wagner himself, likened his obsessive motifs to recurring bouts of neuralgia – an ache of abraded nerves that made the patient conscious of the fraught, intricate wiring under the skin. Wagner suffered from erysipelas, a bacterial infection of the skin once known as St Anthony's fire, and he thought of the inflammation as a by-product of his exquisite receptivity. 'One must pay for everything,' he said about a heat rash that bothered him in 1880; his skin loved fondling soft surfaces, so naturally – in his self-diagnosis – it grew florid as it bristled with excitement. This did not prevent him from raising his internal temperature with spiced-up potions. He craved snuff, and thought of the fumes it sent coursing through his head as a creative stimulus and a spiritual inspiration. Shortly before his death he told Cosima that 'Taking snuff is really my soul.' He meant that it changed his consciousness and conjured up hallucinations, forcing body and mind to admit to the existence of a third, impalpable principle, which, like his music, mediated between bodily sensation and whatever lies beyond its reach.

Leading Elsa to bed as the nuptial music fades, Lohengrin opens the window to admit the nocturnal scents of the flowers, which he likens to the magic that called to him through the air at her time of need. He is actually describing the sensory surfeit – compounded of hearing, seeing and smelling – that Wagner needed to help him compose. He laboured over perfecting olfactory pleasures, and distilled roses into perfumes that he prepared for Cosima's use and called either Eau de Richard or Extract Richard Wagner. His followers came to think of the operas as elixirs that worked on the senses and delivered satisfaction to the entire body. In 1920 a scandalous soprano in Huneker's novel *Painted Veils* feels herself swimming in the Wagnerian scores she studies: the music laps her in 'a magnetic bath' and babbles 'the hidden secrets of sex'. The notion of total immersion would have appealed to Wagner, who after his sessions of self-stimulation tried to quieten his skin with a regime of hydrotherapy. Sometimes he bathed in bran, on other occasions in a solution of coal tar. The waters at Mornex near Geneva calmed his nerves while activating his bowels, which made him aware, as he informed a correspondent, 'of openings (if you'll forgive the expression) which I had completely forgotten about'; his 'haemorrhoidal tumours', as he called them, signalled their appreciation. At home there were daily applications of wet packs, clysters and compresses, rub-downs and dips in a hip bath: a version of the cure prescribed for Amfortas when he is lowered into the woodland pool, though a good deal more intensive. During his work on the heavy-footed, halting march that introduces the Grail ceremony in *Parsifal*, Wagner commented – with a glint of self-mocking self-pity – that it was music for a spa, fit to be played at Marienbad or Ems, where he also had taken the waters. Even the opera's orchestration catered to his comfort, making him feel weightless, as if he had shed his body and its flaring, infected epidermis. The score of the *Ring* was granitic, like a mountain range chiselled into shape. After this he wanted *Parsifal*, as he beautifully put it, to resemble 'cloud layers, dispersing and then forming again', unlike the thundery clots of moisture that thicken above Brünnhilde's lair in *Götterdämmerung* and discharge sparks before Waltraute arrives.

Proust likened Wagner to Vulcan in his forge and pointed out that, although he pretended that his works welled up from obscure metaphysical depths, they were actually the products of 'industrious toil'. Wagner himself once described Wahnfried as 'a veritable composing factory!' His toil was convulsive, a battle – like that inside the steam engines Verdi saw chugging through London – between scalding heat and a cool technical control that tried to prevent an explosion. Siegfried keeps the balance when he forges his sword in Mime's smithy. He pumps the bellows to fan a blaze that melts the splintered steel, hammers it into shape, then plunges it into a trough of cold water, which audibly seethes on impact. But he cannot prevent himself from trying out the blade, and his demonstration of force destroys the equipment he has used for making it: a single blow splits the anvil in half. Whether it belongs to Vulcan or to Mime, the forge is a cauldron that can hardly contain the energy that blazes in it. At Bayreuth, Wagner had planned a temple; what he built was a workshop where illusions were manufactured. Scene changes happened behind a curtain of steam, so that the theatre, as Shaw remarked, smelled like a laundry. A steam engine in the cellars pumped the contents of a reservoir up to iron tanks beneath the roof, from where it could be piped throughout the wooden building in case of fire. Hanslick thought the orchestra pit, 'almost entirely hidden by a kind of tin roof', was 'set so deep that one is reminded of the engine room of a steamship'. These new sources of industrial power made miracles happen. During *Parsifal* in 1889, Shaw spotted a wire snaking from an electric socket to make Christ's blood glow in the Grail. Similarly in Paris in 1867 the monk who rescues the hero in *Don Carlos* appeared in a blaze of electric light, its white glow signalling a supernatural advent.

Like an engine in overdrive, Wagner shuttled between calorific extremes. According to his English friend Frederick Praeger, he worked himself up into an overheated state during the Dresden uprising and despatched a taller colleague – whose legs were long enough to vault over the barricades – to fetch him a refreshing ice. He understood the thermodynamic world view of his era, which computed heat loss and predicted the eventual extinction of the sun. 'The whole thing is a fireworks display,' he said about the universe; like Brünnhilde's pyre, it would soon fizzle out. The light from the stars was already elderly or ancient by the time it reached us, he noted on another occasion. Thinking about steam exhaled from the earth and its return as rain, he drew a desolate conclusion about our tenuous existence and his own creative metabolism. 'This means,' he told Cosima, 'that the human being is nothing but a form of combustion, self-consuming – terrible!' He also brooded about civilization's dependence on the vagaries of temperature: if the Gulf Stream had not been sent into reverse by the extrusion of Panama, Europe would be 'a mass of ice'. Verdi warned his librettists that their words needed to fire him up if he was to produce music. That ignition was for Wagner a matter of life and death, both personal and cosmic. Industrial engineering generated a fiercely propulsive heat, but this only accelerated the engine's breakdown, announced by an equivalent of the chest pains that were so frequent in Wagner's final years. 'With me it is always paroxysms,' he said in 1880 after a night in an unwelcoming Italian bed. He was hyperbolic by nature, but he had physiological and scientific reasons for his exaggerations. His labours used up his life, and at the same time dramatized the fate of the earth, from which heat is stealthily bleeding away. As he worked through the last stages of the *Ring*, he wanted 'every note … to convey the end of the world', and that ultimate climax, with heaven aflame and rivers flooding, had to be an eruption of searing pleasure. Music, he told Cosima in 1881, for him meant ecstasy – an entranced state that can be joyous or tormented, rapturous or morbid, since it expels us from our bodies and either acquaints us with the divine or gives us a foretaste of death.

Verdi concentrated on the combustibility of individual human beings: Otello calls for Desdemona's cooling handkerchief because his brow is on fire, aglow with unreasonable suspicion. The score of *La traviata* keeps track of Violetta's health as she consumes herself, coughing, emitting thready sighs or succumbing to fatigue; the coloratura in her first aria is a feat of fizzy pyrotechnics, a display like that put on by Wagner's effervescent universe, and she hardly recovers from the exertion. At Sant'Agata Verdi had a small working model of the cosmic engine that caused Wagner so much philosophical distress. It was a steam-powered hydraulic pump, housed in a hut on what he called the 'machine lawn'. He imported it from England to regulate the irrigation system that redistributed water from the moat around his property, feeding his plants and refreshing his artificial lake. The pump was unreliable, and its misbehaviour caused him plumbing problems of his own. In 1867 Strepponi blamed his 'intestinal inflammation' and 'stomach upsets' on his rushing to and fro to doctor the engine and its underground conduits.

Balzac explained his teeming output of novels by calling the will a force as irresistible as steam power, and when Verdi went back to work in his seventies, he seemed to be drawing on the same locomotive energy. Ricordi likened him to a dynamo, self-sufficiently generating the electricity he needed. He remained concerned about his stomach, the furnace on which the apparatus depended, and it was wise of Ricordi to proffer a gift of fuel: at Christmas in 1881 he sent Verdi a panettone with a Moor squatting on top of it, in the hope of speeding up the pace of his work on *Otello*, known in their private code as the chocolate project. Strepponi replied sceptically. 'As for cooking the chocolate,' she said, 'while there seems no scarcity of wood, the will to light the fire is lacking.' She was mistaken, perhaps because her frame of reference was the kitchen not the factory. In 1891, hesitating about *Falstaff* after having written no music for four months, Verdi told Boito 'I have not been able to warm up the engine.' Boito assured him that it would soon be boiling, and encouraged him with an industrial injunction: 'Forward! à toute vapeur!' The former galley slave now steamed implacably ahead on iron rails, outstripping all competition.

Two years later, after hearing *Die Walküre* at La Scala, Boito told Verdi that the opera's halting rhythm – bogged down in fatalistic recollection of the past, dragging its cumbrous cargo of motifs – reminded him of a slow train that stopped at every petty station. Verdi, self-evidently, was an express.

# MAGI

When Strepponi wrote to Verdi in 1853 to remonstrate about his mercenariness, she addressed him as 'my dear Mago'. The word charmingly catches her attitude to him: although it marks her almost superstitious respect for his creative power – a magical capacity to extract notes from the air, or from somewhere inside himself – it is edged with the intimate mockery that is only permitted to a lover, and it introduces a little sermon in which she criticizes his potboiling preoccupation with money. Could the magician be a gypsy palm-reader, flattering the client in return for some paltry coins?

Another of Strepponi's pet names for Verdi was Pasticcio, which had the same undertone of affectionate teasing. In the kitchen a pasticcio is a dish of baked pasta with a slathering of ground meat or Béchamel sauce – a good way of recycling leftovers; in music a pastiche is a piece of music anthologically assembled by one composer borrowing from others or by several different composers, like the unperformed *Messa per Rossini* to which Verdi and twelve colleagues contributed. Strepponi knew well enough that he was not an opportunistic dealer in second-hand goods, but her use of the word reminded him that they shared a familiarity with the theatre and its frequently shabby practices and warned him that she, who knew him better than anyone else, reserved the right – in principle at least – not to be impressed by his work. She loved Verdi for himself not for his catalogue of operas, and in a letter written in December 1860 she told him that she was sometimes 'quite surprised that you know anything about music!' When he was in Turin receiving the usual acclaim at the opera house, she remarked in a letter that if the audience had known how well he made risotto *alla Milanese* they would have cheered a good deal louder. Cooking, for the purposes of the joke, mattered more than composing.

Cosima saw herself as a handmaiden singled out to serve genius – to share Wagner's labours, eternalize his name by bearing his children, and police his reputation after his death. He once said to her 'You should have married a god.' She replied 'Well, I did!', and he did not disagree. Strepponi's bond, however, was with a man. 'Everyone agrees that the divine gift of genius has fallen to his lot,' she said when discussing Verdi with his friend Cesare Vigna in 1872; she concurred, but let others do the consecrating. What she valued were his human qualities – his good heart, his charity, his modesty, his proud independence and boyish simplicity. After the premiere of *Falstaff* in 1893, replying to congratulations on his behalf, she said that no one could possess 'greater genius and rectitude of character': the two were equally important, as in her equation between a risotto and an opera. She only regretted, as she added in her earlier encomium to Vigna, that Verdi was a rascal of little faith, luckily not an outright atheist. Because she herself believed in God, she did not make the mistake of deifying artists. This enabled her to manoeuvre her way around Verdi's reverential, intimidated attitude to Alessandro Manzoni, which seemed to have ruled out the possibility of their ever meeting. In 1867 on a visit to Milan to buy furniture, she paid an impromptu call on Clarina Maffei, whom she did not know; she sent a portrait of Verdi on ahead to intercede for her. Clarina proposed a visit to Manzoni. When Strepponi returned home she informed Verdi, who picked her up at the station, that she had found no furniture that pleased her. But, she casually added, 'I'll introduce you to Manzoni. He expects you, and I was there with Clarina the other day.' His reaction was a Wagnerian paroxysm – although Verdi's fit took a comic form, and after flushing and sweating with the effort to control his feelings he removed his hat and 'screwed it up in a way that reduced it almost to shapelessness'. The news of this unexpected social breakthrough managed, like music, to charm and mollify a wild beast. 'The most severe and savage Bear of Busseto,' Strepponi reported, 'had his eyes full of tears.' It is a sweet yet strong-minded story about two women teaming up, almost like a pair of agile, ingenious merry wives, to outwit stuffy men whose concern with reputation and accomplishment inhibits simple human contact.

In their letters Wagner and Cosima renamed themselves Will and Vorstell (short for 'Vorstellung', which means 'representation'). These were the twin forces that in Schopenhauer's philosophy collude to persuade us that the world is real: husband and wife were living out an exalted metaphysical fiction, with Wagner as the strife of desire and Cosima as the embodied image of his quest or the projection of his longing. At other times they enacted Nietzsche's theory of tragedy, with Wagner playing Dionysus and Cosima cast as the priestess of Apollo. Their union was allegorical, a marriage of minds that were subconsciously attuned. She claimed that she was never able to surprise him, because he always intuited what she was thinking. Awake or asleep, they communicated by the exchange of images. In 1878 Wagner reported a dream in which he had stumbled across a funeral procession in Bayreuth. A friend attempted to hold him back, but he broke free, sensing that he ought to be the chief mourner. Cosima knew the meaning of the fragmentary anecdote: 'I prayed fervently for a blessed death, and he receives the vision!' In Verdi's household there was no allowance for the telepathy that allowed Cosima to beam messages into Wagner's dormant brain, or to receive transmissions from him. Instead a fabric cord dangled from the ceiling above Verdi's bed at Sant'Agata; when pulled, it rang a bell in Strepponi's adjacent bedroom. The wiring ran in one direction only, not allowing for Strepponi to send a musical summons of her own. She had to deal with a man who was undemonstrative and unconfiding – but her management of the situation saved him from himself and let him know who actually held the power.

|||||||||||||||||||

Wagner mystified everything, in the theatre and outside it. In his world, as Nietzsche remarked in 1874, there was 'seldom a ray of sunshine, but a great deal of magical wizardry in the lighting'. Hence his recourse to magic, which bewitches the brain by deceiving the eye. He thought of art as a means of altering perception, either aurally or visually (or, in his combination of music and drama, both at once); it worked like a charm, an enchantment. Chemistry could accelerate its effects, which is why Isolde refers to the potions brewed by her mother as 'ihre Kunst', her art. Tolstoy, who fulminated against Wagner's habit of playing on the 'auditory nerves' to overstimulate the brain, likened him to a hypnotist, and suggested that the same result could be 'more quickly attained by getting drunk or smoking opium'. When Mark Twain heard *Parsifal* at Bayreuth, he called Wagner 'the dean magician' who 'from his grave' continued 'to weave his spells about his disciples'. According to this ghoulish whimsy, Klingsor was not content to haul Kundry out of her deathly sleep; he even raised the composer from his tomb as the opera's prelude murmured its insinuations in the dark theatre.

Wagner's first completed opera was *Die Feen*, based on a play by Carlo Gozzi about a family emergency in fairyland. The fairy princess Ada – attracted to earthlings because her mother was 'ein Sterblicher', someone born for no better reason than to die – has married the knight Arindal, who agrees, like Elsa accepting Lohengrin's terms, not to enquire about her origins. Eventually Arindal does ask the forbidden question, and is ejected from her diaphanous realm. Ada follows him back to earth, like Senta who wants either to save the Dutchman or to share his purgatorial afterlife. The fairy king tests his daughter's resolve by making Arindal believe that she has murdered their children: only if he loves her so absolutely that he does not curse her will the match be permitted. He is driven mad by what he sees, and Ada is turned to stone. The magician Groma rearms Arindal for combat against the spirits, and he rescues his petrified wife by playing his lyre like a redeemed, repentant Tannhäuser. Rather than lose Ada forever, the fairy king confers immortality on his son-in-law: couldn't Wotan have spared Siegmund, or intervened to sort things out between Siegfried and Brünnhilde? Before this happy ending, Wagner's fairies are as threatening and arrogant as Valkyries, contemptuous of lowly mankind. It was left to Verdi – in his own belated and startlingly uncharacteristic trip to fairyland – to remember that these creatures are supposed to be lighter and more transparent than we are. In the nocturnal forest at the end of *Falstaff*, Nannetta appears as the fairy queen and sings an aria that is about the genesis of music, a fragrant breeze that seems to be exhaled by another world; the attendant spirits describe the dreaming wood in what sounds like a lullaby whispered by the collective unconscious, afloat on an ocean of buoyant sound. As they softly sing and gently dance, 'Le magiche accoppiando/Carole alla canzon', music pacifies a fractious world. But this after all is an opera by Verdi, unregenerately carnal, so the fairies discard their gossamer wings and start to pinch and bludgeon the cowering Falstaff, who believes that he will die if he looks at them.

*Die Feen* is the unexpected prototype for Wagner's later operas, which are all organized around the passage to and fro between supernatural and mortal worlds. Characters like Senta are eager for transfiguration or resigned to damnation: any fate is preferable to the earthbound ordinariness to which Wotan condemns Brünnhilde. Titian's painting of the Virgin Mary's assumption into heaven, which Wagner often studied while in Venice, describes the course all his people mark out for themselves. Or at least it describes the journey in one direction. In *Eine Mitteilung an meine Freunde*, the essay communicating his artistic intentions to his friends, Wagner wrote about 'the desire of the heights for the depths', which leads his gods to delevitate, like Ada pursuing Arindal or Venus burrowing into a hollowed-out German mountain or Lohengrin coming down from Monsalvat. 'Bin ich ein Gott?' asks the mad Arindal, who thinks he is breathing heavenly air. But madness is not a prerequisite for this promotion: he is already 'mehr als Mensch' because of his irresistible performance with the lyre. Ada, transformed into a fiend to test Arindal, becomes the most liberated of Wagner's superwomen, no longer constrained by the squeamish instincts we call human. She gratuitously commits infanticide by hurling her children into a fiery pit, more than proving Nietzsche's point that Wagner's heroines have no talent for maternity. The contrast with Verdi is inescapable: Azucena in *Il trovatore* commits the same outrage, but by mistake, and even so she never regains her sanity. Of course Ada's infants are restored to life, but by then the taboo has been breached. If God no longer exists, or if godhead can be won by wishing for it or even by singing, then anything is indeed possible.

Wagner returns constantly to the power of magic, which enables his fairies to flout the laws of physics and biology. The words 'Macht' and 'Zauber' seem almost magnetically attracted to each other in his operas. Alberich's curse on the ring equates 'Macht ohne Mass' with 'sein Zauber', and the twinned ideas turn into a Wagnerian definition of art. It is our self-administered immortality, stretching the dull limits of human life and actualizing fantasies. But at the same time it kills off extraneous affections, reduces daily reality to a prosy waste, and estranges the artist from the community of his fellows. This magic power rightly terrifies those who possess it. During her duet with the Dutchman, Senta asks what power resides in her, what mighty magic fires her: 'Von mächt'gem Zauber überwunden/reisst mich's zu seiner Rettung fort./...Was ist's, das mächtig in mir lebet?' She is right to be alarmed, since the Dutchman is the product of her conjuration. Powers like hers ought to be devilish, as they are when Lady Macbeth calls on the spirits who superintend mortal thoughts and asks them – although Piave's libretto for Verdi's opera does not go this far – to unsex her. For Wagner, however, these are the creator's home-grown spells, which turn others into accomplices or agents and compel images nurtured in the mind to take on flesh and blood. Mary, who chides Senta for staring at the Dutchman's portrait instead of working, mistakenly calls the painting 'dem Konterfei'. Art is not the replica of what exists but a vision that reality is challenged to match; the painting and Senta's song about it are both acts of sorcery. She asks the hunter Erik if he is afraid of 'ein Lied, ein Bild?', but his superstitious dread is justified, and she herself gives a small shriek – of victory or perhaps of panic – when the phantasm appears before her.

The advent of Lohengrin provokes a similar response from the chorus, which asks what blessed power ('holde Macht') has spellbound them. Telramund may be right to speculate about a 'Geheimer Buhlschaft', a mysteriously erotic coition between Elsa the visionary and the man she envisions. Emily Brontë wrote a poem addressing her imagination as a male muse, a demon lover who 'by day and night' is her 'intimate delight':

Thee, ever present, phantom thing –
My slave, my comrade, and my King!

Ortrud tells Elsa that she knows how Lohengrin came to her, 'durch Zauber', through magic; Elsa indignantly insists that he is the product of her faith and came 'durch Glauben', through faith. She sings with angelic radiance while Ortrud mutters and demonically rages, midway between speech and song. Elsa's is the romantic approach to religion, dreaming up gods who, like the Olympians, are projections of our desires; she is a companion for Leda and Europa, who cavort in the Venusberg in *Tannhäuser*, and Wagner likened her to Semele, scorched by her flirtation with divinity. Ortrud, apparently more primitive because she worships Wodan and Freia not Elsa's Christian intercessor, is actually a modern atheist who cacklingly derides the word 'Gott' and then, like Feuerbach or Nietzsche, disparages the very notion as a symptom of our moral cowardice. She boasts that her own power will reveal the feebleness of the God who guards Lohengrin and despoil the knight of his shining aura: hers is the intellectual thrust of what the nineteenth century called the Higher Criticism, which secularized Scripture and exposed the irrationality of worship.

Elisabeth in *Tannhäuser* appears to be another victim of enchantment, like Elsa's younger brother Gottfried in *Lohengrin* who is turned into a swan by Ortrud. When she hears Tannhäuser sing, she surrenders 'machtlos' to 'der Macht der Wunder', the power of magic, and in his defence she claims that 'ein furchtbar mächt'ger Zauber', a terrifyingly powerful magic, was responsible for his outburst during the song contest. Wolfram – using the same words, as persistent as a musical motif – asks Tannhäuser to explain the magic or heavenly power that vanquished her: 'War's Zauber, war es reine Macht,/durch die solch Wunder du vollbracht…?' Elisabeth, like Senta or Elsa, has her own reserves of power, exhibited in her prayer to the Virgin. During a conversation in 1892, Italo Pizzi tempted Verdi to ridicule this long, slow aria. Pizzi found the piece so tedious that he wondered why 'our Lord, in front of whose cross Elisabeth kneels and prays, did not swing a leg and give her a boot'. 'To shut her up once and for all!' chuckled Verdi. But the aria is more than abject, protracted puling. Elisabeth's intentions are unlike those of Desdemona in Verdi's own 'Ave Maria', where the plea is generously all-embracing: 'prega nel peccatori' and 'prega per noi' begs Desdemona, praying for our sins even though she is sinless. Elisabeth fixes on the Virgin because of her power, saluting her as 'Allmächt'ge Jungfrau'. Rather than pleading, she demands deliverance, and asks to undergo an Assumption like that of Titian's Virgin – to be spared the fate of sinking into the dust or mouldering in earth and instead directly installed, 'engelgleich', angelically in heaven. She has so far proved to be an ineffectual substitute for the Virgin, or for Christ who, as she says when shielding Tannhäuser from the knights, died to redeem us. Now, in a series of sudden vertical vocal leaps, she asks to be raised aloft, placed where she will be better able to do the work of absolution. It is a self-willed transubstantiation, all the more astonishing because we then watch it happening as Elisabeth, spurning Wolfram's offered help, slowly mounts the hill in a silent epilogue that lasts as long as the aria, walking out of life and into eternity. After she vanishes, Wolfram's aria about the evening star elliptically describes the next stage of her ascent: that single point of light consoles our darkness. He tactfully avoids mentioning that the star to which he sings is also known as Venus, the goddess who ought to be the opposite of Elisabeth's almighty Virgin. Within half an hour her request has been granted and she returns, lying on her bier but – like the Virgin – unburied.

In *Die Feen* an arid wilderness changes into a magical garden, and in *Parsifal* the transformation is reversed when Klingsor's fantastical realm suddenly withers. Did Wagner ever leave fairyland? On occasion it suited him to sign himself Alberich, but he also assumed the role of the sorcerer who presides over a harem of seductive witches: one of his totemic possessions was a music box which he called Klingsor. The pet name acknowledged that his music cast spells, and he sometimes fancied that the same wish-fulfilling abracadabra operated in his daily life. In 1873 in Bayreuth he awoke remembering a dream in which he had been given six hundred francs; he then found that his publisher had sent him a remittance for almost the same sum. Later he went for a celebratory stroll and noticed that a royal gardener was working, for free, on the back gate of his villa. 'Often,' he told Cosima in all earnestness, 'I have the feeling that I am being borne along and sustained by the fairies.'

Henri Fantin-Latour called Wagner's art 'féerique': in his lithograph of the scene when Klingsor revives Kundry, she looks like ectoplasm, whitening in the air at the behest of a medium. Hanslick, however, objected to the *Ring*'s 'exclusion of the purely human factor' in favour of supernatural or subterranean beings and 'their various magic arts'. He was thrilled by the 'colouristic splendour' of the operas and amused by their scenic stunts – the contraptions on which the Rhinemaidens bobbed up and down underwater, Alberich's transformation into a snake and a hopping frog, a rainbow bridge that unfortunately resembled 'a seven-coloured liverwurst' – but questioned whether it ought to be 'the highest ambition of a dramatic composer to make music for a succession of magic contrivances'. *Parsifal* caused Hanslick to worry all over again about the walking trees, the floral nymphs and the dove that pauses in mid-air above the Grail. Wagner's self-glorifying rite was, he decided, 'a kind of superior magic opera … a free play of fantasy revelling in the wondrous'. The wondrous or the merely tricksy? Lohengrin restores the bewitched Gottfried's human form, but by disenchanting the swan he leaves himself with no means of transport. His response is a piece of opportunistic tinkering worthy of a magician who will not let flat-minded reality interfere with his effects: he places the swan's chain in the beak of another conveniently hovering dove, which will tug his boat back to Monsalvat from mid-air.

Verdi had no use for such facile marvels. 'Force still rules the world!' he declared in 1849 when Austria prevailed in the battle against Italian nationalists, and that force belonged to bayonets or battalions, not to Wagnerian sorcery. What Verdi called the force of destiny outweighs the force of magic to which Senta and Elisabeth react with such tremulous terror. Michel Leiris pointed out that 'to drink a love potion as Tristan does is to obey one's destiny, not to inadvertently unleash the "force of destiny"'. For Wagnerian characters fate or fortune is an internal voice that, like the shepherd's ancient tune as interpreted by Tristan, entices them towards the consummation of death. In Verdi the force remains external and arbitrary, like the offstage horn that commands Ernani to kill himself. His characters dose their enemies with poison or imbibe it voluntarily like Leonora in *Trovatore*, but they never bother with potions. Verdi could only conceive of power physically, as the capacity to do others harm or to kill them. Like Machiavelli, he saw lust and fury as unstoppable, incorrigible energies that were peculiarly Italian: in his *Discorsi*, Machiavelli praised republican city-states as breeding grounds for passion, animated by 'greater vitality, greater hatred, more desire for revenge'. Luna in *Trovatore*, who has all those lusty attributes, pauses for an unusual moment of introspection and admits to having doubts about the legitimacy of the death sentence he has passed on Manrico: 'Abuso io forse del poter che pieno/In me trasmise il prence!' – perhaps I'm abusing the power the prince delegated to me. But the qualm passes, and the abuse continues. The power that interested Wagner, by contrast, was mental. His biographer Friedrich Glasenapp, who worked under Cosima's surveillance, credited him with the ability 'to see through people' and a mesmeric talent to control them.

In *Un ballo in maschera* Ulrica, known as 'la maga', is a fairground prophetess with questionable credentials. She tells the sailor Silvano that he will be rich; she is proved right, but only because the king slips some money into the man's pocket. With their jingling antics and their dynastic sideshow, the witches in *Macbeth* detract from Verdi's investigation of moral collapse. He toyed with the idea of an optical machine that would make the apparitions in the cavern cavort on a screen, but he was irritated by the way that these gadgets deceived the eye and bewildered the mind, just as he told the librettist of the prospective *Lear* that he was wary of Shakespearean subjects because the succession of short scenes felt as fidgety and jerky as the successive images in a magic lantern show. The occult and the arcane had to be more than a gimmicky sleight of hand. *Macbeth*'s haunted or spectral effects are produced by instruments newly combined or played in new ways – the bassoons and low clarinets in the witches' den, the muted strings and jarring harmonies as Lady Macbeth wanders through the night washing her hands – or by voices stretched to breaking point. Lady Macbeth enters reading a letter, then after this spoken introduction sings a pealing, scarily forthright homage to ambition and its alliance with evil. In her aria about the dying of the light, her voice steps down into a chesty crypt when, with sarcastic solemnity, she grants the dead the right to a requiem; then comes a jump upwards that is almost a shriek of savage vitality in 'O voluttà del soglio!', as she recoils from such thoughts and excites herself by imagining the voluptuous pleasures of royal power. The opera concentrates on this union of morbidity and sensuality, rather than on supernatural interventions.

Wagner often returned to Shakespeare's *Macbeth* and always found its impact 'crushing', as Cosima reported in 1870. But his interpretation of it – or rather his performance, since he read Shakespeare's plays aloud after dinner, playing all the parts – differed from Verdi's. The challenge the opera sets itself is to elicit sympathy for two utterly reprehensible characters, whose verdicts on their own actions are so unsparing. It does so by showing their pained self-awareness, and almost denies them the saving grace of music. As she sleepwalks, Lady Macbeth whispers or mutters ugly, unavoidable truths that song cannot palliate, and Macbeth finally dismisses his own trumpeting voice as mere bluster, 'vento e suono'. The rest is silence, or the mercy of unconsciousness – death without the requiem that Lady Macbeth allows Duncan and Banquo in her aria. Wagner categorically dismissed such moral and psychological considerations. After rereading the first act in 1878, he told Cosima that Macbeth was a simple soldier, instantly corrupted by his encounter with 'the whole daemonic nature of life'; the demonizing agent might have been music, a Dionysian drive that is hardly represented by the troupe of pretty ballerinas Verdi asked the impresario to supply for the coven. 'The individual,' Wagner said, 'ceases entirely to exist.' Verdi would have found the notion unintelligible, philosophically absurd. He believed neither in gods nor in devils, only in fallible, forgivable human beings.

Others may have worshipped Wagner, but he did not always share their credulous awe. Talking about himself, he could be as impish as Strepponi when she ridiculed or rebuked Verdi. At times Wagner described his work as an act of cosmic genesis, but having grown up in the theatre he knew that it was also a patchy, precarious exercise in make-believe – a display of the conjurer's trickery, not a replica of divine creation. What is Wotan's spear, which causes ructions in the earth and sky when he raises it to menace Mime, but the rune-encrusted rod of a wizard? Theodor Adorno said that Wagner the conductor was a terrorist armed with a baton. If the spear is an overgrown wand, then Wagner's little stick was the wand neatly miniaturized, with no loss of potency.

In 1879 Wagner and Cosima happened to discuss *The Tempest*. Wagner nicknamed her 'Prospera', and she replied by saying 'You are Prospero, you have his magic and his benevolence'. In the exchange of compliments they conveniently forgot that Prospero's cabbalistic art is not entirely benign, and that when he renounces it at the end of the play he crumples into a sadly powerless old man who can no longer whip up the winds. Earlier in 1879 Wagner read Thomas Carlyle's short biography of Alessandro Cagliostro, which in a pseudo-heroic rodomontade praises the self-ennobled charlatan who had wheedled his way into the confidence of monarchs in the late eighteenth century as 'the King of Liars', a character who typified 'this most deceivable of modern ages'. On the same day, after writing one of his craven and obsequiously affectionate letters to Ludwig II, Wagner admitted to Cosima that he felt guilty about the affected language he was obliged to use and the theatrical protestations of eternal love the king expected from him. Did he reflect on the connection between Cagliostro's bamboozling of his royal customers and his own more craven tactics? Two years later Nietzsche scoffed at the 'overloaded bits-and-pieces work' of *Parsifal* and the 'Cagliostricity of its creator'. Paul Claudel, even more disillusioned than Nietzsche, called Wagner a hobgoblin, 'not only a magician but an evil dwarf', as poisonous as Mime.

But for Wagner magic meant more than Cagliostro's fakery. His interest in spirit-summoners and self-transcenders was prompted by existential curiosity and sharpened by an ironic envy. In 1871 he told Cosima he wanted to meet a magician because he fancied being one himself. Why shouldn't he be able to jump over huge distances, as if wearing ten-league boots? The will ought to be capable of outwitting and abridging space. 'My music-making is in fact magic-making,' he said. Once he invited a conjurer with the sadly bland name of Herr Smith to show off his dexterity at Wahnfried. Reflecting on Smith's act, Wagner called him 'a wild character – a flawed rogue', too morally timid for a criminal career, which is why he had to make do with cheating the eye at children's parties. Here too there was an analogy with Wagner's own practices. The Bayreuth theatre looming on the hilltop gave him nightmares, and made him ask, he confessed to Cosima, whether he was not a swindler. Magicians produce rabbits or coins or endless skeins of silk out of nowhere, then cause those trifles to dematerialize all over again: how different was this from Wagner's chimerical moulding of tuned air, or the way he made tinted steam look like raging fire? 'We perform hocus pocus with our art,' he admitted in 1881. Engelbert Humperdinck – who deputized for Wagner by composing a few bars of extra music for *Parsifal* to prolong one of the transformation scenes – had his Witch in *Hänsel und Gretel* quote that ancient, rudimentary gibberish, which may be a garbling of Christ's eucharistic gift of his body, 'Hoc est corpus': if so, the juggler is consciously mimicking and mocking the priest, committing a sacrilege that might have excited Wagner.

At the end of December 1877, reviewing their shared past and speculating about how much future was left to them, Cosima set Wagner the ultimate challenge: could he make her disappear? She asked him whether in his magical researches he had discovered a way 'of making me cease to be, absorbing me into himself'. He answered by pointing in the direction of their tomb, which awaited them behind Wahnfried.

## Two Women and Womankind

For Cosima, marriage was a rehearsal for death, preparing for her permanent incorporation into Richard in the back garden. The mayor of Bayreuth was scandalized by the advance preparations they made, perhaps because they treated death as a public act of consummation, not a penitential sloughing of the flesh. They did not mind that their tomb was ready before the house. Cosima grudgingly accepted the dwelling's comforts for the sake of the children, but said that for her and Richard 'the burial vault would be enough'. While the grave was being dug, Wagner sometimes climbed down into it. He and Cosima tended the site carefully, planting a spruce tree from Triebschen on it, ordering the gardener to keep it swept and to sprinkle birdseed on the vacant mound, taking visitors to see it. Before he settled on Wahnfried as the house's name, Wagner proposed calling it 'The Final Happiness': it was a gateway to their commodious post-mortem double bed. 'When shall we go down to our graves?' he merrily asked Cosima in January 1878, as if proposing an afternoon walk. 'Whenever you like,' she replied. Earlier that day they had been talking about slaves, who were happier in their lot, Cosima thought, than the modern proletariat, and that subject led naturally enough to the jaunty proposal for relaxing in the tomb: living, as the Wagnerian hero of Villiers de l'Isle-Adam's play *Axël* puts it when committing suicide, is best left to the servant class.

They expected the end, when it came, to be blissfully simultaneous. Because Cosima was so much younger, Wagner announced in 1875 – giving dictation to fate with his usual aplomb – that he had made arrangements to live until he was ridiculously old. Then, when they were both ready, they would die together by euthanasia. He had positioned a sofa in his room at Wahnfried for the purpose, and decreed that the last pages of *Tristan* should be played at 'our funeral'. In March 1882 in Sicily, Cosima had an unexpected preview of this joint death. The maid called her to Wagner, who was having a seizure. Seeing him, Cosima fainted in distress. It was her wish, she cheerfully wrote at the end of the day, 'to do everything I could to be worthy of dying with him.... My fainting fit today has given me hope.' It never does to have designs on life, let alone on death. Wagner died alone, as everyone does, even though Cosima was in the room, and she did not instantly and effortlessly join him, like Isolde who is able to will her own expiry. She clung to his corpse for a day, refusing to eat or drink as she waited for her own body to stop going through its habitual motions; her survival bewildered and embarrassed her. Eventually she had to be prised away so that the cadaver could be prepared for its journey back to Munich. She chopped off her hair and deposited it in the coffin as an offering to Wagner and a sign of her nunlike retreat from social existence. In seclusion at Wahnfried, unable to understand why the end had not come to order, she sentenced herself to a living death, and imposed the same rigor mortis on Wagner's legacy. As 'chief remembrancer' – a function that Shaw said was unnatural, because the living cannot stay paralysed in perpetual mourning – she ruled that there should be no deviation from the tempi the Meister favoured and that scenery should remain the same as that which his eyes had looked on. Performances happened under the aegis of what Shaw, dispirited after his visit to the Bayreuth Festival in 1889, called 'the law of death'.

In a discussion of Mozart's final symphonies, Claudio Abbado recently said that for Germans death pervades life and perhaps is life itself, whereas Italians regard death as an outsider and an intruder. Vaughan Williams joked that in Verdi's *Requiem* death, almost personified in the 'Mors stupebit', 'stalks on like a villain in an opera'. Death in Italy is inimical and villainous, whereas Germans with romantic inclinations – to expand on Abbado's premise – befriend it or are seduced by it, like the maiden in Schubert's song 'Der Tod und das Mädchen' who is wooed by the malaise that kills her. In Verdi's operas death is seldom anticipated, as it so ardently is by Wagner's characters – by Elsa for instance, who seeks to prove her love by telling Lohengrin she would die for him, in words that Cosima frequently quoted to herself. Being unwelcome, death in Verdi comes as a shock, even if it has been foretold: Violetta's collapse in *La traviata*, the murder at the party in *Un ballo in maschera*. Characters fight against it, but they are mistaken if they think they can laugh it off, as Giulietta, Edoardo and the Marchesa do in *Un giorno di regno* when they brightly declare in their trio that love will help them to combat an adverse fate. From the Italian perspective, nothing can be gained by thinking about death before you need to. When the final moment comes, the people in Verdi's operas hope it will be quick, and – like Boccanegra as he dies, minutes after being told that he has drunk a slow-acting poison – they counsel the survivors to be brave and to get on with the business of living. D. H. Lawrence reflected on this contrast in behaviour between the two cultures in a letter written in 1911: he damned Wagner's 'bellowings at Fate and death' and added 'I like the Italians who run all on impulse, and don't care about their immortal souls, and don't worry about the ultimate.'

Strepponi died in 1897, a little more than three years before Verdi. He mutely guarded his grief, telling the members of his household 'I don't feel like talking.' This was the same laconic stoicism with which he responded to professional setbacks. When *La traviata* failed in Venice in 1853 he did not feel sorry for himself or blame anyone else, but simply told Ricordi 'Let's not enquire into the reasons. That's the way it is. Addio, addio.' After the second performance he sent an equally terse report to a Roman impresario, and then said, in words like those he used so many decades later after Strepponi's death, 'It's better not to speak of it.' Strepponi left instructions for an abstemious funeral. She wanted a simple ceremony at dawn, so that she could leave the world as she came into it, 'poor and without pomp'. In her will she asked God to do her the favour of reuniting her with Verdi in a better world, which is what Elisabeth and Don Carlos ask for when they part at the end of the opera: did she really expect God to admit to heaven a man who did not believe in him? Left alone, Verdi made an effort to be busy and cheerful, arranged the apportionment of his property, and planned his own minimal funeral. Wagner, whose music is about the amelioration of death, was unable to imagine the event without orchestrating it, but Verdi deprived himself of the mellifluous comfort he extended to his characters and ordered 'No singing and no music to be played' at his obsequies. He also banned flowers, and his body was taken from his room at the Grand Hôtel in Milan in a second-class hearse before the sun rose. Unlike Wagner enjoying the Bayreuth mayor's consternation, Verdi respected the right of the civil authorities to make rules about burial places. He was first placed in a grave beside Strepponi's in the Cimitero Monumentale in Milan; a month later, after the government had given permission, the bodies were transferred to the Casa di Riposo. Their crypt is below the institution's chapel, not trespassing on holy ground.

Cosima gave credence to Wagner's jesting familiarity with the deity – he said that he looked forward to producing *Die Walküre* in the afterlife as entertainment for the Almighty – and reminded herself 'I have to love him like a child or like a god!' since children and gods were alike in their demand for absolute devotion. Strepponi, rather than making an idol of Verdi, judged him as a man. She called him a rascal because he lacked religious faith, and when he was needlessly grumpy she mused that he might be perfect if only he had a little more sweetness and charm. Once she did treat him to an exalted turn of phrase that is almost Wagnerian. In a letter written in 1860 she addressed him as 'O my Redeemer!' and begged him to love her after her death, so she could enlist him as a character reference when she confronted divine providence. The religiosity of the phrase recalls Wagner's comparison between himself and the Flying Dutchman in the *Mitteilung*: he too sought 'das Weib', the archetypal woman who was to be a saviour as well as a partner. Wagner demanded that life should supply him with such a woman, and auditioned a series of candidates for the role. Strepponi, humbler and more patient, did not expect that any man would overlook her past as Verdi chose to do. The redemption he afforded her was not spiritual but moral or even legal, since by marrying her he had restored her to membership of society. 'I wanted to become a *new woman*,' she wrote in 1868. Reformation was her personal responsibility; each of us has to be his or her own redeemer.

In conferring the title on Verdi she had in mind a humanized Christ, the 'Man-God' who prompted her to send kind Christmas wishes to her rival Stolz. In *I masnadieri* Francesco's abominable crimes place him outside humanity, beyond Christian mercy: as he realizes, 'l'Uom-Dio non penò'. Strepponi knew that there should be no limits to forgiveness, even though it may have been harder for one woman to excuse another who had wronged her than for Christ to remit humanity's sins in bulk.

By taking on human flesh, Christ accepted that we are a muddled blend of refined soul and down-dragging body. Romantic critics like August Wilhelm Schlegel found the same tolerant, redemptive spirit in Shakespeare, whose characters are not fatally flawed but spotted with commonness, humanized by their defects or deficiencies. Hamlet is dilatory, Cleopatra is afraid of dying, Caesar is deaf in one ear. Victor Hugo called this openness to the complexity of our nature Gothic: we are sublime but also squalid, which is why Christian cathedrals make room for both angels and gargoyles. Hugo's jester Triboulet in *Le Roi s'amuse*, on whom Verdi based Rigoletto, is the incarnation of this asymmetry. He may look repellent and behave viciously but there is an exquisite tenderness in his love for his daughter, and the fact that he exists to be laughed at does not disqualify him from becoming, in his grief and his self-accusation, a tragic character. True love overlooks aesthetics, and those with hunchbacks, fat bellies or shady sexual pasts have the right to enter heaven. Strepponi absorbed this view of human nature, and her attitude to Verdi had something inimitably Verdian in it. This is why her fondest expressions of love took the form of raillery, as when she described Verdi as a bear growling in its cavern or as an 'ugly, unworthy monster' – a relative of Rigoletto, equally determined to conceal his vulnerability and therefore equally misunderstood.

In 1880 Verdi received a decoration from King Victor Emanuele and the award of honorary citizenship from the mayor in Milan. Left behind in Genoa, Strepponi sent congratulations to him in one of her wittiest, sweetest letters. Almost dismissively, she acknowledged his genius, and derided the official world that had taken so long to recognize it; she also sniffed at the vanity of honours, and exempted herself from joining the chorus of acclaim because she didn't enjoy removing her sandals to tiptoe into the temple and fall to the floor in contemplation of the Highest One. She then chided herself for not shouting hosanna – another of her crimes 'against God and His creatures' – and resolved, in a beautiful image, to 'let the staircase of ovations stretch right up to heaven, so long as you take me with you'. Her ovation avoided the noisy clamour of an operatic audience baying for encores: being 'deeply moved', she spoke 'in a quiet voice'. After this she dispelled any annoyance Verdi might feel when reading such fulsome sentiments by making a joke: she assured him that she would still love and revere him when all his recently converted fans had forgotten his name and were using their breath to blow their noses. Her humour contains an extraordinary wisdom, which enables her to conclude with a reminder that praise is mere puffery. After this, the letter ends by saluting, kissing and embracing Verdi. The endearments are in triplicate because, she says, she is maddened by an amative fever that no doctor has ever diagnosed. Is it possible to imagine an elderly Tristan and Isolde cohabiting with such perfect mutual understanding, and with a combination of adoration and mockery that needs no help from chemicals?

|||||||||||||||||||

Strepponi, after quitting the stage, did not feel that she had subsided into domestic ignominy. Organizing supplies of Italian food and French wine to sustain herself and Verdi during their stay in St Petersburg, she insisted that she had risen 'from the position of singer to that of housewife'; it was an ascent because, thanks to Verdi, she had become respectable. Before they met in 1839 she destroyed all mementoes of her professional life. The aim was not concealment but purgation: she had no interest in the kind of duplicity practised by Cosima, who bore the first of Wagner's children, Isolde, in April 1865 while still living with Bülow and passed the baby off as her husband's. Strepponi played her new domestic role conscientiously, and in 1867, looking back with satisfaction on the five apartments and houses she had furnished for Verdi in Paris, Busseto and Genoa, she said that her only aim was to make his life 'comfortable, agreeable and peaceful'. This, however, makes her sound a little too much like a Victorian angel in the house, recoiling into timorous privacy while her man strides off to deal with the arduous workaday world. It was Cosima who played that cloistered role, which sometimes rankled with her. 'R. writes to the King, I sort out my linen,' she noted in her diary in 1875. A decade earlier, Wagner had moved from Eliza Wille's estate at Mariafeld near Zurich to the villa provided for him by Ludwig II at the Starnbergsee near Munich. Temporarily without a female helpmate, he complained of having to fuss over 'knives and forks, pots and pans, bed-linen and so on. I, the glorifier of women! How kind of them to leave me to deal with their chores.' As her reward for taking charge of such matters, Cosima was assigned her own heroic 'fight with the dragon', as Wagner put it – though it hardly matched Siegfried's feat. Her battle was fought with the household accounts, in a failed attempt to restrict his spending.

When Verdi was irascible, Strepponi felt like his blameless victim, but she was also aware of her own power and – a little like Desdemona nagging Otello to reinstate Cassio – did not scruple to use it. Wagner blessed Cosima as the enabler of everything he achieved, but it was Strepponi's advocacy that helped to start and subsequently restart Verdi's career. In 1830 she convinced the impresario Bartolomeo Merelli, whose mistress she then was, to stage *Oberto* at La Scala, although because of a contractual tiff she did not sing in it. Three years later, after the failure of *Un giorno di regno*, she accepted the part of the blasphemous harridan Abigaille in *Nabucco* and persuaded the baritone Giorgio Ronconi to withdraw from another commitment to take the title role. She sang Abigaille again in Parma in 1843, even though the role's declamatory hectoring tore her already damaged voice to shreds. Having been partly responsible for the beginning of Verdi's career, she also wanted to preside over its end. Hence her doubts about Boito's intrusion on his retirement. The homes she made for her husband were meant to be his reward, and she regretted that he did not allow himself to enjoy them.

His sullen self-containment also frustrated her: he kept his emotions for his music, just as she prudently saved up her most lavish protestations of love and sent them by letter, which spared her (she suspected) from having to see him grimace in disgust. Strepponi sometimes wanted to warm Verdi up. Cosima, by contrast, increasingly saw it as her 'sacred task' to cool Wagner down, to calm his medically inadvisable tantrums. Strepponi allowed herself to complain, whereas Cosima's relationship with Wagner – once they got beyond the secret liaison that hoodwinked Bülow and scandalized Ludwig II – involved a slavish self-abnegation. Music was Cosima's penance, as she said in 1870 when a piano reduction of a Beethoven symphony played by Hans Richter sent her to bed sobbing about her treatment of Bülow. Later that year she punished herself for still having a mind of her own, and grovelled after committing 'the blackest of sins'. Her crime was to disagree with Wagner about the proper tempo for another Beethoven symphony. Not having unlearned the habits of the Catholicism she gave up to live with him, she used her diary as a confessional box, apologizing to her children, its predestined readers, for wickedly contradicting their father.

Like Strepponi when Verdi married her, Cosima became a new woman thanks to Wagner, although she thought of the change more as a reincarnation than a renovation. In 1870 she called their union a palingenesis, a transmigration of the soul that delivered her 'from a previous erring existence'. Leaving Bülow involved sacrifice, the abandonment of 'religion and all else besides', but she insisted on thinking of adultery as a spiritual rebirth that brought her 'nearer to perfection'. Rehoused in another existence, she settled into a routine that was cosmological rather than domestic. Wagner told her that she was the earth and he was the sun around which she revolved. He agreed, he said, with the oriental equation between woman and the ground we tread on: Cosima should think of herself as the ploughed field in which seed would from time to time be sown. At least the sun, at this stage in their partnership, had a fructifying influence. By the last year of Wagner's life that sun had turned into a remoter, colder planet, and Cosima was no longer the maternal soil but merely an invertebrate creature peeping out of it. This was how she responded in March 1882 when Wagner played her a melody he was tinkering with: she hardly dared to say that the music recorded the state of her soul, though she hoped that 'the yearning gaze of a worm' bore 'some relationship to the shining blessings of a star'. On another occasion she joined Wagner in repudiating 'up-to-date rubbish' about the emancipation of woman, who should, he declared, have 'nothing to do with the outside world'. Cherishing her reclusion, Cosima lamented his decision to raise money by giving concerts of the *Siegfried Idyll*, her own private possession that belonged, she believed, in the closeted sanctity of her home. 'Great sorrow on my part to see it performed in front of so many strangers,' she noted in Basle in 1871. Later she was so distressed by the report of a performance of the piece in Mainz that she retired to her room to weep, bemoaning the fact that 'what I cherish must be yielded up as too sublime for me' and concluding that she had no right to be happy.

When she and Wagner were photographed in Vienna in 1872, she sat while he stood beside her, holding her hand as she gazed up at him with a look of adoring compliance. His free hand gripped the back of her chair to signal ownership; her free hand, open and useless if not required by him, lolled on her lap. The pose diplomatically disguised the difference in height between them, but Cosima was unhappy about it. Her 'rightful position' in front of the camera, she said, should have been on her knees before him. She might have profited from the example of Strepponi, who warned Verdi in her 1880 letter that she disliked prostrating herself; so did Verdi, who said when he finally met Manzoni that he 'would have knelt before him if it was permissible to worship men'. The remark was not pious but staunchly democratic: men cannot worship other men because they are equals. Wagner set the terms for Cosima's dealings with him, and made his creativity depend on her obsequious service. When she praised a section of *Parsifal* that he played to her, he replied 'Yes, one must be good to me, then everything is all right.' Although she did not quarrel with this definition of her function, she fretted about her adequacy. 'Am I worthy of being good to you?' she asked: a covert request for praise or a plea for further exactions? Avid for pain, she indirectly ordered Wagner to hurt her; it reminded him that he could not do without her, and with luck it would make him feel guilty about their mutual dependence.

Married couples usually establish separate, complementary areas of existence and expertise, as Strepponi and Verdi did. She grew flowers in her portion of the garden, while he planted trees and cultivated his vegetables. She had a pet peacock, he dealt with the less decorative livestock. Indoors she looked after the furnishings, but it was he who ordered the iron grilles for the windows at Sant'Agata, and in their Genoa apartment he served as carpenter and locksmith. Such odd jobs were not so different from his creative labours. Boito appealed to his craftsmanship when he likened the task of revising *Simon Boccanegra* to repairing a table with a wobbly leg; Verdi agreed, and in steadying the rickety structure hoped he would also be able to 'straighten … the many crooked legs of my notes'. Wagner by contrast admitted in the *Mitteilung* that the legends he cobbled together in *Der fliegende Holländer* did not quite fit, and said that 'the joinery of the situations is … imperfect'. The phrase was a boast in disguise: unlike Verdi, he had no desire to be a domestic handyman. Love of the Wagnerian kind involves an interpenetration of bodies and minds, not a division of labour. Tristan and Isolde announce during their love duet that they have become each other: he is Isolde, she is Tristan. Brünnhilde tells Siegfried that she is his soul, which means that he is both Siegfried and Brünnhilde. Assuming that she had been absorbed into Wagner, Cosima behaved as if they shared sensations as well as thoughts, and sometimes transferred his miseries to her body. In the Tuscan heat in 1880 his skin reddened and chafed and his nerves tormented him. She longed to suffer in his place, like a baroque martyr begging for the stigmata: 'I beseech the heavens, ecstatically accept a night of violent toothache, and pray, pray, pray that he be allowed to rest.'

Despite the inequality between herself and Wagner, Cosima was convinced that they were almost androgynously merged. One night during the same Italian summer she felt 'my whole being immersed in his, in the richly consoling sea of his thoughts, and both of us silently lost in the still, mild glory'. What she described was a double drowning. She may have subscribed to the theory more whole-heartedly than Wagner, who knew that sexual tastes are conditioned by culture as well as by our personal quirks. In 1870 he discussed with her the subject of Greek love, 'which we cannot ourselves envisage': could he – after his pederastic play-acting with Ludwig II – really not have envisaged the homoerotic reading of his work by admirers like Aubrey Beardsley, whose Tannhäuser in the pornographic romance *Under the Hill* tires of Venus and prefers to frolic with his catamites? In 1904 in his misogynistic tract *Geschlecht und Charakter*, Otto Weininger noted that Wagner, Ludwig II and Liszt were accused of unwholesomely close friendships, then went on to call *Parsifal* 'the greatest work in the world's literature' because it exposed the horror of coitus and exhorted men to destroy the women who were so greedy for their seed. Wagner conceded that in Greece the love between men produced 'the highest qualities of aestheticism', then asserted that 'the adoration of women' was a new belief, 'which divides us entirely from the antique world'. He attributed the novelty to his primitive German forebears, who identified women with nature 'rather in the way the Egyptians worshipped animals' and declared them to be untouchable. Wagner had a menagerie of pets – among them a succession of dogs, a hare, pigeons and a raucous trumpeting peacock, along with a horse called Grane like Brünnhilde's mount – which he saw as transmogrified gods; all the same, his theory does women no favours, and his lecture on the history of sexuality soon turned into a rant about modern females who wore fetchingly impractical bibi hats and twined their hair into chignons that exposed the nape of the neck and made them only too touchable.

Wagner doted on his generic woman, although that infatuation was self-love by other means. He admitted in the *Mitteilung* that he developed as an artist 'along the path which we must designate the feminine' and came to conceive of Siegfried – 'the male-embodied spirit … of the doer of truer deeds, of manhood in the utmost fullness of its inborn strength' – by imitating the girlish daydream of Elsa in *Lohengrin*. His ideal female remained faceless, a principle not a person, 'hovering before my vision as the element of Womanhood in its widest sense'. Every woman, because she possessed a particle of that gynocratic mystique, had a claim on his attention. A man can spend a long weekend with Venus, then go home – though not for long – to Elisabeth. In a legalistic quibble before she lights the pyre, Brünnhilde says she is Siegfried's true wife and dismisses Gutrune as his temporary paramour. Although she slights the pretender, she does not dispute her husband's right to have both 'Eheweib' and 'Buhlerin', consort and mistress. Multiplicity is irresistible. A myth, as Wagner understood, is the sum total of every version or variant that tellers – himself included – make up when relaying it; an archetypal hero has a thousand faces, and so does an archetypal heroine. Why else does Don Giovanni need to keep a catalogue of his conquests? Wagner revered *Don Giovanni*, although he bizarrely argued that Mozart composed it in the persona of 'an unconditionally loving woman', a feminized musician who pined for union with a male poet; he also enjoyed Byron's more casually pro-miscuous *Don Juan*, even if when he read it with Cosima they dismissed Juan's sojourn in the harem as material for a scurrilous comic opera. Despite his affected disapproval, Wagner consciously followed the example of those universalizing rakes. Cosima's love for him was exclusive, yet he loved not only Cosima but also Minna, Jessie, Mathilde, Judith – and perhaps even Carrie Pringle, the flower maiden from *Parsifal* with whom he was supposedly flirting in the months before his death. Each love was different, which is why he had to sample them all. The statement about 'Womanhood in its widest sense' is a libertine's manifesto.

He treated the young actress Minna with callous bravado, and in 1835 told his crony Theodor Apel with a smirk that she was 'so completely free with her favours with me, almost to the point of excess, so that I feel increasingly strong & well'. Cockily confident, he wondered whether he should test his power by deceiving her: 'Would that not be a masterpiece of behaviour on my part?' This could be Don Giovanni reflecting on Donna Elvira's flattering but ultimately tiresome obsession with him. As a virile epicurean, Wagner was enthusiastic about Minna's career: 'one can only live like that with an actress; – this disregard for middle-class values is something you can find only when the whole basis is one of imaginative freedom & poetic licence'. The retired Strepponi looked back on such looseness with discomfort, but for Wagner it was an advantage, a pleasing by-product of art. Minna had been seduced by a guardsman at the age of fifteen and left with a daughter whom she passed off as her younger sister; performers were professional dissemblers, not constrained by the moral codes of polite society. They were also, like Wagner himself, experts at simulating emotion, and when

Minna departed for an engagement at a theatre in Berlin he let the punctuation of a love-famished letter he wrote to her speak for him: 'A large beautiful city, ---- oh – I can't go on! – '. In fact Minna got her own back by deceiving Wagner, and before his appointment in Riga, soon after their wedding in 1836, she ran off with a merchant. She made the mistake of returning to Wagner four months later, and decades of misery followed, with squabbles when they were together and jealous rages at a distance after he deserted her. Planning to escape to Greece and the Orient in 1850 with Jessie Laussot, he disposed of Minna easily enough: 'I expressed a wish that she might remain in Zurich, draw a small garden plot, look after our dog and bird and, as far as possible, live a life of hope.' The bird was a parrot that specialized in croaking 'Richard Wagner, you are a great man', so it would have made a handsome memento of him. In 1859 he took a coldly malicious revenge on Minna in a letter written from Paris to their doctor in Dresden. Her mental problems, he confided, derived from his 'having ceased to have sexual intercourse with her'; he withdrew conjugal privileges, he claimed, because of her poor health. He asked the doctor to enforce a medical 'Liebesverbot', imposing 'a ban whereby she must consider not only herself but me as well'. The prohibition cost him little personal anguish. Strepponi was more calmly resigned and Verdi more taciturn when coping with such matters. Their relationship fairly soon ceased to be sexual and grew more stable and settled as a result, although she sometimes ruefully referred to the way things were in 'the active part of our lives'. In 1874, tormented by his indiscreet visits to Stolz, she made a long-suffering allusion to the drought, telling him 'I have the right at least to your respect, if not to ask for your caresses'.

In our society music functions as a sexual aid, so the popular assumption is that composers must be enviably proficient lovers. In 1925 a biography of Wagner's 'vie amoureuse' was published in a perfumed French series called *Leurs Amours*, and in 1955 in a film called *Magic Fire*, based on Bertita Harding's biographical novel, the Wagner of Alan Badel romanced a lush succession of Hollywood sirens – Yvonne De Carlo as Minna, Valentina Cortese as Mathilde, Rita Gam as Cosima. The film's publicity campaign forgot that the magic fire surrounding Brünnhilde is a chaste cordon meant to debar potential suitors, and made the blaze more ardent than Wotan intended. 'His Passion For Beauty Set A World Aflame!' its poster proclaimed. Luckily Wagner himself did not have to live up to this priapic reputation, and he was startled as well as gratified by the way his music pandered for him. After being sent an allowance in 1849 by Jessie Laussot and Julie Ritter, the widow of another merchant, he told Uhlig that his art had 'always found favour with women's hearts' because 'women are the very music of life'; he assumed that they admired his work rather than coveting his body. Libertines usually pursue sex because they feel unworthy of love, and the young Wagner bragged about Minna because his success was astonishing proof of his capacity to excite desire. 'I have fired her to the very marrow of her being,' he told Apel, adding that 'she loves me to the point of sickness; I have become her tyrant'. He nowhere mentioned any reciprocal feelings. At the end of his life he made a more honest self-assessment. He first told Cosima that 'love has never been offered to me directly'. Then a few months later he compared her with Minna and complained, she wrote, that 'Nature had never given him anything completely his own, he had always taken things over from someone else'. Although the self-pity is distasteful, as is the unchivalrous slight to both wives, the remarks cut deep, edging Wagner closer to the unlovable Alberich who is rejected by the Rhinemaidens and has to buy sex from the woman who gives birth to Hagen. Wagner calculated that married women would be easier to win because he could capitalize on their current unhappiness or boredom, and someone like Minna – already used and discarded by the officer who impregnated her – could be relied on not to be choosy.

Verdi's love life was less busy, certainly more reticent. There must have been a showdown with Strepponi about Stolz, who – as the biographer Mary-Jane Phillips-Matz points out – retreated to a prudent distance during 1876. But there were no reprisals and no permanent breach. Strepponi renegotiated the triangular relationship with the kind of finesse exhibited by characters in the novels of Henry James, and henceforth Stolz mostly wrote joint letters to Verdi and his wife, rather than to him alone. At her most distraught, Strepponi had vowed to Verdi that she was prepared 'to love [Stolz] frankly and honestly', and she now made good on this pledge. She and Stolz sent one another presents and even shared clothes, making light of the way that Verdi had previously treated them as interchangeable. In her will Strepponi left some jewelry to Stolz, whose friendship helped Verdi through his bereavement.

Verdi withdrew into himself and waited for the crisis to abate, like the tenors in his operas who leave pairs of female rivals to fight it out. In *Oberto* Riccardo seduces Leonora, then abandons her to make a more politically advantageous match with Cuniza. Leonora wants revenge, but Cuniza decides that sisterly amity should come before passion; when Riccardo flees, the women make common cause. In *Il corsaro* Corrado vacillates between two very different muses, fortunately situated at different ends of the Mediterranean. On his Aegean island he has Medora, who in her aria 'Non so le tetre immagini' sings to her harp as she patiently awaits his homecoming. She is herself as passive as an Aeolian harp, animated by Corrado's love and causelessly doomed to die when she believes she has lost him. Further east in a Turkish harem he captivates Gulnara, who is not self-sacrificing but murderous and kills Pasha Selim to help her new lover escape from prison. Corrado has to choose between archetypes: the weeping woman whose fate it is to be played on like an instrument and then set aside, or the infuriated woman who takes charge of her fate with the dagger as her instrument. Byron's roaming Don Juan would simply sail from one to the other; Conrad in Byron's *The Corsair* is relieved of the pair of them because both die, which frees him to wander off alone on the homeless, mercifully undomestic sea. Corrado seems to want neither woman. He abandons Medora, but he also quarrels with Gulnara's plan to free him, and says it would be dishonourable to kill Selim while he sleeps. Corrado's reluctance forces Gulnara to do it – and for a moment she sounds as scathingly indignant as Lady Macbeth, wondering how a pirate acquired such scruples. He returns with her to his island, where Medora, convinced that she will never see him again, has taken poison. She survives only long enough for a final trio, in which there are no recriminations. The Muslim Gulnara asks Medora to intercede for her in the Christian heaven, but she is denied the chance to enjoy Corrado, who guiltily jumps into the sea. Verdi's men are seldom erotically reckless or impetuous, like Walther in *Die Meistersinger* when he plans to elope with Eva, or Siegfried when he overcomes his fear and kisses Brünnhilde awake. Don Carlos backs off in dismay when Eboli offers herself to him. He is in love with his stepmother, and Eboli is only his father's mistress, which is not quite the same thing. Eboli saves Carlos during the uprising in the prison, but not for herself. Neither woman gets him: he readies himself to go off to war in Flanders, though he actually takes refuge in the monastery. Radamès is equally passive, allowing Aida and Amneris to argue over him. Bold under cover of darkness, he agrees to flee with Aida, but when surprised by Amneris he thinks only of his blemished reputation. The priests give him the chance to defend himself but he remains silent, leaving Amneris to denounce theocracy on his behalf. The opera begins with an aria in which Radamès fantasizes about victory; it ends with a prayer for peace muttered by Amneris – a plea for respite from drama, which is lashed into motion by our vainglorious dreams and our self-wasting feuds with others.

In 1933 the German critic Paul Bekker boldly claimed that Verdi's operas have little interest in sexual love, which is Wagner's obsessive subject. Verdi, 'thoroughly masculine' according to Bekker, had a particular affinity with his baritones, who tend to play fathers not lovers. His sopranos are most affecting when cast as daughters – or ersatz daughters like Violetta, who asks Germont to embrace her paternally – and his tenors, for good or ill, are frequently under the thumb of baritones, like Carlos schooled by Posa, Otello led astray by Iago, and Alfredo bullied by Germont. The female counterweight to the authoritative baritone is the mezzo-soprano, who gives voice to 'life's darker forces'. The complementarity is a little like Wagner's notion of himself as the sun and Cosima as the earth, although fertilization is not Verdi's aim. Bekker's examples of the elemental Verdian woman include the infanticidal Azucena in *Il trovatore* and Ulrica in *Un ballo in maschera*; he might have added the rabble-rousing Preziosilla in *La forza del destino*. Lady Macbeth belongs in this psychological company, as do termagants like Abigaille in *Nabucco* and Attila's nemesis Odabella, though they sing in a different register. Eboli and Amneris, whom Bekker does name, contradict his typology because they are women in love, not Amazonian warriors or Italianate Erdas.

The scheme is approximate, but it corresponds to Verdi's own emotional compass. His uprightness and inflexibility were baritonal, as was his angry growling; he had little of the high-strung emotionalism we expect of tenors. Who would be the right female partner for such a man? Not Abigaille, the role that excited Strepponi's enthusiasm, and not any of the earth mothers or man-eating goddesses listed by Bekker. Surely not Violetta, although sentimental readings of Verdi's life often present *La traviata* as his defence of the fallen woman he raised up. Strepponi was never a whirligig hedonist like Violetta the party-giver, and she lacked the penitent Violetta's zeal for martyrdom. As her letters reveal, Strepponi possessed an array of precious qualities not shared by any of Verdi's heroines: she was witty, playful, insubordinate yet deeply loyal, on occasion – as in her comments about inheritance – almost brutally pragmatic, and she adjusted herself to her husband's taciturnity by keeping her own deepest feelings in reserve, to be expressed only in an emergency. If she were put into an opera, it would have to be a comedy, composed by Mozart or Rossini not by Verdi. She offered him an antidote to the fury of his music, which may have been why he loved her.

Wagner told Cosima 'You are Elisabeth, Elsa, Isolde, Brünnhilde, Eva in one', as if any human being could simultaneously be a Madonna and a mystic, a wild Irish sorceress and a winged deity, with the role of a merchant's daughter thrown in for good measure. He was forever casting her in one or another of these roles: one day in the summer of 1870, when she returned from Lucerne to Triebschen by boat, Wagner greeted Cosima from the shore singing the tune that the shepherd pipes to announce Isolde's arrival at Tristan's deathbed. Both challenged and diminished by his music, she felt that his expectations would, as she said, be 'the death of me'. Cosima exerted herself to live up to the daunting emotional standards set by opera; Strepponi tried equally hard to live them down.

## At Home

In 1887 during his winter sojourn at the Palazzo Doria in Genoa, Verdi received a visit from the critic Étienne Destranges. Boito had to act as an intermediary, since Destranges was a proselytizer for Wagner and his French acolytes, especially Vincent d'Indy (who as a special favour had been permitted to tiptoe into Wahnfried and peep through the study doors at the preoccupied Meister). None of Verdi's operas before *Aida* impressed Destranges, many of them positively annoyed him, and he thought that they all had justly been forgotten; later, in 1895, he was to declare that only the last three deserved to survive because they showed that Verdi had humbly restudied his art at the feet of 'the Bayreuth Titan'. Ushered into the drawing room of the Palazzo Doria, Destranges found Verdi to be 'unsophisticated', which meant that he was taken in by the old man's claim to be a simple rural fellow, now wearily superannuated. When Destranges wrote up the interview, it concluded with a fateful question: what did Verdi think of Wagner? 'Ah, him!' Verdi replied, and sagaciously said no more. His tone was respectful enough to placate Destranges, who merely wanted to have his prejudice confirmed.

Destranges' partiality even conditioned his view of Verdi's decor. In a city, in a home fit for a prince or a magnate, Verdi abandoned the bucolic persona he assumed at Sant'Agata, where he kept an eye on sales of wheat or wine and relaxed by sitting on a rock beside his lake pensively angling for carp. Destranges, however, sniffed at the framed prints on display in the antechamber, 'of the type that English newspapers give away for free'. While waiting for Verdi to appear, he snobbishly appraised the gilt chairs, the bronze ornaments, and 'a couch with a cushion, tapestried in garish colours and representing a pheasant'.

It was fortunate that he did not get a glimpse of Verdi's 'Sala turca', furnished in Byzantine style and bedecked with oriental hangings and a painting of a lolling odalisque, along with trinkets from Turkey and Egypt. But the couch and its cushion were enough for Destranges. The room, he said, had 'an atmosphere of profound bourgeois luxury', which he placed at the opposite extreme to 'the majestic severity of Wahnfried'.

He was judging Wagner's house from its blank facade: 'built from the inside', as Cosima said, it deliberately snubbed the street. Wahnfried was consciously majestic, with Wotan on a sgraffito above the entrance and a bust of Ludwig II in the front garden – but did Destranges know that Wagner had toyed with what Cosima called 'Arabian-style construction plans' for a forecourt, dreaming about a glazed conservatory and a grove of transplanted palms that would have swallowed up his benefactor's bust? Destranges' comparison between the two residences implied that Verdi lived like a retired banker, whereas Wagner occupied the austere laboratory of a true creator. In fact it was Wagner who obeyed the bourgeois rule by separating work from home, public from private life. Across the river on a hill above the railway line, his Bayreuth theatre was a gaunt utilitarian box of brick, occasionally likened to a brewery; his home might have been a merchant's refuge in the suburbs, named for its plush, swaddling comfort – here he sought peace ('Fried') from the madness ('Wahn') of his professional domain.

Walter Benjamin described the house of the typical bourgeois as 'a box at the theatre of the world', a cubicle in which the householder could be the detached spectator of society's mayhem. Wahnfried was Wagner's personal equivalent to the row of boxes he placed at the rear of his theatre for royal visitors and other notables who expected special treatment. George Bernard Shaw approvingly noted that the Festspielhaus had 'no draperies, no cushions, no showy colours'; at home Wagner made up for this lack of florid upholstery and for the bland palette of the auditorium, described by Shaw as 'a light dun, as of cream colour a little the worse for smoke'. Snakes writhed and tangled in a frieze around Wahnfried's hall, and the drawing room was a jungle of greenery, with peacock feathers in vases and a gutted polar bear sprawled on the floor. Bluebirds plummeted from the sky on the peppermint-green wallpaper, and a chandelier reached halfway to the floor, like a crystal tree growing upside down from the embossed ceiling. Upstairs Cosima had her own sanctum in a lilac salon. In Genoa Verdi occupied only a slice of a subdivided palace, but Wagner built himself a palace in miniature, decorating the walls of the vestibule with paintings of the Nibelungen saga copied from the originals in Ludwig II's Residenz in Munich. The verandah of Verdi's drawing room in the Palazzo Doria overlooked a private park with a baroque fountain, then surveyed the harbour: it was this vista that he commended to the scene painters for his revised *Simon Boccanegra*. He had the backdrop for an opera outside his windows; Wagner, however, lived inside the set. The tall, viewless vestibule imitated the lobby of the Wesendonck villa in Zurich, where concerts were often performed. A gallery protruded beneath the skylight, but there was no visible means of reaching it: a staircase hidden inside the walls separated the stage from the family's private space on the upper floor, as if limiting access to the wings or the dressing rooms of the actors.

Although he enjoyed his view in Genoa, Verdi also took an ironic pride in the flat, dank terrain of the countryside around Sant'Agata, boasting that it was 'impossible to find an uglier place than this'. Strepponi, grimly jocular, called it 'the Athens of Italy'. They referred to their ample, comfortable villa as a hut, a hovel, a shanty, and when improvements were carried out Verdi pretended that there were no architectural plans because it would have been absurd 'to build anything artistic in so unpoetic a spot'. It was the frippery of art and poetry that he slighted, not his home: a house is a functional shelter like a bear's cave, with lambrequins as an optional extra. The entrance to Wahnfried may have been an informal concert hall, but at Sant'Agata music was superfluous, and when the critic Filippo Filippi proposed a visit Verdi warned that he risked 'finding a piano not only out of tune but without any strings'. Even after the house was remodelled, he still thought of it as 'four walls in which to take shelter from the sun and inclement weather, amid the vastness of the fields'. An Italian assumes that life should be lived in the open, on the communal stage of the piazza; only when it is too cold, hot or wet do you need to skulk indoors. But a German house needs to be a fortress, insulated against the harsh winter. Wagner preferred refuges like the Venusberg that Ludwig II installed in a pavilion outside his rococo palace at Linderhof: you walk through the gardens, open a door, and are suddenly in an artificial cavern with walls of decoratively crinkled plaster, a shallow lake on which scallop-shell boats bob, and a mural that rosily depicts the revelry of the nymphs who attend on the goddess of love.

Verdi built a chapel at Sant'Agata to spare Strepponi a lengthy journey to attend Mass. Personally, he had no use for it. In Milan or Genoa he drove her to church, then left her alone to commune with the God she believed in, just as Wagner told Cosima – almost as if accusing her of infidelity – to give her saviour his greetings. The chapel was a functional section of the house, like the library or the kitchen, the stables or the cantina where the wine was stored; Wahnfried needed no devotional annex, since the whole house was a temple. After deciding on its name Wagner said he had christened it, and individual rooms were readied for use with pseudo-religious rituals. In 1874 the dining room was 'consecrated', as Cosima said, though not with a dinner: a conference about the inaugural festival was held there. Beethoven had composed an overture for the consecration of a house, *Die Weihe des Hauses*, although the house in question was the new Josefstadt Theater in Vienna, and Wagner later defined *Parsifal* as the work that would ceremonially confer holiness on the stage of his Bayreuth theatre. It was a different matter to lavish such honours on a domestic space, or to baptize a family dwelling: the ceremonies announced that Wagner was presiding over his own cult.

This atmosphere of aesthetic holiness transformed life at Wahnfried into a sacrilegious charade. At Christmas in 1880 the Russian painter Paul von Joukowsky arranged the younger Wagners into a Nativity scene, which he later painted; his group portrait hung high on the wall of the music room, as if the figures it depicted were hovering just below the ceiling. Joukowsky cast himself as Joseph, with Daniela, Cosima's oldest daughter, as the haloed Mary, her hands clasped in prayer. Her sisters Eva, Isolde and Blandine were concertizing angels. The infant Jesus was the young Siegfried, as soft and dainty as his sisters, with ringleted hair and fluttery eyelashes. He is seen using Joseph's carpentry tools to plane a cross, well in advance of need. Perhaps Joukowsky was attempting to portray the inner child of the elder Wagner: spending time with him 'in the intimacy of his home' convinced Joukowsky of his host's 'childlike goodness', and he agreed with Cosima when she said that she thought of Richard as 'the child with the orb whom St Christopher carries across the stream'. The orb, in Cosima's reading, was the imaginary universe he bore within him; the house that contained this family was to be a cosmic womb.

The sgraffito incised above the front door by Robert Krausse completed the ordination. Directed by Cosima, Krausse personified the constituent parts of Wagner's artwork of the future. The three-cornered tableau showed off a new and heterodox version of the Trinity. At the apex, Teutonic myth is represented by Schnorr von Carolsfeld, with Wotan's ravens hovering behind his slouch-hatted head. He raises one hand in a gesture traditionally used by John the Baptist when summoning converts, but the other grips a spear, which establishes his hostility to Christianity. Placed slightly below him on either side is a pair of muses, like a bigamist's wives. The role of Tragedy, holding a classical mask, is played by Wilhelmine Schröder-Devrient, the singing actress whose performances excited the adolescent Wagner. Music, cradling a lyre, is Cosima. Wotan may have unseated Jehovah, but he still needs the Virgin Mary in duplicate to bear the myth's artistic offshoot. On behalf of both women, Cosima shows off the first fruits of this marriage of arts and epochs – young Fidi, dressed for play in a Grecian kilt and a winged Germanic helmet, with a blunt, stunted sword over his shoulder. The sgraffito made the inhabitants of Wahnfried accountable to a destiny that few human beings would feel capable of fulfilling, and Siegfried inevitably shrank from his role in this genealogical saga. Forced to wear his operatic namesake's bearskins for a photograph taken after the first *Ring* in 1876, he limply holds up a horn he has no intention of blowing; despite possessing his mother's aquiline nose and his father's pugilistic chin, he looks wan and wistful. To the dismay of his parents, he enjoyed rearranging his elder sisters' hair, and Wagner on one occasion destroyed his toy theatre, worried by his dreamy effeminacy. He expected Siegfried, his appointed swordsman, to possess a 'world-conquering quality', although he once told the boy – jokingly as Cosima insisted, though the remark was later inked over in her diary – that he looked like an amiable cretin.

The mystique cultivated by Joukowsky's painting could easily be twisted into parody. Karl Marx pointed out in 1876 that Wagner's family was far from holy: in a letter to his friend Jenny Longuet, Marx chuckled over Cosima's marital history and remembered that she was the illegitimate daughter of a notorious reprobate, now a Catholic abbé. These entangled affairs, Marx said, would have made an excellent subject for an operetta by Wagner's detractor Offenbach, who was more at home with the loose-living Olympians than with the thundery Germanic gods. Caricaturists were quick to expose the self-mythologizing imposture of Wagner's house. In 1879 Constantin Grimm drew him as Siegfried, who has just slain a dragon that deputizes for his jeering critics. Like a hunter on safari, he props his foot on the beast's scaly back, and affects not to notice the money bags of treasure – profits from performances of the *Ring* – that now belong to him. Behind Grimm's Wagner, Wahnfried has a new set of tutelary deities. The pillars that support it are Hans von Wolzogen and Heinrich Porges, apostles or evangelists who explicated the operas by tabulating motifs and policed approved interpretations. The house is held up by sycophantic hot air, and a notice attached to the front door clarifies the conditions of entry to this unecumenical temple: Jews, it announces, are unwelcome.

|||||||||||||||||||

Planning the layout of space at Wahnfried, Wagner placed an embargo on views. As Cosima recorded, he insisted that from his workroom he 'must not be able to see the garden paths, which lead outward – that is too definite, it disturbs concentration'. At Triebschen he permitted the mountains to obtrude outside the window, but they were further off, therefore less of a temptation; they also counted as his own creation, since Judith Gautier on her first visit in 1869 identified the pastoral slopes of Rigi as Monsalvat and said that Pilatus, with its stark cliffs and cloudy peak, must be Valhalla. Wahnfried, however, was to be an introverted house, where Wagner could disappear into his dreams. This made it the opposite of the villa at Sant'Agata, which communicated with the world instead of debarring it. Before his return home in 1878 Verdi sent instructions to his housekeeper to 'open the windows just before we get here, so that we can see things easily'. He turned windows into doors, and treated the paths that led outwards as extensions of the corridors inside the house. His bedroom and Strepponi's opened directly onto the garden; they unconventionally chose to live at ground level, not on the so-called *piano nobile* upstairs, which was occupied by guests and servants. Steps leading up to the front door of Wahnfried raised it as if on a stage. At the rear another set of steps led down from the music room, allowing Wagner, his family and their dogs to pose for photographs in graduated ranks. Needing no elevation and no bare, defensive facades, Verdi and Strepponi lived more casually: they were often photographed lazing with visitors on garden chairs just inside the gate of the property, a few feet from the road.

A fence divided Verdi's ornamental garden from his fields, but a gate opened onto an avenue of plane trees down which he strolled when inspecting the crops. Wagner's terrain was more strictly and repressively delimited. Wahnfried backed onto a royal park, laid out by the Markgravine Wilhelmine, Frederick the Great's sister, and although Wagner disapproved of garden paths he wanted to be able to take his exercise there in the afternoon when his work was done. Courtly bureaucrats first disputed his rights, at last grudgingly gave permission, then procrastinated about fitting a gate behind Wahnfried. Verdi could 'play the czar in that garden of his' as Strepponi said, and he even imitated the God of Genesis who shaped the inchoate earth and divided water from dry land when he constructed an island in his artificial lake: in 1865 she reported that he had 'made the necessary arrangements' for the little outcrop of soil and rock to protrude above the surface, as if he were a deity who preferred not to get his hands dirty. Wagner enjoyed no such liberty. As a result, his walks in the Hofgarten were acts of defiance, strategically planned so that he could magnify the cramped area and convince himself that it was a personal fiefdom. On one occasion in November 1878 he and Cosima walked 'for an hour without going twice along the same path'. The palace gardens were a theatre of power – a symbol of autocracy because of their exclusiveness, and an experimental battlefield where manoeuvres could (in musical parlance) be conducted or rehearsed while military bands played. In 1880 Wagner issued orders of his own as he passed the parade ground. 'Arm yourselves with cannons,' he said, 'so that the French shall on no account occupy Bayreuth!' Avoiding such martial flourishes, Verdi took a mock-heroic view of his domain. It was an excerpt from the featureless plain that he fondly called 'my desert', and it owed its quaint topography – the meandering paths and the groves of magnolias, the summits of piled-up earth and the subterranean grotto with its tunnels of smoothed boulders – to his scenic imagination. His lake started as 'a muddy puddle' before earning what he admitted was its 'pompous title'. In 1869 it underwent a demotion when he and Strepponi almost drowned after the boat in which they were rowing overturned; in her account of the misadventure, she reduced it to 'the infamous dirty pool'.

Like Franz Werfel finding in Verdi a combination of Garibaldi the enthusiast and Cavour the organizer, the librettist Antonio Ghislanzoni saw the garden and the fields beyond it as a map of the proprietor's dualistic nature. The lachrymose willows at the front gate and the 'tortuous and melancholy' lake vouched for Verdi's moody creativity; the lands outside the fence, a model of 'agricultural science' as practised in England and France, testified to the practicality and discipline with which he prosecuted his career. As evidence of Verdi's romanticism, in the garden there is a sculpted hump of earth with a thicket of shrubs growing on top of it – not, as it happens, another contrived lookout, since a path leads down to a door that opens beneath it and reveals that the soil carpets a ceiling of bricks. The interior is an egg-shaped hollow, dim and dank. It could be mistaken for a hermitage like the one occupied by Leonora in *La forza del destino*, but this in fact was Verdi's home-made refrigerator, testimony to his other, more practical persona: the ice that crusted the lake all winter was raked off and stored here under layers of straw, then brought out during the sweltering summer to preserve food and to doctor the sprains and swellings suffered by workers in the fields. The shaggy beauty of the mound was a camouflage for its usefulness. Even when absent, Verdi checked on the seasonal routines at Sant'Agata. In the spring of 1849 his father sent a report on the calving of the cows to him in Paris. Back in Paris in the autumn of 1866, Verdi gave his agent instructions about felling the exact quantity of poplars required for construction on the property. He was equally thrifty when it came to his horses: they were to be fed on Sant'Agata hay, and their manure – 'on which,' Verdi said, 'I am counting greatly' – had to be stockpiled.

At Bayreuth Wagner drilled a small army of musicians and technicians while simultaneously courting the donors who made the enterprise possible. Verdi's dependants were a community of tenant farmers and peasants to whom he distributed school supplies, clothing, or servings of polenta doled out from the villa's kitchen. He established dairy farms to provide employment for two hundred labourers, and was proud that this dissuaded villagers from emigrating to the cities or to America. When the flooding of the nearby Po ruined harvests of wheat throughout the district in 1879, he conducted the *Requiem* at La Scala to raise funds for relief. Wagner was excited by the idea and the spectacle of revolution; Verdi lived through one and – in reaction to riots in the impoverished countryside – did his best to assuage the misery that caused it, making charitable benefactions and lowering rents or waiving payments that were overdue. The rules of Wagner's gift economy permitted him to repay a patron's subsidy by delivering an opera, but Verdi settled musical debts with the fat of his land. In the summer of 1890, after the annual ritual of killing the pig, he packed a case that he sent by train to Stolz. It contained two shoulders of ham, one of them for Ricordi. He added instructions for preparing the meat after soaking it for half a day in lukewarm water to dilute the salt, and cautioned Stolz not to overcook it. He had no trouble envisaging the soprano he so admired as Leonora in *Il trovatore* – who subsists on the rations left for her once a week by the Padre Guardiano – supervising the procedure in her kitchen. Which human function is more important, singing or eating?

Rather than Verdi's ploughed, sown and reaped fields, the ideal Wagnerian location is a conservatory, like the hothouse in the third of the *Wesendoncklieder* where artificial, non-native growths exude tearful moisture and twitch their homesick tendrils in the humidity, fingering a void. Snatches of melody associated with the writhing languor of the sick Tristan underlie Wagner's setting of this poem, since the hero and the emerald-canopied plants are both victims of a life force that is dumb but dogged, mindless and pointless. In 1871 Wagner and Cosima visited the aquarium in Berlin, which they saw as a lesson in Darwinism: man was merely 'an animal with desires', and the dissatisfied grabbing and groping of organic life, made manifest in the aquatic plants, seemed 'horrible'. Verdi, as Strepponi joked, talked to his trees and flowers, encouraging them to grow. Wagner might have coaxed them to commit suicide: the watery shrubs in the tank reminded Cosima of the urgent need to renounce existence. Nature pleased him more when it put on an immaterial show, with bodies dissolving into flickery radiance. In Bayreuth in July 1881 the children took their parents to see glow-worms give 'a wonderful display of *Midsummer Night's Dream* magic' in the Hofgarten. A few evenings later, Wagner strolled off and returned 'like a shining Wotan' with a glow-worm in his hands, which he gave to Cosima. As always, she assumed that a random happening must be a quotation from one of his operas, although actually it is Hans

Sachs, brooding about the affray on Midsummer's Eve, who attributes the disturbance to a goblin or a glow-worm in search of its mate. The female firefly emits
light to attract the male, and what Wagner held was a small emblem of the carnal
urgency that impels comedies like *Die Meistersinger* or Shakespeare's *Dream*.

Verdi synchronized art and gardening by planting trees to commemo-
rate the stages of his career: a plane after *Rigoletto*, an oak after *Trovatore*, a willow
after *Traviata* (although this is also Desdemona's tree, and Boito noted that Verdi
first alluded to it in *Nabucco*, when the slaves sing about mute harps hanging
in willows). He gradually took root among this sturdy, sheltering plantation.
Backstage at La Scala in 1893 he complimented Nellie Melba on her performance
as Gilda in *Rigoletto*. She said she was honoured to meet him, and – as she later
wrote – 'he bowed, slowly, almost sternly … like a tree trying to bend'. The image
beautifully catches the creaky stiffness of old age, and also conveys her respect
for this gnarled elder, whose 'impenetrable reserve' made conversation awkward.
Wagnerian trees behaved more demonstratively, hysterically tossing their heads.
During summer gales in Bayreuth in 1881, Cosima noticed 'the eternally denying,
head-shaking trees', which displayed 'a sad picture of life'. Their agitated foliage
seemed to be repeating the advice inculcated by Schopenhauer: 'resign yourself,
resign yourself'. The arboreal Verdi bent without breaking, and executed his bow
to Melba with a dignified courtesy. On the day of his death, a placard displayed in
Busseto by the municipal council spoke with forgivable hyperbole about a toppled
colossus and a star extinguished in the sky, but it came closest to the truth in a
third metaphor, which likened him to a great tree felled by lightning.

||||||||||||||||||

When not hardening into a tree, Verdi liked to impersonate a wild beast prowl-
ing through dark forests. In 1865 in a bust by the sculptor Jean-Pierre Dantan he
mutates into a lion, its paws planted on a piano, its looped tail flicking the keys.
'Otello recovers himself and stands erect like a lion,' he told Boito when outlining
the episode he wanted to add to the opera's third act. But, he wondered, could the
debilitated man 'again become the hero of earlier days' and fight off the Turks? It
was a question Verdi must have been asking himself as he resumed his career. By
the end of his life he resembled Dantan's affectionate caricature, and the composer
Giovanni Tebaldini, who saw him at Sant'Agata two months before his death,
marvelled that his white-maned head could still proudly strike 'a leonine pose'.

Streponi thought Verdi was ursine, and in 1848 he agreed that he was
'more of a bear than before' despite living in Paris, where snarling animals were

meant to learn better manners. The best he could do in that line was to undergo a grumpy, reluctant domestication. In his correspondence with Arrivabene he often adopted the persona of a dog, which referred to Verdi as its 'majordomo, factotum and secretary', refusing to recognize him as a master, let alone a maestro. On one occasion the canine Verdi sent fraternal greetings to Arrivabene's dog with 'wide open jaws'. Like bears, dogs only smile when they are about to bite, and Strepponi was briefly alarmed by his reaction to the report of her unauthorized visit to Manzoni in 1868: he displayed 'a great row of teeth, including the wisdoms!', which prompted her to explain in a hurry.

Although Verdi said that he preferred the company of quadrupeds, animals confirmed his humanism, or at least enjoined him to behave humanely. To call a man a lion is to pay him a compliment, to make him a king among men; to call a man a bear chides him to be better than a wild creature. The birds and beasts in Wagner's extended family intrigued him for a different reason. They seemed to demonstrate the slippery relativism of humanity: did spirits migrate through species, using the human form as one costume among many others? Praeger was puzzled by his affection for 'brute creation' and thought his attitude to his gigantic Newfoundland dog was positively paternal. He remonstrated with Wagner about his 'illogical and intemperate' decision to cast animals in the *Ring*. Siegfried introduces himself by bringing a bear into Mime's smithy, and Brünnhilde addresses the last section of her funeral oration to her horse. Elsewhere there are rams, ravens, a frog, a serpent, a dragon, a bird with the gift of prophecy and a trio of mermaids. Praeger rightly argued that animals were a distraction onstage because they couldn't act while actors representing animals were even more embarrassing, but he missed the point when he assumed that Wagner's aim was 'a mistaken realism'. On the contrary, the purpose of the small zoos in the *Ring* and in Wagner's household was to undermine the notion of an exclusively human reality, a phylogeny in which we award ourselves first place. While Verdi enjoyed pretending to be a bear, Wagnerian characters like Siegmund and Siegfried actually wear bearskins. For Wagner, this was no tribute to their talent in hunting or in skinning their kill. Fur, as he remarked to Cosima, demonstrated the superiority of animals. They grow the clothes they need, whereas humans have to load themselves with encumbering garments stolen from other creatures. He might have been thinking of the pelts in which the glum Verdi was photographed during his winter trip to St Petersburg.

The Christians in *Parsifal* call Kundry a beast; she indignantly asks whether animals, in these sacred precincts, are not holy. Parsifal learns respect for life after spearing a swan. As Gurnemanz chastizes him for his crime, the orchestra – which catches the lulling, rocking rhythm of relaxed flight and marvels at the wonder of suspension in its trills – passes on this education in empathy. Wagner praised 'the animal divineness of the Greeks', with their tales of metempsychosing gods, and thought that the hero's blind dog Argos was the finest, most emotionally profound character in the *Odyssey*. He enjoyed evidence that the gaps between the species could be bridged: the guests of honour at a childrens' party at Triebschen in 1870 were a troop of fifteen poodles, dressed – as Cosima noted – in 'fine jackets and pink hats', with a barrel organ to accompany their choreographed antics. In 1880 in Sicily, Cosima responded to bad news from home by writing up a necrology of departed friends. Along with the dean of Bayreuth, the wife of an obliging banker, the municipal gardener and the Wahnfried bricklayer who had tumbled from a scaffold, she listed two of their dogs. All were 'good souls, both human and animal', equally entitled to respect. Wagner's collaborators were not rewarded with gifts of salted ham: his strict vegetarianism derived from ethical principle but also from an almost primitive superstition that he might be eating a soul that was in transit through the body of a cow or pig. On a drive in 1881 he mused about his Darwinian relatives, with none of the shame or disgust felt by English believers who were affronted by the theory of evolution. His daughter Eva looked to him like a tortoise, and her sister Isolde identified Cosima as an elephant. Wagner preferred to think of his beaky consort as a pelican, or 'an ostrich with me the Moor sitting on its back'. As for himself, he was sure he had once been a flea, the most irritating of parasites. Etymologies, he fancied, preserved traces of our links to these ancestral spirits, and compound words experimented with an impossible grafting of species. When Cosima saw a raven, he told her that it was 'the chief bird of the Germans', and went on to call Wolfram 'the most exalted name' because it combined 'the two sacred creatures, wolf and raven'.

In Wagner's judgment, humans did not disgrace themselves by acting on feral impulse. The coital encounter between Siegfried and Brünnhilde, he said, should resemble two animals mating, with none of the courtly prevarications that complicate matters for Tristan and Isolde. In *Götterdämmerung*, Siegfried tells Gunther that he has no property and has inherited only his body, which he uses up as he lives. This is the boast of what Émile Zola called 'la bête humaine', a creature not beholden to the past or mindful of the future, indifferent to the achievements and possessions that we hope will anchor us to the world and perpetuate our presence. Wagner was delighted when Cosima said that the dying Siegfried seemed to her less a person than a stricken animal. That, for her, is what made the incident – set, significantly, during a hunt – so piteous. Like an animal, Siegfried is surprised by the very idea of death; he has been spared our anxious lifelong forethought, and has none of the self-pity or regret that this knowledge induces. He is as far as possible from Otello's sadly human efforts to blame others and to erase his errors by repeating the kiss he gave to Desdemona at the beginning of the opera. Once in Sicily Wagner saw a lizard fasten on a beetle, which made a brief, futile effort to free itself. The incident summed up what he called 'the tragedy of existence', probably with more justice than the collapse of a great general.

Strepponi surrounded herself with an aviary of fellow singers, alliteratively named Poli-Poli, Pretin, Prevost and so on. A parrot perched on her shoulder when she walked in the garden, and after its death was stuffed and mounted in a glass case as a reward for good behaviour. Wagner kept poultry at Wahnfried, and sometimes insisted on breakfasting at the chicken house to enjoy the cackling and crowing and to listen for quotations from his scores: his children told him that one of the cockerels sang an excerpt from the *Siegfried Idyll*, and another male, more spiritually inclined, screeched a diminished fifth that reminded Cosima of the prelude to *Parsifal*. Birds interested Wagner less for their prowess in laying than as pretexts for poetic metaphor and satirical metamorphosis. A cock with dishevelled feathers seen at an agricultural show in Bayreuth resembled the untidy Beethoven. Another cock, showily bewigged and given to nervous twitching, was a dead ringer for Berlioz; when it moulted, its bare head made Wagner wonder whether Berlioz had reconsidered his vocation and entered a monastery. The resident Wahnfried turkey prompted one of Wagner's most gloriously paradoxical whimsies. 'A butcher's shop in front, a fashion magazine behind,' he said. The rear view of their peacock with its tail spread confirmed his republicanism. 'Just like royalty,' he remarked when he saw the puny stump that supported the ceremonial display. 'All pomp in front, fear behind.'

He took a more solemn view of swans, which for him as for Tchaikovsky and Sibelius were proud, potent spirits, emissaries that revealed the contradictions of a world poised between white and black, grace and gloom. In 1861 in Paris he wrote a piano piece, 'Ankunft bei den schwarzen Schwänen', about two black swans seen in a pool. It begins morosely, with drooping harmonies that sound like an elegy for Tristan on his sickbed. But Wagner saw the swans in their pool while he was staying in a guesthouse attached to the Prussian Embassy, so the baleful music changes key and spells out Elisabeth's jubilant greeting to the hall of song from *Tannhäuser*: the birds of ill omen swiftly change their plumage. At the end of his life, they underwent another change. Travellers often compared the gondolas gliding on Venetian canals to coffins; to Wagner they looked like black swans, which were equally funereal. The Italian habit of gunning down or trapping birds infuriated Wagner, whose first act after he arrived in Sicily in 1881 was to free some captives from cages smeared with birdlime. The following spring, when the landscape again resounded with tinny potshots, he remarked on the lack of birds, which were either dead or exiled to the gentler, more clement north. The silence provoked a portentous generality about the conflict of cultures and the national provenance of art. 'The world of sound,' he said, 'has fled to Germany.' Verdi was less squeamish, and although he banned hunting at Sant'Agata he wrote to Escudier in 1860 about the new sporting skills he had acquired during the winter in Genoa: 'when I see a bird, *Bang!* I shoot; if I hit it, good'.

Verdi and Strepponi doted on their fluffy, beribboned Maltese terrier Lulù. When the dog died, Verdi felt he had lost a 'faithful, inseparable companion', and Strepponi wept as she wrote about her loss (though she acknowledged that 'some perhaps may laugh' at her distress). Lulù was a replacement for the children Verdi had buried and those Strepponi had given away; he was, Verdi said, a 'true friend', by implication making up for the false friends he had to deal with in the theatre. Wagner mourned Cosima's pet dog Koss in similar terms – 'Such a good, friendly creature, so dependent on one!' – although what he emphasized was the dog's devotion to him, rather than paying tribute like Verdi to a more egalitarian friendship: a dog loves its master whether or not he is a genius or a celebrity, and it responds to goodness not greatness.

Verdi could only think of dogs as honorary human beings, whereas Wagner was fascinated and metaphysically puzzled by their remoteness from us. Where, Cosima asked, would the soul of Koss go? To a friendlier world, Wagner tactfully assured her. Strepponi grieved over Lulù's 'atrocious suffering', and Verdi said that his own suffering as he watched the dog die had been 'atrocious'. The adjective – a standby in operatic libretti, used by Otello as he reflects on the idea of Desdemona's infidelity – equates the victim's torments with the helpless emotional pain of the witnesses, and cements the same fellow feeling that makes us pity Violetta. But Verdi would not have agreed with Wagner's assertion, made in a letter to Mathilde Wesendonck in 1858, that the sufferings of men were less affecting than those of animals. Wagner's reason was that animals cannot be redeemed by the agonies they undergo, whereas human beings are capable of attaining salvation. The idea took on a more sombre inflection when he lectured Mathilde on man's 'need to suffer' and his own willingness to go 'to lengths of great cruelty' to ensure that this happened. This was not the confession of a sadist or a psychopath; it simply rationalized the acute nervous strain of his music. Perhaps Wagner's kindness to animals was his compensation for the way he so delectably tortured the rest of us.

Lulù remained unique and irreplaceable, like any creature that is loved. With dogs as with women, Wagner was a generalist and a generalizer, intrigued by the variety of canine breeds. For a while, the grey pug Koss cohabited at Triebschen with the Newfoundland Rouzemouk, familiarly Russ. Wagner walked them together, after donning what he called the 'fearsomely large Wotan hat' that identified him as a god – not quite a creator, possibly a breeder who amused himself by making genetic experiments. He used a startlingly comic Verdian image to describe the disparity between the miniaturized Koss and the gigantic, lumbering, hirsute Russ: they were, he said in a letter to Ludwig II in 1869, 'Falstaff with his page!' Improbable as it might have seemed, Koss and Russ were related, since both breeds remotely derived from some primal wolf. When Verdi came to consider the relationship between Falstaff and his page two decades later, he arrived at an even more happily unexpected conclusion: they were one and the same, temporally and physiologically continuous, not separated by centuries of genetic tinkering. In *Falstaff* the fat knight rebuts Alice's complaint about his corpulence by remembering when he served as the Duke of Norfolk's page and was so supple that he could slip through a ring. In time, the agile youth has thickened into the bulging, wheezing old man, but the process is miraculously reversed as the seasoned baritone sings a fleet, wispy scherzetto lasting less than thirty seconds in a voice that is thin and nimble, belying his bulk and his age.

Verdi was toying with a Shakespearean mystery – the revelation that as time passes a single man plays many parts, serially changing his mind and body if not his species – while Wagner studied a Darwinian conundrum. In 1872 Russ broke free during a walk and attacked another dog; Wagner disengaged him by tugging at his tail. In Cosima's diary entry for that day, the brawl is sandwiched between religious and scientific speculations. Immediately before the canine dispute she describes Wagner asking whether Wotan or Siegfried was the greater character and deciding that Wotan was 'the more tragic, since he … is atoning for the error of creation'. Immediately after the incident she notes that 'Darwin is giving [Wagner] pleasure' by proving that we have made moral progress because we now accept animals as fellow creatures. Dogs were perhaps a way of rectifying the creator's error or nature's miscalculation. In *Deutsche Kunst und Deutsche Politik*, published in 1867, Wagner accepted man's descent from the ape, but wondered why 'the last step from animal to man' did not happen by way of 'the elephant or dog, which possess decidedly more developed intellectual faculties than the monkey'. Would Verdi have agreed with this alternative genealogy? What mattered to him musically was emotional force not intellect, and the rare references to the animal world in his operas occur when people are at their most impassioned. Ulrica in *Un ballo in maschera* prophesies over her cauldron while the owl hoots and the salamander hisses, and Monterone in *Rigoletto* roars like a dying lion beset by curs.

The Wotan hat that Wagner wore when he exercised his dogs was a thinking cap as well as a ceremonial emblem of status. He knew that 'the error of creation' could not be blamed on a creator, since his reading of Darwin had persuaded him that nature muddled along without divine direction. In Bayreuth in June 1882 he exchanged a volley of witty, whistling calls with a downcast blackbird whose efforts to mate were doused by the wet weather. At the end of the duet he said to Cosima, 'The creatures are better than their creator.' Reproduction in the animal world brought him close, he believed, to the obscure moment of genesis; because the spectacle was sexual, it evoked his own adaptations of classical myth, not the bodiless creativity of the biblical God. When his Newfoundland Faf had a litter in 1881, Wagner compared her romping puppies to the amorous cupids who disport themselves in the Venusberg in *Tannhäuser*. His only regret was that they remained earthbound, unable to take flight and fire their flaming arrows from mid-air. Later he likened them to suckling human infants, whose squalling demand for milk is 'the most drastic expression of the will to live'. As soon as the hungry urgency is sated, he noted, the live things tumble into a stupor that is tantamount to death: here, in both the kennel and the nursery, the self-defeating coital action of *Tristan und Isolde* was re-enacted.

Once again creation seemed to be a mistake. But at least Wagner allowed creatures to increase and multiply, whether or not there was any point in doing so. In her letter persuading Verdi to work less hard, Strepponi said 'We shall have no children', which dispensed him from having to provide for heirs. She went on to describe Sant'Agata as 'the Eden of the earthly paradise', where like Eve she kept company with her pet birds, the draughthorses Solfarin and Menaffiss, and the rest of the animals. The absence of children was proof of her good fortune; childbirth, as she knew, was a punitive consequence of expulsion from the garden. Despite the pessimism Wagner absorbed from Schopenhauer, his Darwinian interest in genetics made him more inclined than Verdi to hope for the amelioration of mankind. All it would take, he calculated, was the modest study of man's best friend. In 1880 he announced that he regarded the dog as 'the human being's finest achievement'; since our remotest ancestors had bred dogs out of wolves, we ought to be able to refine our own species. Cosima asked who would be capable of humanizing humans. 'Ah!', said Wagner, 'the founder of a new religion.' He was of course nominating himself. Verdi bred horses and developed a bloodline that was named after him, but he ignored human eugenics. In 1865 when he and

Strepponi returned to Sant'Agata after a winter in Paris, they received an adoring welcome from the watchman's dog. Her gloss on Darwin was more sceptical than Wagner's: 'I don't know whether a monkey is a degenerate man,' she wrote, 'but certainly man, where the heart is concerned, is far from being a perfected dog.' Breeds can be improved, and man might even be surpassed by a superman like Siegfried or Nietzsche's Zarathustra; it is less easy to alter human nature, whose incorrigible passions provoke Verdi's music.

When Lulù died in 1862, Verdi and Strepponi buried him under a weeping willow, with an epitaph – 'Alla Memoria D'Un Vero Amico' – carved on a column. When Russ died in 1875, he was transferred to a mossy tomb behind Wahnfried, near the vault that awaited Wagner and Cosima. His memorial stone alludes to the baleful vigilance of Hagen, who in *Götterdämmerung* sits up at night like a mastiff to protect the Gibichung hall against enemies. Hagen snarls 'Hier sitz' ich zur Wacht', which on the grave becomes 'Hier ruht und wacht Wagners Russ'. The dead dog not only rests but watches, as unsleeping as a vampire. A nearby stone commemorates another Newfoundland, whose special talent was to clatter his teeth as if he wanted to talk: this was 'Wahnfrieds treue Wächter und Freund, der gute schöne Marke', named after Tristan's cuckolded uncle. Verdi simply valued a friend. Wagner, having founded a new religion, needed not only disciples but also a kennel of guardians and sharp-fanged protectors.

# 4 | *Duets or Dualities*

## Genesis in Music

Wagner, who set himself 'the cruelly difficult task of creating in my mind a non-existent world', understood his obligations: before the first notes of an opera could be composed, creation itself had to be reimagined. Music must have been present, he told Cosima in 1872, at 'the genesis of things', and it could therefore 'always start again from the beginning', as his operas do with their circumlocutory motifs that move the action forward while sending it into reverse. Audibility precedes visibility, and the drama starts when music travels gradually towards us across a yawning distance that is both temporal and spatial. The pilgrims in *Tannhäuser* trudge slowly in our direction; a glimmering speck of radiance in *Lohengrin* grows into a solar blaze. Sounds drift forward like the glow of dawn glimpsed far off by the Norns at the start of *Götterdämmerung*, or perhaps like incense stealthily suffusing the air. There is no single punctilious moment at which light is switched on, as in the Bible: that conceit, as Ludwig Feuerbach sneered, derived from 'Hebrew egotism', which pretended that there was a God whose decision to create the world put a sudden stop to formlessness and the void. We can eavesdrop on the beginning, as we do when the river wells up with the help of the booming bass in *Das Rheingold*, but the process actually began long, long before our ears picked up the first murmurs or our eyes caught sight of the undulating motion of the waters. Wagner's world is primordial, never entirely settling into fixity and liable at any moment to revert to chaos, as it does when gales buffet Daland's ship in *Der fliegende Holländer*.

The place of origins is always buried deep. Doubting that *Tristan und Isolde* would ever be performed, Wagner called it 'a mystical pit', a private underworld reserved for initiates. At Bayreuth he concealed the orchestra in just such a lidded gulf so that music could spread through the air like 'vapours rising from the holy womb of Gaia' at Delphi, where the oracle was housed in a cleft of the earth. What the crevasse disgorges can be terrifying: creation is not always accompanied by the shining haze that announces Lohengrin. At the beginning of *Siegfried* music materializes out of a grimmer chasm. Insidious rumblings and stirrings or metallic rustlings make palpable the darkness of the forest, its obscurity challenged by Siegfried's horn and the industrious clatter of Mime's hammer. Elsewhere Wagner's music articulates the unknowable; here it terrorizes us by evoking the unknown and making us afraid of shadows. When fire discolours the air in the first act, Mime shrieks in alarm, though what causes him to gibber and yelp is nothing but light combined with sound, the product of Wagner's scenic imagination. The prelude to the second act is even more threatening, as menacing low strings and braying brass take us into the black cavity of Neidhöhle where the dragon lurks. After apparent aeons of combat with nocturnal fears, we finally reach a moment of enlightenment that is almost an exorcism. The awakened Brünnhilde's shining address to the day in the third act – 'Heil dir, Sonne!/Heil dir, Licht!' – is a decree that arrogantly co-opts the fiat of the biblical creator, Feuerbach's contemptible Jehovah who imagines that he has a monopoly of power. We hear Brünnhilde inventing the sunlight, which she captures in the brilliance of her effulgent tone.

With his workmanlike approach to composition, Verdi was spared the agonies of gestation that Wagner volunteered to suffer, and could dispense with cosmic preliminaries. Following the preference of classical theorists, he began his operas *in medias res*, with the action already underway. In *Aida* Ramfis and Radamès are discussing the choice of Egypt's military leader, with the priest replying to a question we have not heard the warrior ask; in *Rigoletto* the Duke and one of his pimps are hurriedly completing arrangements for a seduction. Even if there has to be a summary of the immediate past – a Wagnerian excursion into memory, like Ferrando's narrative at the beginning of *Il trovatore* – it is soon jerked back into the urgent present, here interrupted by the bell that disperses the quaking soldiers. Verdi's beginnings are calls to attention, like Ferrando's alert to the troops or the noises of a party in progress that dispel the thready, strung-out musings of Violetta in the *Traviata* prelude. The action of *Falstaff* is almost literally kick-started by a swashbuckling upbeat. *Otello* leaps impatiently into the fray, vaulting over the Venetian intrigues that take up the first act of Shakespeare's play. The stormy opening scene gets its reeling impetus from a sudden, apocalyptic discord produced by bass drums, cymbals, an organ and a gong; it seems to split the sky open like forked lightning.

Endings are equally peremptory. In *Rigoletto* Sparafucile agrees to kill whoever next knocks at the door and immediately does so; a bell punctually sounds for Vespers and cues the massacre. Such dread finality was incomprehensible to Wagner. Discussing with Cosima his decision to bring back Sieglinde's hymn of praise to Brünnhilde at the conclusion of *Götterdämmerung*, he said that music 'has no ending' and 'is never really complete'. Individual characters die but music continues, because its function is to conduct them on the next, unseen stage of their journey. In Verdi such an epilogue counts as an error, an impropriety. Riccardo in *Un ballo in maschera* is stabbed during a dance. The room is crowded, so the stage band continues playing its mazurka; when the news circulates, the strings falter, the tune turns wispy, and the music falls helplessly silent.

Verdi's *Requiem* starts with a whisper not a bang, as the chorus, sunk in some profound hollow of grief, mutters a prayer for rest. But the effect is not like Wagner's long view down into a remote recess as he follows a river back to its source in *Rheingold*. Verdi listens for human longings that remain unspoken, rather than pursuing a trail of metaphysical and scientific enquiry. Before the Rhinemaidens can start to sing, they need to invent the idea of language. Sound changes from babble to patterned letters and then into words, although their chant of 'Weia! Waga!/Woge, du Welle' is still hardly separated from the onomatopoeia of the physical world. Alberich then sneezes to expel water from his nostrils: the unlyrical noise disrupts this liquid symphony, and melody is wracked into meaning. Kundry labours through the same evolution in *Parsifal*. She mumbles hoarsely when awoken by Klingsor in the second act, and sounds – according to the stage directions – as if she were learning to speak all over again. By the time she accosts Parsifal in the garden, she knows how to sing. Roused by Gurnemanz in the third act, she once more groans and yelps in alarm, then utters her last two penitent words of service, 'Dienen, dienen', after which she says no more. Silence is here a state of beatitude, beyond both speech and song. When the soloists in the *Requiem* make themselves heard over the chorus, the long history traced by Wagner is abbreviated. They are not afraid to address a louder, more commanding appeal to God and Christ; like tribunes, they stand up for people who cannot speak for themselves, and they supply an immediate reassurance, because we hear them boldly and beguilingly negotiate our salvation.

The storm in *Der fliegende Holländer* is not only bad weather. It is another of Wagner's guesses about the turmoil of creation, an elemental mayhem that will recur, as the Dutchman puts it in his monologue, when an annihilating blow cracks the world asunder on doomsday. Wagner often likened his orchestra to the ocean, and even his more landed, grounded operas made early listeners feel seasick. Hanslick called the overture to *Die Meistersinger* a 'tonal typhoon', and the modulations in *Parsifal* gave him an attack of aquatic nausea. The water, lashed by gales, overwhelms people or turns them into vessels for this turbulent energy, like the hallooing sailors, Senta when she mimics the storm in her keening cries of 'Johohoe! Hohohoe!' and 'Hui!', or the Dutchman as he orders his ship back to sea with a shrill whistle. Nature's boiling confusion cannot be soothed and solidified by the biblical God who so tidily divided water from dry land. The Dutchman's crew jeer at the mundane carousing of Daland's sailors; the ghosts have their own theory of art, and during their pandemonium they shout 'Sturmwind heult Brautmusik,/Ozean tanzt dazu!' – the hurricane sings, and the pitching ocean, on which no one can stand upright, dances. The Steersman prematurely announces that Daland's ship has firm moorings, but is then jolted by a crash like a thunder-clap as the Dutchman casts anchor; the hunter Erik clings to the earth, staring from a cliff at a wet, unformed infinity over which no one has control. Wagner was doing more than reliving his voyage from Riga in 1839: he was picturing the contents of his mind when roused to creative fervour. Isolde's first outburst is a sudden, vocally jagged appeal to magical powers that will, she hopes, whip the sea into a maelstrom and rip Tristan's ship apart. Then, with a scornful blast of breath, she commits the fragments of wood and canvas to the winds. Wagner had to work himself into such a state before he could persuade music to pour forth. Spitting out imprecations and creating her own small tornado of maddened air, Isolde mocks the idea that art, rather than disturbing people with its experiments in disintegration, should have a humane, benign purpose. Her mother's sorcery now produces only 'Balsamtränke' – medicinal draughts, like the kind of art that weak-mindedly tries to ease our fears and reconcile us to reality.

The characters Verdi took from plays by Schiller sometimes indulge in such apocalyptic tantrums, but he had a way of humanizing them, reducing their rhetoric to flustered exaggeration. In *I masnadieri*, based on Schiller's *Die Raüber*, the women who flee from Prague after the terrorist Carlo torches the city scream 'Il finimondo certo è venuto!' The end of the world has not come, but in the circumstances they can be forgiven for their operatic hyperbole. When his father seemingly returns from the dead, Carlo sarcastically salutes 'caos eterno', the broiling mess that preceded creation: the words are mere expletives. Luise in Schiller's *Kabale und Liebe*, blackmailed into marrying the odious Wurm, vows to strangle him on their wedding night and then submit gladly to the punishment of torture. Verdi's heroine in *Luisa Miller* is more temperate. She complains to God about her misery in a heart-tearing aria, then quietly submits. Nor does she possess the radical instincts that Schiller admired. In the play Luise reacts with snarling indignation to the snobbery of Lady Milford, but the operatic Luisa keeps her feelings to herself when the duchess Frederica purloins the man she loves. She has no need to speak out, because Verdi composes a quartet in which the orchestra falls silent so that we can overhear Luisa's anguish, her rival's relief, and the muttered satisfaction of her two male persecutors.

Verdi's longing was for rootedness, stability, not the heaving Wagnerian flux that gave Hanslick qualms. A river for Verdi was less a primal source like the Rhine than a convenient means of disposal. Sparafucile in *Rigoletto* flushes away the bagged corpses of his victims in the Po, and Aida thinks about drowning herself in the black vortices of the Nile. Most Verdian storms soon blow over, like the one in *Attila* that clears so that foundations can be laid on the marsh. Only the hurricane in *Otello* flares into something like Wagner's sublime catastrophes, prompting the chorus to shout 'Spasima l'universo': the universe is convulsed. The verb is telling, because contemporary criticism linked Verdi to the so-called 'spasmodic school' of romantic poets, who followed Byron in allowing neuroses and fits of self-induced anguish to dictate their verses. A San Francisco reviewer in 1859 described *Il trovatore* as the distempered production of a 'spasmodic composer'. But the spasms in *Otello* turn out to be those of the epileptic hero, not a symptom of universal upheaval, and although the orchestra lurches in sympathy as Montano sees Otello's ship swallowed by gulfs and then vomited skywards, the opera is a contest between this disorder and the more rational imperatives of art and of civic propriety, which Verdi, unlike Wagner, struggles to uphold.

The nature exposed by the glaring crash that starts Verdi's opera is a civil war of combative elements: Otello is the voice of the roaring wind, whereas Iago, who calls himself a critic and is as subversive as Wagner's Loge, has the flickering destructiveness of the fire that is lit to celebrate victory. We might be watching a speeded-up version of the conflict between civilization and barbarism that Mazzini remembered when he surveyed the ruins in the Roman Campagna; classical art can never let down its guard, since anarchy is forever returning. Otello's arrival calms the tempest, but he then has to subdue a riot on land when the drunken Cassio picks a fight. The bonfire is meant to be a 'Fuoco di gioa', although energy and joy soon bleed out of it. The heat falters, its light dims, and the chorus chronicles this small death in phrases that ebb and lose vigour, leaving Iago to rekindle society in his drinking song. The world's survival seems to be at stake whenever the dramatic conflicts explode. 'Per l'universo!' swears Otello when vowing to punish Desdemona. As he throws her to the ground, bassoons, trombones and horns open up a sonic gorge, with spaced-out, concussing chords as portentous as the thudding of Wotan's spear when he makes the earth shudder to frighten Mime. During the ensemble that follows this assault, Cassio remembers the storm. He imagines a lightning bolt of annunciation above his head, and says that he owes his promotion to a tidal wave stirred up by a hurricane, which has heaved him out of 'l'abisso del mar'.

In *Das Rheingold* the world slowly, steadily evolves from that initial orchestral pulse, and its collapse in *Götterdämmerung* has an equally dignified deliberation, happening almost at the pace of a funeral march. In *Otello* the world is created instantaneously in a blinding flash, and it can be extinguished just as tersely. To finish his atheistic Credo, Iago confounds creation by uttering the word 'nulla' and laughs at the senile fantasy of heaven. All that remains, when the echo of his mockery dies out, is a sonorous vacancy.

Verdi pretended not to be interested in genesis or in music's transcription of that mystery. In 1864 he laughed about a proposal to erect a monument in Arezzo to Guido Aretinus, the medieval monk who devised a new system for musical notation and codified solfeggio by relating notes to syllables taken from the first stanza of a Latin hymn. Why not, Verdi asked, put up a statue to Pythagoras, who mathematically regulated the tuned intervals of the diatonic scale, or to Jubal, the biblical ancestor honoured by all who play the lyre and pipe? Despite these joking denials, opposed myths about music clash in *Otello*. The first act ends with a charm or benediction that quietens the discord of the stormy opening. Otello and Desdemona gaze up at the constellations in their duet and sing about Venus and the Pleiades, the seven sisters, consorts of the gods, who nursed the infant Bacchus. The harp, oboe and trilling violins sketch the velvety, scintillating sky: this is the music of the spheres. Iago's earlier drinking song invokes a different account of origins when he refers to the 'morso/del ditirambo', a dithyrambic nectar. Liquor inflames the brain and body like a Dionysian song, and Iago, who obsessively repeats this refrain, disseminates a giddy delight as if he were Pan on the rampage. In his description of drunkenness, the world palpitates, jerking and staggering rather than throbbing as at the start of *Das Rheingold*; it frees the drunkard to defy the gods and the fate they prepare for us. Cassio too experiences inebriation musically and likens himself to a lute, impulsively tingling. Boito's text – to which Verdi responded with a romping, clattering orchestral and vocal uproar, leading unstoppably to the fight and the shouted glee of the chorus – almost paraphrases Nietzsche's theory about Greek tragedy and the birth of drama from the uproarious, irrational spirit of music.

Wagner placed that birth on view in the Bacchanale he composed for the Paris *Tannhäuser*: it matches the brawl in *Otello*, although for Wagner the motive is erotic whereas Verdi's scene is driven by the crackling animosity between men. In the Venusberg nymphs induce youths who hold goblets to exchange drinking for dancing. A troop of Bacchantes encourage the revellers; the Graces, whose inter-locking circular dance emblematically acts out the bond between heaven and earth, are aghast at the rout but powerless to quell it. The orgy soon turns into the kind of battle over which the corpse-scavenging Valkyries preside, as putti discharge arrows into the throng and the Graces nurse the dancers who are wounded by their barbs. In Wagner's synopsis the Graces inform Venus that a gentler force has pre-vailed over the madness of the libido, but that is not quite what we see or hear. The dance froths, flails, then slumps into post-coital lassitude, and the Graces cannot heal the lesions left by the venereal arrows. The creative act, whether performed by a deity or an artist, is indistinguishable from the sexual act; it is a craving that lapses into lethargy as soon as it is sated, then recovers to go through the motions all over again. Here music expresses frustration rather than the endless, never-complete infinitude that Wagner spoke of to Cosima.

In 1933 Thomas Mann pointed out that in *Tristan und Isolde* God is replaced by 'the cosmogenical myth in which the longing motif summons the world into being'. When Isolde tells the story of creation to Brangäne, she dethrones Erda, the matriarch who manages nature in the *Ring*. Frau Minne, as Isolde cosily calls the goddess of love, is now 'Des Weltenwerdens/Wälterin', governess of the world's unfolding; her task, as if she had taken over the work of the Norns, is to weave opposites together, plaiting joy and sorrow, pleasure and pain, love and death into an amalgam. Is this an account of creation or a jus-tification for suicide? Wagner may have fancied that composing operas was like begetting and bearing children, but the dying Tristan – whose father died after begetting him and whose mother died in bearing him – repudiates this notion of creativity when he curses the aphrodisiac drink, Shaw's musical 'brandy of the damned'. His tormented motto is an abbreviation of life: 'sehnen – und sterben!', to yearn and then to die. Tristan does not so much summon the world into being as urge it towards nullity, though without Iago's sardonic glee. His revulsion provoked Otto Weininger's notorious treatise, which declared that 'every form of fecundity is loathsome' and dispensed men from their 'moral duty to provide for the continuance of the race'. In 1903 the twenty-three-year-old Weininger fol-lowed what he took to be Wagner's orders and shot himself through the heart.

Verdi was not given to metaphysical speculation, but in one case his music sketched the penumbra of existence. The synopsis for *Aida* was prepared by the Egyptologist Auguste Mariette; although Verdi said that he had no par-ticular regard for the culture of Egypt, the strangeness of its gods may have made them more amenable than those who were closer to home. Amonasro accuses the Egyptians of having profaned Ethiopia's temples and altars; the word he uses is 'immite', which suggests that they have been demythologized. Verdi, imagining Egypt's temples and altars, does the opposite: he restores their sanctity, and treats them as sanctuaries for music. Radamès is taken to Vulcan's temple to receive the sword he will take into battle, but before the ceremony an unseen priestess is heard descanting on 'possente Fthà, del mondo/Spirito animator', after which her prayer trails off into an ecstatic vocalise. Fthà, also anglicized as Ptah or Peteh, was the creator who dreamed the world and then, like the biblical God, spoke it into being; as the priestess meditates on the holy name, her male colleagues mutter an awed recollection of earth's emergence from 'nulla', here a softer, hazier state than the hollow absence that Iago mocks. Another contingent of temple maidens then performs a scampering dance that choreographs the process of creation, with the planets circling the sun. The dancers are lighter-footed than the Bacchantes in the Venusberg in *Tannhäuser*, and there is no chance of Wagner's proposed intercourse between music and drama, since Verdi keeps the sexes prudently apart: after the sinuous windings of the priestess's voice, the male choir, led by Ramfis, is boomingly officious, and the men harness the creative spirit to their own destructive uses when they bless the sword.

Fthà means 'opener': in obedience to the god's behest, Egyptian priests prised open the mouths of the dead to let out the spirit. The Italian word is an exhalation, like the 'phut!' with which we blow out a candle, and the breath it expels is a vibrant trampoline, a support for the fluctuations of melody. Wagner had his equivalent to this mythological fancy, defined – with the help of some queasily surgical metaphors – in *Oper und Drama*. He called speech 'a defunct organism', but prescribed a means of revival, a way of 'healing the wounds with which the anatomist's scalpel has gashed the body of speech, breathing into it the breath that may animate it with living motion'. That breath, of course, was music. As Aida falls unconscious in the crypt at the end of the opera, she says she sees heaven opening to her ('Già veggo il ciel dischiudersi'). The priestess is then heard repeating her praise of Fthà who liberated the ghost trapped inside the moribund body. Above the airless vault is a statue of Osiris, whose descent to earth to couple with Isis caused the Nile to overflow and – to use a word from the priestess's hymn – fecundated the desert. Aida was wrong to describe the flooding Nile as a tomb. Egyptian religion brings life out of death by fertilizing the land; she and Radamès, expending their last breaths with exquisite slowness in their shiningly attenuated repetitions of 'O terra, addio', transform suffocation into something like Wagner's idea of an endless melody.

In 1872–73 Cosima kept track of the building works for the Bayreuth theatre. Wagner was pleased by the excavations, and savoured the green and pink colours of the churned-up earth. 'There is the Venusberg already,' he said. For Cosima the path onto the site descended into an underworld that was not quite so uterine. She thought she was surveying 'the foundations of an Egyptian temple!', and when she clambered onto the unfinished stage she noted 'pillars ranged like sphinxes' and imagined the wings opening into corridors that might have led to sealed mortuaries. She could have been describing the set for the final scene of *Aida*, first performed in Cairo in 1871 and then in Milan, Parma and Naples during 1872. On another visit to the site she remained outside and stared up at the scaffolding: 'it all looks to me like a grave (the Pyramids!)', she wrote. Cosima hoped that the auditorium would give visitors the sense 'of being inaugurated into the mysteries'. For Mark Twain, it did so only too well. Stultified during the performance of *Parsifal* he attended there in 1891, he thought he was sitting 'with the dead in the gloom of a tomb', and was relieved when the cadavers around him stirred to life and applauded. Despite the whispered contemplation of Fthà, the temple in *Aida* is a less sepulchral place. Verdi told Italo Pizzi that he disliked the 'ecstatic silence' that Wagner demanded of his audience. He enjoyed the noise the public made in response to his music; for him, the theatre was a civic arena, a forum where ballerinas can skip and pivot, warriors swear bloody oaths, and bigoted priests conduct political trials. As Ramfis implies when he calls Isis 'la Diva', the enigmatic priestess may simply be a soprano whose voice is the only supernatural thing about her.

|||||||||||||||||||

Opera begins when note and word come together – but do words call notes into being, with music as the natural extension of speech, or does music predate words, which clumsily paraphrase melodies and harmonies that remain elusive? When revising *Simon Boccanegra*, Verdi asked Boito to deliver verses in exact lengths to a set metre, and said that, although he was sure the words would be beautiful, it wouldn't matter if they were ugly. They were a pretext for his music, and it was their destiny to be not heard, or at least not properly understood. Verdi was testing Boito to see whether he could be treated as dictatorially as previous librettists; he knew well enough that opera was a collaboration and sometimes a competition between song and speech. The two pairs of characters in the *Rigoletto* quartet from the third act bicker about this very matter. The Duke starts off with another sample of his honeyed, artificial and unfelt lyricism in 'Bella figlia dell'amore', but Maddalena's derisive dismissal is almost spoken. Gilda's reactions are elaborately musical, tugging at the rhythm to give herself time to lament, eventually soaring above the disreputable situation into heady coloratura altitudes as she announces her willingness to die. Rigoletto, rougher and more realistic, drags her back to the solid ground of speech by telling her that tears are useless and ordering her to be silent.

Wagner, being his own librettist, only had himself to argue with, but the internal dispute was fierce. Music alone was never enough. As Wagner explained to Ludwig II, Siegfried insists on knowing what the Woodbird's chirruping in the second act means; he therefore kills the dragon, and this violence inadvertently teaches him to understand birdsong. It is a strange theory of linguistic evolution, but there is a telling logic to it. Words disrupt the instinctual calm of nature, establishing human control. Music meanwhile lends its voice to the wordless suffering of creatures that cannot speak. In Sicily in 1880 Wagner listened in astonishment to the braying of a donkey, a wheezing plaint that was presumably meant to communicate pleasure. 'The tragic thing,' he said, 'is that it seems ridiculous': a Shakespearean observation, acknowledging the proximity of joy and misery. A few weeks later, during a discussion of Parsifal's reaction to his mother Herzeleide's death, he told Cosima 'Everything *cries*! ... Everywhere this cry, this lament'. It is the same point made by Banquo in Verdi's *Macbeth* when, in a brief arioso before the discovery of the murder, he says he felt the earth tremble beneath him during the storm and heard voices moaning in the pitchy air. One cry stands out: the screech of a predatory owl, ominously registered by oboe and clarinet. The frisson is alarming, but to Verdi it represents abnormality, an upheaval in nature. For Wagner such a cry was the original musical noise, omnipresent in nature. It resounds from Brünnhilde as she bewails Siegfried's treachery. With wrenching force, she takes a single, exclamatory word – 'Ach Jammer! Jammer!' – and cracks it in half as if her own mighty voice were breaking. 'Weh'! ach Weh'!' she continues. To say she is woebegone hardly does justice to a despair that language cannot adequately translate. Before drinking the potion Isolde angrily vociferates; at the end of the opera she rhapsodizes to the bystanders, eloquently describing a vision they cannot see. But her truest, most heart-rending moment is a cry that is not verbalized – the throttled monosyllable 'Ha!' that escapes from her when she finds Tristan dead.

Verdi established a musical hierarchy whose gradations overcome such rawness. In 1887 in a letter to Ricordi he illustrated his vocal theodicy by arranging the characters of *Otello* in a triangle: Otello howls, Iago declaims, and Desdemona sings. In 1878 Wagner, talking about Shakespeare's play, mentioned Othello's 'shattering cry of pain' when Iago makes him doubt Desdemona's fidelity: shatteringly set to music by Verdi in Otello's 'Miseria mia!', it is less a complaint about cuckoldry than a sudden and inordinate reaction, as Wagner said, to 'a cruel world hitherto unimagined'. Iago meanwhile talks, and is lyrical only if he wants to deceive Otello, as in his lulling lies about Cassio's dream of Desdemona. For Verdi, the irrational bellowing of the one and the rational, witty chatter of the other cancel each other out. Song, Desdemona's prerogative, has a sweet serenity unavailable to the men.

The Wagnerian cry is not necessarily distressed. It can express hilarity, an ebullient liveliness that presents the mere act of breathing as a huffing and puffing demonstration of strength. Hence Siegfried's hallooed refrains – 'Hoho! Hohei!', 'Hoho! Hahei!', 'Heiaho! Heiahohoho! Heiah!' – as he works the bellows to stoke up the furnace and rhythmically hammers the molten steel of his sword in the first act. Like the Woodbird's song before he deciphers it, this music is vocal without being verbal. It semaphores emotion, making opera, in the rude forest, a survival of some unfallen paradise where communication could happen through the exchange of melodies. Resident in Eden at Sant'Agata, Strepponi communed with her 'beautiful peacock, that stands watching me', and remembered the messages of 'affection and fidelity' transmitted by Lulù's bulging eyes; Wagner, when Siegfried listens to the murmuring of the forest, notates those silent conversations.

Despite Siegfried's efficiency at dragon-slaying and marching through fire, the opera's real concern is his aesthetic education. He first acquires language, then goes on to grapple with the more complex and baffling phenomenon of music. At last, inventing opera in his own way, he brings the two together. His aim when setting out on his adventures is to learn the meaning of fear; what he actually learns is the meaning of Wagner's art, which is fearful because of the erotic and psychological mysteries it lays bare. Long before his encounter with the Woodbird, Siegfried questions Mime about birdsong. He wants to know about mating rites in spring, and as he describes the nesting of birds and the pairing of foxes and wolves, the orchestra swells into a brief pastoral symphony, a pendant to the more elegiac Good Friday music in *Parsifal*. The passage speculates about music's purpose in the natural world, and explains it as a reproductive lure. Hence Siegfried's muddling attempt to charm the Woodbird by piping a reply to its greeting, like Wagner during his whistled conversation with the Bayreuth blackbird. Siegfried imitates its song, like Rameau who mimicked a hen's pecking in his *Pièces de clavecin*, or Beethoven who set the flute and clarinet to imitate the quail and cuckoo in his *Pastoral* symphony, or Messiaen who composed pianistic arias for the oriole, the buzzard, the curlew and a global aviary of warblers and whistlers in his *Catalogue d'oiseaux*. 'Nach liebem Gesellen lockt' ich mit ihr,' Siegfried says of the pipe: he appeals for reciprocation, calling for a comrade if not a mate. This is Wagner's rougher equivalent to the serenade of Fenton in *Falstaff*, who sings his lilting line about a kissed mouth and its savouring of sensation – 'Bocca bacciata non perde ventura' – in the hope that he will hear an immediate reply. You cannot kiss yourself; love has to be a duet, and Nannetta enters on cue to complete the couplet from Boccaccio. Siegfried has no such luck, and grumbles that his attempts at musical seduction only attract wolves and bears. Nature – or perhaps his adoption by an Italian composer – endows Fenton with irresistible tone and accurate pitch, whereas the English horn squawks and flattens when Siegfried blows through his reed. But development depends on trial and error, and his breach of melodic rules may strike a blow for creative liberty, as do the scandalous novelties of Walther's first free-form song in *Die Meistersinger*.

Undeterred, Siegfried advances from reed to metal by blowing his horn. Having failed to attract a mate, he succeeds in provoking an enemy, as Fafner grumbles at the disturbance and lumbers from his cave. The dragon's spilled blood does more than translate birdsong; it also allows Siegfried to hear the murderous thoughts of Mime, whom he also idly slays. Killing precedes coupling: Siegfried's mental initiation and his progress to adulthood depend on violence, an instinct more innate – and perhaps, in Wagner's view, more liberating – than the desire for sex.

Wagner rightly called the amniotic waves at the beginning of *Das Rheingold* 'the world's lullaby'. More deviously, Mime tries to lull the grown-up Siegfried by describing how he clothed and fed the hapless infant and supplied him with toys; his mewling voice sounds as if he is rocking his charge's inquisitive brain back to sleep. As opposed to this syrupy cradle song, when Wotan intervenes in the action he uses music as a 'Wecklied', a wake-up call that interrupts dreams and compels us to face reality. He first prods Fafner out of his drowsy stupor, then cries 'Erwach!' as he raises Erda from her somnolent refuge beneath the earth. Fafner resists being dragged back into consciousness, but Erda responds to the alarm and says 'Stark ruft das Lied': the song is powerful. Siegfried awakens the sleeping Brünnhilde, as he explains, so that he too can wake up, presumably by casting off the mental indolence of childhood, and when he kisses her he repeats Wotan's cry of 'Erwache! Erwache!' Yet the association between words and music remains problematic. Language defers to a power that is at once lower and higher, able to convey feelings without needing to analyse them and also able to combine opposed feelings, like fear and desire. Brünnhilde puzzles Siegfried by identifying him with the sunlight that banishes nature's sleep, and she goes on to call him the incarnation of Wotan's forethought and of her own fantasy. He reacts like someone hearing opera for the first time. 'Wie Wunder tönt, was wonnig du singst;/doch dunkel dünkt mich der Sinn,' he says: the sound of her voice is wondrous, though its meaning remains obscure. What matters is that her song has moved him, taught him the value of awe. His bewildered self-discovery and sense of emotional affinity are more important than being able to follow what she is singing about.

Verdi had no interest in music not made by human beings, but on one occasion he came near to Wagner's fascination with the lyricism of nature. In *Falstaff* female laughter, so infectious that it becomes almost choral when the wives giggle and chortle together, sounds like Wagnerian birdsong. As Alice and Meg compare the identical letters Falstaff has sent them, they flit up and down the scale: laughter announces a mood of happiness or frivolity or hilarity or – in this case – delighted superiority that can do without words. The weeping of Nannetta, whose father has forbidden her match with Fenton, is dispelled by a similarly mellifluous reiteration of 'No!' This is all it takes to place Alice, Meg and Quickly in charge, helping nature to renew itself by assisting one of the courtships between animals that Siegfried observes in the forest. The ensemble in Ford's garden – with a posse of men plotting reprisals against Falstaff while the women conspire separately and Fenton has a whispered colloquy with Nannetta – absorbs Verdi's characters into a continuum as impersonal as the orchestra or as Wagner's sprouting, burgeoning springtime landscape. Quickly refers to the tongues of the three women as instruments, livelier than clicking castanets; Ford hears the mob as a swarm of wasps or buzzing hornets. The irony is that none of these witty words are audible, and Ford, as if speaking up for the self-sacrificing Boito, even makes an alienatory joke about the different priorities of drama and opera. 'Se parlaste uno alla volta/Forse allor v'intenderò,' he says to his gabbling companions: if you spoke one at a time, I might be able to understand you. But Ford – a tormented man who has strayed out of a tragedy, like a refugee from *Otello* – has missed the point. The opera's fugal conclusion partly answers his complaint: now they can all sing the same words because they are voicing a universal truth about human folly.

Wagner's characters slowly gain wisdom by listening to music, after which they struggle to put this understanding into words. Parsifal is chastened by Gurnemanz's lecture about his killing the swan, but his response to the news of his mother's death is another act of violence, followed by a faint. Verdi did not expect words to articulate the mystery of music (as perhaps only Isolde, in her 'Liebestod', succeeds in doing); they tend to be afterthoughts, pondering the enigmatic harmonies that spread through the air, able to do no more than add tame, trite captions. Hence the miraculous passage in which Falstaff, arriving for his tryst in the forest, actually hears the chimes at midnight – something that Shakespeare's character in *Henry IV* only refers to, alluding to nights of roistering long ago. Verdi imagines that moment and stops the action to recreate it; he makes it a meditation on the passage of time, which is the medium of music. A distant bell strikes twelve times, and Falstaff checks on his punctuality by counting the strokes out loud. It is a simple operation that, in this very fast-moving comedy, takes up almost a whole minute, during which Verdi weighs the different powers of music and words. Falstaff as he enters is introduced by a heavy, zigzagging motif whose repetitions evoke his stumbling path through the tangled wood to the place where the dangerous encounter – sensual or perhaps mystical – will occur. Then the bell sounds, tolling one predictable note at precise intervals and challenging the singer to make his simple recitation of numbers into a graph of what he feels. The words shiver or balefully echo through the gloom, and the arrival at the end of the sequence should probably be terrifying, since a lifetime spent waiting for this conclusion has been almost used up. But no words can match what the orchestral strings do as they punctuate the twelve regular, identical strokes. The reharmonization – which Benjamin Britten called 'astounding' – advances through a series of shocks, including a lapse into nervy dissonance; dynamics vary, rhythm falters or accelerates, while the first and second violins and the viola momentarily go their separate ways. This busy minute serves as a small manifesto for music: it finally brings us home and reassures us about the world's stability, but along the way, like the 'alte Weise' of the shepherd in *Tristan*, it makes us feel anxious, disoriented, uncomfortably aware that number, time and language are systems for imposing a fictitious clarity on the surrounding darkness.

Here music almost literally undermines words. More usually Verdi expected words to provoke music; this leads at once to action, not to the prolonged, self-searching orchestration of thought as Brünnhilde waits on her rock for Siegfried's return in *Götterdämmerung* or Sachs broods in his workshop in *Die Meistersinger*, indifferent to the bustle and chitchat of his apprentice. Wagner imagined music and words coming together in a fusion or fertilization. Verdi thought of that creative encounter as a kind of ignition: perhaps a divine spark, perhaps the kind of firing-up that happened when an industrial engine like the pump at Sant'Agata started into life. He often used this image when describing the kind of excitement he looked for onstage. He told Escudier that routine stultified singers at the Paris Opéra and snuffed out 'the fire that transports and carries one away'. He praised the 'fire and enthusiasm' of Stolz and the tenor Mario Tiberini in *La forza del destino*, and demanded an inspiring, electrifying 'spark' – a flashpoint that the composer alone could not supply – from anyone cast as Amneris in *Aida*.

Verdi was quick to notice when libretti gave him words that were suitably flammable. A small example is analysed in his letters to Antonio

Ghislanzoni about *Aida*. Amneris, having tricked Aida by telling her that Radamès is dead, studies her reaction and then vengefully spits out the truth, 'Radamès *vive!*' Ironically, the word has to sound like a lethal blow, because it strips off Aida's mask of indifference; in a flare-up of unguarded joy, she repeats the incendiary verb. Verdi claimed that what attracted him to *Nabucco* was the text of 'Va, pensiero', but apart from this pensive episode – which Zaccaria reprimands when he harangues the apathetic chorus – Temistocle Solera's text keeps words in a state of white heat. 'Fulmine' and 'furore' recur, especially when Abigaille's growling, slashing voice fulminates: her rages are thunder and lightning. This is what Verdi, in his instructions to Ghislanzoni, called 'la parola scenica': a word that is dramatically impetuous, turning instantly into a deed when a singer utters it. At the beginning of *Nabucco* Zaccaria appeals to the God of Abraham to kindle a breath of fire – 'un soffio accendi' – in his followers. That Pentecostal flame is meant, he says, to scorch the infidel; in 'Come notte a sol fugente' he adds an aspirated flourish to the word 'vento' when he describes the false gods being scattered by the wind. What began as a fiery breath ends, after the chorus joins in, as a cyclone.

Watching for the spark, Verdi wanted performers to surprise him. He sometimes wrote that spontaneity into the drama, in little gratuitous acts that allow characters to alter the balance of power. Ernani twice breaks cover by announcing that he is 'il bandito Ernani', and Manrico emerges from nowhere to rescue Leonora as she is about to enter the convent. More humorously pushy, Riccardo in *Un ballo in maschera* boasts that he has unaristocratically arrived in the witch's den before his courtiers. 'Arrivo il primo!' he says, and when Ulrica orders her customers to leave he exempts himself in another cheeky aside, 'Non me!' Such momentary upsets are ruled out by Wagnerian drama. Alberich foretells the future, after which the ring automatically destroys whoever touches it. Unscripted actions that ignore this foresight are immediately fatal, as when Siegfried laughs off the warnings of the Rhinemaidens and tosses a clod over his shoulder to show his contempt for mortality. This is the blundering of a character who has been deprived of free will: the plot of *Götterdämmerung* depends on the drink that temporarily erases Siegfried's memory, because only someone with no capacity to make rational choices could be so easily misled. Abigaille in *Nabucco* rips up the parchment that testifies to her ancestry, but she does so to ease her ascent to the throne. Cancelling the past sets her free, rather than making her, like Siegfried, the dupe of others. History in the *Ring* consists of helplessly retold stories and mistakes made all over again; nature alone is cyclical not circular, self-renewing not repetitive. By the end – when Brünnhilde performs the actions foreseen by Waltraute in her warning, to the sound of motifs that are recovered memories of previous events – everything is a doom-laden recapitulation.

Neither music's regularity nor the story's predictability inhibit Verdi's characters. The theatrical excitement and moral courage of *Stiffelio* derives from this determination to go beyond the book, to make decisions that have no precedent. The book in this case is holy, supposedly infallible; it should set down penalties for the adultery that Stiffelio's wife Lina has committed while he was away on his evangelizing rounds. But Verdi makes room for the improvised behaviour of live human beings and for astonishing acts of self-transcendence like Stiffelio's last-minute decision to pardon the sinner. As a minister of God, Stiffelio feels that he is a divine ventriloquist. 'Di Dio/Ora parlo nel nome,' he cries when forbidding Lina's elderly father Stankar to fight a duel with her seducer, Raffaele. Before making his judgment known to the congregation, he asks to be prompted by the same source: 'Dio, a parlar loro ispirami'. Inspiration is the act of breathing in – or of receiving what Cicero called 'afflatus', a supernatural impulse – and without it respiration, in the form of song, is impossible. But is song a theological marvel or a more human physiological skill? Stankar still seeks revenge, and rails about dishonour in an aria that, according to Verdi's instructions, should be panted breathlessly. Passion seems to have winded the old man, as he admits before he makes a last, loud threat: 'La voce ed il respiro/Mancar già sento a me!' – he feels his voice failing, his breath running out. It is a touchingly honest acceptance of limits, which contradicts Stiffelio's assertion that the breath he emits is an irate blast of heavenly wind.

After her startled 'Ha!', Isolde berates the dead Tristan and tries to detect a last fluttering sign of life, 'eines Atems/flücht'ges Wehn!' Then in her final outpouring she joins her breath to that of the entire world, 'des Welt-Atems/wehendem All', in an oxygenated version of the flood that begins and ends the *Ring*. With odd exceptions like Stiffelio, Verdi's characters cannot make use of Isolde's numinous gale; they have only their own unaided breath, but that is all they need. Leonora's scene beneath the tower where Manrico is imprisoned in *Il trovatore* is a singing lesson as well as a lesson in the emotional, moral and spiritual powers of song. Her aria – which is about her 'sospiri', the mournful sighs from which the music is made – ends with a trill, as she describes the pangs that afflict her heart. Trills temporize between two notes and stop time for as long as the alternation continues; this one matches but also stabilizes Leonora's agitated heartbeat, so that musical technique makes it possible for her to control her emotions. An unseen chorus of monks then begins a 'Miserere', praying for the condemned Manrico, while a bell tracks time and reminds Leonora that it is running out. She says that grief is choking her, stilling her heart, and complains of palpitations. But the triplets she sings to defy the monastic dirge and the brave, heady elation of the cabaletta in which she vows to save Manrico mark the difference between chant and song, between the grim strictures of theology and the soaring freedom of lyricism. The 'sospiri' and 'palpiti' that afflict Leonora are music's ardent sources and its vital signs, her defence against the verdict the offstage voices pronounce as they recite from their liturgical script.

Verdi's 'parola scenica' had to be kinetic, cueing a physical movement. Wagner wished he could call his operas 'ersichtlich gewordene Taten der Musik', deeds of music made visible, but those Wagnerian deeds are usually invisible, performed by the orchestra and pictured internally by us: Siegfried's journey on the Rhine or his funeral procession, Tannhäuser's pilgrimage to Rome, Parsifal's expiatory wanderings on the way back to Monsalvat. The music travels; the characters, as Verdi complained when he saw *Lohengrin* in Bologna, are fixed to the spot. For Verdi, that meant paralysis, the denial of drama. In 1881, discussing with Boito the scene in the council chamber that they were adding to *Simon Boccanegra*, he worried about giving muttered asides to Gabriele Adorno, because while voicing such comments he would have to remain immobile, an observer of the action not a participant. Verdi returned to the principle five years later when wondering whether *Otello* should be entitled *Iago*. As he told Boito, Iago was 'the demon who moves everything' – though he is an unmoved mover without a plausible motive, and after setting up his plot he stands apart and lets it take its course. Otello, however, was 'the one who acts', which meant that the opera had to be named after him: Iago proposes, Otello disposes. The distinction would have meant nothing to Wagner, who cultivated the immobility that Verdi dreaded. Parsifal and Gurnemanz advance from the forest to the temple by walking on the spot. Without budging, they wait for the painted trees to move aside; the orchestra, as Gurnemanz points out, turns space into time, and the tolling bells that advance from the distance and recede again measure the ground they have notionally covered. During *Parsifal* at Bayreuth in 1897, Arthur Symons marvelled at seeing people for the first time utterly still onstage, and paid this 'metaphysical music' a paradoxical compliment. Here, he said, 'Wagner realized the supreme importance of monotony'.

Inertia was for Wagner the ideal dramatic condition, because it made his characters concentrate on the music. The Steersman in *Der fliegende Holländer* drifts in and out of sleep while on his watch: a dereliction of duty, but his dozing makes it clear that the opera is a phantasmagoria, with the Dutchman's ship rearing up in his dream. Action is severely rationed, reaction discouraged. Elsa in *Lohengrin*, summoned in the first act to defend herself against the charge of murder, enters with unperturbed slowness and responds silently, with understated nods, to the five questions the king puts to her, just as Parsifal, when he wearily returns to Monsalvat at the end, communicates with Gurnemanz by bowing his head or shaking it before he removes his helmet. Elsa's aria about her vision of Lohengrin breaks off between each of its stanzas, and – indifferent to the dramatic emergency – she has to be coaxed into continuing by the lengthy interventions of the men. How many times in the first act does Brangäne have to ask Tristan, who remains stubbornly motionless, to go to Isolde? When he finally relents, the dramatic encounter is delayed, or transferred to the orchestra, by two long minutes of stasis as they study each other, Isolde gripping her couch to steady herself, Tristan hesitating before he moves closer. A further two minutes of physical stillness and vocal silence follow their drinking of the potion, while the music records what is happening inside them: it churns, writhes, briefly relaxes, after which the unresolved chord from the prelude returns to announce that there will be no immediate relief.

This unpropulsive, interrupted rhythm, with its frustrating postponements and its brooding retrospectiveness, obeys a musical law. 'The eloquent pause – that is the province of music,' Wagner told Cosima in 1878. Such pauses, in which the dramatic action is suspended so that the music can impart information the characters lack, are the most eloquent passages of *Die Walküre*. The orchestra is aware of the attraction between Siegmund and Sieglinde before they express it, so there is a tactfully soft anticipation of her aria 'Du bist der Lenz' when she hands him the drink. The orchestra identifies Wotan during Siegmund's account of his childhood and again when Sieglinde describes the stranger at her enforced wedding. Even after a command to hurry up – like Hunding's gruff order to Sieglinde 'Fort aus dem Saal!/Säume hier nicht!' – things proceed at the same calm, thoughtful pace. Wotan admits to feeling paternal remorse only after putting Brünnhilde to sleep, and then, in referring to her as 'meines Herzens/heiligster Stolz', what he emphasizes is the loss of an alter ego, his other half. It is in the orchestra, during the pause before he sings 'Der Augen leuchtendes Paar', that his regrets surge up. At such moments, characters audibly if not visibly mutate. After her argument with Wotan, Brünnhilde reluctantly gathers her weapons and – as the softened, sensitive modulations hint – begins to feel a human empathy that estranges her from the pitiless gods. Music establishes a living connection between people who seem to have nothing in common. The 'Todesverkündigung' – the dialogue in which Brünnhilde, materializing like a phantom, predicts Siegmund's death – is another of Wagner's mesmeric exercises in what Symons called monotony. It takes the form of a 'ritornello', an iterated refrain or, in Nietzsche's terminology, an eternal return. Occupying fixed positions, the goddess and the warrior repeatedly go back to first principles and restate their cases with slight variations: Brünnhilde offers Siegmund a hero's death, he refuses it because he will not desert Sieglinde. Then, after twenty minutes, the situation suddenly and violently turns upside down. Disarmed by love, Brünnhilde decides to protect him rather than waiting to collect his corpse. The dramatic reversal is hasty, scrambled and in the event disastrous; what matters is the musical premeditation and moral reappraisal that lead up to it.

Wagner's characters are what Claude Lévi-Strauss called 'chromatic beings', with moods that modulate like notes or like light passing through a prism. Lévi-Strauss, who honoured Wagner as an amateur anthropologist, used the term to describe symbols that could alternate between opposite meanings. His example was the opossum, which is a negative agent in some South American legends and positive in others. He might also have cited the spear in *Parsifal*, which first gives a wound and then heals it; it is profane and punitive when wielded by Klingsor, but hallowed when Gurnemanz calls it 'O wunden-wundervoller/heiliger Speer!' Similarly, flowers are blowsily erotic when they flaunt themselves in Klingsor's garden in the second act but chaste when they bloom in the meadow at Easter in the third. Chromatic beings change colours kaleidoscopically, which is why Wagner's characters often come in sets, with each of the interrelated members of the group representing a different stage in the continuum, like the tinted spectrum of the rainbow at the end of *Das Rheingold*. There are three Rhinemaidens, three Norns and nine Valkyries in the *Ring*, as well as four Brabantian nobles in *Lohengrin*, six minstrels at the song contest in *Tannhäuser*, and a dozen Meistersingers. Individuals are mutable, a compound of divergent selves that alternate without ever merging. Lévi-Strauss archly calls Isolde 'an opossum function' because she varies along a chromatic scale between black and white, sometimes hating Tristan, sometimes loving him, sometimes – as when she finds him dead – feeling both ways at once. Brünnhilde has the same variability. Awoken by Siegfried, she veers from maternal solicitude to virginal trepidation, from divine scorn to sexual frenzy. Appropriately enough she decides, after experiencing all these alterations, 'Brünnhilde bin ich nicht mehr!' She is no longer Brünnhilde – but who then is she? The psychological alterations happen as quickly as the slithering key shifts and instrumental figurations that accompany them in the orchestra. Kundry in *Parsifal* vacillates between attempting to corrupt Parsifal and begging him to save her. The critic James Huneker thought her a 'ridiculous hag', so psychologically incoherent that he compared her, as his ultimate insult, to a Verdian character: 'she is Azucena when she reveals to Parsifal his parentage – perhaps Wagner had heard of *Il trovatore*! ... She is of the opera operatic.' His slur missed the orchestral connection between motives that drama alone cannot reconcile. Leonora in *Il trovatore* derives music from her racing pulse and her irregular breathing. Wagner's heroines are also made of music, though their composition is more ambiguous and unstable: they have dissonant, tonally irresolute minds.

In Verdi's operas, music works more single-mindedly, breaking down the resistance of drama, as when Violetta's soft singing convinces Germont to reconsider his judgment of her. Such an epiphany is inconceivable in a novel. In *I promessi sposi* Manzoni either despairs of making miracles happen or, if they do occur, begs pardon for not explaining how or why. The hero Renzo goes to work in a silk mill. His success pleases his cousin Bortolo, who can afford to be generous because the illiterate young man is no threat to his own position. 'Perhaps, reader, you would prefer a more ideal Bortolo?' asks Manzoni. 'If so, then all I can say is, make one up for yourself. This one was like that.' A cardinal berates the parish priest whose refusal to marry the betrothed couple has been responsible for their misadventures, tells him he should have martyred himself for their sakes, and awaits a reply. Manzoni, as dumbfounded as the priest, prolongs the pause, starts a new chapter, then stops again to wonder whether it is reasonable to expect such noble altruism of human beings. On one occasion the improbable transformation does occur. A nameless bandit chief, who has the heroine Lucia in his power, reviews his life, seeks forgiveness, and ends his reign of terror. To account for this stretches Manzoni, who was dealing with an obdurate, irredeemable reality; for Verdi, it would have been easy. Music can sponsor sacrifices like that which the parish priest cannot bring himself to make. Offering up her own life at the end of *Rigoletto*, Gilda rushes in where angels, let alone characters in novels, fear to tread.

Changes of heart in Verdi's operas are like an intercession of grace. Music does the work of religion: it impels people to act uncharacteristically, turns them inside out, gives meaning to the impalpable notion of a soul. It is the conscience of drama, overriding the realist's assumption that characters are necessarily flawed and feeble like Bortolo. Wagner's chromatic beings flicker through all the colours of the rainbow; in Verdi, black turns to white as we listen.

|||||||||||||||||||

For Wagner, music drama was the consummation of a marriage. He described the union of the two arts as a sexual encounter, with language as the rationalizing male force that invades and is then absorbed by the sensual body of music, which he took to be female. Wagner identified both with his male protagonists and with the females they wooed, although his divided aims meant that the lovers always quarrel on their way to consummation. Tristan, so guiltily self-aware during his delirium, exemplifies the poet's need for understanding and the dramatist's attraction to conflict. Isolde is the spirit of music, the embodiment of what Søren Kierkegaard called its 'sensuous immediacy'. After upbraiding her lover for inconsiderately dying, she advances to her own solitary orgasm, which is a hymn in praise of music – of its sightless radiance and its immaterial volume, of its synaesthetic transformation of sound into sight or even into smell, and of the vibrancy by which it makes manifest the respiration of life itself.

Or the sequence could be reversed, making music the matrix that gave birth to drama, as in Nietzsche's genealogy of tragedy; music was a baby nourished, Wagner told Cosima in 1872, by its mother's blood. Either way, the insemination took place inside Wagner, whose art required him to perform a double biological duty. Mime lies when he says he is both Siegfried's father and his mother, but Wagner claimed exactly this when discussing the parentage of his operas.

'Deeds of music' sound like heroic masculine achievements, comparable with dragon-slaying, but Wagner preferred to describe his creativity gynaecologically. In 1860 he wrote to Liszt about the lying-in that would usher *Tristan* into the world: the location of the event was still 'a mysterious secret', but the opera's 'birth would be simplest … if I were to entrust its confinement to the King of Hanover'. It was Ludwig II, of course, who became the midwife, helping Wagner through the last stages of his labour. He spared no detail when likening his work to the gory business of expelling a new life from the body inside which it has been nurtured. Early in 1882 he and Cosima had a meal to celebrate his completion of *Parsifal*, although because he had finished composing it three weeks earlier he announced that 'this was the afterbirth'. The metaphor did not spoil their appetites: some animals and human beings in a few societies eat the placenta, a magical act that returns the incriminating evidence of creativity to its hiding place. Wagner superimposed this mystery onto another one, which dealt with reproduction in heaven. He was intrigued by August Friedrich Gfrörer's analysis of Christian myth, and in 1873 summarized for Cosima his gendering of the Trinity: 'God the Father, masculine; the Holy Ghost, feminine; the Redeemer as the world stemming from them.' Wagner then made a connective leap to Schopenhauer's metaphysics, identifying the three persons of the triangle as 'will, idea, and world emerging out of the division of the sexes'.

The world evolves from differentiation; family trees fork and branch outwards, like the exponentiating breeds of dogs. One becomes two, then many.

Wagner was a creator who worked backwards, attempting to reach the androgynous state that had predated division. Hence the oddities of the family romance in his operas, which are more interested in fusion than in fission. Incest, committed by the Wälsung twins, comes naturally to these characters, who overlap inside their creator. Fricka contemptuously describes Brünnhilde as the bride of her father Wotan's wishes, and he calls her 'meines wunsches schaffender Schoss', the womb in which his plans are shaped, a surrogate mother for his ideas. Even after he abandons her on the flame-encircled rock, Wotan controls Brünnhilde at second hand: the only man able to win her is his grandson, so she gives herself to her nephew. When Siegfried appears, Brünnhilde cancels the distance between them by telling him 'Du selbst bin ich': you are myself. Sex is the reunion of sundered halves that, like music and drama, should never have been split apart.

Verdi, an adamantine character who claimed that he lacked nerves, never thought of music as something painfully extracted from inside himself. During preparations for *Macbeth* he wrote out the text in prose, then made his librettist Piave versify it: someone else's words had to prod the music into existence. In 1844, while composing *I due Foscari*, he ordered Piave to 'work yourself into a proper state of feeling and write some beautiful verses'. He would never have expected to find himself in the same tipsy, elevated state – unlike Wagner who, when revising the Venusberg scene in *Tannhäuser* for Paris in 1860, wheedlingly told Mathilde Wesendonck that 'in order to compose the music, I shall need to be in a very good mood indeed'. The music came to Verdi no matter how he felt or what else he was doing: he jotted down a phrase for 'Immenso Fthà', the sacerdotal chant that recurs throughout *Aida*, on a scrap of paper memorializing that day's sales of firewood and wine at Sant'Agata. But his instruction to Piave contained a challenge. The librettist was to transmit his excitement to Verdi, which meant puncturing his reserve, perhaps weakening him.

He was modelling their collaboration on the play that was their source, Byron's *The Two Foscari*. Byron emphasizes the stoical self-containment of the Doge and his son Jacopo, who both die of despair without physical cause. The wracked Jacopo is 'a sufferer, but not a loud one', and the Doge's composure amazes the Venetian politicians. One of them asks *'Feels he*, think you?' and another replies 'He shows it not.' They might have been discussing Verdi, who incidentally told Piave that he did not want Jacopo to be tortured onstage. For Puccini, the application of pain was a sure way of eliciting song – or the more untuned screams of Cavaradossi in *Tosca* when the spiked steel of Scarpia's torturers tightens around his forehead, or Liu in *Turandot* when her arm is twisted to make her blab out her secret. Opera requires characters to express what they feel, but Verdi preferred not to apply the pincers and hooks employed by Puccini's thugs. *I due Foscari* breaks down the resistance of Byron's stoics by mobilizing Jacopo's wife Lucrezia, who appears at intervals with her moist-eyed children, hoping to soften the accusers and to make her father-in-law intervene on her husband's behalf. The Doge, obliged to uphold the laws of Venice, says he has no more tears to shed, but with her vocal blandishments Lucrezia succeeds in proving him wrong. As a proxy for Piave, she was meant to entice the same reaction from the composer, who whispered to Clarina Maffei when the revolutionary leader Mazzini died, 'Don't tell anyone, but I sometimes weep!' Yet the emotion released by music proves fatal to both Foscari: although Jacopo's life is spared, he dies of homesickness as he sails into exile, and his father the Doge collapses, heartbroken. Verdi had good reason for his temperate demeanour.

Wagner told Liszt that 'music (as a woman) must necessarily be impregnated by a poet (as a man)', which made creation a kind of self-seduction. Verdi kept the roles further apart and fudged the genders: was the librettist a female who could be easily dominated, or was it the composer who had to be wooed into submission by the other man's words? The stories he told about the origins of *Nabucco* in his anecdotal memoir may over-dramatize the details, but they reveal the intricacy of this power play with his collaborators. When the German composer Otto Nicolai declared Solera's text to be beneath contempt, the impresario Merelli fobbed it off on Verdi, who also returned it. Merelli stuffed the pamphlet into Verdi's coat pocket, then shoved him out of the office, slammed the door and locked it. This supplied Verdi with a way of apologizing for his first success: he was bullied into composing the score because Merelli would not take back the libretto. Even in jest, Verdi disliked appearing to be the loser, so he adjusted the balance by coercing Solera, adapting the tactics Merelli had used. He wanted to add a prophetic aria for Zaccaria, but Solera declined to write it. He was persuaded to relent, then hummed and hawed about when it might be ready. Verdi expedited matters by locking the door of the room they were in and pocketing the key. He told Solera that he would only be released when the prophecy was written, and passed him a copy of the Bible. Solera glowered at his jailer, but the words were ready in a quarter of an hour.

Wagner expected a fanciful impregnation, the union of his complementary sexual selves; for Verdi, composer and librettist were both strong-willed, competitive men, fighting – like tenor and baritone in his operas – over a woman who surely knew in advance which of them would be the victor.

# 'That song conquers me'

Drama watches characters in action, who make choices and confront the consequences. Opera changes that formula: drama now is a reaction to music. The brash jubilation of trumpets prompts a patriotic oath in Verdi's *La battaglia di Legnano*, and Wagner's Rienzi tells his followers to foregather when they hear the long, clear note of the trumpet. Meanwhile an organ inside the Roman basilica propounds a different set of values, threatening the tribune with religious reprisals. Another organ prompts Luisa Miller's last prayer, and in the respectable Wartburg the sweet, insidious figurations of violins drag Tannhäuser's memory back to his underground orgy with Venus. Bells, ritualizing time with their regularity, call Parsifal and Gurnemanz to a temple that resounds with unseen voices: a dying man in a burial niche, children somewhere above, an oracular contralto even higher in the dome. A different religious ceremony, the auto-da-fé in *Don Carlos*, is interrupted by an ownerless soprano voice from the air, dispensing comfort and the promise of salvation with the aid of a rippling harp and an ethereal harmonium. In the darkness Brangäne listens for the horns of the hunting party that seems to her to be dangerously close, while Isolde's ear is attuned only to the nocturnal stirring and rustling of the garden and what she calls the laughter of the fountain, like the bubbling of her agitated blood. Otello rebuffs Iago's insinuations when he hears Desdemona seraphically singing with a chorus of children as a mandolin tinkles. 'Quel canto mi conquide', he says, conquered by the song. Opera is less about what people do than what music makes them feel.

The drama of *Die Meistersinger* investigates music's uses – its ecclesiastical function and its role as a social fixative, its easing of labour and its mythical capacity to restore paradise, the teasing oddity of an art that is so impalpable.

The singing lesson that David gives to Walther, like Siegfried's experiments with the reed, situates music somewhere between nature and culture. His classification of tones cites the nightingale, lark and finch as models of lyrical spontaneity, but there are also modes that have no auditory equivalent, named after metals, herbs, paper and ink: music can only be described by dragging in extraneous metaphors. Defying Wagnerian protocol, David even indulges in some Italianate vocal ornamentation when explaining 'Blum' und Koloratur', and he manages to make sense of these synaesthetic terms. Sounds can bloom and blossom, and though unseen they have colour. Thus, to Baudelaire's ears, the Venusberg harboured 'a rosy light which came not from the sun', and Liszt when he heard the *Lohengrin* prelude visualized a cathedral with golden doors, asbestos joists and opaline columns, seen through a rainbow-toned cloud of incense. Unfortunately Walther learns little from David's encyclopaedia of frills and flourishes; Ford is an apter pupil when Verdi's *Falstaff* offers him an abbreviated tutorial in vocal technique. Ford has been trying to woo Alice, as he says, by singing a madrigal. He utters the word with a ricocheting decoration that is almost like flamenco, but his oscillation gets nowhere until Falstaff takes it up in an impromptu melody to which Ford adds assenting repetitions. Soon Ford attempts some vocal flitting and darting of his own. Falstaff – to paraphrase the compliment he pays his own wit in Shakespeare's *Henry IV* – is not only musical in himself but the source of music in other men.

Wagner designed *Die Meistersinger* as a rebuttal of Italy's claim to have invented opera. In Germany artisans not courtiers take credit for the art, and a thronging open field outside Nuremberg replaces the exclusive palaces of Florence and Mantua where Peri's *Euridice* and Monteverdi's *Orfeo* were staged in the first decade of the seventeenth century. Fending off accusations of Wagnerism late in his career, Verdi made a point of re-establishing Italy's pre-eminence in *Otello* and *Falstaff*. Boito reminded him that Shakespeare's tragedy had its source in a tawdry tale from Giovan Battista Giraldi Cinthio's *Hecatommithi*, and later sneakily traced the character of Falstaff back to *Il pecorone* by Ser Giovanni. Here was a mythic source as primordial and as elusive as any of Wagner's – not a saga or a folk tale but a digest of anecdotes compiled in Florence during the fourteenth century by an anthologist so obscure that he might have been anonymous. Verdi, according to Boito, had restored Falstaff to his proper 'Tuscan source'; the score correspondingly remembers the Tuscan source of opera. Hence Ford's madrigal, or Alice's decision to take up her lute as she waits for Falstaff's arrival. When he arrives, his courtly verses fondle the tune with which he greets her as delicately as a Renaissance singer. He then releases his eager, ardent full voice in 'Ed or potrò morir felice', applying weight to the melody until it echoes the love duet from *Otello*: a vaulting leap ahead from the early seventeenth to the late nineteenth century. Before the masquerade in the dark forest in *Falstaff*, Nannetta promises to sing 'parole armonïose' – harmonic, harmonizing words – and her aria is a rare case of music that apparently filters down from the sky and falls like dew on our overheated, disruptive world. Verdi preferred, however, to marvel at the music produced by bodies, human and otherwise, so that when Falstaff calls Ford an ox – 'un bue!' – the orchestra lows like the beast. In *Die Meistersinger* intemperate noise threatens to upset the precious, precarious order imposed by music: Sachs shouts as he hammers the shoe to disrupt Beckmesser's serenade. But the most musical sound in *Falstaff* is a noise made neither by voices nor by instruments. The kiss exchanged by Fenton and Nannetta is another deed of music made not visible but audible, delicate yet resonant enough to be overheard by everyone in Ford's crowded house, and it renders words unnecessary because it provokes a dramatic climax more succinctly than any 'parola scenica' could do.

In planning an opera, Verdi always thought ahead to the music's emotional outcome, the pay-off for him, for his singers and for us. His letter to Salvatore Cammarano in 1850 about *King Lear* asked for a 'very singular, moving scene' in the hovel on the heath, a 'touching little duet' between Edgar and Gloucester, a 'moving scene' when Lear and Cordelia are reunited in prison, as well as some therapeutic 'soft music … behind the scene' when Lear awakens with his reason restored. Classical tragedy aimed at purgation, and Aristotle's catharsis was a medicinal cleansing that violently harrowed the soul. Verdi's designs on his audience were less drastic, though devastatingly efficient: he wanted to make us cry.

The tears of his characters are an unmiraculous equivalent to the liquefying blood of Saint Gennaro in his Neapolitan shrine. They are a proof of life, a moral credential, even a spiritual assurance. In the *Requiem*'s 'Lacrymosa' the soloists toil through their account of Judgment Day as if they were wading through an ocean of tears, and the chorus adds a wailing descant that seems to rise up from an afflicted, beleaguered world. Human history is not the annals of bloodshed but an archive of lachrymose woe. Elisabeth in *Don Carlos*, during the aria she addresses to the former emperor, asks whether the dead weep in heaven, implying that tears are a symptom and symbol of our earthly lot. Aida suffers, as she says in her first aria, because she cannot openly cry for her Ethiopian compatriots, and the most malevolent trick Amneris plays on her is to encourage her tears by pretending that she shares them: 'Ben ti compiango,' she purrs as she entices a confession from her slave. During the triumph, Radamès honours Aida's tears, her 'pianto adorato'. Desdemona's willow song begins with two words that make singing and weeping synonymous, 'Piangea cantando'. Tears like laughter are a defining attribute of humanity, which is why Iago does not believe in them: in his atheistic Credo he dismisses crying along with kisses as the acting-out of an emotion that only fools believe to be heartfelt. Otello, less anaesthetized, knows that tears confer value. He remembers that the tales of his exotic exploits were ennobled by Desdemona's solicitude. His phrase is 'Ingentilìa di lagrime', which implies that her moist eyes softened his rude stories, made them gentle but also rendered them genteel and worthy of the august company in her father's house. When he mistreats Desdemona, she responds with a melody that manages to demonstrate her goodness while pointing in its measured cadences to her forthright dignity and quiet indignation. She sings about her tears, the first she has ever shed to express grief, and as she reaches into the air for a high note on 'le prime lagrime' the dazzling arc of sound seems to pluck her from the ground. These tears, she specifies, are not self-pitying, and this is what gives them such moral force; she cries on Otello's behalf, and as she bedews the dust she prays for him and has the satisfaction of seeing him weep as well. 'Tu pur piangi?' she asks. Briefly pitying her, he has regained his humanity, which for Verdi means a capacity for commiseration.

Later Otello knocks her to the ground in front of the Venetian ambassadors. Desdemona is crushed by a volley from the bass, and a gaping interval between notes opens a pit for her to fall into. She tries, thanks to Boito's beautiful verbal image, to see her grief as part of a cycle in nature that will eventually bring healing: she notices that the sun is impartially gladdening the sky and sea, though she doubts that it will dry the bitter drops shed by her eyes. Yet if the soprano's voice is as 'sereno e vivido' as the warming light to which she refers, Desdemona effectively rises above her plight. Opera, at moments like this, does more than amplify emotions by increasing their volume; it enlarges them, shares them with the whole of the sentient world. The tears we quietly and perhaps shamefacedly shed for theatrical characters testify to our literal, physical membership of one another, which prompts us – as proof of our emotional generosity – to cry over the simulated distress of fictional people. Rulers in Verdi assume responsibility for this emotional economy. Riccardo in *Un ballo in maschera* says that power means drying the tears of his subjects – although what this means is providing them with entertainments like the masked ball, or making surreptitious handouts like the tip he slips into the pocket of the loyal sailor in Ulrica's den. Verdi's priests want to make tears flow rather than staunching them. Stankar in *Stiffelio* dismisses his daughter Lina's tears as if they were those of an actress, but Stiffelio condemns her for not crying, which to him is the symptom of a hardened heart.

Wagnerian tears are less frequent, less appreciated, more easily wiped away. Elsa cries in confusion when challenged by Ortrud during her bridal procession, but Lohengrin, controlling the situation with the help of a musical modulation, orders her to shed tears of joy: 'Komm, lass in Freude dort diese Tränen fliessen!' After Kundry's baptism in the last act, Parsifal listens to the music that describes the warming of the stark earth in spring and then, fining down his hefty voice in a delicate pianissimo, delivers a benediction that usurps her grateful tears and banishes regrets: 'du weinest! – sieh! Es lacht die Aue' – you are crying, but look, the meadow smiles. Nature has stealthily changed the winter's tale of tragedy – trees like corpses, soil stiffened by ice – into the burgeoning comedy of spring. There is no opportunity for the mute Kundry to respond, and no reason for her to do so: the opera has passed beyond human fates and beyond humanity, contemplating a life force as impersonal as the fluent, pulsating Rhine. Here, looked at with hindsight, is Wagner's equivalent to the fugue in *Falstaff*. But Boito's refrain has to be revised to fit this achingly regretful post-mortem review of a world that the characters in *Parsifal* seem already to have quit. In 'Tutto nel mondo è burla' Boito describes life as a jest; for Wagner life is an illusion. Man the jester whirls around, as Falstaff and all the others admit – a rational creature who behaves irrationally, exhilarated by insanity. Wagner stops the comic carousel, releasing his characters from the burden of human existence. Verdi's people, in the relay race of their fugue, compete with each other to have the last laugh, and conclude in a braying, hooting explosion of mirth that is cacophonously taken over by the orchestra in the final rampant bars. Instead of that loud hilarity, Wagner asks us to listen to the silent, metaphorical laughter of the meadow.

Verdi and Wagner use corresponding terms to describe the benison of music. Rigoletto tells Gilda that her mother loved him 'per compassion' despite his deformity, then instantly adds that she died. Kundry begs Parsifal for 'Mitleid', which means mercy or pity or charity, and he becomes wise – as the voice from the dome of the temple predicts – by acquiring this sympathy for others. Compassion is literally the sharing of passion, the gift of reciprocation, just as condolence means to partake in doleful feelings that are not monopolized by the person who is bereaved. The 'mit' of 'Mitleid' likewise adds a conjunction to 'leid', which means pain. But can a Wagnerian character shoulder another's misfortune and try to relieve it, as Rigoletto's wife did? The 'mit' is as problematic as the connective 'Wortlein "und"' that puzzles Isolde during her second-act duet with Tristan, and he takes the compound word to pieces when he says to Kurwenal, 'mit leidest du,/wenn ich leide'. His gratitude for his retainer's sympathy does not last long, because Tristan goes on to deny that the Verdian transfusion of feelings is possible: 'nur was ich leide,/

das kannst du nicht leiden!' Kurwenal respects this solipsism and apologizes for dying beside Tristan. The words used by Verdi and Wagner, apparently parallel, make moral assumptions that are incompatible. Rigoletto's remark about compassion suggests that love has a necessary element of pity: to feel sorry for someone else is to take responsibility for them, which means, among other things, wanting to make them happy. Shakespeare's Othello says that he loved Desdemona because she pitied the agonies he underwent when sold into slavery. Boito took that complacent, self-congratulating remark and shared it between Otello and Desdemona; when she repeats it, coaxing extra repetitions from him near the end of their love duet, it testifies to a mutuality that eludes Shakespeare's characters, since Desdemona in the play is not asked to second Othello's recollection. According to Schopenhauer, 'Mitleid' was the highest of virtues, which is why Wagner esteemed it, but its value had little to do with the generosity of Violetta when she donates her last coins to the poor. The awakening of this virtue to the wounds of others was futile and self-cancelling. Because there is something perverse in volunteering to share an anguish that is after all incommunicably locked up in the bodies of other creatures, Schopenhauer thought that 'Mitleid' led us towards the recognition that existence is intolerable. Philosophically, it readies us for suicide. In 1872 when Wagner saw a dog run over and killed on the quay in Lucerne he thought about what the proper response should be rather than responding instinctively, as Violetta does when she remembers those even less fortunate than herself. 'A human being should not feel pity,' he announced after due deliberation. 'Nature doesn't want it; he should be as cruel as the animals.'

In Wolfram von Eschenbach's *Parzival*, the medieval romance that was one of the sources for Wagner's opera, the ignorant hero is sent on a quest that involves asking a question. He is puzzled when he sees the stricken Anfortas in the Grail castle, but because Gurnemanz has rebuked him for being inquisitive he does not ask the obvious question, which would have restored the sick king to health. As Wagner retells the story, the quest is about acquiring empathy not information. Gurnemanz makes Parsifal grieve for the swan he has wantonly killed at the outset; his rending cry of 'Amfortas!' after Kundry kisses him in the second act announces that he now knows how it feels to have your flesh torn, your corruptibility exposed. But his response is a form of identification like that performed by the player who sheds spurious tears for Hecuba in *Hamlet*; it is supposed to match Christ's acceptance of his grievous mission, although Christ did more than assure the downtrodden that he felt their pain. Parsifal pities the swan but shows no such commiseration to Kundry, and when she begs him for sympathy – 'Mitleid! Mitleid mit mir!' – he pushes her aside. Returning to Monsalvat in the third act, he refers to the path of suffering he has trodden, 'der Leiden Pfade'.

The stabbing intervals of the third prelude describe a lamed, limping tour of the world, but we know nothing about what happened during this emotional apprenticeship. In 1905 in his *Stories from Wagner* J. Walker McSpadden invented just one mawkishly Christian anecdote to fill the interim: Parsifal rescues a stray lamb, returns it to the ewe, and is rewarded by fortuitously finding his way back to the Grail castle. Wagner's Parsifal has to learn compassion, which is not, as it is for Verdi's characters, an inborn aptitude, and when he is honoured by Gurnemanz as 'Mitleidsvoll Duldender,/heiltatvoll Wissender!' the compound words incongruously bunch together ideas that ought to be kept further apart. According to this tribute, he is a pitying sufferer who can heal because he is enlightened. But, after his reaction to Kundry's troublingly incestuous kiss, what does Parsifal suffer? Is there sufficient wisdom in the vegetarian doctrine Gurnemanz preaches when mourning the swan? The funeral march that introduces the first Grail ceremony moves us, just as it enables Parsifal and Gurnemanz to glide from the forest to the temple by walking on the spot: emotion means movement, a motion inside the body, but this unblocking of sensation does not guarantee moral growth.

Wagner wrote what he called 'the music of transition', like the endless melody that conducts us between desolate numbness and a scarcely believable joy as Gurnemanz describes Good Friday. The sounds are malleable, and as we listen one idea coils, twists, collapses and reforms as something else, stretching us to recognize an affinity between opposites. Likewise in the interlude between the first two scenes of *Das Rheingold* the glowering motif that denominates the ring dissolves into the more forthright and officious motif announcing Valhalla. Transitions like this were too fickly metamorphic for Verdi, and also too reversible. The moral and emotional bonus of his music was conversion, an instantaneous change of heart. The Spanish king in *Ernani* and the Peruvian governor in *Alzira* gratuitously forgive the political opponents who have plotted against them, Riccardo in *Un ballo in maschera* even pardons his assassin. When the context is religious, the new faith of Verdi's characters depends on human sympathy not divine clemency, and it comes to them through music. In *Nabucco* the despot and blasphemer is instantly forgiven when he begins his wrenching minor-key plea, 'Deh perdona'. He later asks for pardon from the Hebrew God he insulted, with the cello sombrely vouching for his remorse and the flute catching the glint of grace that flutters like a dove's wings. In *La forza del destino* it is the 'sublimi cantici' of the monks that pacifies Leonora, and as she dies in the Milan version she soothes Alvaro with a seraphically floating melody that is like manna made of air. She promises that God will forgive his crimes; he promptly repents, explaining 'A quell'accento più non poss'io resistere' – how can he resist her voice?

The accord is hard-won because Alvaro has to live with his guilt and with the loss of Leonora. It was easier for Wagner to resolve the *Tristan* discord in the last bars of the opera because a final transition has carried off both Tristan and Isolde to a world of sound and light that is as bodiless as music. Wagner felt no duty to be consoling. In 1859 he wrote a cheerfully distraught letter to Mathilde Wesendonck declaring *Tristan* to be *'terrible'* and predicting that it would be banned – not for political sedition or moral laxity, which made the censors object to *Rigoletto*, but because it threatened mental stability and physical health. Verdi's art helps his characters endure life, whereas Wagner's prods us to recognize that it is a dead end. Music in one case cures distempers, and in the other enlightens us by ravaging our timid, flimsy sanity.

| | | | | | | | | | | | | | | | | | | | | |

Verdi and Wagner often agreed about subjects that were suitable for operatic treatment, although their different views of the characters that attracted them forced them instantly apart. Was Barbarossa a menacing vandal or a guardian of rude racial virtue? Was Rienzi a dreary politician with no private life or a man who nobly personified the state? Was Macbeth merely ambitious or the victim, as Wagner told Cosima, of demonic forces?

In his comments on Schiller's plays, Wagner seems to be engaged in an oblique dispute with Verdi, reclaiming characters that belonged rightfully to him. He praised the 'dignified tone' of Schiller's *Don Carlos*, and his motto, when in a contented mood, was 'Life is beautiful after all!' – a quote from Schiller's Posa, who blesses the world as he leaves it, pleased that by entrusting his mission to Carlos he has contributed to making it a better place. The libretto for Verdi's opera gives Posa a paraphrase of that line in the aria he sings as he dies, but the operatic scene does not end in resignation: the king, who in Schiller remains impassive and unrepentant, joins Carlos in an angry elegy for the dead man. The line Wagner quoted is wistful but serenely selfless; Verdi pressed beyond this quietism and made the survivors raise their voices in lament and protest. Cosima had her own designs on the two female characters in *Don Carlos*, and at the start of her life with Wagner she told him that 'the queen has always been my ideal of womanhood, the princess just a charming example of femininity'. The comment made her betrayal of Bülow seem like Elisabeth's selfless decision to give up Carlos for reasons of state; it was hypocritical of her to sideline Eboli, whose secret affair with the king is a closer analogue to Cosima's own behaviour. Verdi would not have recognized either character from Cosima's description. His Elisabeth is no poised angel of renunciation but a woman tormented by her decision to be untrue to herself, and his Eboli – so recklessly vivacious, so sexually aggressive, at last so overcome by self-loathing – is not a conventional feminine charmer. A few weeks before his death, Wagner was again reading Schiller's play aloud. He commended Posa's 'Aryan ideality', and said that the king's morose, funereal monologue was 'Shakespearean', although by then he might just as well have called it Verdian. 'Elle ne m'aime pas' – the nocturnal despot's long, grim self-revaluation, introduced by the threnody of the cellos – is a soliloquy rather than an aria, since music offers the king no respite from his sadness. Perhaps Wagner felt too close a kinship with the insomniac king who, surrounded by guttering candles, imagines his own internment in the Escorial; cautioning against over-excitement, his doctor forbade him to continue with the one-man performance.

Verdi's first setting of Schiller was *Giovanna d'Arco*, loosely based on *Die Jungfrau von Orleans*. Wagner considered the play to be 'den Gotteswunderbaum', a divine and miraculous growth; it was probably a mercy that he did not know the opera. He compared Schiller's Joan of Arc with Parsifal, since both were icons of a spiritual virginity who showed how Christianity might 'be preached to the world with renewed purity and truth'. Reading *Die Jungfrau* in 1870, he criticized Schiller for allowing Joan to be distracted from her 'awesomely sacred calling' when she is wooed by her British enemy Lionel. He worried about the relevance of this detour, and in 1878 he preferred to stress the heroine's immolation – 'Joan in chains, her liberation, then the victory, her death, the recovery of the flag to serve as her shroud' – which made her a Gallic Brünnhilde, intent on national glory. Verdi's Giovanna could indeed be a premature critique of Wagner's armour-clad Valkyrie. What interested Verdi was the relationship between the militant maid and her disgruntled father, although Giovanna and old Giacomo are the moral antithesis of Brünnhilde and Wotan. Wagner's god cannot forgive the weak-minded sensitivity of his disobedient daughter, and he punishes her by sentencing her to a menial domestic fate. In Verdi, the father refuses to accept his daughter's rebellion against her homely role, and he sees her military career as a sign of mania. He approves of the funeral pyre, which will burn away her wickedness rather than cauterizing the world like the flames in *Götterdämmerung*. Ultimately she comes to agree with him. The 'diva donzella' wants to desert the army, disbelieving in the 'applausi' of her admirers, and she tries to shed her divinity by removing her chain mail. Wagner emphasized Joan's sanctity; Verdi could only think of her as a human being who, like a diva of the operatic kind, may possess exalted powers but longs to shed them and retire to her rustic home.

Verdi and Wagner both revered Shakespeare, each in his own way. For Verdi, reading him was ancestor worship, a Latin homage to a familial god: he referred to Shakespeare as 'il Papà'. Wagner was less adept at humbling himself before an antecedent. In a letter to Mathilde Wesendonck in 1859 he explained his impudent attitude to a writer he regarded as an equal: he enjoyed fraternizing with 'the world's great' when he read, and – grousing as usual about his professional setbacks – said that this helped him to surmount 'life's misadventures'. In a smugger moment, he told Cosima in 1881 that Shakespeare must have been a cheerful fellow, 'somewhat like me'. Even racially they were akin. Wagner, who spoke a Saxon dialect, considered Shakespeare to be a product of the resurgent 'Anglo-Saxon spirit', no longer squashed by Norman Catholicism. At the age of thirteen, he even garbled Shakespeare's name so as to make him a Wagnerian embodiment of embattled heroism: he thought the plays he was reading were by Shicksper, and believed that both syllables – the first alluding to 'Schicksal' or fate, the second pointing to a spear – were auguries.

Verdi called Shakespeare 'the great searcher of the human heart', a secular priest who listens to our collective confessions but prescribes no penance. It was typical of Verdi to assume that all hearts were laid bare by this scrutiny. Wagner required a more private audience, and in 1882 he called Shakespeare 'my only spiritual friend'. Although in his readings he played all the parts, the characters he favoured were Shakespeare's tragic egotists. One morning in 1880 Cosima reported that he was worn out after having raged through Lear's imprecations the night before. As well as assuming the role himself, Wagner could cast someone else in it, if that suited his psychological purpose. A month before his death he was annoyed by Liszt, then a guest at the Palazzo Vendramin, and told Cosima that her father was 'just like King Lear, his acquaintances the hundred knights'. It was a sinister remark: he referred to Lear's refusal to relinquish the trappings of powers when he visits himself and his rowdy entourage on his daughters, and he may have been slyly suggesting that Cosima should treat her father as harshly as Goneril and Regan do. That night Cosima heard him murmuring 'King Lear, horrible man' as he lay in bed. Tragedy, looked at like this, narrows to monodrama; it is about the individual's mistaken sense of his eminence, and his fury when others encroach on his domain. Verdi, by contrast, recognized that *King Lear* rebukes such a desire for monopoly. What made the play unworkable as an opera was his insistence, when he prepared his outline of the action in 1850, on dealing with all of its snagged, intersecting plots. There would have to be five principal parts, he told his librettist Cammarano, though he immediately added four more, with Goneril as a second prima donna. He understood the play's breadth but was defeated by it, although later, in *Simon Boccanegra, La forza del destino* and *Don Carlos*, he brought to opera something of Shakespeare's extended time and amplified space.

Summing up Shakespeare, Wagner ignored the empathy valued by Verdi and replaced it with airy omniscience. 'How wonderful is Shakespeare's fine mockery! this godlike contempt for human foibles!' he told Mathilde. Was he equating Shakespeare with the Duke in *Measure for Measure*, the absent but disgusted god he actually eliminated when he adapted the play in *Das Liebesverbot*? After another dizzy associative leap, Wagner's Shakespeare metamorphosed into a Parsifal figure: now he represented 'the highest level of spiritual composure, attained only by genius – or by sainthood, and saints don't even need a sense of humour!' Yet the *Henry VI* plays left Wagner convinced of 'the dreadfulness of life', and made him call Shakespeare 'the greatest pessimist'. So was Shakespeare smilingly contented or acidly supercilious? It depended on how Wagner himself felt, since in attributing a philosophy to Shakespeare he was extrapolating from his current state of mind. Verdi had a better understanding of Shakespeare's impartiality because, without presuming to say so, he shared it, dispensing his characters from having to act out his own theory of existence (which is not to say that he had one). When Wagner cooled down, his critical intelligence informed him that while generalizing about Shakespeare he had been looking in the mirror. He reacted angrily, like an unrequited lover. Shakespeare, he told Cosima, was 'unbearable' because 'unknowable': how could his idol be so unWagnerian?

By coincidence, the Shakespearean characters most frequently mentioned by Wagner in the later years of his life were the protagonists of Verdi's last two operas. Wagner twice greeted Cosima by quoting Othello's remark that, unless he loves Desdemona and she is worthy of that love, 'chaos is come again'. There were devious displacements in this use of the play: Desdemona is blameless but Wagner was not, since Cosima had discovered his epistolary romance with Judith Gautier, so in adopting the role of Othello he was perhaps seeking forgiveness. Failing that, he excused his own conduct by sharing out the guilt. In 1879, forcibly extinguishing a cigarette, he was reminded of Othello stifling Desdemona, and Cosima repeated a remark he had made earlier – 'that O. killed Desdemona because he knew she must one day be unfaithful to him'. She accepted his presumption of guilt with her usual meekness. 'I am like Othello,' Wagner said again a few days before his death, and quoted the hero's self-aggrandizing obituary for himself. Whereas Verdi sweetened Otello's end by allowing him a recollection of the earlier love duet, Wagner rightly saw how comfortless the play's conclusion is. He omitted the last scene from his reading in 1879, and said that only 'a brute like Shakespeare' could write something so disconsolate.

Wagner is seldom endearing, which makes his admiration for Falstaff both peculiar and uniquely revealing. He quoted the domestic chitchat of *The Merry Wives of Windsor* with 'laughing delectation', and was simultaneously touched and amused by Mistress Quickly's report of Falstaff's death in *Henry V.* The character's extravagance and indebtedness of course appealed to him. After *Götterdämmerung*, the epic that he mock-modestly called 'this little opus', Wagner said that he would get by, like Falstaff, with only two shirts. The quotation was a warning that he had no intention of living more frugally or composing on a more modest scale. What pleased Wagner was Falstaff's incorrigibility: during a cure in 1878 he sneaked a glass of brandy between doses of spa water, and cheerfully misquoted Falstaff's nonchalant reply when he is censured by the Lord Chief Justice. Beyond Falstaff's verbal inventiveness and his wicked audacity, Wagner considered him to be a genius: an artist whose supreme creation is himself. Perhaps it was the global bulk of the man that made him speculate in 1881, on a day when he was reading *Henry IV*, about whether 'a true genius' could ever be fat. He decided against it – genius, in his view, had to be self-consuming – but the example of Falstaff suggested that there might be another kind of art, derived from a gluttonous enjoyment of life not a struggle to renounce it. Verdi stopped short of using Falstaff to justify unpaid loans and illicit drinks. In 1894, however, Verdi did borrow a hundred lire from Edoardo Mascheroni, who had conducted the first performances of *Falstaff.* He needed the money to buy a train ticket but apparently forgot to repay it. He laughed off the lapse in a letter to Mascheroni that transcribed the giggling of the merry wives – 'Ha! Ha! Ha! Ha! Ha! Ha!' – and repeated the fugal motto about the nonsensicality of the world. He had already arranged to reimburse Mascheroni through interme-diaries, but his chuckling conveyed a wish that life could consist of play, with time suspended, debts waived, sins remitted.

Wagner told Cosima that, as an adolescent, he wanted to find 'a mystical meaning in Falstaff'; he was excited by the uncanny – Hamlet's ghost, Macbeth's witches – so he found it hard to accept the down-to-earth physicality of comedy. Returning to Falstaff during the years in which he was completing *Parsifal*, he resumed his campaign to spiritualize the bibulous rascal. It was not an absurd undertaking, as Franz Werfel implied when he compared the works with which Wagner and Verdi concluded their careers: '*Falstaff* is the comedy of overcoming the world, just as *Parsifal* is the mystery play of overcoming the world.' An entry in Cosima's diary during February 1880 supports Werfel's analogy. 'R. talks about sainthood and withdrawal from life … and in connection with that plays the prelude to *Parsifal*,' she notes. To conclude the evening, Wagner performed the scene in which Falstaff outwits the Lord Chief Justice. The disparity between saint and sinner was musically harmonized: 'we found little difficulty,' Cosima reports, 'in passing from the Saviour to Sir John!'

Coping with Wagner's unpredictable temper and his frequent medical crises, Cosima took up one of Falstaff's sayings: 'like Falstaff, I could wish it were bedtime and all well'. She was hoping to get through the rest of the day, although the mantra inevitably sounds like a Wagnerian wish for unconsciousness – and in *Henry IV* Hal replies by telling Falstaff that he owes God a death. Verdi, on the other hand, adopted a motto used by his own Falstaff and made it announce his determination to get through the rest of the life that was left to him after he completed his valedictory opera. The line he chose as his personal epilogue was 'Va, vecchio John', which Falstaff sings – with a jerky rhythm that tells of the effort it will take to squeeze a little sweetness out of his ancient flesh – as he prepares for his rendezvous with Alice. Extrapolating from Boito's text in what he called 'le ultime note di Falstaff', Verdi looked beyond Falstaff's anxious concern with virility, and in a sheet left in the autograph score he wrote a genial, generous farewell to a character who would, he knew, outlive him:

> Tutto è finito!
> Va, va, vecchio John …
> Cammina per la tua via
> Finche tu puoi …
> Divertente tipo di briccone
> Eternamente vero, sotto
> Maschera diversa, in ogni
> Tempo, in ogni luogo!!
> Va … va … cammina, cammina,
> Addio!!!

With everything at an end – the opera, and perhaps the composer's life – Verdi sends old John off on his way for as long as he can continue. Falstaff will potentially last forever, since the character recurs wearing different masks in all times and all places; although he may seldom tell the truth, this amusingly typical scoundrel is eternally true because he shows us one aspect of our human nature. As the tribute develops, it disproves the opening line of the envoi, a tag recited by tragic characters like Aida and Radamès in their tomb. Everything has not ended. Falstaff is one of the few Verdian protagonists still alive at the end of the opera, and Verdi here entrusts him to the safekeeping of the theatre, a place of revivals and resurrections where all demises are temporary.

## Lovers and Heroes

In 1869, soon after leaving Bülow in order to live with Wagner, Cosima likened herself to a camellia. It was a flower to which Verdi could have claimed proprietary rights: Violetta in *La traviata* is based on the heroine of *La Dame aux camélias*, who bedecks herself with the invitingly open blooms. The courtesan Marguerite Gautier in the novel and play by Dumas fils rejects bouquets of roses and lilies, sickened by their perfume. Camellias appeal because they are foreign growths, blowsy and voluptuous; their lack of fragrance suggests a deficiency in her, confirmed by her professional approach to sex. Verdi ignores the floral symbolism, but has Violetta present the puppy-like Alfredo with a camellia from her corsage and tell him to bring it back to her when it has faded. Camellias wither quickly: it is her way of agreeing to an assignation tomorrow.

The camellia in Cosima's diary is not a love token or – since flowers are the genital organs of plants – a signal of sexual availability. It is sickly, a 'fleur du mal', and it sums up the difference between Wagnerian eroticism and the way Verdi's men and women conduct their affairs. Cosima remembers watching camellias unfold; she might be Dalila in the opera by Saint-Saëns telling Samson that her heart opens to him as flowers do when kissed by the dawn. What Cosima sees, as soon as the flower displays its private parts, is 'the evil worm, a black-and-yellow dot, lying in its heart'. The canker is her regret about the husband she deserted, and this remorse, she concludes, is 'as much a part of Nature's intention as the flowering of the plant itself!' Here is the art of transition in organic life, with death as a consequence of growth, treachery as a concomitant of love. The image enabled Cosima to deal with the distressing situation in a conveniently Wagnerian way. She laughed off Liszt's 'childish' expectation that she should atone for her action; instead, as she wrote a few months after her commentary on the camellia, a 'fellow suffering' like that of Parsifal for Amfortas oppressed her heart, so that her sympathy for Bülow dispensed her from having to endure further punishment.

The camellia dies obscenely. It does not merely fade, as Violetta tells Alfredo it will; it turns brown and rots before falling off the bush in a putrid heap. The consumption that afflicts Marguerite and Violetta was a romantic disease, supposedly bred within over-excited bodies that consumed themselves. Verdi, however, never implies that his heroine's illness is a judgment on her. Although Germont disapproves of her lax morality, no one calls her tainted or foul. The notion of the lady of the camellias suggests the spoiling of Catholic sanctity, like Jean Genet's Notre Dame des Fleurs (who happens to be a male hoodlum, the lover of a transvestite called Divine); the nickname has little relevance to Violetta, who is a martyr to Christian hypocrisy. Cosima's diary entry makes it possible to imagine a Wagnerian setting of *La Dame aux camélias*, which would ignore the sweetly ordinary routines and sheltering affection of Verdi's characters: Violetta and Alfredo in their country retreat, Germont's growing sense of paternal responsibility for the woman he at first condemns. The novel by Dumas fils contains a series of episodes – all of them eliminated by Verdi – which seem anachronistically Wagnerian. The hero Armand falls victim to Marguerite because of an 'affinity in fluids' that accelerates his heartbeat whenever he sees her; like Tristan and Isolde, they are drawn together by an occult emotional chemistry, and after Marguerite's death Armand suffers from a brain fever like Tristan's, with nervous seizures that produce stammerings and ravings. At his most demented, he exhumes her body to make sure that she is dead, and has to contemplate the pitted face with its greenish hollows, more nauseating than the flower with its black and yellow sore: it is a moment that Wagner comes close to staging when the unburied body of Elisabeth is carried on, when Amfortas dismays the knights by opening Titurel's coffin, or when the corpse of Siegfried raises its arm in a post-mortem malediction. The sickroom in *La traviata*, with a doctor in attendance, is a model of sanitary rigour when set against these funerary tableaux. Decay had no fascination for Verdi, who left decadence to Wagner.

The critic Massimo Mila described *Un ballo in maschera* as 'Verdi's *Tristan und Isolde*, translated into Italian and relocated beneath a fiery, passionate sky'. It may be the translation or the warmer weather, but the comparison works better as a contrast. Mila was not entirely accurate about the climate, because *Ballo* – first set in Sweden, then transferred to colonial Boston when the censor forbade any allusion to the assassination of King Gustavus III at a ball in Stockholm –

properly belongs on a cold latitude where passion cannot afford to go naked. Verdi's characters lack the compulsiveness of Tristan and Isolde; Riccardo and Amelia, sharing Verdi's own emotional discretion, would rather not be in love. He is one of Verdi's playboys – like the Duke in *Rigoletto* or Belfiore in *Un giorno di regno*, who is a knave promoted to philosopher-king, luckily for only a day – and the flirtation with his political colleague's wife is an escapade. She wants only to be rid of an unwelcome infatuation, and asks the sorceress Ulrica for an antidote to love, not an elixir. Like Tristan and Isolde, both have their confidants. Instead of the wary, mistrustful Kurwenal, Riccardo relies on the androgynous page Oscar, sung by a sparkly coloratura soprano; this irresponsible Cupid betrays the secret of his master's disguise at the masked ball and is responsible for his death. Brangäne becomes a reluctant pander when she pours the wrong potion, and cannot forgive herself for propelling Isolde into Tristan's arms. But Ulrica does her duty as a forbidding superego: whereas the hedonistic Oscar lives only in the present, she sees into the future, predicts retribution, and frightens Amelia into repentance.

Unlike the rendezvous of Tristan and Isolde in the garden, the midnight meeting in *Ballo* should not have happened. Amelia goes to the heath to gather a herb that supposedly sedates desire, and Riccardo is only able to surprise her there because he has overheard her conversation with Ulrica. Their encounter takes place under the aegis of death, because the herb grows beneath the gallows – but death for Verdi is the ultimate prohibition, not the aphrodisiac that entices Wagner's lovers to speculate about the last refinement of erotic experimentation, snuffing out life itself. Verdi's scene is the product of a strange self-censorship: its distant source must be some ancient fertility rite in which a naked woman might roam through the nocturnal landscape to gather the ingredients for a love potion, though here every detail of that scenario is negated. Rather than being warmed by desire, Amelia says that she freezes in trepidation, and she dreads the change that the drug may induce in what she calls her 'mente convulsa', her convulsed mind. As if the gallows were not enough of an impediment to love, she further terrifies herself by invoking God, who will punish her – as she predicts in her aria – for breaching the sacrament of marriage. By contrast, the potion in *Tristan* kills off all moral scruples. When Tristan bounds on in response to the quenched torch, there is a yelping exchange of high notes, including two high Cs from Isolde, to signal the immediate physical union of the lovers. But Riccardo's arrival starts an argument, as Amelia tries to manoeuvre away from him and in her desperation calls on Christ to rescue her from shame and usher her towards salvation. Riccardo tunefully ingratiates; she is reduced to babbling incoherence, and when he tricks her into admitting that she loves him she immediately begs to be protected from herself.

After her confession, Amelia returns to the Wagnerian equation of love and death, though she interprets it in her own more mistrustful Verdian way. She was lying on her funeral bed, she says, dreaming of relief from her wound – more like the ailing Tristan than the ardent Isolde. She cannot understand why she is unable to succumb to this feeling, which involves reversing or overturning her spirit, 'versar quest'anima', and she asks whether love can only be put to sleep by death: the gallows remain her moral support. Verdi praised the librettist Antonio Somma for catching the 'disordine' of passion in the text he provided for the duet, and it is indeed a disorderly vocal collaboration. Riccardo in 'Non sai tu che se l'anima mia' performs a little aria that sounds immaculately rehearsed, as if it had been used before with other women. Amelia strikes out in a divergent musical direction in her prayer, which reaches for spiritual heights with its grand aspiring phrases and then subsides into another example of the baffled, disconnected conversational phrasing that reveals her panic as she tries to repel him: 'E tu va – ch'io non t'oda – mi lascia'. An interruption follows, as startling and embarrassing as the return of the nocturnal hunters in *Tristan*. Melot exposes Tristan's treachery to King Marke; Amelia's husband Renato appears to warn Riccardo of the conspiracy against him, and hustles his veiled wife away. During Marke's long monologue of recrimination the unresponsive Tristan quietly condemns himself to death. The equivalent anticlimax in Verdi turns out to be brilliantly unexpected: perilous love is sidetracked into comedy when Amelia is unveiled, and the conspirators laugh at Renato for taking a moonlit walk with his disguised wife. Mockery – by contrast with Melot's jealous anger or Marke's sense of betrayal – is a more efficient analgesic for passion than Ulrica's herb.

Don Carlos and Elisabeth de Valois might have a better claim to be Verdi's Tristan and Isolde, because their relationship, developed in three tortuous and achingly inconclusive duets, is a study in dramatic frustration and musical sublimation. They are denied their tryst in a dark garden because of an almost farcical misunderstanding: the message summoning Carlos is sent by Eboli not Elisabeth. Chance, not fatality or the involuntary pressure of an obsession or a drug, determines the lives of Carlos and Elisabeth, who have to cope with external demands – duty, morality, family, foreign policy – that Tristan and Isolde ignore. Verdi's characters are brought together by an arbitrary diplomatic arrangement that turns out to be emotionally right: their parents decree that they should marry to cement an alliance between Spain and France, and when they meet at Fontainebleau they find, to their amazement, that they actually like each other. They reflect on their good fortune in a section of their first duet that is slow, sober, utterly unWagnerian in its lack of frenzy. Their separation, when Philippe

II sends word that he prefers to keep Elisabeth for himself, matches the moment when Tristan's ship reaches port and Marke arrives to collect his bride. By then the drugged Tristan no longer recognizes a reality that conflicts with his desires, and when told that the king is waiting he dismissively asks 'Welcher König?' Elisabeth, however, listens to attendants who prevail on her to accept a marriage and end a war. Because Philippe has allowed her to make her own choice between himself and his son, it is a moment of vertiginous dramatic freedom without an equivalent in Wagner, whose characters are always in the grip of memories, motifs, compulsions. Isolde solves the problem by asking 'Muss ich leben?' and falling in a faint. Elisabeth has no Brangäne to license the id by administering a drink, and she shares the customary Verdian craving for peace, sought by Leonora in *La forza del destino* and Amneris at the end of *Aida*. She therefore gives her consent, in a voice that is hardly able to utter the monosyllable 'Oui'. Although Wagner sang the praises of renunciation, none of his egotists would be capable of such a sacrifice; Wagnerian suicide is easier than this stoical resolve to live without happiness or hope. Wagner's sailors, shouting 'Heil!' to greet Marke, are noises off, a brash irrelevance. In *Don Carlos* it is the pained exclamations of Elisabeth and Carlos that go unheard by the chorus acclaiming the armistice.

In their second duet they are at cross purposes. Carlos is still the lover, but Elisabeth has graduated to the role of honorary mother, and even foresees a Pietà with her stepson dead of anguish in her arms. Despite her discouragement he comes close to experiencing the little death of the Wagnerian orgasm, and his instant of pleasure is so intense that he collapses in a fit; the swooning instrumentation – which includes, in some versions of the score, the wail of the tubular ophicleide – contributes to his loss of control. In Wagner, this would be a delicious reverie, like Brünnhilde remembering Siegfried as she gazes at his ring before Waltraute's arrival or Siegfried remembering Brünnhilde as he dies. In Verdi, it is more like a nervous breakdown. Again adopting the safe and sacrosanct maternal role, Elisabeth revives Carlos, although it sounds as if he has arisen from his grave, with trombones and a grim rhythmic tattoo on the drums hinting at retribution. He abuses the God who restores him to consciousness of his misery, and then, like Alvaro in the St Petersburg *Forza del destino*, calls for thunderbolts to pummel him. His extremism prompts an equally fraught reaction from Elisabeth: she dares him to commit parricide and then to ravish her – a curse or a wild incitement? The attempt at a duet is violently ruptured when he rushes away, which leaves her free to make the soaring announcement that God has watched over them. For once she is grateful to have been invigilated from above; she needs no Brangäne to sing offstage warnings, because her conscience is an internal guardian, always on duty.

Philippe cannot punish Elisabeth for keeping dubious company, because she has already frightened Carlos off. Lacking Marke's forbearance, Philippe humiliates her at second hand by banishing the attendant countess who left her alone. Elisabeth is allowed a solo in reaction to the king's insult, 'Ne pleure pas', but it hardly qualifies as an aria because her words are veiled, impersonal, as she concentrates on cheering up the disgraced, weeping countess. As so often in Verdi, responsibility to others overrules personal feeling. This scene helps to explain Wagner's claim in *Deutsche Kunst und Deutsche Politik* that the characters in Schiller's play are more 'unforcedly highbred' than those of Shakespeare, whose royal personages have to unlearn the etiquette of rank and imbibe wisdom from yokels. It was Verdi, however, who composed music worthy of the nobility to which Elisabeth, Posa and eventually Carlos aspire.

In the third duet Elisabeth draws on the lofty euphemisms of religion, recommending Carlos to God and even, in the Italian translation of the text prepared for Milan in 1884, calling him a pilgrim: she now resembles Wagner's Elisabeth, and she despatches the reprobate not to Rome but to Flanders, where he will redeem himself through political action rather than by requesting a papal pardon. To sanctify their relationship is her way of denying the truth about it, and Carlos at once contradicts her by equating love with death. But that Wagnerian truism is unacceptable here, because life is not so easily discarded. She therefore resurrects Posa, a convenient symbol of duty and sacrifice, and reminds Carlos of a political obligation that has not concerned her until this moment. The martial section of their duet sounds discordantly vigorous, with its harp strummed like a guitar, but this declares Elisabeth's determination to reorchestrate her stepson's emotions. The belligerence soon falters, and Carlos is triumphant when he sees her crying; she counters him by calling her tears 'pleurs de l'âme', tears of the soul shed by women in tribute to fallen heroes, not those of a woman saying farewell to her lover. At last there is agreement and unison when they sing about a happiness that will be forever deferred. The crudely pious Italian text translates this as peace in the arms of the Lord, but the French original speaks of 'cet éternel absent qu'on nomme le bonheur'. Joy is an eternal absentee, like the God in whose name the opera's political murders are committed. Their voices tail off, since the words are too painful to declaim out loud, while the violas and clarinets murmur sympathetically and the horn emits a choked sob. Comfortless, they have only the resignation of their simple melody to ease their pain, and ours.

When Toscanini heard Bruno Walter conduct the second act of *Tristan* at Salzburg in 1936, he said 'If they were Italians, they would already have seven children, but they're Germans, so they're still talking.' Quite apart from the touchy matter of national habits in lovemaking, there are complications if the remark is applied to Wagner and Verdi. How many children do we imagine Verdi's married couples producing? Amelia in *Un ballo in maschera*, whose husband intends to kill her because of her presumed adultery, suddenly mentions one: in her aria 'Morrò, ma prima in grazia' she offers to die but asks first to embrace her only son, who will have the job of closing his dead mother's eyes. The unseen child is a ploy, her means of bargaining for her life, but at least she is able to invoke the idea of family as grounds for leniency. No Wagnerian heroine could win an argument by remembering her phantom offspring, since – except for the infanticidal Ada in *Die Feen* – all his female characters are infertile, as Nietzsche noted. The only Wagnerian matriarch is Erda, the indiscriminate earth mother. Other mothers are either dead, like Herzeleide who wastes away when Parsifal abandons her, or merely notional: Parsifal may have begotten Lohengrin, but who bore him? The erotomania of Wagner's characters is an end in itself, not a prelude to procreation. W. H. Auden refused to believe that any heterosexual man could be as emotionally demonstrative as Tristan, and liked to claim that he and Isolde were undercover lesbians. (It is probably significant that the eight-year-old Auden sang through the love duet with his mother: she was Tristan, he was Isolde.) Alternatively, Auden suspected that a 'homosexual triangle' linked Marke, Tristan and Melot. What the old man cannot forgive is that his catamite has deserted him for a woman; in addition, on the evidence of a grammatical quibble about the accusative 'ihn' and the ablative 'ihm', Auden intuited that Tristan has been seduced by Melot, whose fury is that of another spurned lover.

Wagner's couples seldom coincide or unite as music and drama were supposed to do. Tannhäuser spurns Venus and mortally injures Elisabeth. Lohengrin expels Elsa from the marriage bed, the Dutchman accuses Senta of infidelity. Isolde meekly returns to Marke when Tristan is wounded, Siegfried makes love to Brünnhilde and then forgets he has done so. Duets soon fall apart into quarrels, which is why Wagner's theory legislated against them. The critic Hanslick complained about the lack of 'multiple-voiced pieces' in the *Ring*, where characters testify 'as in court proceedings, one after the other'; he rightly thought that music's advantage over drama – so excitingly exploited in Verdi's ensembles – lay in its capacity to permit 'two or more persons, even whole masses' to be heard at once, polyphonically. If characters sing over each other in the *Ring*, the result is mere hubbub: the hysteria of the Valkyries when Brünnhilde is disgraced, the brutish guffawing of Hagen's vassals. The 'monodic' scruple, as Hanslick called it, was one that Wagner adhered to in his private life. As a lover, he told Cosima in 1872, 'I spoke in monologues'. He said that his relationship with her was an exception, although her diaries disprove it: Wagner talks while Cosima listens, agrees with him, castigates herself when she does not, then silently transcribes the day's stock of dogmatizing monologues.

A Wagnerian duet is apt to be a double soliloquy, like the dialogue – most of it unspoken – between the Dutchman and Senta. He is a portrait come to life, and to him she too is a mute portrait, 'dieses Mädchens Bild', an image not a person. Their match has been agreed on before they meet: she is infatuated by the ballad, and he resolves to make her his wife the moment Daland mentions that he has a daughter. The whispered stealth of the music follows two streams of consciousness. They do not exchange words until halfway through the long duet, and then, rather than conversing, they listen to each other's thoughts. She murmurs to herself that she wants to be his saviour; he somehow intuits this and gives thanks for her sacrifice, though in a prayer that is not directly addressed to her. It is the converse of Boito's procedure in the first act of *Otello*, where a Shakespearean monologue – the self-glorifying and perhaps untrustworthy verbal aria that Othello delivers to the senators in the first act of the play – was taken to pieces and divided between Otello and Desdemona. In *Othello* she listens to him in silence; the operatic duet makes Verdi's Desdemona, who has insisted on being taken to the war zone for her honeymoon, a participant in his adventures, a co-creator of his mystique. As he cradles her, Otello momentarily sounds like Tristan. 'Venga la morte,' he says when ecstasy seems out to obliterate his consciousness. But Desdemona is no Isolde, and rather than sharing Otello's attraction to 'il momento supremo' or 'l'attimo divino' she asks heaven to grant them a love that will not change with the unchanging years. Music gives the Shakespearean words the force of a spell: she elongates the two syllables of 'anni', which is her way of ensuring that time passes slowly and that happiness has no end. Continuity matters more to her than unsustainable climaxes.

Verdi's characters are two ill-matched individuals trying to coexist; the typical Wagnerian couple consists of two aspects of a single self, like Jung's animus and anima or the mysteriously self-divided creative mind of Wagner himself. Elsa repeatedly says that she wants to disappear into Lohengrin, who has himself appeared from somewhere inside her, and she asks him to take everything she is: 'In dir muss ich vergehen,/vor dir schwind'ich dahin'. After the wedding she wants to dissolve when he looks at her, to wind round his feet like a stream, to be trodden underfoot like a flower – metaphors that anticipate the abasement of Kundry, who bathes Parsifal's feet and dries them with her hair. 'Ist dies nur Liebe?' she asks: is this only love? No, it is probably both more or less than that; it is a collusive fantasy, as she perhaps suspects because she questions the word, which is as unspeakably wonderful ('unaussprechlich wonnevoll') as his name, and equally beyond her ken. Yet despite this worshipful self-humbling, Elsa continues to harry Lohengrin, asking the forbidden questions about his identity and his origins. Under pressure, he says that he comes from 'Glanz und Wonne', splendour and delight, as if he were the key of C major personified. This may be all that it is prudent for him to impart about music; Elsa, however, is tormented by his elliptical remark, because if he derives from such a radiant heaven he will surely want to return there, leaving her behind on an earth that is the dark, conflict-ridden ground of drama.

In 1908 the Viennese satirist Karl Kraus made a tart comment about 'Zu neuen Taten', the phrase with which Brünnhilde farewells Siegfried at the start of the duet when they emerge from her cave in *Götterdämmerung*. They have been together, presumably, for just one night, but she packs him off to perform new deeds, donates her horse to speed him on his way, and assures him she is letting him go because she loves him. Domestic cohabitation is not an option (which is why Kaspar Bech Holten's production in Copenhagen, in which Brünnhilde cooks for Siegfried in a mountain-top cabin and survives the immolation to bear his child, looks so false). 'This,' Kraus said, 'is the voice of Wagner's women.' He found Brünnhilde's attitude preposterous: 'She should inspire not deeds but love, then the deeds would follow.' Even Wagner thought that the abrupt sundering of the lovers needed explanation, and he told Cosima that Siegfried was leaving to get 'tributes from a few kings!' It was a wickedly sardonic reference to his own plundering of Ludwig II's treasury, but in fact Wagner's Siegfried – unlike the hero of Fritz Lang's *Nibelungen* film, who subdues twelve kings and seizes their booty before wooing Kriemhild – has no interest in riches and no idea of what the Nibelungen hoard is worth. Obsessively retrospective like every Wagnerian character, Brünnhilde charges him to go on remembering what has already happened – his passage through the fire, his removal of her armour. She calls herself Siegfried's soul, and he is proud to serve as her arm or perhaps as her armament, an extension directed by her from her vantage point on the peak. Though apart, they are inseparable, cooperating as Wagner wanted soulful music and active, energetic drama to do. Theirs is not a marriage but an aesthetic alliance, which once more proves unequal. Siegfried stumbles through the drama making dim-witted mistakes and is subsumed by music when he dies.

Verdi's couples may be denied a continuing life together, but at least they are able to imagine it happening outside the confines of the opera. Radamès would leave arid Egypt with Aida; Leonora would elope with Alvaro on the horses tethered below her window, be married by the priest he has waiting, then sail off to his kingdom in what he vaguely calls the Indies. The only future Wagner's couples can comprehend is a blissful extinction. After the interrupted duet, Marke asks why Tristan has dishonoured him. Tristan replies that he cannot say, although the *Tristan* chord gives a wordless answer. He then asks Isolde to follow him – but into darkness and non-existence. She seems not to understand, and says that her home is with him: perhaps she expects him to take her to his castle in Brittany. He disabuses her by kissing her gently but chastely on the forehead, after which he goads Melot to attack him and drops his sword to ensure that he receives a wound. Isolde remains silent when Tristan falls, then presumably goes off with her unloved husband. She resists drama's temptation to act and react, choosing the 'motionless life' that Maurice Maeterlinck argued in 1896 should be the subject of modern tragedy; she ignores what Maeterlinck called 'the violence of the anecdote' (summed up, in his view, by the ranting brutality of Shakespeare's Othello). For Verdi's Carlos and Elisabeth, parting is death. For Wagner's characters, life means apartness, and death is the only inseparable union.

|||||||||||||||||||

'I want a hero,' Wagner said to Cosima in 1875. He was quoting the opening line of *Don Juan*, in which Byron chastizes the unheroic times for offering him no protagonist worthy of an epic; he has to settle for an amiably shallow adolescent who lacks the mad rapacity and heaven-defying courage of Mozart's Don Giovanni. Wagner's appropriation of the phrase referred to his search for a Siegfried – not for the hero himself, but for a tenor with the lungs and legs to perform the role in the first Bayreuth performances the following year.

Wagner persisted in imagining heroes who might save the world, although like Siegfried they always fail to do so. Verdi, on the other hand, knew he was living through the twilight of heroism: in *I masnadieri* Carlo watches the sunset and remarks that it reminds him of a hero's decline and fall. As a dramatist, Verdi preferred people with divided loyalties, whose principles are at odds with their passions. Studying the libretto for *Les Vêpres siciliennes*, he objected to the monolithic nature of the rabble-rouser Procida. The other characters in the opera turn out to be almost embarrassingly complex, juggling political allegiances and the more seditious insinuations of erotic or familial love, and Verdi's music follows their twisting manipulations. Hélène is a duchess, before whom the Sicilian patriot Henri prostrates himself as a humble soldier. She tells him that if he avenges her brother's death, presumably by assassinating the French commander Montfort, she will think him nobler than any king: a bargain worthy of Lady Macbeth. Their duet is a negotiation not an avowal of love, with sour harmonies and some balefully emphatic decelerations to ensure that Henri understands the deal she is making. The intended victim is his father, though Henri self-righteously rejects his heritage when he adheres to the radical cause. Then at the ball, just as Hélène is about to strike Montfort down, Henri prevents the attack and betrays his colleagues. His excuse is that he was merely cancelling a debt: he owes his life to Montfort and has paid restitution by intervening, but is now free to hate him again. Montfort, frustrated by Henri's refusal to reciprocate his love, stages an execution to extort an avowal from him: Hélène will be beheaded unless Henri calls him father – which of course, after a tormenting delay prolonged by an ominous drumbeat, he finally does. Can you torment someone into loving you? And should Hélène have been relieved or disgusted to be spared at the price of her lover's capitulation? Montfort then impetuously dismantles the apparatus of occupation by agreeing to let Henri marry her. Far from reconciling the factions that squabble over possession of the island, his gesture provokes a disaster by giving Procida his cue for the massacre. The domineering pomp of grand opera matters less in this case than a plot that works like a psychological torture chamber, tearing characters apart.

As Henri's failure of nerve demonstrates, for Verdi emotional bonds outweigh political loyalties. Wagner too had doubts about the brawny mystique of heroism. Offering the role of Rienzi to the tenor Joseph Tichatschek in 1841, he said that the character was 'a hero in the full sense of the word', although he was severely diminishing the word's traditional meaning: he called Rienzi 'a visionary dreamer', and ignored his performance on the battlefield as a holy cavalier. In a programme note for Beethoven's Third Symphony, written in Zurich in 1851, Wagner again stretched the definition of heroism and argued that the nickname *Eroica* referred not to military prowess but to 'the complete man in full possession of the purely human feelings of love, suffering and power'. It is difficult to see why Gutrune, when Hagen encourages her to fantasize about a match with Siegfried, calls him 'der herrlichste Held der Welt'. The orchestra sycophantically sounds his motif as she utters the slogan, but all he has done to justify the accolade is kill a dragon. He fails to repeat his success when hunting with Hagen, has to beg food because the boar he was tracking escaped him, and blames the waterhens – which is what he takes the Rhinemaidens to be – for distracting him. In April 1869 Wagner pondered the meaning of Siegfried's fearlessness, which, he tendentiously claimed, clarified the meaning of Christ's words about clothing the lilies of the field and feeding the sparrows. The scriptural quotation allowed him to ignore Siegfried's brutality: the hero represents 'the human being who truly lives for his own calling alone', and this notion of 'an inwardly secure being' is perpetuated 'in the legend of Siegfried and the fairy tale of Tom Thumb'. So were the muscular oaf and the noisy fairground midget interchangeable?

Despite his reputation, Siegfried is not as inwardly secure as Wagner implied. His knowledge of taxonomy makes him mistrust Mime's claim to have bred him: no toad can father a fish. Never having met any other member of the same species – since Mime, he assumes, is subhuman – he cannot understand what or who he is, and likens himself to a fish, a finch, then to the carefree, unhoused wind. Every creature he encounters is a nonpareil. When Mime prods him into battle with Fafner in the second act, Siegfried first asks whether the dragon has a heart, then where in his body it sits. After he removes Brünnhilde's armour in the final act he is comically surprised to see that she is not a man; he may also be wondering whether she is human. There is callow comic innocence in this, but also analytical wonder. Siegfried cannot take the human prototype for granted, and he might be dealing with the kind of aliens concocted by science fiction – H. G. Wells's Martians who consist of brain-boxes with metallic pincers attached, or his invertebrate lunar Selenites who are blue-skinned brainless heads. Wells invented such beings as a reproach to what he called 'our incurable anthropomorphism', warning human beings not to fancy that we set the pattern for organic existence, and Wagner was also challenging the self-satisfaction of our species. In an interview with a Berlin journalist in 1899, Verdi remarked that he had never met any of Wagner's deities or demons. It was a polite, jocular evasion, but it also marked his undaunted faith in human nature, at the very end of a century in which, according to Nietzsche, Spengler and Wells, mankind had reached the end of its tether.

A month before his death, Cosima heard Wagner talking – with scarcely credible lucidity – while he dreamed. 'If He created me,' he said, 'who asked Him to? And if I am man in His image, the question remains whether I am pleased about that.' A God no better than Wagner himself was hardly worth believing in. Even so, his own recipe for the gestation of characters was perhaps an improvement on the chancy, dangerous routine of biological reproduction. In January 1871 he thanked Cosima for helping him to fulfil 'Nature's purpose', which was 'to bring a son into the world'. A few days later, studying the son he had named after his operatic hero, he toyed with ways of outwitting mammalian nature. 'If nothing comes of this one,' he said, 'then the devil take child-making; one will have to try it like Wagner with the homunculus.' He was referring to his namesake in Goethe's *Faust*, an alchemist who breeds a miniature man, a sort of Tom Thumb, in a test tube. The idea appealed to Wagner, who told Cosima that the homunculus was 'the German spirit' seeking to escape from the scholar's study and fly free in nature. When he heard a tiny bird chirping in early spring, he said that it was asking 'to be brought into the world like the homunculus'. Goethe's homunculus, however, is a brainchild not a fledgling chick, a thought not a growing body, and its birth is disastrous. It is released from its glass container by Proteus, the shape-changing god who came to mind when Heinrich Porges reflected on Wagner's habit of impersonating his own characters; unable to settle into a body, it is swallowed up by wide, windy open space.

The fable helps to explain why Lohengrin says when leaving Elsa that the Grail wants him to return: like the homunculus, he needs a sealed, hermetic environment. In 1881, returning to the subject of his own quaint progeny, Wagner gaily compared Lohengrin to 'the mandrake being pulled out of the bottle (the Grail the bottle)'. The mandrake was a compound of vegetable and animal, growing out of the soil though with human features, allegedly liable to scream in pain when it was uprooted. Wagner called this hybrid by its German name, 'Galgenmensch': the word helpfully explains the mandrake's origins, since this little man of the gallows was reputedly spawned by the semen that hanged men ejected in their final throes. Suddenly there is a coincidental link between the imaginative laboratory in which Wagner's fantastical mutants are conceived and Verdi's more normal world. Could the magic herb that Ulrica sends Amelia to pick beneath the gibbet in *Un ballo in maschera* be a mandrake? Is this why Amelia imagines that she sees a head rising from the ground? She even shrieks, supplying the cry of mandrake as it is pulled out of the ground. Self-censorship by librettist and composer or scepticism about the bizarre superstition muddle up the incident, so that what might have been deviant risks seeming merely nonsensical. Amelia does not find the herb because there is no such thing, and the hovering head, reattached to a body, turns into Riccardo, who is only too embarrassingly real. Wagner, like a god or like Goethe's alchemist, assumed the right to revise nature; Verdi could not allow the laws of biology to be so easily flouted.

# A NEW RELIGION

Looking back on a creative labour that had, as he pointed out, produced a new world, Wagner sometimes allowed himself a spell of divine complacency, like God pausing to declare that his handiwork was good. When he perused his scores, he told Cosima, he felt like Jehovah reading the Bible. The *Ring* was his Old Testament – a story of creation and catastrophe, grimly predestinate even though it narrated the decline and retirement of its god – and it had to be supplemented by a New Testament that rewrote the contract between God and men. Hence his plan to spend his last years inventing a new religion, its gospels being *Parsifal* and *Die Sieger*, a drama first sketched in 1856 and based on the life of the Buddha. Verdi the agnostic dispensed with God and had no ambition to supplant him, in either his paternal or filial roles. In 1865 he wrote to Piave about Wagner's music of the future and derided the desire for 'music that is pure, virginal, holy, spherical': the adjectives he underscored came from a rhapsody about the sublime written by the young and Wagner-besotted Boito, who wanted to restore music to the refined, remote spheres from which it first sifted down. Verdi – whose scriptural citations usually had an undertone of blasphemous ridicule, just as he sometimes ended letters with mock-papal blessings – was sceptical about this Second Coming. 'I look upwards,' he told Piave, 'and I await the star that will show me where the new Messiah is born, so that, like the Magi, I may go to adore him. Hosanna in excelsis!' During the rehearsals of *Don Carlos* in Paris, Jules Claretie likened Verdi to 'some Assyrian god'. Others saw him as a biblical patriarch: the journalist Blanche Roosevelt said that his expression when conducting resembled 'that of Moses when he smote the rock'. He paid no attention to such pious fawning.

Verdi did share Wagner's belief in the artist's prerogatives, but he expressed it more sardonically. In 1871 he protested against the encroachments of singers who 'made bold to "create" (as the French still say) their parts, and in consequence made a complete hash … out of them'. He was discussing a report on the reform of conservatories, and balked at its allowance for 'conductors' inspiration' and 'creative activity in every performance'; his response to these notions was a flat, fundamentalist 'No'. 'I want only one single creator,' he told his publisher Ricordi. Since Verdi did not believe in the biblical God, it is clear who that sole authority was. Dante's poem about the Virgin – set by Verdi as the sacred motet 'Laudi alla Vergine Maria' in his *Quattro pezzi sacri* – calls the creator 'Fattore', and the word is given an enthusiastic emphasis by the four female soloists. As Verdi knew, it was he who fashioned or fabricated the characters that were distributed among the singers, he who jotted down the notes that were his commandments to conductors. It angered him when Mariani raised the volume of the brass in the overture to *La forza del destino*, which distorted the meaning of the piece by making it belligerent not meditative: the conductor's inspirational whim was an offence against the creator's monopoly. He denied that 'either singers or conductors can "create", or work creatively – this … leads to the abyss'. Theologically, the abyss is perdition; Verdi had his own theatrical equivalent, a pit to which he irately consigned pretentious colleagues.

German romantic philosophers expected God to wither away, like the state after the revolution. The theologian Friedrich Schleiermacher said in 1789 that religion could survive in God's absence by redefining itself as 'pure contemplation of the universe'. Brünnhilde arrives at this understanding when she awakens and hails the sun, the light and the resplendent earth; so do Otello and Desdemona when they gaze at the stars, and in their ebullient way the characters of *Falstaff* experience the same grateful recognition when they sing the praise of folly. Alternatively, God became superfluous because man replaced him. Friedrich Schlegel argued that 'every good man ceaselessly becomes more and more God', which is what happens when Parsifal or Stiffelio officiate as redeemers. Verdi's singers in the 'Laudi alla Vergine Maria' carefully spell out Dante's word 'nobilitasti', which refers to Mary's spiritual promotion when she was chosen to bear God's child; she is a specimen of the humanity that the biblical creator ennobled when recreating himself in human form. Lohengrin's embassy on earth illustrates a different closure of the gap. Wagner's gods, as he said in the *Mitteilung*, are anxious to descend to our world – more like the Olympians flirting with nymphs or Wotan (as Fricka complains) whoring on earth than like God ordering his only begotten son to undergo a mortal birth and death. Wagner had no respect for the notions of a virgin womb and a chaste, unerotic act of creation. He emphasized the 'finite, physically sure embrace' that joins gods with mortals, and he understood the dangers of this coition. 'Must not the god dissolve and disappear?' he asked. 'Is not the mortal, who had yearned for god, undone, annulled?' Lohengrin and Elsa accordingly destroy each other, as do Wotan and the humanized Brünnhilde.

In a letter written to Ludwig II on Good Friday 1865, Wagner spoke of a day of redemption and of 'God's suffering!!' He was referring both to the crucified Son and to the Father, who ought, like Wotan, to be atoning for his guilt. But Wagner's god suffers out of sight after Siegfried brushes him aside; it is Verdi who shows God grieving. The Inquisitor in *Don Carlos* reminds Philippe II of 'la foi du Calvaire' and advises him to sacrifice his son for political reasons. Philippe has little enough compunction about handing Carlos over, but he does bewail the loss of Posa in a lament that Verdi used again in the 'Lacrymosa' section of the *Requiem*: are these God's tears of remorse for a power he has misused, matching Elisabeth's approximation to a Pietà when she grieves over the collapsed Carlos? The New Testament story is here the grim prescription for a family tragedy, with the son shuttled between an abusive father and a bullied mother. Already in *Jérusalem* – the revised version of *I Lombardi*, performed in Paris in 1847 – Verdi and his librettists seem to be conducting a post-mortem on Christianity disguised as a pilgrimage to the site of Christ's death. The crusaders travel to see the holy sepulchre, which, as they suggestively remark, guards a souvenir of God's farewell to the earth. Roger sermonizes about the lugubrious valley of Jehosaphat where the angel presented the bitter chalice to Christ, but in the previous scene Gaston, unjustly disgraced, complains about his own 'calice d'amertume': he is a Christ condemned without reason by Christians.

Heinrich Heine, aware that the Christian monopoly was weakening, proposed that his contemporaries should be allowed a 'free trade in gods', and the characters in Verdi's early operas behave as if this were already their right. In *Alzira* the Peruvian tribesman Zamoro and the native woman he loves sing with bouncy flippancy about their self-interested choice of belief: 'De' nostri infidi numi/cadde il fallace impero' – the false empire of their faithless gods has collapsed, and they now resolve that each of them will be a god to the other. Why bother with a remote, unreliable deity when you can deify a lover? Nabucco charges into the profaned temple on horseback and asks who dares to mention God in his presence; later in a series of swaggering pronouncements he declares that he has elected himself God and demands that the crowd bow before his idol, a brazen 'simulacro'. Abigaille taunts the warrior Ismaele when she finds him with

Nabucco's daughter Fenena and asks, with a vocal flourish like the laceration of a whip, which God can save him. She expects him to make a tactical choice: religion is a by-product of politics and a preparation for war. Zaccaria airily dismisses Baal and in his place sets up the God of Abraham, whose recommendation is the quivers of lightning bolts he can discharge. Boosting morale, he promises that God will come to our aid 'nell'estremo evento', in an occasion of moral and physical peril. But the opera consists of extreme events that God is not always quick enough to muffle or defuse: the priest himself takes Fenena hostage and threatens to kill her in the temple.

The feud between Christians and Muslims in *I Lombardi* is less a theological combat than an exercise in name-calling. The Lombard contingent ridicules 'Stolto Allhà', whose followers in Antioch salute him as 'Allhà terribile' and beg him to pummel the invaders with thunder. The Archbishop of Milan considered the opera's libretto sacrilegious because, among a catalogue of other outrages, its unordained characters perform a baptism. He protested to the police and tried to have the production cancelled; Verdi's single, slight, contemptuous concession was to alter the words 'Ave Maria' to 'Salve Maria' in the heroine's first prayer. Giselda's address to the Virgin is in any case ineffectual, as the stealthy, nervous instrumental commentary predicts it will be, and it is followed at once by the burning-down of her house and the parricidal murder of her uncle Pagano (who later turns up, not dead at all, as a hermit in the desert). She is a freethinker whose mental intrepidity is expressed in violently flamboyant harangues, with slashing rhythms and wildly elated coloratura. When she questions the justice of the bigoted expedition to Jerusalem, her father Arvino accuses her of treason. The hermit trusts that his sword will raise the toppled Cross to affright the infidel, and insists that this is God's will: 'Dio lo vuole'. But Giselda shouts down his militancy in her reply, 'No, Dio non vuole, no, no, Dio non vuole!' She goes on to expound her own more tolerant gospel, praising 'Il Dio degl'uomini' – the god of mankind, the benevolent spirit venerated by nineteenth-century positivists. Arvino's response is another of the librettist Solera's extreme events: he draws his dagger like Zaccaria, and says he will kill his daughter to silence her obscene raving.

Giselda and Pagano perform the scandalous baptismal ceremony beside the Jordan river, making a Christian of her lover Oronte, the son of the heathen tyrant of Antioch. Oronte tells his mother that his attraction to Giselda is responsible for his conversion: does this mean that the one true god is Eros? In his aria 'La mia letizia infondere' he swooningly sings about floating among the harmonic spheres and flying to heaven with her, but his new faith does him little good. He is wounded in battle, which prompts Giselda to reproach the cruel God of her fathers. After he dies, she sees him in her sleep, installed in the Christian paradise. He is a very palpable spirit, because he thanks her for her brokering his salvation and tells her to urge on the crusaders. She awakens, and asks whether she has had a vision or has merely been deceived by a hopeful fantasy. This is Elsa's question to herself in *Lohengrin*, and it is paraphrased by Parsifal as the flower-maidens scamper off; the same query – the anxious self-inquisition of all romantic poetry and fiction – occurs to Keats in his ode when the nightingale flies away. Giselda overcomes the uncertainty in an outburst of crazed vocal vehemence, denying that it was a dream and officially classifying it as a miracle: 'Qual prodigio!' Man invents God, or gods. Why shouldn't a woman – even if her father has already accused her of being demented – cheer herself up by imagining the afterlife? In her cabaletta Giselda transforms delirious rapture into military fervour by rally-ing the Christian troops. Verdi went further when he adapted the opera for Paris. He took advantage of the city's worldlier atmosphere by giving the crusaders a drinking song in which they look forward to being welcomed to Palestine by the Emir's harem girls, who as expected perform a sinuous ballet in the third act. The Holy Land has its unhallowed pleasures.

Nietzsche thought that the elderly Wagner was not creating a new religion but surrendering to the old one, with its sickly slave morality and its revulsion from the sinful flesh. In 1878 he decried the text of *Parsifal* for being 'limited to Christian times' and containing 'too much blood (particularly in the communion scene)'. But Wagner had earlier dissociated himself from Liszt's Christian reading of *Lohengrin*, which could equally well be retelling the story of Cupid and Psyche, a classical myth that warns of the discrepancy between the divine and the human, and *Parsifal* too is far from orthodox. Gurnemanz's survey of the flowering meadow on Good Friday is more pagan than Christian, despite his allegorical description of dew as 'des Sünders Reuetränen', the sin-ner's remorseful tears. What crime did the landscape commit, and why should nature need to have its sins cleansed? Gurnemanz calls the earth's resurrection magical, but Christianity's magical feat – its vanishing act, like that which Cosima challenged Wagner to perform when she asked if he could make her disappear – occurred on Easter Sunday, not Good Friday.

Wagner was not so much espousing Christianity as annexing it. This did not mean that he had supplanted the Saviour, as Otto Weininger suggested when calling him 'the greatest man since Christ'. For Wagner, the New Testament's sermons pointed towards the greater glory of art rather than glorifying the artist. 'Music is the new religion,' he announced in 1871, and on another occa-sion he ordained Beethoven as its high priest. He had already demonstrated what he meant in 1843 in *Das Liebesmahl der Apostel*, performed in the Frauenkirche in Dresden by twelve hundred male choristers and a hundred instrumentalists. Wagner later described the long, unwieldy piece as a 'miracle play': the miracle was the delayed intervention of the orchestra, hidden behind the choral masses until at last, after more than fifteen minutes, it responds to the pleading voices of the downcast, persecuted Apostles at their Pentecostal feast. They have splintered into factions as all revolutionary movements do, and at first, in a cappella exchanges between the assembled groups, they concentrate on consolidating their brotherhood. With unanimity at last regained, they can compel the orchestra to make itself manifest. It does so after an elemental agitation: the voices describe the air rustling and ringing as the earth shudders, then the strings tremble, and at last a contingent of brass – horns, trombones, bassoons – accompanies a public pronouncement by the Holy Ghost. Hidden behind the choral ranks, mystically invisible as in the Bayreuth pit, the orchestra represents the unseen spirit. Does it descend to them from on high, like the purer voices of the boys and the far-seeing contralto in *Parsifal*, or is it generated by the cooperative needs of all those men, who have closed ranks and pooled emotions like the adherents of Mazzini's Young Italy when they swore their revolutionary oaths? The sociologist Émile Durkheim argued in 1912 – when the idea was still startling – that rites of consecration are a desperate request sent out by those who want to be charged with supernatural energy, 'electrized' like a battery. In *Das Liebesmahl* it is just such a shared belief that begets a god. Wagner's Apostles overcome their paranoia when the aerial spirit assures them that Christ's word will prevail; asking 'Ist den Jerusalem die Welt?', it reminds them of their universalizing mission. But they ventriloquistically voice that command themselves, and when they disperse it could be Wagnerism not Christianity that they set off to promulgate throughout the earth. George Sand imagined a similar epiphany in a letter to Liszt in 1835. Music, she said, 'is prayer, it is faith', and she assumed that when the disciples gathered together to remember Christ they first testified one after the other, then felt the need to 'call in unison' upon the fiery-tongued spirit. At that point, she thought, they must surely have burst into song, inventing the notion of a 'harmonious concert'.

In a series of comments recorded by Cosima, Wagner treated Christianity and music as parallel phenomena, a dual blessing for the human race. These, he said in 1869, were the two forces that had most enriched the world since the decline of classical culture. In 1870 he returned to the subject when he received a letter from a French prisoner of war in Erfurt asking for lessons in harmony. 'Yes,' he said, 'music has affected everybody, it is a destroying, uplifting force

– like Christianity when it first emerged.' The pairing of epithets is significant: Christianity smashed idols and killed off old gods before unveiling its own version of the truth, which is why Ortrud in her imprecations in *Lohengrin* objects to the discrediting of Wodan and Freia, and music too, as Wagner always insisted, has to drive us mad or make us ill before we become worthy to understand it or to profit from its ministrations. He elaborated on the link when professorially musing about 'my treatise on the philosophy of music', which sounds as if it would have imposed the same radical decrees as the *Communist Manifesto*. Church and state, he had decided, could both be abolished, because 'religion has assumed flesh and blood in a way quite different from these dogmatic forms'. In 1873, after reading about the execution of a murderer, Wagner fancifully orchestrated capital punishment: it should be 'entirely the work of religion, which, like music, starts with the first scream, proceeds to lamentation (and the artistic display of lamentation), and ends with salvation'. The ceremony was emotionally satisfactory, he added, because the criminal had consented to his punishment and an entire community took part in exterminating one of its members. The same can hardly be said of the decapitation that Montfort sadistically devises in *Les Vêpres siciliennes* or the auto-da-fé in *Don Carlos*. Verdi found it less easy to transform the scream into a lament; for him the spectacle of judicial murder was not purgative, and it saved no souls.

In his treatise Wagner intended to show that music was 'the direct product of Christianity, as is the saint, like Saint Francis of Assisi'. His remark casually expunged the Italian Renaissance and denied music's logical advance from church polyphony to the monody of Monteverdi. Verdi accepted the logical necessity of that development from sacred to profane, which he summarized at the start of the *Requiem*. The slow, soft, deferential murmuring of the chorus in 'Te decet hymnus' pays homage to Palestrina, for Verdi the source of the Italian musical tradition; here there would have been no disagreement with Wagner, who in 1848 prepared an edition of Palestrina's eight-voice *Stabat Mater* for use by larger choirs. But then the soloists rise to their feet, exhibit their operatic voices one by one, and rite gives way to drama. The only section of the *Requiem* that does without the quartet of vocalists is the 'Sanctus', which may be why it is the shortest and the most unambiguously joyful: here Verdi imagines the angels singing, free from the uncertainty and distress that assail his human characters. The soloists by contrast are plangently personal, ignoring the decorum of a church service in their cries of 'Salva me', and as they alternate between 'eis' and 'ego' they place the emphasis on individual men and women, not the indiscriminate mass of mankind.

Their voice types provide Verdi with a quartet of readymade allegorical characters, who retain traces of an earthly past that they do not pretend to
have lived down. The tenor, first to be heard, brazenly proclaims his primacy; like
Alfredo in *La traviata* or the ingratiating Duke in *Rigoletto*, he relies on his irresistible lyrical persuasiveness when he makes his honeyed entry in the 'Hostias'
of the 'Offertorio' or asks to be classed among the sheep not the goats. The bass
is an authoritarian, charged like Zaccaria in *Nabucco* or the Padre Guardiano in
*Forza* with enforcing the fear of death, except when in the 'Dies Irae' – suddenly
as pitiful as Silva in *Ernani* or the sleepless Philippe II in *Don Carlos* – he broods
on his own end, 'mei finis'. Like Amneris in *Aida*, the mezzo-soprano upholds the
law as she reads from the book of fate in 'Liber scriptus', though she subverts
her own prescriptive message when she stalls on the word 'nil', as chilling as the
'nulla' with which Iago nullifies creation in *Otello*. The soprano's task, discharged
by both operatic Leonoras or by the reformed Violetta, is intercession. She wafts
above her colleagues in the 'Lacrymosa', and gives a long-breathed imitation of
Michael the standard-bearer by treading air in the 'Offertorio'. Her sustained
pianissimo in 'de morte transire ad vitam' enacts that mysterious transition from
death to life by attenuating the last word so that she almost makes us believe in
a resurrection when breath will be extended beyond gasping mortal respiration.
Yet her half-spoken admissions of fear at the beginning and end of the 'Libera me'
reveal how stricken and dubious she actually is, despite her valiant air of certainty
when she sings.

The soprano has a more reticent colleague in Verdi's 'Te Deum', one of
the *Quattro pezzi sacri*. Here the basses proclaim the Church's universality and
address the big-battalioned Lord of Hosts, with God unfolding into the three-
personed Trinity, supported by cohorts of Apostles, prophets and martyrs. The
same militaristic din accompanies, boosts and then censures Scarpia's lecherous
musings during the 'Te Deum' in Puccini's *Tosca*, performed in a Roman church to
give thanks for Napoleon's defeat. Baroncelli in Wagner's *Rienzi* also complains
about the way the tribune bludgeons his opponents with 'Festepomp': by ordering
a 'Te Deum' to be performed, Rienzi passes off his brutality as divine vengeance. Verdi had no interest in this brassy dogmatizing, and told the musicologist
Giovanni Tebaldini that the hymn should sound like man's appeal to God, not
God's proclamation of power. At the end of his 'Te Deum' a single, distant female
voice therefore utters a phrase that admits what underlies the loudly jubilant
demonstration: her abject words are 'In te, Domine. In te speravi' – in you I have
hoped, God. The piece should end, as Verdi said to Tebaldini, 'in pathos, darkness,
mourning and even in terror'. There is no compulsory adhesion, as in Wagner's

*Liebesmahl.* An anonymous individual shyly detaches herself from the hubbub of the multitude, and her prayer not to be eternally confounded goes unanswered.

The *Requiem* comes close to exemplifying Wagner's theory about music as Christianity purged of dogma and doctrine. It is both destructive as well as uplifting, as Wagner expected. A world crashes in ruins in the 'Dies Irae', with the bass drum orchestrating an avalanche, and although the soloists appeal for faith, the uplift they purvey is vocal not theological. We have to be satisfied with melody, just as Matthew Arnold advised Victorian doubters to read the Bible for its poetry. By the time he composed *Otello*, Verdi was able to admit God's redundancy and to accept that music offered our only access to a higher, better world. Boito's libretto seems at first to have resituated Shakespeare's characters in a Catholic society: Iago's sarcastic 'Credo' makes a devil of him, and when an 'Ave Maria' is attached to Desdemona's willow song it sounds as if she is placing her trust in a Madonna who succours mortals. But in fact the operatic Iago is a Darwinian materialist who believes he was spawned in 'il fango originario', the primeval slime, and his rhyming of 'germe' and 'verme', germination and worms, recalls Darwin's study of earthworms, agents of nature's morbid creativity that breed new life out of decay. Verdi also thought of Iago as an ape not a demon. He told the painter Domenico Morelli that the character should look simian, with 'eyes set close to the nose' and a head that bulged out behind as signs of his regressive nature; the comment potentially turns *Otello* into a Darwinian beast fable, the battle between a proud lion and a devious, smirking monkey. On another occasion Verdi said that he imagined Iago as a Jesuit, which enabled him to attack the sophistry of the established Church. He took an equally unspiritual view of Desdemona, even though the children who present her with lilies liken her to the Madonna and bedeck her as if she were a sacred icon in a niche. Verdi told Ricordi that he considered her 'the type of goodness', a being who 'existed in part' but had been 'poetized and deified' by Shakespeare: she owes her apparent divinity to art, not religion. He was even clearer about this when he wrote to the conductor Franco Faccio in 1887. The willow song, he said, required a soprano who must be 'like the Holy Trinity', able to 'produce three voices, one for Desdemona, another for Barbara (the maid) and a third for the "Salce, salce".' This Trinity is not ethereal, and all of its persons are lodged in a human throat; here too is another example of drama's multiplication of our singleness, as one woman plays many parts, having a dialogue with herself and then somehow finding an extra voice for the drooping, mournful willow tree.

In 1889 Verdi made his fourth setting of the 'Ave Maria', published as part of the *Quattro pezzi sacri*. This time, rather than allowing a character like Giselda or Desdemona to pray for calm, he merely set himself to solve a technical puzzle by harmonizing a crabby scale worked out by a Bolognese musician. Verdi called the scale 'graceless', a word that temporizes between aesthetic and religious meanings: the intractable sequence of notes – C, D flat, E, F sharp, G sharp, A sharp, E – lacked grace because of its awkward transitions, but his aim in matching it with a sacred text was to make it symbolize the grace embodied in the Virgin. In a letter to Boito, Verdi joked that he undertook the exercise in the hope of being beatified after his death; Boito replied that many more Ave Marias might be needed before the pope would pardon him for Iago's rascality. Verdi persuaded the irregular intervals to sing, in a haze of shining tone exhaled by four muted soloists. If the awkwardness of the contrivance showed through, so much the worse for the deity who was being praised: the composition had to make do with what Boito called a 'rickety scale', an ill-made stepladder. 'Scale' is the same word as 'Scala', since the opera house in Milan was built on the site once occupied by the church of Santa Maria della Scala, 'Our Lady of the Ladder'; Boito's remark about the shakiness of this particular scale implied that music could no longer automatically climb into the sky, as it did in the days of Palestrina or Bach.

When the fire blazes up at nightfall in *Götterdämmerung* and Brünnhilde hears Siegfried's horn, she hastens towards him, leaping up to her god or trusting that she will be lifted weightlessly aloft like Titian's dead Virgin: 'Auf! – Auf! Ihm entgegen!/In meines Gottes Arm!' But her greeting deflates into a scream of fear, and she falls back to earth. Verdi's seven notes reach only so far. Further up, the sky is empty, or filled, as Brünnhilde says when the disguised Siegfried swoops down on her, by nocturnal birds of prey.

|||||||||||||||||||

Wagner did not forget his promise to endow the world with a new religion. On an evening in late 1877 he quizzed his American dentist Newell Sill Jenkins about Mormonism, which like Wagner's own cult had its self-appointed prophet, its revelatory texts and its hilltop tabernacle, built at the end of a long trek across country. He was curious about Brigham Young, who had recently died after leading the Mormons to Utah, and asked Jenkins to explain 'the secret of his power'. Could a religion depend on the self-righteous certainty of one man, whether it was Wagner himself or Young's predecessor Joseph Smith, founder of the Latter Day Saints movement? The angel Moroni presented Smith with a series of gold plates on which the Book of Mormon was engraved; Smith locked up or buried them, after using seer stones to help him translate a language he called 'reformed Egyptian'. The story suggests that religion is best understood as an aesthetic lie validated by our credulity. This was a dangerous discovery, which in time filled the world with false prophets, one of whom cited Wagner as his source. Hitler, during a nocturnal concert of Wagner excerpts on the gramophone, told his colleague Hans Frank 'Out of *Parsifal* I am building my religion.' He went on to specify what would be excluded from the cult: 'the solemnity of the Mass without theological party-bickering', the bass note of brotherhood with no meek admixture of Christian humility – a religion that imposed a political doctrine and made no mention of God.

But was Wagner inventing a religion or reinventing mythology? After scoring the moment when Gurnemanz explains the transition from forest to temple by telling Parsifal that time has become space, he remarked to Cosima that he had set a philosophical precept to music. Claude Lévi-Strauss was more specific: in an essay written for the programme of Wieland Wagner's *Parsifal* at Bayreuth, he said that Gurnemanz's phrase was a succinct definition of myth. Presumably what Lévi-Strauss meant is that myth studies events as if they were spatial structures, contiguous but not necessarily consecutive, bundled together in space like the staves in a musical score rather than unfolding in a temporal sequence as stories or histories usually do. Myths are allowed to be improbable, but there is always a logic to the marvels they relate; though they seek to propound universal laws, their method is to take parallel stories from disparate cultures and graft them onto one another.

Like Foresto in *Attila* linking Venice to the fabled phoenix, the characters in *Die Meistersinger* rely on myth to bolster their city. Anxious to establish Nuremberg's centrality to Germany or the centrality of their own trades within the city, they play devious games with history and geography. The stories they tell are what we call urban myths – apocryphal tales that connect us to other members of our chosen group while detaching us from those who belong elsewhere and circulate legends of their own. As he hammers shoe leather, Sachs sings about the divine provenance of his trade, wittily revising Genesis: now boots not fig leaves are God's pitying gift to footsore humanity. At the festival, the tailors have a smug song about an ancestor who during a siege frightened off Nuremberg's enemies by dressing in a goatskin and cavorting on the city's walls. David's song about Johannistag stretches sacred history and makes a biblical pedigree depend, as so often in Wagner, on the etymology of a name. A woman from Nuremberg, he claims, traipsed to the Holy Land to have her son baptized by Saint John; when she got home, the boy who had been named Johannes in the saint's honour naturalized himself in Germany as Hans. The song splices Hans Sachs to the Apostle whose namesake he is, and arranges a confluence between the Pegnitz, Nuremberg's river, and the Jordan. In its smilingly fictitious way, it is as much of a scandal as the illegitimate baptism that infuriated the archbishop in *I Lombardi*.

Mythic characters have a bewildering multiplicity; as archetypes, they beget a teeming offspring of variants, scattered through time and space, and Wagner relied on his musical transitions to connect these disparate selves. He happily acknowledged the synthetic tricks of his trade. Hence his analysis of the Dutchman as a rough amalgam of the Wandering Jew and Odysseus, figures belonging in two utterly incompatible myths: is Wagner's hero forever condemned to wander lovelessly on the seas, or is he searching for a wife who will make a home for him? Senta's offer waives the curse and turns the eternal outcast into a husband, which proves how conveniently manipulable myth can be. But that reconciliation of the contradictory stories risks triviality: Senta therefore changes her mind and chooses to share the Dutchman's perdition – though this too, when Wagner revised the orchestral ending, changes to a sublimated love-death. The sagas contain two independent heroes, welded together in the *Ring*. One is the dragon-slayer Siegfried who marries Gutrune, known in the sources as Krimhilde. The other is Sigurd, who in the Norse narrative awakens Brunhilde and takes her as his wife. Superimposing them results in a tricky inconsistency, covered up in *Götterdämmerung* by the potion that makes Siegfried selectively amnesiac. Another less troublesome consequence is Siegfried's sexual double-dealing, as irresistible as the incest in *Die Walküre*: morality sets up barriers between the different kinds of love represented by Brünnhilde and Gutrune, but myth reveals the embargo to be artificial because love is at once innocent and depraved, tenderly selfless and hungrily carnal.

In Gottfried von Strassburg's *Tristan*, the medieval courtly romance that was one of the sources for Wagner's opera, the hero has a choice of Isoldes. The sorceress who brews the potions is Isolde the Wise; her daughter Isolde the Fair becomes Marke's wife and Tristan's mistress. After Marke discovers their affair, the banished Tristan meets Isolde of the White Hands in Normandy and marries her. But when he is wounded, he sends for Isolde the Fair, the only one who can heal him. To give the trio different names might clarify matters, but it would obscure their complementarity: they represent potentialities that coexist inside every individual. Wagner conflates all three characters, which makes his ragingly self-divided Isolde an all-inclusive study of the necessary attraction and the equally necessary antagonism between sex and death. There is only one Tristan in the opera, but he duplicates himself with the aid of an anagram. The knight who kills Isolde's lover Morold calls himself Tantris, though when he reappears to woo her for Marke he reverses the syllables and becomes Tristan, hoping that this new identity will rescind the incriminating past. Myths consist of modules, like the two halves of that name, which can be chopped up, jumbled, recombined at will. Isolde finds the verbal riddle easy to solve, and she clinches the point by a forensic experiment that removes a fragment from one place and fits it into another. A splinter of metal had lodged in the head of the dead Morold; she slides it into a notch on Tristan's sword, which proves him to be the killer.

Kundry is another dualistic creature, a composite of devout messenger and diabolical witch or of tender mother and seductive temptress, and she exchanges identities, bodies and voices without warning. By merging divergent sources or bringing together characters who remain separate in Wolfram von Eschenbach's *Parzival*, Wagner creates a woman who is at odds with herself, dramatizing conflicts that threaten to tear us all apart. Klingsor in the second act lists some of her previous incarnations: Salome's mother Herodias is one, Gundryygia – an orthographic and perhaps genetic relative – is another, while in the third act she resembles the penitent Mary Magdalen. In the first act she describes to Parsifal the death of his mother Herzeleide, then gives him a kiss that is not maternal even though she bestows it in her name. She owes her mixed motives to Wagner's recombination of happenings taken from the romance: when Wolfram's Gamuret dies, Herzeleide suckles Parzival as if the child were her lost husband.

Parsifal does not know what he is called until Kundry labels him, and he tells Gurnemanz that he has had many names, all of which he has forgotten. No sooner has Kundry christened him than she rearranges the syllables of his name and, like Tristan adopting the alias of Tantris, refers to Parsifal as Falparsi, which supposedly defines him as the pure fool, 'der reine Tor'. The derivation is spurious, as Wagner confessed to Judith Gautier. 'The "Araby dialect" in which "fal" is supposed to mean fool or uncouth was my invention,' he said, although credit for the guess actually belonged to the philologist Joseph von Görres. Wagner shrugged off aspersions of inaccuracy: 'What do I care about the real meaning of Arabic words?' Elsewhere he speculated that the name's origins might be Greek, since – as Cosima gullibly noted – 'the Celts (Germans) came first of all into contact with the Greeks'. Actually Parsifal is Perceval, he who pierces the vale, the hero who ventures into the valley where the Grail castle hides and penetrates its mystery. Some of Wagner's etymological hunches were accurate enough. He understood that the enigmatic figure of the fisher king derived from a misspelling of 'roi pêcheur' ('pêcheur' meaning fisherman, 'pécheur' sinner): the king is sinful, so Amfortas in the opera has no need to spend his time fishing. In 1879 Cosima, walking with the children, saw a blue bird beside the river, recognized it as what the English call a kingfisher, and wondered about its connection with the sinful king. Wagner was not present, otherwise he would surely have extemporized a theory. The truth was occasionally obliging. Composing the Good Friday music, Wagner redistributed the accents on 'Kar-Freitag' because he wanted to make it sound like 'Klag-Freitag', a Friday given over to mourning. Cosima urged him to change the word, but Wagner hesitated to do so. The following day he was informed by Hans von Wolzogen, the propagandist who edited the *Bayreuther Blätter*, that 'Kar' was not Hebrew but 'an old German word meaning "care" or "lament"'. He and Cosima were gratified.

Theodor Adorno argued that Wagner's music is atomized, broken down into terse, short-breathed mottoes or motifs that can be arranged in any order or grafted onto each other in compounds that express new ideas. His language is equally atomic. Wagner's reading of Jakob Grimm – the philologist who studied German grammar and went on to collect folk tales with his brother Wilhelm – convinced him that words, as he told Cosima in 1873, evolve in the same way as myths; or perhaps, rather than evolving, both words and myths go through a series of permutations that work by breaking down wholes into parts and trying new ways to make the splinters interconnect. Brünnhilde tells Sieglinde that her unborn child should be called Siegfried, and explains that the name is a compound of the words for victory and joy. Introduced to Gutrune, Siegfried applies the same analytic procedure and asks whether those are good runes that he reads in her welcoming eyes. Like these words, the symbols in the *Ring* are forever being recycled, smashed up to serve other functions. The clump of gold is beaten into a ring. Brünnhilde collects the broken bits of Siegmund's sword so that Siegfried can later solder them together. Meanwhile Mime is cooking one of his indigest-ible stews: Siegfried melts ingredients in a crucible and Mime mashes them in a pot, so that both imitate Wagner's eclecticism. The sword shatters the spear cut by Wotan from the cosmic ash tree, and the felled tree itself is chopped into logs that are heaped by the hearth in Valhalla to fuel the last blaze.

In his essay on what it meant to be German, Wagner referred to 'myths of native gods woven into an endless web of sagas'; and at the beginning of *Götterdämmerung*, when the three Norns recite the world's history while spooling out the rope that holds the collapsible chain of events together, he put that verbal image into action. To plait the cord is to plot history, to make contingent hap-penings inevitable and predictable. Time once more is being turned into space: the Norns might be moving those scenic trees that give Parsifal the illusion he is walking towards the temple. Sensing that the end is near, they imagine the beginning, which is the purpose of myth. The first Norn, whose memory is the longest, can sing of holy things because she witnessed the creation. Wotan tore the branch from the ash to make his spear and a spring welled up, lisping wisdom like the river in *Das Rheingold*; then after aeons – though within only a few seconds in her narration – the wounded tree died and the spring ran dry. The compulsory chore of recapitulation is soon underway, and the Norns tell us all over again what we already know: Wagner, as E. M. Forster put it when discussing the motifs, wrote 'music that reminds', tugged backwards into remorseful retrospection. The third Norn worries that they are not conscientiously spinning as they sing, and asks her sisters whether they want to know when the end of the world will occur. They give her no direct answer, since this is information we are better off without; it comes as a shock to Siegfried when the Rhinemaidens, in a terrifying abbreviation of the epochal story, tell him that he will die later that afternoon. Twined around the bodies of the Norns, anchored to a fir tree and secured by its attachment to Brünnhilde's rock, the rope, like myth, should set bounds to the world and stabilize it. But the multiplicity of stories retold by these three narrators disentangles and separates the cord into strands, and Wagner's image of the web recurs as the Norns struggle to maintain their hold on the rope. What they are passing on to each other is a text, a composite thing defined, like a textile, by the threads that have been woven and knotted into it. The first Norn worries that the weft ('das Geflecht') is tangled, the second complains about snags from the sharp-edged rock that snarl its texture ('verwirrt ist das Geweb'). The cord snaps, leaving them only with remnants – like the shards of the sword, the battered halves of the spear, the piled lumber that was once a tree: all the fragmentary constituents of Wagnerian myth.

There is an equivalent in Verdi, also intricately and deceptively manufactured by women. This is the veil about which Eboli sings in *Don Carlos*. It is flimsier than Wagner's yarn, which has to yoke the universe into consonance; its only function is to cover the face of the Moorish king's mistress. But the refrain of the female courtiers echoes the third Norn's injunction and toys with the same link between text, texture and textile. 'Tissez des voiles,' the women sing as they describe the weaving of veils in the Paris version; this became 'Tessete i veli' in the translation prepared for Milan. Myth is a filmy tissue of fictions, and the rope in *Götterdämmerung* frays, subjected to too much intellectual pressure. More impatient, the king in Eboli's song takes the initiative and rips off the veil, then cries out to Allah in dismay as he recognizes his wife, who has adopted the disguise to entrap him. In Wagner, the outcome is the confounding of history and the end of time; in Verdi, a moment of comic confusion is soon overcome – although the anticlimax in Eboli's song hardly matches her enraged reaction when she removes her mask in the garden and disappoints Carlos.

Wagner enjoyed making jokes about the infirmity of his myths. The rainbow bridge in *Das Rheingold* is a mental artefact, extending Verdi's ladder to heaven; it rewrites the biblical covenant that arches across the sky after Noah's flood, because it allows Wagner's supercilious gods to retreat from the earth rather than accepting responsibility for what happens on it. But how solid is a symbol whose building blocks are merely droplets of iridescent vapour? Froh tries out the rainbow before treading on it; he assures the gods that it can support their weight, but the need for a test encourages us to doubt it. Myth was Wagner's charter of imaginative liberty, permitting him to make anything happen anywhere. Writing to Mathilde Wesendonck from Paris about the Bacchanale in *Tannhäuser*, he said that he transferred Venus from the warmer south to the Wartburg because he wanted to tell two stories at once, connecting the classical goddess with the Nordic fiddler Strömkarl, whose violin-playing had devilish powers. It amused him, he said, to complicate the mixture, and he wished he had brought in another analogous myth by casting some ballerinas as the Bacchantes who murdered Orpheus and having them toss the severed head of the first singer into a waterfall.

On the evening when he quizzed his dentist Jenkins about Brigham Young and Joseph Smith, Wagner showed off his gift as a mythmaker by elaborating a whimsy about a heaven as stuffed with material benefits as that of Mahomet. Celestial bliss, he said, was to come in different gradations, to be enjoyed on separate tiers; tickets for the various levels of the hierarchy were to be purchased from priests, who would only accept hard cash. The expenditure would be worthwhile, because the services of worship were to be 'magnificently choral'. As he developed the conceit, Wagner relished the shocked reaction of another visitor, a dour Lutheran mathematician. Jenkins, however, who explained Mormonism by saying that it delivered sanctity on earth and made the western desert bloom, enjoyed the 'extravagant jest': Wagner was describing a theatre, like the temple he had built for himself and consecrated with performances of *Parsifal.* Verdi might have been less amused, not because Wagner travestied religion but because he made the theatre religiose. In the French *Don Carlos* Posa describes the mission of Flemish liberation, for which he enlists Carlos, as 'notre oeuvre'; in the Italian translation this became their 'grand'opera' – a bathetic joke, given Verdi's opinion about the conservative grandiosity of the Opéra. But although Wagner may have been teasing his humourless guest, he spoke in earnest. After the gods had faded into twilight, there could be no religion but opera.

# 5 | *A Death and a Regeneration*

## THE MAN OF THE EVENING

While occupying a cottage in the grounds of the Wesendonck villa in Zurich during the 1850s, Wagner often strolled over to the main house late in the afternoon to try out excerpts from his day's work on Mathilde's Bechstein piano. Because he usually arrived between five and six p.m., he called himself 'der Dämmer-Mann'. 'Dämmerung' can refer either to sunrise or sunset, but Debussy tidied up the ambiguity by describing Wagner's music as 'a beautiful sunset that was mistaken for a sunrise': he belonged to the weary evening, and was almost an augury of the sun's extinction. Mathilde's poem 'Schmerzen', set by Wagner in 1857 as the fourth of the five *Wesendoncklieder*, worries about the sun's fate, which preoccupied scientists after geology demonstrated the age of the earth and thermodynamics calculated that the loss of heat dooms all living things. Although Kurwenal comforts Tristan in the third act of the opera by saying that 'der alten Sonne' still shines on him at Kareol, the phrase is not reassuring: what if the old sun is as close to expiry as Tristan himself? 'Schmerzen' is about the elevated pain that comes with this foreknowledge of an end. The song addresses the sun and reflects on its daily death, with red eyes luridly smearing tears across the sky as it slumps into the sea; although it rises again like a proud Siegfried – 'Wie ein stolzer Siegesheld!' – the singer refuses to be dismayed by the prospect of eternal darkness. The critic Paul Bekker called the chromaticism of *Tristan und Isolde* 'a nocturnal phenomenon': it blurred the contours of things, and made them disappear into 'mere tonal vibrations'.

This twilight extended around the world. In the 1870s Ruggero Leoncavallo planned his own equivalent to the *Ring*, a trilogy consisting of separate operas about the Medici brothers, Savonarola and Cesare Borgia. He called his prospective epic *Crepusculum*: only Wagner could have convinced an Italian to see the Florentine Renaissance as a time of dusk not dawn. Despite the militancy of Wagner's *Rule Britannia* march, the novelist Arnold Bennett even implicated him in the fatigue of the overextended British empire, described by the statesman Joseph Chamberlain in 1902 as a 'weary Titan'. After a Covent Garden performance of *Tristan und Isolde* – which he considered an hour too long for the human physique to endure – Bennett applied the phrase to Wagner and said 'the Weary Titan made a point of wearying others', adding that 'he did it on purpose'. For Oswald Spengler, the Wagnerian malady went beyond exhaustion; it announced a cosmic ending. His encyclopaedic threnody *Der Untergang des Abendlandes* was translated as *The Decline of the West*, although the title literally meant the going-under of the evening land; a related verb, 'untergehn', is used by Mathilde in 'Schmerzen' to describe the sun slipping into its grave. Spengler made Wagner a scapegoat for the West's terminal state. He likened the *Ring* to the Pergamon Altar, the Hellenistic monument with its frieze of Olympian gods battling giants that German engineers excavated in Turkey in the 1880s and took back to Berlin. The gigantism of the altar, with its daunting staircase for intimidated worshippers, marked the top-heavy conclusion of an ancient culture, and Wagner's 'ruthless bombardment of the nerves' and his cultivation of a 'towering greatness' announced the depressing, demoralized finale in modern times. Greek art, according to Spengler, built structures that confirmed the geometrical rationality of creation. Wagner's music abandoned that humane, civilizing task and left us to float off into a 'bodiless infinity'. Spengler decided that 'the last of the Faustian arts died in *Tristan und Isolde*. This work is the giant keystone of Western music … a finale'. He called the arts of the West Faustian because they derived their energy from the striving, thrusting will, which had been weakened by 'senility' – a charge even more damaging than the sadism that Max Nordau imputed to Wagner in *Entartung*.

Decadence meant dissolution. In his description of the *Tristan* prelude, Spengler might also be referring to the start of *Das Rheingold*: what he heard was 'strange surgings.... The motif comes up out of dark terrible deeps. It is flooded for an instant by a flash of hard bright sun.... It laughs, it coaxes, it threatens, and anon it vanishes.' A 'whole world of soul' melted away, he said, in the first three bars of *Tristan*, just as the solidity of nature was broken up into 'strokes and patches of colour' by Edouard Manet or the impressionist painters. Spengler offered no evidence for this connection between the arts, though his point could be illustrated by Renoir's portrait of Wagner, painted in Palermo in less than an hour in 1882, days after the orchestral score of *Parsifal* had been completed. It might be a study of the 'rich, hoary voluptuary' who, along with the invalid, was another of the typical degenerates described by Nordau. As seen by Renoir, the jutting planes of Wagner's cranium, his craggy nose and pugnacious chin – the insignia of determination, respected even by the sculptor of the bust in Venice's Giardini Pubblici – turn squashy. His unfocused eyes recede and narrow to slits, with weary shadows bunched beneath them like overstuffed valises. His skin has an unhealthy pallor, though his mouth, pursed or pouting, is flushed, still eager for sensation. Thicker brushstrokes touch in his white hair, too heavy for a collapsible head that is as fragile as an eggshell. When he was shown the result of the accelerated session, Wagner remarked that he looked like 'the embryo of an angel, an oyster swallowed by an epicure'. Both images were wittily and terrifyingly apt. Was he unborn in the womb, or dead and buried inside a glutton's body? Either way, he no longer recognized himself as a human being. Pictorial dissolution had overcome him, just as he wished a sonic dissolution on the objects – swords, castles, lumps of gold – that his music translated into tremulous air.

After he changed his mind about Wagner, Nietzsche suggested that a typical telegram sent home by a festivalgoer might read 'Bayreuth: bereits bereut' – already rued. But it was too late for repentance; the theatre on the hill was a cenotaph, testifying to what Nietzsche called in 1878 'the death agony of the *last act*'. Thomas Mann's *Buddenbrooks* examines that Wagnerian agony as it fells successive members of a mercantile clan. The organist Pfühl warns Gerda Buddenbrooks against experiments with harmony, and denounces Wagner's music as 'demagoguery, blasphemy, and madness! It is a fragrant fog with thunderbolts! It is the end of all morality in the arts!' Despite this frothing, Pfühl cannot resist the vice and secretly arranges the 'Liebestod' for a chaste combination of violin and piano. Young Hanno is unmanned by being taken to *Lohengrin*, which leaves him 'plunged into shame': music is the equivalent of masturbation, draining the boy's vitality. Improvising at the piano, Hanno refuses to resolve the *Tristan*esque dissonance, and in the rhapsody he composes just before his death he takes a precociously erotic delight in postponing the climax. When the theme is finally restated, his pointless self-titillation reveals that he has been propounding 'the cult of nothing'. Mann calls Hanno's performance of the piece brutal, depraved, cynically crazed, and his febrile imaginings are characterized by metaphors that allude to Wagnerian epic: 'Was he slaying dragons, scaling mountains, swimming great rivers, walking through fire?' No, he is only playing the piano. Siegfried Wagner, another specimen of what Isolde calls an 'entartet Geschlecht', felt diminished in the same way by the virility of his namesake, and apologized for the imposture in his memoirs: 'No anvils have I smashed, no dragons have I slain, no sea of flames have I traversed,' he wrote, paraphrasing Mann's mockery of Hanno. History happens first as tragedy, then as farce; first as heroic action, then as an impotent aesthetic replica.

Thomas Buddenbrooks is deaf to Wagner's enticements, and his wife Gerda mocks him for liking insipid tunes that confirm his optimistic world view. But he suffers his own moral collapse when he reads a volume by Schopenhauer, which convinces him – as it convinced Wagner – that life is an illusion sustained by the mendacity of the will, and that individuality, the highest of values for nineteenth-century novelists, is an error of perception. Turning the pages, he is exposed to a silent performance of *Tristan*. The Buddenbrooks clan resembles Mann's own family, which he left behind in Lübeck when he set himself up as a writer in Munich; confessing a personal guilt, the novelist argues that decline or decadence occurs in a bourgeois household – and by implication in a commercial nation – when it spawns an artist. Art, dreamily fulfilling our wishes, is the antithesis of the puritanical self-denial on which the accumulation of wealth depends. It is a revenge on prosperity and even on fecundity, which is why the very young novelist took such pleasure in arranging the deaths of his joyless, toiling characters. Despite his own warnings, Mann continued to find Wagner's music irresistible, and even a synopsis in prose could be powerfully exciting. In his story 'Tristan' an enthusiast plays the love duet from the opera on a sanatorium piano, using the score to woo a female patient. Mann's exclamatory words envy the pulse of instrumental sounds: 'Oh, tumultuous storm of rhythms! Oh, glad chromatic upward surge of metaphysical perception!' The mere thought of the orchestra and voices is risky, and the young woman soon dies of her disease – killed by Wagner, not by consumption.

What if the music were to be suppressed, as in the spoken theatre? Then Wagner's characters could be diagnosed as deluded neurotics; deprived of their aural drug, they would have a chance of curing themselves. This is the case with Henrik Ibsen's heroine in *The Lady from the Sea*, first performed in 1888. Ellida, a lighthouse-keeper's mentally unsettled daughter, is Senta without an orchestra to support her fantasies and whip up the winds. Her Dutchman is a wooer called the Stranger, who tells her she is a sea creature and attempts to spirit her away with him. Rather than longing like Senta to save the demon, Ellida wants to be saved from him. The official meliorism of the nineteenth century comes to her aid: she steadies herself when told that, though we may have begun in the ocean, we have now acclimatized ourselves to life on land and cannot regress. With calmer nerves, she watches from the shore as the Stranger's steamer disappears.

In the last two decades of the nineteenth century the novelist Romain Rolland attended concerts of excerpts from Wagner's operas at the Cirque d'Hiver in Paris. Huddled with an audience of the poor and deprived, he found a thrilling energy that was otherwise missing from his life, an antidote to the moral debility of the times. Wagner's gift to the wretched of the earth was *Siegfried*, which in Rolland's opinion breathed 'perfect health and happiness'. Was he right? Leo Tolstoy, who saw the opera in Moscow in 1896, thought that its manly primitivism was the cover for mincing effeminacy: he complained that the tenor who sang Mime had 'white, weak, genteel hands' and none of the muscles needed by a smith – shaming evidence of the West's lost impetus. Rolland too was dismayed when he found out how the cycle continued, and like Shaw he condemned Wagner for succumbing to fashionable despair in *Götterdämmerung*: 'How fine a more optimistic poem from the revolutionary of '48 might have been.... Why should it be truthful to depict life only as a bad thing? ... What inspiration there is in the laugh of a great man.' Verdi came to the century's rescue when he dispensed that sustaining joy in *Falstaff*. Rolland admiringly repeated an anecdote about Richard Strauss who, when Kaiser Wilhelm II called *Falstaff* feeble, insisted on the marvel of Verdi's self-renewal. Lacking the vital delight that modern men needed, Wagner was relegated to the past. 'It is the voice of a century of tempest that passes with you,' Rolland declared in a funeral oration for his youthful hero.

The Wagnerians in the stories James Huneker collected in 1902 in *Melomaniacs* have more trouble laying their tormenter to rest. 'Dusk of the Gods' is the reverie of a music lover who dozes while a virtuoso pianist free-associates through the history of music, starting from the fugal algebra of Bach, advancing to Mozart's graceful dances, then thunderously saluting Beethoven. When the recital reaches Wagner, tones become colours and a sonic seduction washes over the listener's ravished body. The 'degradation and effeminization of music' has begun: the art is 'a modern Circe ... whose wand transforms men into listening swine'. Huneker's listener even imagines that these silken, polychrome sounds have an evil, mephitic smell. Like Nietzsche he identifies Wagner with Klingsor, who 'tears down, evirates, effeminates and disintegrates.... The art nears its end; its spiritual suicide is at hand.' Suicide is here a matter of form, as music forgets its own rules and takes to imitating painting or poetry, but in other decadent narratives Wagner provides the soundtrack for mad acts of self-destruction. In Villiers de l'Isle Adam's *Axël*, written in 1885, a love like that between Tristan and Isolde is the excuse for a suicide pact. The degenerate aristocrat Axël and the defrocked nun Sara meet in a castle crypt, draw daggers to kill each other and then, instantaneously infatuated, decide to drink poison together: it is as if the opera had ended before the conclusion of the first act, with Brangäne excused from having to swap elixirs. Theirs is what Siegfried and Brünnhilde call a laughing death, because it spares Axël and Sara satiation, ennui, the impotence of old age – and also saves them from the tedious rigmarole of making love. *Axël* concludes with a nihilistic misreading of *Götterdämmerung*. Wagner rounded up survivors who stare in wonder at the spectacle of the burning hall, but Axël's last words express his hope that the rest of the human race will die as unregretfully as he does; while Wagner's orchestra sets nature free in an exultant, cleansing overflow, Villiers asks for a benumbed silence, disturbed only by a distant wind, 'vibrations of the awakening of space, the surge of the plain, the hum of life'. Reduced to a hum, life is background noise, vexatious and irrelevant.

Wagner's own death inaugurated the fin de siècle, and therefore had to be staged as a public ritual, a spectacle like the excruciation of Christ or the funeral of Siegfried. In fact it happened behind closed doors, while the rest of the household was at lunch in the Palazzo Vendramin. Gabriele d'Annunzio therefore anticipated the moment in his novel *Il fuoco*, published in 1900, and made sure that this rehearsal for Wagner's death happened in full view of the hero Stelio Effrena, a poet who sees himself as an Italian equivalent to Wagner, a prophet of national renewal.

Stelio advertises his credentials by delivering a lecture – or rather a wild-eyed rant – in Venice in the autumn of 1882. The setting is the council chamber of the Doge's Palace, where Shakespeare's Othello had confronted the senators and Byron's Foscari dealt with their political and personal dilemmas; now the seat of power is occupied by an artist. Being Latin, Stelio is the legimate heir to an ancient civilization, and he therefore quibbles about Wagner's right to claim Greek tragedy as a model for of the *Ring*. Italy, he insists, remains the homeland of music: the anguish of Amfortas is already present in a Palestrina motet, which is 'purer and more virile' than Wagner's chromatic heavings. Even so, Wagner, who has 'foreseen and forwarded the aspiration of the German race to the heroic greatness of empire', can teach the Italians about art's contribution to national glory. Stelio quotes the king's summons to the warriors in *Lohengrin*, declares that Wagner deserves as much credit as Bismarck for the Prussian victories at Sedan and Sadowa, and challenges Italy to ape the heroic efforts of 'the barbaric creator'. He campaigns for a theatre dedicated to Apollo to be built on the Janiculum Hill in Rome; the dramas he intends to write for performance in this neoclassical Bayreuth will be 'a constructive and determining power in the third Rome' – a city that is to supersede the Rome of the emperors and the popes. Stelio is a homegrown Rienzi, with better credentials than Wagner's Germanized interloper.

After the lecture, someone mentions that Wagner is in Venice, with an ailing heart. Stelio, returning from the Lido on a stormy day in late November, notices him on board the steamer, attended by Cosima and Liszt. He looks wan, frail enough to be blown away by the gale that flails the lagoon; Stelio silently sings the boisterous shanty from *Der fliegende Holländer* and imagines this exhausted figure in the guise of the angry young exile who dreamed up the Dutchman as the symbol of 'his furious struggle, his supreme hope'. Cosima is anxiously protective, Liszt mutters a prayer to quieten the winds. Suddenly Wagner is stricken. He cries out, collapses, and is laid on a bench, clammily sweating but scarcely able to breathe. When the steamer reaches San Marco, Stelio and a friend offer to carry him ashore. To their amazement, his short, bent body is as weighty as bronze, and they feel they are holding aloft the effigy of 'the Hero … the Revealer who had laid the essences of the universe, in infinite song, before men's worship'. It is a funeral procession even more doleful than that of Siegfried, but it has a startling, miraculous result: Wagner's 'sacred heart' begins beating again as they lift him onto the jetty. He is revived by the solicitude of his handlers, who ensure his immortality.

The news of Wagner's actual death comes a few weeks later, preceded by a cacophony of bells. The world does not end on cue, but all valour and value bleed from it, as d'Annunzio notes. Stelio asks Cosima's permission for himself and five helpers to carry Wagner's crystal coffin to the boat waiting outside the Palazzo Vendramin, then to the railway carriage. A posthumous smile on the face of the corpse leaves the pallbearers with 'a wondering fear that made them religious'. When they reach the station, bunches of laurel brought from the Janiculum are strewn on the coffin by two artisans, 'shaped in the mould of the ancient Roman race', who are building Apollo's temple. The offering is less a mark of respect than a signal that a transmission of power is taking place. Bavaria in February, where Wagner's corpse is to be taken, remains under its pall of frost, but the branches are evidence of an early Roman spring. 'He has conquered; he can die,' says Stelio of Wagner. Now it is to be Italy's turn, under his own leadership.

Ten years after publishing the novel, d'Annunzio and his nationalist troops seized control of the city of Fiume (now Rijeka in Croatia) and declared it an independent state. The poet was its self-proclaimed Duce, and when he elaborated a constitution for his fiefdom he gave music a corporate role as religion's rival, representing 'the kingdom of the spirit'. D'Annunzio's adventure made Wagner seem like a fair-weather revolutionary: he never organized his supporters into a paramilitary band, or proposed that Bayreuth should secede from Bavaria and threaten the rest of the unWagnerized world with reprisals.

Most other Wagnerians marvelled at their hero's audacity and despaired of ever equalling his achievements. D'Annunzio alone behaved as if Wagner had not gone far enough.

|||||||||||||||||||

Stelio's oration declares that Wagner – promoted from artist to demagogic Messiah – will be crucial to Italy's moral and cultural rearmament. French Wagnerians, remembering the war with Prussia, had more trouble justifying their partiality. Saint-Saëns refused to discount Wagner's odiously gleeful lampoon about the siege of Paris, and held him accountable, as Germany's 'national genius', for the Prussian massacre of women and children, the bombing of hospitals and the desecration of cathedrals. When Charles Lamoureux conducted *Lohengrin* in 1887, a caricaturist portrayed him as an obsequious monkey handing bags of French gold to a sneering Wagner; police had to control mobs of protesters outside the theatre. The same opera was staged at the Palais Garnier in 1891, translated into French as a gesture of appeasement. Again patriots chanted the 'Marseillaise' in front of the Opéra, while police patrolled the auditorium, ready to eject hecklers. Even Romain Rolland bridled in 1905 when the final scene of *Die Meistersinger* was performed in Strasbourg at a festival that was meant to arrange an accord between German and French music. Given the quarrel between the two countries over Alsace-Lorraine, Sachs's hymn to the holiness of 'Deutsche Kunst' was a diplomatic gaffe. Rolland felt that Wagner's 'arrogant music … reflected his military, middle-class nation', oozing good health and self-satisfaction.

There was no doubting the devotion of Emmanuel Chabrier, however: Vincent d'Indy heard him muffling his sobs during a performance of *Tristan* in Munich in 1880, and Chabrier explained that he had waited a decade to hear the cellos play their A in the prelude. But such a surrender was only possible while the lights were out. When Chabrier came to recall the pilgrimage six years later in his piano quadrille *Souvenirs de Munich*, he treated the score with flippant sarcasm, picking out elements of derisive humour that usually pass unnoticed. His digest returns several times to the ditty Kurwenal sings to taunt Isolde, which is taken up by the jeering sailors. A snatch of the love duet is left unmolested by the adaptation, though it ends prematurely with a little decorative twiddle by the two pianists, who have not been captivated by the witchery. The quadrille turns everything into a dance, and Chabrier's summation of *Tristan* ends with a frantic gallop: the languishing, enervated opera is speeded up, made fit for use on a social occasion. After the *Ring* at Bayreuth in 1896 Gabriel Fauré felt like a self-flagellating penitent, 'convinced of universal misery, eternal suffering, and that is all!' But his *Ring* quadrille, already composed with André Messager eight years before the Bayreuth trip, is upbeat and ebullient. The piece begins with the forging of Siegfried's sword, here polished off without effort; it goes on to Brünnhilde's announcement of Siegmund's death, accelerated and thereby robbed of its leaden gravity; Siegmund's spring song tinkles out elegantly and is interrupted before it can spread the erotic instinct through all of nature. Finally the magic fire spells out Siegfried's motto, but for just a few seconds. Deprived of his longueurs, Wagner is not quite trivialized but certainly robbed of his capacity to engross our time and take over our lives.

In the years after Wagner's death, what worried (or in some cases delighted) commentators was his amoralism. Decadence or degeneration meant a loosening of the religious and ethical strictures that regulated bourgeois society, and Wagner's music inflamed those who heard it. The young Alfred Stieglitz, a musician before he became a photographer, made a note in a private album on his twentieth birthday in 1884, confiding that it was his ambition to live 'in Venusberg' like the sated Tannhäuser. Listening to *Tristan*, he imagined he saw the singers coupling as their voices blended. The censors who examined Verdi's libretti before the operas could be licensed for performance worried about political sedition, which is why locations were transposed: *Giovanna d'Arco*, for instance, could only be performed in Rome in camouflage, so it became *Orietta di Lesbo*, about a Genoese freedom fighter assailing the Turks. The puritans who fiddled after the event with Wagner's stories were not bothered by his revolutionary sympathies; their concern was his erotomania. The prudish J. Walker McSpadden – a gentleman amateur from the American South who supplemented his *Stories from Wagner* by compiling a *Boy's Book of Famous Soldiers* and a volume on *Pioneer Heroes* – treated the myths as a patrimony that was to be handed down from fathers to children, which is why he systematically bowdlerized them. All suspicion of sex was removed, leaving the characters in the *Ring* limply unmotivated. Siegmund and Sieglinde are childhood playmates reunited, not incestuous siblings. Fricka has no need to reproach Wotan for begetting the Valkyries during his affair with Erda: he rides away from Valhalla and returns after many years with a mounted troop of female guardians, whose provenance is never questioned. The announcement of Sieglinde's pregnancy is eliminated, and instead Brünnhilde whispers 'words of tenderness and balm' that McSpadden refrains from imparting. When Siegfried awakens Brünnhilde they do not make furious love but sit and talk for a long time, after which – with no night spent in the cave – he departs on the Rhine. McSpadden cannot retell *Tristan* for his innocent readers without mentioning the love potion, but he ensures that it does not quieten Isolde's conscience. Pleading indisposition like a hypochondriac opera singer, she persuades Marke to delay their marriage, which means that she is at least not committing adultery with Tristan.

Altering the stories may have satisfied Verdi's censors, but in Wagner's case the problem lay in the music – in what Hanslick called its sensual fascination and its power as 'a direct nervous stimulant'. Tristan and Isolde, he said in 1883, were hostages to 'a chemical power'. What they called love was 'a purely superficial pathological process'; the pathogen was the potion, their quaintly medieval equivalent to hashish or absinthe. In *Painted Veils* Huneker was even more explicit. A bigoted reviewer in the novel denounces a moral rot that he traces back to Wagner: 'What else is *Tristan und Isolde* but a tonal orgasm? … Musical erethrism, I tell you.' Hanslick's concern was the way those lubricious harmonies appealed to 'the female audience particularly'. Men could cope with such a seductive onslaught, or perhaps were entitled to enjoy it; Wagner's crime was to provoke an erotic response in women, who were officially supposed, if they were decent, to be above such things. When the pianist performs his Wagnerian pastiche in 'The Dusk of the Gods', Huneker's shocked listener asks 'Was art a woman's sigh?' That sigh is presumably one of pleasure, never heard before: it is the sound of a woman relishing sex, like Venus in Beardsley's *Under the Hill* when she masturbates her pet unicorn and laps up its semen. In 1893, after attending a performance of *Tristan* in Paris, Beardsley drew an audience of Wagnerites. The women have tropical jungles of hair, ripe labial mouths, bare shoulders and white swelling breasts; two unvirile men are squeezed between them – one a bald bespectacled intellectual, the other with a grotesque pinched face and a transvestite coiffure – and they shrink from their ardent, exotically fleshly companions, whom they are incapable of satisfying.

Nietzsche wondered 'What is a female Wagnerian, medically speaking?' Beardsley's diagnosis would have been clear enough: a Wagnerienne – as the critic Paul Rosenfeld called the most fervent female acolytes – is a nymphomaniac. Physiologically speaking, there were defining signs, at least in the eyes of timorous men. In George Moore's novel *Evelyn Innes*, published in 1898, the young soprano preparing to sing Isolde and Brünnhilde has one disqualification: 'the Wagnerian bosom was lacking'. Her aristocratic protector encourages her career, but worries about the 'extravagant growths of flesh' that will develop as a by-product of the strong lungs demanded by Wagner. A plush bosom is to him 'a dreadful deformity', but he reconciles himself to it if the protuberant breasts – already placed on show in Beardsley's sketch – are 'musical necessities'. The tipsy male connoisseurs in *Painted Veils* appraise a balancing set of plump curves when they gossip about another nubile Wagnerian soprano, Easter Brandès. A sceptic complains about her impulsiveness, but says that women 'think with their matrix.... They are the sexual sex.' The critic Ulick Invern wants to hear more about Easter's art. 'And less about her coda – there's a musical term for you,' jokes the raunchy Alfred Stone. We like to laugh about fat ladies in opera; the tittering may derive from our fear of women whose art, lodged inside their bodies, makes them totems of engorged fertility.

Apart from *Tristan*, the opera most often accused of sponsoring depravity was *Tannhäuser*. With the debate about religion and the artist's social identity removed, it was treated as a guide to sexual deviation. Oscar Wilde's Dorian Gray sits alone in his box at Covent Garden listening 'with rapt pleasure' to the prelude, in which he hears 'the tragedy of his own soul'. No Venus menaces Dorian, whose demons are epicene male dandies: Wilde customized the Venusberg to suit more rarified tastes. Beardsley's foppish Tannhäuser in *Under the Hill* leaves Venus with her priapic unicorn and takes his pleasure with the serving boys who share his bath and then apply 'delicious frictions' to his private parts when towelling him down. His truest love affair, however, is with himself, and before entering the perfumed bordello he titivates his peruke, fluffs up his ruff, and says 'Would to heaven I might receive the assurance of a looking-glass...!' The more conventional Tannhäuser called Reggie in E. F. Benson's *The Rubicon*, published in 1894, is at least subjected to a tug of war between two women. He deserts his fiancée Gertrude – a 'breezy' girl, belonging in the healthy outdoors, 'fond of hunting, lawn-tennis, animals, hymns' – and takes up with the adulterous Eva, a pagan creature who holidays in Algiers and is rumoured to smoke cigarettes. He recognizes his error when Eva invites him to *Tannhäuser* at Covent Garden – perhaps the same performance in which Dorian Gray found a representation of his own corrupt career? All it takes to recall him to duty is the sound of the pilgrims plodding towards redemption; before the curtain rises on the Venusberg, the bashful Reggie blurts out 'You are a wicked woman' and escapes from Eva's box. Wagner's goddess is infuriated by Tannhäuser's rejection, but Benson's aristocratic wanton takes Reggie's condemnation to heart and makes amends by drinking prussic acid. In 'Tannhäuser's Choice', one of the stories in Huneker's *Melomaniacs*, the medieval characters crop up again in fashionable London and adapt to its different sexual ethics. Harry Tannhäuser, a heroic tenor, offends the chaste Elizabeth Landgrave by spending dissipated afternoons in a house off Piccadilly with his ageing Venus, named Mrs Holda in honour of the matronly goddess praised by Wagner's shepherd for bringing spring to the meadows. The

English Elizabeth reacts more sensibly than her operatic namesake: she gets engaged to the brewer's son Wolfram, and announces that they will travel to Rome for their honeymoon. 'Oh, these affected Wagnerites!' giggles the goddess, having disposed of the competition.

Almost by definition, a Wagnerian soprano counted – both to the guardians of a threatened morality and to the proponents of a new, modern amoralism – as a vixen. The disappointing truth is that the greatest Wagnerians tend to be level-headed professionals, unincandescent once the performance is over, like the matronly Kirsten Flagstad or the earthy, humorous Birgit Nilsson. But in the nineteenth century, women who went on the stage were, like Strepponi, apt to be stigmatized as loose characters. Cosima was hypocritically horrified when Hans Richter suggested that her daughter Eva might have a singing career, and threatened to repudiate the girl. Another of Huneker's melomaniacs, a bossy American matriarch whose daughter has been engaged at Bayreuth, vows that the girl 'shall never sing Isolde with *my* permission'. She is outraged by the 'dreadfully immoral situation', and by the costume of gauzy cheese-cloth Isolde is expected to wear. Easter in *Painted Veils*, whose senses are 'narcotized' by Wagner, jettisons respectability when she sings Isolde, Brünnhilde and Kundry at Bayreuth. She prepares for the engagement by changing her name to Istar, the Assyrian and Babylonian goddess whose temple maidens were sacred prostitutes; as a Wagnerian specialist she is self-evidently akin to 'the daughter of sin'. The singers in Huneker's stories do their best to augment the spicy varieties of sex they find in the operas. Madame Stock in 'Brynhilds Immolation' has a daughter, Hilda for short, who trails around with her as she sings Brünnhilde and Isolde. In the wings Hilda is kissed by a beefy Hungarian tenor, her mother's partner on- and offstage. The girl is prepared for 'a Siegmund and Sieglinde love' – not quite incest but even more complicated, since the tenor proposes sharing his favours between mother and daughter. Madame Stock generously hands Herr Albert over to Hilda, then strides off to sing *Götterdämmerung*: the immolation announces her sexual retirement.

Chastity offstage is no safeguard against the intimate ardour of the music. In 1936 Marcia Davenport, the daughter of the soprano Alma Gluck, published *Lena Geyer*, a novel about another of these alarming female careerists. Geyer's Isolde is breathlessly described as 'the distillation of erotic passion'. But after some ill-advised, vocally damaging bouts of sexual indulgence, she decides that she can live either for love or for art, not for both; she chooses to protect her talent by forswearing sex. 'I am only a throat,' she says as she deflects a prospective lover. Of course she is required to pay for her defiance of nature, and she dies of cervical cancer while listening in a morphine-induced stupor to the 'Liebestod' on the radio, conducted by a man who long ago broke off with her because of her rule of continence. Too late, Geyer enjoys consummation, and her 'cracked and shrivelled lips' silently mouth 'the whispered notes that had drawn her soul sighing to her lips'. Thea Kronborg in Willa Cather's *The Song of the Lark*, published in 1915, may not be wicked but is certainly wild. She grows up in mountainous Colorado and first hears Wagner at an orchestral concert in Chicago. Her Wagnerian career begins, however, when she is caught in a storm while hiking through a canyon in Arizona. She hides in a cave among powdery relics of earlier cultures; emerging, she leaps over crevasses, her energy recharged by her exploration of the ancient earth. She now knows how to play a goddess, 'with only a muscular language'. Established as a prima donna at the Metropolitan Opera, she looks like a sophisticated savage in her furs: walking through Central Park during a blizzard, she resembles 'some rich-pelted animal, with warm blood, that had run in out of the woods'.

The most lurid of these imaginary careers is that of Margarethe Styr in Gertrude Atherton's *Tower of Ivory*, published in 1910. Atherton, born in San Francisco, was described by a reviewer in 1898 as the chronicler of 'emancipated American womanhood'. Despite her liberal sympathies, she declined to meet Oscar Wilde, whom she associated with 'the decadence, the loss of virility that must follow over-civilization'. *Tower of Ivory* extends that slur to Wagner. Styr enthrals the callow young Englishman Lord Bridgminster, who hears her in *Götterdämmerung* in Munich and feels, as Wagnerites so often did, that he is voluptuously drowning. She belongs to Ludwig II's operatic troupe, and gives two performances that are supposedly in the king's presence (although he remains out of sight), both in the middle of the night. At Neuschwanstein she performs by moonlight on what is now known as the Wagner bridge, a specimen of dizzy Nietzschean engineering that spans a ravine near the palace; the programme is all climaxes, with the ravings of Kundry followed by Brünnhilde's war-cry. Back in Munich she repeats the complete *Götterdämmerung* in the Residenz, with the king as the sole auditor. The private performance begins at midnight and lasts until dawn, with no interval between the acts so that life will not perturb the insane illusion of art.

During her affair with Bridgminster, they often discuss Wagner. He rather vacuously suspects that 'Wagner's music changed the nature of the void itself', and Styr agrees that it induces madness by setting up 'a vibration in the nervous system' that 'lifts us bodily from the plane of the normal'. As Isolde, she allows herself to be scorched by close contact with 'the most licentious opera ever written'. The audience, responding to her ferocity in the first act, seems to be overtaken – as Atherton sensationally calculates – by a cataclysm like those ancient convulsions of the earth that 'annihilated millions and buried continents'. Styr unleashes the same 'primal devastating force' in another performance of *Tristan* after she learns that her lover has married a demure young Englishwoman of his own class with the bucolic name of Mabel. Bridgminster is lured back to Styr, and his wife dies in childbirth during his absence. He then proposes marriage to his mistress; suddenly remorseful, Styr tries to dissuade him by confessing the full extent of her sinfulness – a childhood of poverty among the coalmines of the American West, seduction at the age of fifteen, escape to New York, a career as a streetwalker with the proceeds from her grubby outings sagely invested in stocks, the exploitation of rich protectors like those who support Violetta, and so on. Bridgminster ignores her tawdry revelations, as if he wanted to repeat Verdi's action in rehabilitating Strepponi. The only way Styr can save him from the mistake of ennobling a former harlot is to give one last, purgatively realistic performance of *Götterdämmerung*, at the end of which she rides into the flames and incinerates herself. Atherton does not say whether she dismounted from her horse before this suttee.

George Moore's *Evelyn Innes* has a similar plot, though a different resolution: it ends not with a bonfire but with a whimper of submission. Evelyn's father is the organist in a Catholic church in London. His mission is to revive Palestrina's music; the talent Evelyn inherits inclines her towards opera, but he warns her 'how dangerous the life of an opera singer is' and prays that she will not betray 'our holy religion'. The dangers are social – her titled admirer Owen Asher belongs to a class that lives 'for balls and dinner parties, for love-making and the opera' – but also insidiously musical. Evelyn knows that 'to sing Isolde and live a chaste life' is an impossible contradiction, and spends months of study and rehearsal 'seeking the exact rhythm of a phrase intended to depict and rouse a sinful desire'; the score of *Tristan* has a shuddering sensuality, even when Owen plays snatches of it on a dry-toned harpsichord. 'That music maddens me,' Evelyn says when still reeling after a performance of the second act. Brooding about the iniquity of her profession, she reflects that 'the restriction of sexual intercourse is the moral ideal of Western Europe', which makes Isolde, armed with her concupiscent potion, the most scarlet of women. Evelyn's Brünnhilde is also eagerly carnal, and her interpretation offends Cosima, who complains that she forgets that the character is a goddess. Unlike Verdi with Strepponi, Owen has no plans to make an honest woman of his mistress, which is why he casually remarks that he 'doesn't care much for the nuptial music' from *Lohengrin*. Besides, marriage would mean the curtailment of Evelyn's career: 'Lady Asher as Kundry? Could anything be more grotesque?' Maria Waldmann – who sang Eboli, Amneris and Preziosilla for Verdi, as well as appearing in the first performances of the *Requiem* – married an Italian duke, but only after prematurely quitting the stage at the age of thirty-one; even in Italy, the roles of diva and duchess were incompatible.

The young composer Ulick Dean, who has 'recanted his own Wagnerian faith', coaxes Evelyn to question her enthusiasm for Wagner. He has imbibed some of Nietzsche's prejudices, and describes *Parsifal* as 'the oiliest flattery ever poured down the throat of liquorish humanity'. But whereas Ulick dabbles in the Kabbalah, it is 'our old religion', as her father calls it, which comes to Evelyn's rescue. Disgusted by her professional and personal life, she suspends performances, retreats to a convent, and consults a Monsignor, who places an interdiction on singing Isolde. It is the kind of advice usually given to sopranos by those worried about their vocal health, though in this case what is at issue is Evelyn's moral condition. Her spiritual advisor permits her to give concerts, and in principle does not object to her engagement at Bayreuth for the role of Kundry, who ends as a grovelling penitent. Singing Isolde, however, is tantamount to perdition. At last, tired of compromises, she abandons music altogether and becomes a nun. Moore – an unrepentant Wagnerian who made the pilgrimage to Bayreuth, met Huneker there, admired d'Annunzio's Wagnerian novel *Il trionfo della morte*, and tried to imitate Wagner's 'endless melody' in his prose – regards her decision with mystified awe.

The novelist Jules Barbey d'Aurevilley gave decadents two ways out of their predicament: either suicide or prostration at the foot of the Cross. Styr opts for self-cremation, while Evelyn – after toying with an overdose of a sleeping draught – decides on the chillier purification of the cloister. If they had specialized in singing Verdi, they might have been spared such drastic remedies. But perhaps the fatal exultancy of Wagner was preferable to the lowlier pleasures of his rival. In 1904 in Willa Cather's story 'A Wagner Matinée' a woman visiting Boston from the dreary prairies is taken by her nephew to a concert of orchestral excerpts from Wagner. She spends an afternoon being tossed on stormy seas and singed by magic fire, after which she is reduced to sobbing misery as she remembers the flat, vacant vista of normality to which she must return when her holiday is over. Verdi cannot compete with Wagner's excitements, although the woman's nephew ineptly tries to brighten her mood by saying 'Well, we have come to better things than the old *Trovatore* at any rate!' At the end of Moore's novel, Evelyn is equally snobbish when the Reverend Mother, politely making small talk, asks about her Italian repertory. 'Wagner I have never heard,' the nun explains – it would hardly be consistent with her vow of chastity – but she wonders whether Evelyn ever sang any operas by Verdi. Although Evelyn denies it, the Reverend Mother persists: 'Surely you admire *Trovatore* – the "Miserere", for instance. Is not that beautiful?' In her innocence she probably reckons that it is safe to praise a scene containing a monastic chant. Evelyn's reply is unChristian in its lack of charity, but it sums up the almost pitying view of Verdi taken by the aesthetes of the fin de siècle. 'The "Miserere",' she concedes, 'is no doubt very effective, but it is considered very common now.' 'Ah,' replies the Reverend Mother, which could mean many things. The Angelus bell fortunately breaks off their discussion.

|||||||||||||||||

The reformed Evelyn thinks of the 'delicious death' and 'swooning ecstasy' of *Tristan* as moral crimes. More grievously, Owen Asher describes those musical enticements as 'sins against life'. He is voicing the evolutionary spirit of the late nineteenth century, an ideology that counteracted the drift into dissolution. Life, he says, is a gift from nature, and we have a duty to make the best use of it. Starting from such truisms, Aryan racial theorists like Houston Stewart Chamberlain, Wagner's son-in-law, developed a policy of eugenic progress, expounded in their 'Regenerationslehre': to revitalize society it would be necessary to purify the national breed and eliminate tainted Jewish blood. For Chamberlain, Wagner was 'the victorious commander in the second "Battle of the Nations"' – a campaign to root out the Semitic enemy within.

Wagner himself pondered the philosophical impasse of the declining century in some diary entries he made in 1880 and 1881. He was reluctant to accept the full stop at which the culture and his own music had supposedly arrived; he found no certain answers to the problem, though eventually these were supplied by Verdi, whose return to creative life in the years after Wagner's death was the best evidence of regeneration in action. After each of Wagner's pessimistic speculations, it is possible to imagine a curt rebuttal by Verdi. Wagner praised the Italian Renaissance for 'aestheticizing … an immoral world', and was excited by 'beautiful beasts of prey: tigers, panthers!' The appropriate response is Iago's scornful 'Ecco il Leone!' as he stands over Otello. Surely animality is not the best hope for the played-out human race? Wagner worried about over-population, and saw war as a hygienic method for reducing numbers – though he feared that it had also weakened the race by eliminating the tribal Goths. Verdi's Falstaff replies to this sinister proposal in his monologue about the absurdity of quarrelling over honour; his sluggish cowardice offends the combatants in Shakespeare's *Henry IV* plays, but in the opera he has been demobilized and can wisely devote himself to preserving the body and catering to its appetites. Wagner calculated that 'the strength of moral exertion for regeneration would have to be equal to the physical revolution caused by the degeneration of the human race'. Verdi placed his trust in physical recovery, not frantic intellectual efforts: a beaker of mulled wine restores Falstaff after his dunking in the river. 'History will have to begin from the beginning,' Wagner warned, 'in order to teach us anew.' That was the reason for the unprogressive cycles of myth. But why can't history simply continue, as the fugue at the end of *Falstaff* allows it to do? In another entry Wagner lamented miscegenation, which allowed 'the blood of the nobler males' to be adulterated 'by the baser feminine element: the masculine element suffers, character founders, whilst the women gain as much as to take men's place'. He parenthetically added '(Renaissance)'. The merry wives of Windsor, who save society from the male obsession with property and propriety, are sufficient refutation. Finally Wagner proposed that the genius – exemplified by Christ, 'a most noble poetic fiction', and probably by the holy fool Parsifal – might be our saviour. But in *Falstaff* the fool is saved rather than nominating himself as saviour, and he modestly makes no pretence of holiness.

In 1894 d'Annunzio published *Il trionfo della morte*, his most dementedly fervent homage to Wagner. *Falstaff* had its first performance the year before, and Verdi's last opera – the product of his regeneration – is a marginal presence in d'Annunzio's novel, needing to be demeaned and ridiculed so that the world can end in the approved Wagnerian manner. At the time, the only person who noticed the connection between the two works was the actress Eleonora Duse. She happened to be Boito's current mistress, although before long she moved on to d'Annunzio, who portrayed her as Stelio's rejected muse La Foscarina in *Il fuoco*. She found the productions of both men unsatisfactory. After seeing *Falstaff* in London she described it to Boito as 'sad stuff', unwontedly melancholy. D'Annunzio's novel was worse, because Duse believed that the self-destructiveness of its hero Giorgio, whose brain is addled by his addiction to *Tristan*, libelled 'every heroic effort *to put up with life* – all the great agonizing sacrifice which is *to live*'. She ended by wiping her hands of both: 'neither *Falstaff* nor d'Annunuzio'. Perhaps, knowing Boito, she was right to interpret the opera so negatively. Did the librettist see Falstaff as a fatter Iago, a spirit of denial like the devil in his own opera *Mefistofele*, first performed in 1868 when Boito still worshipped Wagner? Falstaff can certainly be described as a degenerate figure; what Duse failed to acknowledge was that Verdi's music gives him a jovial ebullience he does not possess in *The Merry Wives of Windsor*. About d'Annunzio's novel she was exactly right: it is a sin against life, for which Wagner is expected to take the blame.

Giorgio embodies the biological depletion that preoccupied Max Nordau. He is unable to 'accomplish an act of vigour' when his mother goads him to stand up to his father and secure his inheritance. 'I live, I breathe,' he remarks with a certain disgust, 'but what is the substance of my life?' He destroys himself a little every day, feels 'like a half-empty bladder', and in his mid-twenties is impatient to die. He needs a remonstrance like Falstaff's 'Va, vecchio John', which Verdi himself took to heart. But instead of Falstaff's strutting rejuvenation, what Giorgio sees is the puffy, repellently pallid physique of his father, sweaty and stinking, wrinkled, pimply and hairy. Fat, which for Falstaff means fullness of being, is even more obscene: at dinner Giorgio's younger brother scoops up food with downy, flabby hands and shovels it into his mouth. The kiss that suddenly quietens the uproar in Ford's house in *Falstaff* loses its charmed power here, since sex is viral, 'refermenting the venoms … that, since immemorial ages, the purplish sinuous mouths of women had poured onto eager, subjugated males'. The children his father sires with a mistress are healthy and robust, which turns Giorgio's stomach. He is equally nauseated by the sterility of his mistress Hippolita, who cannot obey 'the terrible will of the species' that demands 'the perpetuation of the race' and will therefore, he believes, 'attain the supreme perfection of her beauty' as an anaemic, marmoreal corpse.

At the end of the novel a piano is delivered to the remote house near Ortona on the Abruzzo coast where Giorgio and Hippolita are living, and they spend two sensually glutted days playing through the score of *Tristan*. The opera is their induction into a netherworld, not the round, capacious 'mondo' of Verdi's fugue. The instrument cannot convey the torrential surges of the music, and it is from 'the eloquence, the enthusiasm of [Giorgio's] exegesis' that Hippolita learns about its 'tragic Revelation'; his rabid words supersede Wagner's music. Of course he violently traduces the work he purports to be translating into Italian. The anger of the spurned Isolde becomes a 'homicidal mania', and Tristan in listening to the shepherd's lament rejects the 'eternal evil' of Darwinian procreation. After the 'Liebestod', Giorgio asks Hippolita whether she would like to die in the same way. She calls it a nice idea, but adds that on earth such hydraulic transfigurations don't usually happen. He finds the response revoltingly vulgar: with the music no longer casting its spell on her, she has reverted already to 'low lasciviousness'. He pours wine into her and feeds her peaches, which squirt juice over her face. When she offers him the bluest veins of her wrists to kiss, he threatens to slash them with a knife; she dares him to do so. Here and elsewhere, d'Annunzio gives

Wagner's more introverted and intellectual characters a Latin carnality and a taste for carnage. In his play *Francesca da Rimini*, the story of Tristan and Isolde acts as a pandar: Francesca and Paolo give in to their illicit desire while reading a romance about their predecessors, and lust makes them bloodthirsty in ways that have no precedent in Wagner. Paolo works off his frustration by committing indiscriminate rapine, and aims an arrow through the gullet of the braggart who mocks his brother. During the battle Francesca is fascinated by Greek fire, a sulphurous weapon that like an elemental carnivore can consume rock, iron and diamonds as well as flesh. The operatic characters are tame by contrast: Tristan either drops his sword or asks Isolde to use it against him, and the torch she extinguishes cannot compete with the blaze in Francesca's cauldron.

After his preparatory skirmishes with Hippolita, Giorgio suggests a cooling stroll along the cliffs, where he predictably pushes her towards the edge. She struggles, curses, scratches, bites, and fights for her life 'like a beast', since only a beast – in d'Annunzio's estimation – would react so unoperatically. To underline the distance between their foul world and Wagner's ideal realm, a dog barks at them as they grapple. Giorgio finally grabs Hippolita's luxuriant hair and drags her with him as he plunges over the precipice. Although they repeat the dual leap of Senta and the Dutchman, there are significant differences: in Senta's case the end is voluntary, and when Giorgio and Hippolita crash onto the rocks no music proclaims their redemption.

## An Evergreen

In Franz Werfel's *Verdi* the composer gloomily concludes that 'the day of the north' has come: he and his hearty, tuneful native culture have been made redundant by Wagner. This foreboding gave advance warning of events in Werfel's own time, when the Wehrmacht advanced to the sound of Wagner. But the fictional Verdi's phrase also corresponds to the way Italian musicians saw their predicament in the last decades of the nineteenth century: they were a band of partisans gallantly resisting a mightier power. In 1885 T. O. Cesardi began his study of Wagner by quoting the slogan that Garibaldi's followers chanted as they battled to expel foreigners from Italy. Would the same anathema work against a musical colonist? By 1910, when Scipio Sighele published a collection of propagandistic essays on nationalism, it was a lost cause, and the outcome could be summed up in musical shorthand. Sighele heard a bell tolling for 'the imminent funeral of the Latin race', while blaring fanfares – comparable perhaps to the brassy triumph of the Egyptians in *Aida* as they parade their captives – welcomed 'the victorious and invading German race'. The order of nature had been overturned, as if antipodally. The sun now shone from the north, and 'we, the Mediterranean peoples', Sighele said, were cast into the shade.

The result was a slump. In 1877 Carlo Magnico wrote a study that contrasted Italian and German music, with Rossini and Wagner as his binary or even bipolar pair. Magnico argued that Rossini was synonymous with joy, Wagner with dejection; Rossini exuded irony and scepticism whereas Wagner was about faith, in the worst, most dogmatic sense. An atavistic pagan happiness, supposedly resident in Italy, was under threat. Hence Verdi's indignation when critics said that he had capitulated to Wagner by relying on motifs like Quickly's 'Reverenza' or

Otello's 'Un bacio ancora' and by merging arias in a fluently continuous melody. Shortly after the premiere of *Otello* in February 1887 he was interviewed by Gino Monaldi, who suggested that Italy had lost its 'creative fertility'. Verdi denied it, then indirectly complained about imperious German fads. Young composers were encouraged to treat the voice as a mere instrument; they forgot that the texts they set ought to be poetic and idealistic, not – although Verdi did not say so – the grubby low-life anecdotes favoured by verismo composers.

When he heard Puccini's *Le villi*, Verdi cautioned against the foreign symphonic influence in this Slavic fairy tale. Puccini dated his musical vocation from a performance of *Aida* that he attended in Pisa as a teenager; he represented Lucca, his birthplace, at Verdi's interment; in 1905 at Ricordi's behest he composed a brief *Requiem* to be sung at La Scala on the anniversary of Verdi's death – a modestly scaled, perhaps intimidated piece for a small choir, organ and the mournful but not grief-stricken voice of a viola. Despite these genuflections, his operas ignored Verdi and measured themselves against Wagner instead. The orchestral intermezzo before the third act of *Manon Lescaut*, a description of the heroine's penitential journey to Le Havre, turns the yearning of *Tristan* into a masochistic prostration; Minnie in *La fanciulla del West* is a pistol-wielding Brünnhilde of the California backwoods. At the end of his life, struggling to conclude *Turandot* with a love duet that might stand beside that in *Tristan*, Puccini acknowledged the fatality of this influence. He sneaked a look at Wagner's score, and soon wished he had not. 'Enough of this music!' he wrote. 'We are mandolinists, amateurs; woe to him who gets caught by it! This tremendous music destroys one and renders one incapable of composing any more.' The mandolin is a plebeian instrument, played by Neapolitan street singers and by the Cypriot and Albanian sailors who serenade Desdemona in *Otello*. How could it compete with the sleek collectivity of the Wagnerian orchestra? Amateurism too is retrograde – unprofessional, pre-industrial.

This sense of Italian inferiority had economic and political sources, and music was merely a symptom of the malaise. Unification in 1870–71 invigorated Germany, which rapidly acquired colonies in Africa and in the Pacific; this was the empire for which Stelio in *Il fuoco* gave equal credit to Bismarck and Wagner. But Italy stagnated after the Risorgimento, beset by bank failures, riots, and the usual scandals about sleazy politicians. When the country belatedly tried to grab a share of the imperial spoils in Abyssinia in January 1887, the result was a humiliating military defeat at Dogali. Hanslick, writing about the first performance of *Otello* the following month, remarked that Verdi was expected to sustain Italian morale. He likened the event to the first *Ring* at Bayreuth in 1876, but with an important proviso: publicity had boosted Wagner's festival for years in advance, whereas Verdi forbade such puffery and worked on *Otello* in secret, so the response, when it came, was more spontaneous – an expression of gratitude to the composer, but also a patriotic celebration demonstrating that Italy's glory was not, like that of Otello, a thing of the past. Hanslick reported that the premiere at La Scala was 'a matter of national importance, and the governmental crisis was forgotten, along with the military disasters in Abyssinia'. It was as if Otello's 'Esultate!', which announces the sinking of the Ottoman fleet, could make up for the slaughter of Italian troops at Dogali. Verdi, who was dismayed by Italy's behaviour in Africa, might not have appreciated the connection.

After the opera was performed in Venice in May 1887, Boito saw it as a vindication of the levelled hero – 'Otello triumphs also in his adopted country, before the real lion of St Mark's,' he told Verdi – and predicted a benignly imperial future for the work. Saved from his downfall, the hero would 'continue his great flight in space and time'. Following the first performance in London in July 1889, Boito confirmed 'a worldwide victory'. Military analogies came naturally in discussing *Otello*, though Boito also described the success of *Falstaff* as a Napoleonic conquest. He wrote to Verdi in March 1893, six weeks after the premiere at La Scala, to report that the Milanese had all become 'citizens of Windsor'. This did not mean that Italy had been culturally colonized by England: Verdi was convinced that he had repatriated Shakespeare, and when *Falstaff* reached Paris in 1894 he bluffly assured an interviewer that it was based on 'an ancient Italian comedy, written in a very ancient language long before Shakespeare!' Having established that all of Milan was either crammed into the Garter Inn or camped out in Windsor forest, Boito went on to praise the tonic effects of the music. On this occasion Verdi's responsibility to the nation was medicinal, and never had an opera so penetrated 'the spirit and blood of a people'. Boito believed that 'this transfusion of joy, strength, truth, light' would 'produce a great benefit for art and for the public'; he saluted Verdi as a healer, 'the Physician of Art'. Taking over the Aryan jargon of Chamberlain and the latter-day Wagnerians, he went further by calling *Falstaff* 'regenerative therapy' and declared himself pleased that a production in the capital would soon extend its curative powers to 'those most degenerate Romans'. It seemed like a simple, infallible recipe for restoring Italy to what Boito called 'intellectual health'.

The country needed only to be true to itself, which meant staying true to Verdi rather than straying towards Wagner. In his interview with Monaldi, Verdi restated his own belief in a national genius that must not be traduced: 'What I can tolerate least of all is for an Italian to write like a German, and a German like an Italian. An Italian must write as an Italian, a German as a German.' In practice this was no longer easy. Verdi acknowledged the new internationalism of music in the interview, and his *Inno delle nazioni* promulgated this creed (although only by lining up separate national anthems: there is no overarching hymn for the universal brotherhood, 'un mondo di fratelli', that Boito's text describes). But his advice restricted the range of choices available in a larger, less nationalistic world. Arturo Toscanini, for instance, began as a renegade, an enthusiast for Wagner who took Verdi for granted. In 1884 he played in the orchestra when *Lohengrin* was performed in Parma, and like so many others was 'overwhelmed by magical, supernatural feelings'. Appointed principal conductor of La Scala in 1898, he chose operas by Wagner – whom he provocatively called 'the greatest composer of the century' – to open his first three seasons. His career as a conductor began with *Aida* in Rio de Janeiro in 1886 when he was just nineteen, but during those early years in Milan he concentrated on *Otello* and *Falstaff*, in which Verdi was thought to have paid his dues to Wagner; at this stage Toscanini had no time for the earlier, unreformed operas. When he wanted to stage *Trovatore* in 1902, Ricordi, suspecting him of a plan to gloomily Wagnerize it, at first withheld the rights.

Two composers who grew up in Verdi's shadow – Ferruccio Busoni, born in 1866, and Ermanno Wolf-Ferrari, born in 1876 – had even more intimately divided loyalties. Busoni's father was an Italian clarinettist who concocted instrumental fantasias on *Trovatore*, while his mother was a half-German pianist; he spent his childhood in Trieste, itself the subject of a competitive tussle between Italy and Austria. He was grateful that his father had dosed him with Bach and trained him as 'a "German" musician'. Yet the elder Busoni had dogmatically Italian tastes. He wore a Garibaldian beard, affected to despise German beer, wine and music, and fought with his son over the competing merits of Verdi and Wagner. Ferruccio's Wagnerism – starting with a pensive, subdued piano transcription of the *Götterdämmerung* funeral march in 1881 – was an almost automatically Oedipal rebellion. In 1887 he reviewed *Otello*, speculating that Boito had suspended his work as a composer in order to serve as Verdi's librettist because 'he wants to remain an Italian' and 'wishes, perhaps unconsciously, to play his trumps against Richard Wagner'. The phrasing suggests that for Busoni this was a quixotic gesture. And why would a musician who had studied Bach and the last Beethoven quartets want to remain an Italian? Then, after hearing *Falstaff* in Berlin in 1894, Busoni had to recognize his own Latin heritage, and wrote a letter to Verdi, which he never sent, hailing him as a kind of paternal grandparent. He explained that his musical education had been German, but said that '*Falstaff* provoked such a complete spiritual and emotional upheaval, that I can honestly say it marked the beginning of a new era in my life as an artist'. Nevertheless there was no homecoming. As an operatic composer, Busoni temporized between the two cultures: his *Turandot* was based on the 'commedia dell'arte', but in *Doktor Faust* he attempted to do justice to the mysticism and metaphysical ambition of Goethe's hero.

In Wolf-Ferrari's case, Wagner not Verdi provoked the upheaval, which almost aborted his musical career. His father was a Bavarian painter, his mother Venetian; he began life as Hermann Friedrich Wolf, though in his early twenties he revived his mother's maiden name and called himself Ermanno Wolf-Ferrari. When he was thirteen an aunt who lived in Bayreuth invited him to attend the festival, where he heard *Tristan, Meistersinger* and *Parsifal.* 'The commotion,' he reported, 'proved too great for my young brain.' He fell ill and for a time gave up his musical studies, though during a later attack of Wagnerism he made an adolescent attempt to compose 'a kind of *Tristan*'. Under his father's influence he entered the Accademia di Belle Arti in Rome in 1891 to study painting, then transferred in 1893 to the Akademie der Tonkunst in Munich. Returning to Milan, he met Boito and Verdi. The vocal music he composed was better received in Germany, but its literary sources were almost exclusively Italian: comedies by Goldoni, or Dante's *La vita nuova.* He resolved to rely on the gifts he had inherited from his mother, which were Italian staples: 'a sunny disposition' and 'strong nerves' like those of which Verdi boasted. He became an Italian-German composer, whereas Busoni's blend was German-Italian. The hyphenated mixture broke down in 1915 when Italy sided with the Allies against Germany and Austria-Hungary, which left Wolf-Ferrari painfully aware of the split within his 'chromatic or ... enharmonic soul'. At the beginning of the nineteenth century, north and south kept their distance. By the end of the century, they had begun to overlap, with confusing and – in Wolf-Ferrari's case – distressing results.

||||||||||||||||||

For Nietzsche, the will to power was a biological drive, present in the lowliest insects that struggle to breed and in the genius who projects himself into the future by perpetuating his ideas. This was the instinct at first encouraged and then belied, as Nietzsche decided, by Wagner's music: a Dionysian riot gave way to the nihilism of *Parsifal.* The catchphrase sounded its rallying cry in Italy as well. In 1869 Michele Lessona – a naturalist who gave his name to the species of frogs and lizards he studied – published *Volere è potere,* a biographical anthology of Italy's most prominent achievers. His subjects were models of Darwinian evolution and adaptation at work: they demonstrated that the fittest survived, and that they did so by ingeniously overcoming obstacles and relying on the spirit of enterprise that the social reformer Samuel Smiles called 'self-help'. The volume contained Lessona's admonition to his newly unified country, which is why it was topographically organized in a series of chapters that climbed from south to north, from Palermo to Turin, from an agrarian to an industrial culture. Reaching Parma, Lessona paused to devote an entire chapter to Verdi. He embellished the fable of self-improvement by making the composer begin life as a barefoot waif; this enabled him to end by reporting that Verdi in prosperous middle age had the justified contentment of 'a man who was able to assert his will'. For Wagner, instructed in these matters by Schopenhauer, the will was tantamount to original sin, as its craven puling persuaded us that life was worth the bother. In Lessona's view, Verdi demonstrated the error of that philosophy: will was the very sap of life.

When Lessona published his book, Verdi was in his mid-fifties, soon to complete his career (as he thought) by composing *Aida*. Hence Lessona's claim that he was 'at the height of his powers, which he uses nobly'. The Darwinian ideology placed a premium on youth; it was unlikely that an old man could regenerate himself, let alone do the same for an entire country. Even after hearing *Otello*, Hanslick was doubtful about Verdi's reinvigoration. Antagonistic as always, he thought that the elderly Verdi's virtues were at best negative: he had learned restraint and now avoided vulgarity. But in opera, 'the most sensuous of musical creations', Hanslick thought that 'the wisdom of old age is seldom so rewarding as the genius of youth' – though how many composers before Verdi had written an opera in old age? 'And,' he regretfully added, 'youth in music is melody', which he found lacking in *Otello*. Shaw too was unconvinced. In 1901 he described Verdi as 'a thorough unadulterated Latin', who was never 'Wagnerized' but only took back from German music 'what Italy gave'. The greater finesse of the last operas was explained, Shaw argued, by 'the inevitable natural drying up' of Verdi's 'spontaneity and fertility'; he got away with *Otello* because Shakespeare's play was an ersatz Italian opera, in Shaw's opinion no better than a libretto. Ten years earlier, reviewing *Otello* at Covent Garden, he had hilariously detected the same loss of 'vigorous and passionate impulses' in the lazy, stilted performance of the tenor Jean de Reszke, who grappled with Victor Maurel's Iago from a discreet distance and made the audience 'feel how extremely obliging it was of Maurel to fall'. Then, supposedly knocked down by epilepsy, de Reszke arranged himself on the floor 'with a much too obvious solicitude for his own comfort'. Shaw hoped that when de Reszke's good looks paled and he had to compete with younger tenors, he might 'gain more as an actor than he will lose as a singer'. The comments draw attention to the fact that live performance is a battle with time, marshalling and recharging energies that drain away as we watch the singers or actors exert themselves. For the same reason Shaw jeered at the mothballed *Parsifal* he saw in Bayreuth in 1889. 'Wagner is dead,' he proclaimed, which should have been good news for the theatre, freeing it to rethink his legacy. The festival, however, remained a temple of defunct traditions, not 'an arena for live impulses'.

The law enforced by Darwin's reproductive will decreed that the old must give place to the new. Shaw accordingly praised Verdi's 'docility' in respecting the finer taste of Boito, 'a younger man' who helped him to chasten his 'coarseness', but he could not have been more wrong about the balance of power in their relationship. Rather than bumptiously dictating terms to the old man, Boito deferred to Verdi at considerable personal cost, giving up work on his own opera *Nerone* to prepare the libretti for *Otello* and *Falstaff.* Verdi the gerontocrat always prevailed in their metaphorical trials of strength. 'You are healthier than I, stronger than I,' Boito told him in 1884. 'We have pitted the strength of our arms against one another, and mine bent beneath yours.' It is an extraordinary image: Boito had arm-wrestled a septuagenarian, and was pleased to have lost. Even Verdi's handwriting counted as a demonstration of physical force, like a blow from a fist. In 1889 Verdi re-addressed a letter sent by Duse to Boito, who had been staying at Sant'Agata. Boito noted that 'a strong hand that knows how to command obedience from the pen' – and, by implication, from the writers to whom he dictated orders – had made the change on the envelope. The superimposition of Verdi's script on that of Duse looked, he said, like 'a lion's paw on a swallow's wing'. The old lion may have enjoyed pretending to be senescent, but Verdi secretly believed that longevity was a matter of Darwinian will. In 1880 Strepponi encouraged him to 'try to live to the age of Methuselah (996 years) if for no other reason than to please those who love you'. Taking her point, Verdi chastized Arrivabene late in 1886 for fancying himself ill. 'It's the fashion now,' he wrote, 'to live to 90, 115, or 139 years. I was reading last night of a woman of that age who left two baby children, one 85 years old, the other 94.' Arrivabene could not be jollied into continuing, and died two months later.

Having coaxed Verdi back to life for *Otello*, Boito had to do so all over again when convincing him to consider *Falstaff.* He appealed to Verdi's 'will to work', and also suggested that Verdi should administer to himself a dose of the medicine with which he eventually treated Italy's moral ailments. A tragedy like *Otello*, he said, 'morbidly excites the nerves', whereas 'the joking and laughter of comedy exhilarate mind and body'. With wise prescience, Boito even allowed tragedy an envious sideways glance at comedy when Otello gears up for revenge.

Critics since Thomas Rymer in the seventeenth century had ridiculed *Othello* because cuckoldry is a subject for low comedy: would a tragic hero fuss about handkerchiefs and soiled sheets? Boito allows Otello to dispose of that objection when he decides to kill Desdemona: 'Tu alfin, Clemenza, pio genio immortal/dal roseo riso,/copri il tuo viso/santo coll'orrida larva infernal!' – You, Clemency, sacred immortal genius, rosily smiling, cover your sainted face with the horrid mask of hell! Otello here acknowledges that mockery is an option, but he elevates and sanctifies comedy even as he expels it from his personal drama. The spirit of clemency returns, however, at the end of *Falstaff*, making light of misdemeanours and defusing conflicts. Falstaff in his list of Alice Ford's fetching attributes praises her starry eyes and swan-like neck, then calls her lips a flower that laughs, 'un fior che ride'. He goes on to say that the smile she gave him – and the strings quiver as he utters the word 'rise' – semaphored her availability. Her charm resides in what Otello calls her 'roseo riso', whether or not she is sarcastically smirking. Now it is tragedy that must be sent packing: the saturnine Ford rages about his own supposed cuckoldry as noisily as Otello, but the end of his aria is anti-climactically deflated, derided by the nimble, almost mincing musical footwork of Falstaff as he returns dressed up for wooing.

Verdi was won over by Boito's argument about the elixir of youth. 'Let us do *Falstaff* then!' he replied. 'We will not think for the moment about the obstacles, age, illnesses!' There were physiological setbacks. Verdi's legs failed for a time, though he was pleased to report that his stomach and head remained sound; on another occasion he and Strepponi were felled by an influenza epidemic; Boito once or twice had to convalesce after crises with Duse. But the helpers and friends who died of their illnesses during these years – Emanuele Muzio who developed dropsy, Franco Faccio who suffered a mental breakdown, the politician Francesco Piroli – were all younger than Verdi. He seemed to have defeated duration, reversing the cycle of the seasons that leads from springtime comedy to the sad tales that are, as Shakespeare put it, best for winter. In April 1854, during negotiations to buy a parcel of land at Busseto, Verdi hesitated about whether he should pay immediately or wait until Saint Martin's summer – a treasured time of warmth in November, named after the unseasonal blooming of the riverbanks as the saint's corpse was ferried down the Loire on a boat. Almost forty years later, Falstaff associates himself with this same rural festivity. He denies that he is superannuated, claims instead that he is enjoying his personal Saint Martin's summer, and illustrates the point by swooping up to a heady climax at the end of the phrase. The moment allows Verdi to bask in the glow of a receding sun, to luxuriate in his own late flowering.

Falstaff refuses to accept his own decay and even manages to recover from the Wagnerian decadence. He seems most at risk of giving in to this cosmic fatigue when he drags himself out of the river at dusk. Dumped in the water, he almost suffers death by dripping, 'un stillicidio continuo' – a squalidly comic variant of Wagnerian dissolution. 'Tutto declina,' he murmurs, then sings a dignified lament for the lost 'virilità dal mondo' as the orchestra trudges through a funeral march. Energy ebbs, as when the gods in *Das Rheingold* are deprived of Freia's golden apples. At this point, as Falstaff notices the darkness of the air, there is a naughtily pertinent musical quotation from Wagner: it is the scurrying motif that introduces the agitated Klingsor as he prepares to send Kundry into combat with Parsifal. Julian Budden calls this a coincidence and denies any connection to Wagner's opera, but the association is surely clinched by Falstaff's preceding phrase about virility. Klingsor is self-emasculated, as Kundry reminds him when she asks whether he is chaste. Later in the forest the women pray to God to make Falstaff chaste, which will keep him from being a nuisance in the future; he counters this by begging them or God to spare his belly – 'Ma salvagli l'addomine!' – since eating is more important to him than sexual pleasure. Outside the inn he is downcast but not disabled, and after the chilling reminiscence of Klingsor's deficiency he recuperates by downing a beaker of wine. It is music that saves him from deterioration, as an orchestral trill gives audible form to one of Boito's quirkiest metaphors. A cricket, Falstaff says, seems to chirp inside a man's body when he is drunk; the flute at once imitates the sound, the strings multiply it, the winds amplify it, and finally, with all the instruments raucously concurring, the revivifying trill spreads through the world, which Falstaff – who could be referring to his own warmed-up, expansive bulk – calls the jocund globe. The calorific death feared by Wagner has been postponed.

The will to live loudly resounds in verismo operas, although for Puccini it resembles the fallacy that Schopenhauer taught Wagner to mistrust. The condemned heroine of *Manon Lescaut*, stumbling parched through a desert, cries 'Non voglio morir, non voglio morir! No! No! Non voglio morir!' Despite her protests, she dies five minutes later. The same self-deception persuades Cavaradossi in *Tosca* that his execution is a theatrical stunt; he soon discovers that the firing squad is not shooting blanks. This desperation to go on living is seldom warranted by the lives these characters currently have: a routine of aching toil in *Il tabarro*, an eternal vigil sustained by false hope in *Madama Butterfly*. Although verismo claimed to be realistic, it was closer to the naturalism of Zola, whose novels treat men and women as animals, still embedded in what Boito's Iago calls the primal mud. *Falstaff* too begins in a greasy tavern as Caius exchanges insulting names –

Lulù painted by Filippo Palizzi, 1858

Portrait bust of Verdi as a lion by Jean-Pierre Dantan, 1866

*Wagner and his Creations* painted by Karl von Schweninger

Verdi considering the Neapolitan censor's objections to the
libretto of *Un ballo in maschera*, caricature by Delfico, 1858

Wagner, caricatured by Faustin, using
a Prussian helmet as his podium, 1876

Verdi rehearsing *Un ballo in maschera* with the tenor Fraschini and
the soprano Fioretti (seated), caricature by Delfico, 1858

Verdi by Vincenzo Gemito, 1872

Wagner by Auguste Renoir, 1882

# Aus Bayreuth.

Aeschylus und Shakespeare, nach Porges die beiden einzigen Bühnendichter, welche Wagner an die Seite gestellt
werden können, machen im vorschriftsmäßigen Frack dem Meister ihre Aufwartung.

At Bayreuth in 1876, the Meister receives the homage of
Aeschylus and Shakespeare; caricature published in *Der Ulk*

Verdi sketched by the tenor Enrico Caruso

*Darwinian Evolution* by T. Zajacskowski from *Der Floh, c.* 1875: the orthodox Jew
Roof Wagele from Leipzig, brandishing a shofar, evolves into Richard Wagner,
who wields a baton in place of the ram's horn used at the synagogue

Cartoon of rehearsals at Bayreuth with Mussolini as Isolde and Hitler as
Lohengrin, published in the *New York Times* on 16 August 1942

Siegfried Wagner in his father's shadow

Katharina Wagner's vision of her great-grandfather, from Act III of her Bayreuth
production of *Die Meistersinger von Nürnberg*, 2007

Hans-Jürgen Syberberg's film of *Parsifal*, 1982: Klingsor's flower
maidens cavort inside the hollowed-out and sectioned skull of Wagner,
with the composer's death-mask keeping watch from above

Wagner on the night before his death, sketched by Paul von Joukowsky

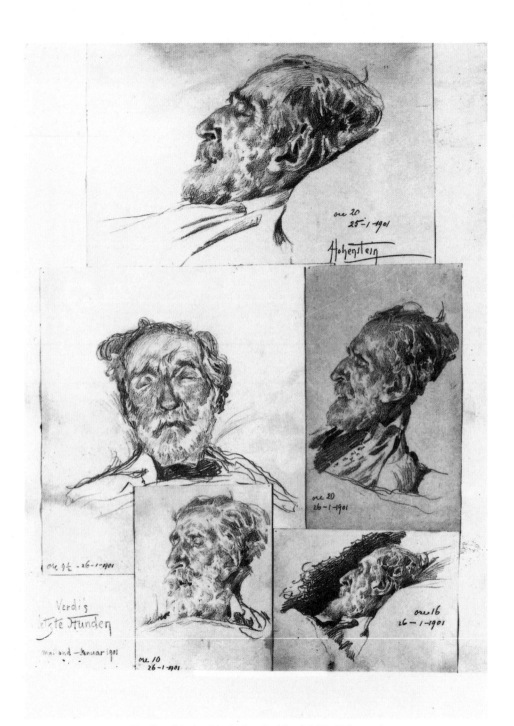

Verdi on his deathbed, sketched by Adolfo Hohenstein

Verdi's state funeral in Milan, 27 February 1901

Verdi on the commemorative monument in Parma, sculpted by Ettore Ximenes, *c.* 1913–20

Verdi by Enrico Butti, 1913, on the
monument outside the Casa di Riposo in
Milan

Verdi by Luigi Secchi, outside the opera house named
after him in Busseto

The unveiling of the Wagner monument in the Berlin Tiergarten,
painted by Anton von Werner in 1908

Arno Breker's bust of Wagner
at Bayreuth, 1939

The composer with his characters: Pasquale Civiletti's monument
in Verdi Square, Broadway at 73rd Street, New York, 1906

beast, dog, gnome – with Pistol and the red-nosed Bardolph. Falstaff swelters in a laundry basket under piles of dirty linen, and is dumped in a dirty stream as if he were a blind kitten being drowned at birth. Having looked down on this sordid new environment, Verdi effervescently rises above it: in *Falstaff* the will prevails through grace, levity, alleviation, not by holding onto life with deadly tenacity. Camille Bellaigue beautifully described the opera's melodic texture as 'handfuls of sonorous dust' caught by the sun, which makes 'thousands of atoms unite and form a ray of light'. Dust here does not imply decomposition; the sonic atoms are lighter than air.

The philosopher Henri Bergson had a remedy for the expiring century, a progressive impetus that he called the 'élan vital'. There was no need for Darwin to imagine the species breeding in a bed of corpses; what kept the race going was a vitality as irrepressible as Boito's alcoholic cricket or the mellifluous merriment of the wives in *Falstaff*. Bergson reproved Darwin by remembering that man was once defined as 'an animal that laughs', and he relied on that laughter, as Verdi does in his fugue, to keep us moving ahead. In 1884 Bergson delivered an academic lecture asking why we laugh and what we laugh at; he went on speculating about this humane mystery, and in 1900 published a book in which he acclaimed laughter as an evolutionary conscience and a control on automatism, predictability, inflexibility – the sclerotic forces that inhibit our freedom and cramp our growth.

Bergson's literary references were mostly to Molière, although he did mention *Othello* in order to establish that jealousy is a comic folly not a tragic affliction, and he must have been thinking of Falstaff's crony Bardolph when he asked 'What is there comic about a rubicund nose?' He also wondered in passing why 'excessive stoutness' is thought to be laughable; he assumed it was because a fat person's body is an encumbrance, an evolutionary disqualification. Falstaff, who in the last scene of the opera looks forward to bursting his belt, shows up the limits of the thesis: for Shakespeare and Verdi, comedy is about unique, ripely idiosyncratic individuals, not people who harden into types like Molière's miser or his hypochondriac. Near the end of his book, Bergson considered comedy in the context of biology and the other sciences that popularized pessimism in the late nineteenth century. Drama, he argued, is about 'contrary electricities', 'strong attractions and repulsions ... followed by ... that electrification of the soul known as passion', which could almost be a description of Verdian opera. The problem, Bergson added, is that society forbids such 'outbursts of violent feeling'; mankind's 'slow progress' has dampened down our 'inner fire', 'just as the life of our planet has been one long effort to cover over with a cool and solid crust the fiery mass of seething metals'. Wagner shared this entropic vision, but Verdi did not.

If the cool crust was formed by the intellect, Verdi regretted its interference with the body's spontaneity. In 1892 he warned the fastidious, over-studious baritone Maurel, who was learning the role of Falstaff, that 'In art a predominant tendency towards reflection is a sign of decadence.' The final moments of *Falstaff* – especially the very last bars, when the voices fall silent and leave the orchestra rambunctiously rejoicing – evoke a chaos that is the source of creation, the elemental ferment that goes on sparking and roiling inside the brain of an artist. Vincenzo Morello, in a d'Annunzian rhapsody about Verdi written in 1900, called his music 'hot and smouldering', and said that the notes were 'like knives sparkling in a brawl, and blood [that] flows from lacerated hearts'. The homicidal scenario suits verismo – the knife fight in *Cavalleria rusticana*, Don José menacing Escamillo with his blade and stabbing Carmen – better than Verdi. Bergson, using similar imagery, saw volcanic eruptions as evidence against the inevitability of our stealthy thermodynamic death, and thought that the earth probably dreamed of such 'sudden explosions', which allowed it to 'resume possession of its innermost nature'. Fits of laughter are equally eruptive, and they shed no blood.

Shaw ridiculed the 'Life Force worship' that led Wagner to invent the disastrous superman Siegfried and to forget about the need to reform institutions and redistribute wealth, but in his metabiological drama *Back to Methuselah* he adopted Bergson's doctrine of creative evolution, and it was he who applied the vitalist theory to Verdi. He made the connection in 1917 in a review of *Trovatore*, which even includes an aside about *Parsifal*. Shaw considered Verdi's opera to be 'void of intellectual interest', and declared that if you thought about it for a moment 'it would crumble into absurdity like Klingsor's garden'. Given this irrationalism, Shaw proposed that the next revival of *Trovatore* 'should be supervised by Bergson; for he alone could be trusted to value this perfect work of instinct, and defend its integrity from the restless encroachments of intelligence'. But it is *Falstaff* that best suits Bergson's notion of drama as the rampage of a 'living energy'. Verdi at first had doubts about the rumpus being made by Big Belly, as he called his hero. 'I let him frisk a bit,' he told Boito in 1891, 'but if he persists I will put a muzzle on him and a straitjacket.' In his reply Boito suggested that all disciplinary strictures should be removed: 'Give him free rein, let him run; he will break all the window-panes and all the furniture of your room, no matter … Let everything be turned topsy-turvy!' The pandemonium in Ford's house is first silenced by an overheard kiss, then brought to a synchronized halt by the splash of the hamper and the cascades of laughter it provokes. The nocturnal melee in *Die Meistersinger* lasts much longer, is more doggedly laborious, and only stops when shouted down by the Watchman's horn, as censorious public order quells

Bergson's 'fiery mass of seething metals'. Sachs, in his inquest the next morning, decides that the uproar, like the much briefer orchestral postlude to the fugue in *Falstaff*, had a kind of creative excitement – but he only reaches this conclusion after long, anxious thought, not by trusting human nature like Verdi and Boito.

Touring Europe, *Falstaff* undertook a mission to heal or at least to pacify and cheer up the world. Ricordi informed Verdi that following several months of anxious insomnia he had been granted the mercy of a good night's sleep after hearing the opera in Trieste. 'So then,' he proposed, 'in certain cases: *Prescription: Falstaff!!!*' From the same city, the conductor Mascheroni reported on a reconciliation with the temperamental Maurel. They were staying on the same floor of a hotel, and one morning at eight coincided at the lavatory in the hall. Maurel was emerging, holding up his trousers with his hand and looking pleased to have made his daily deposit. Mascheroni, carrying the newspaper, pretended that his need was not urgent and shifted from foot to foot as they exchanged pleasantries through clenched teeth. After a while, recognizing the commonness of their plight as creatures with bodies, they shook hands, embraced and, as if acting out the fugue, laughed at their absurdity. 'Peace was sworn at that sacred altar,' wrote Mascheroni, 'not too well perfumed as it was.'

Well-wishers encouraged Verdi to perform the miracle all over again, and rumours again circulated about an operatic *King Lear*. But by the turn of the century, he had outlived his will, and – after complaining to a friend about his dim eyes and his tottering legs – asked 'Why am I still in this world?' It was his own decrepitude that he bemoaned, whereas Wagnerians like d'Annunzio's Giorgio and Villiers de l'Isle Adam's Axël condemned a decrepit world in which they no longer wished to live. Three weeks after asking that weary question, he suffered a stroke in his Milan hotel. He was buttoning his vest when the moment came and, puzzled by the sudden uncooperativeness of his fingers, he remarked 'One button more or one button less' before collapsing – a more nonchalant version of the dying Lear's request, 'I pray you undo this button.' Verdi lay unconscious for almost a week, making death wait rather than rushing towards it in the Wagnerian manner. Boito kept watch, but was so grief-stricken that he could not describe what he saw until a couple of months later: he then explained his muteness by saying that the loss had left him – the younger man, the survivor – deprived of 'vital warmth' and crushed by a 'paralysis of the will'. Looking back, he imagined the inert Verdi valiantly struggling. With his sterterous breathing, he held out long enough, Boito told Bellaigue, to leave the reaper with a scarred scythe – an agricultural image that Verdi would surely have appreciated.

The moment d'Annunzio heard about Verdi's death on 27 January 1901, he began to write a commemorative ode. He undertook the task for his own purposes, in his self-appointed role as the nation's bard. His true sympathies were with Wagner, as his novels and *Francesca da Rimini* reveal, and in different circumstances he could just as easily have gone onto the attack, since his own politics repudiated the parliament to which Verdi was elected. During the 1880s d'Annunzio's allies were a group of writers whose work appeared in the *Cronaca bizantina*: Byzantine rather than Roman, they portrayed themselves as luxuriously depraved, not virtuous and civic-minded men of the people like Verdi. Nevertheless, the occasion presented d'Annunzio with an opportunity and he seized it. He worked on the ode while travelling by train to a rendezvous with Duse in Nice, completed it late in February, and recited it in public three days afterwards in Florence. Perhaps the setting explains the Florentine references in the poem, which installs Verdi – referred to only as 'il creator estinto' – in a local pantheon beside Dante, Leonardo and Michelangelo. The company is not too august but perhaps too unearthly. Verdi told Boito that he preferred Correggio to Michelangelo, whose giant figures frightened him, and he might have been happier with Manzoni as his colleague in immortality. No specific operas are mentioned. Instead their characters merge in what d'Annunzio calls 'un immenso coro/di popoli', chanting Verdi's 'melodia suprema' up and down the peninsula. This was more than verbosity. A few days after the poem was recited, when the bodies of Verdi and Strepponi were transported from the cemetery to the Casa di Riposo, the crowds on the streets of Milan were said to be the largest ever seen in Italy; d'Annunzio's immense chorus – consisting, to be precise, of eight hundred singers – performed 'Va, pensiero', with Toscanini conducting.

In 1913, for the centenary of Verdi's birth, Mario Albani made an adaptation of Verdi's other patriotic chorus, 'O Signore, dal tetto natio', sung in *I Lombardi* by the crusaders who pine for their native hearths. They are homesick for the brooks and vineyards of Lombardy; in *Jérusalem* oak trees replaced vines to make the nostalgia more resonant for Parisians. Albani's 'Epicidio' dispenses with all such topographical markers. The evergreen homeland is now Verdi's music, and the composer – addressed as 'O Signor della gran melodia' or 'O Signor delle liriche scene' – supplants a God whom the crusaders quietly rebuke for uprooting them. Solera's original words are dispirited. The crusaders have been humbled, and they appeal to Christ not to let his paladins be mocked. Their consolation lies not above but below, as in a burning desert they dream of the peaceful, fruitful landscape they have left behind. Albani's imagery by contrast is airier, less terrestrial. He imagines the muses elegiacally sighing over Verdi, speculates about the mystical harmonies he might now be hearing up above, and ends with something like a Second Coming. The last stanza of 'O Signore, dal tetto natio' is angry: the singers are punished by their memories, and their reverie makes arid reality harder to bear. Albani concludes with the resurrection of Verdi, whose choruses are performed by the cherubim in heaven, who lives on in Italian hearts, and whose name has been eternalized by history:

> Ma tu vivi, lo dice il concento
> Dei Cherubi ne' cieli di Gloria,
> Tu ben vivi ne' Cuori, e la storia,
> Gran Maestro, il tuo Nome eternó!

At the end of *Falstaff*, calling for the recently married couples to unmask, Ford uses an extravagantly theological word. 'Apoteosi!' he cries, though an immediate fusillade of laughter reveals his error. Under cover of the coy veils, Caius has been spliced to Bardolph, and the forbidden match between Fenton and Nannetta has also been solemnized. All the same, Ford has a point. An apotheosis is the making of a god. Wagner learned about the process from Feuerbach and showed it happening in the transfiguration of Isolde, Brünnhilde and Parsifal. Now Verdi is apotheosized, though not by being exempted from our common human lot like Wagner's characters: he is deified by popular acclaim.

# 6 | *Their Second Century*

## UPS AND DOWNS

The twentieth century began, a little belatedly, with the death of Verdi, followed before long by an assault on Wagner's corpse. During the 1920s Verdi unexpectedly came back to life in Germany. Then in the 1940s Salvador Dalí, in a self-promoting tabloid newspaper he produced in New York, sensationally announced 'RICHARD WAGNER REPORTED KILLED', as if this were recent news. In 1951, marking the fiftieth anniversary of Verdi's death, Massimo Mila reported that he was actually still alive, dominating and belittling the later generations that ought to have equalled or surpassed his achievements. Verdi, Mila said, was 'a father who is younger and more vigorous than his sons', the ultimate Oedipal nightmare.

Bernardo Bertolucci's film *1900*, a chronicle of the twentieth century's first half in Italy, obeys the classical precept by starting in the middle, after which it reverts to the true beginning of its story. It opens on the day of liberation in Milan in 1945, with reprisals against fascist collaborators in the vicinity of Parma, which is Bertolucci's home territory as it was Verdi's. The narrative then jumps backwards, with the directive 'Molti anni prima' written across the screen. The entrancing phrase is like a fairy tale's promise to tell us what happened once upon a time: without knowing how many years we have retreated, we are happy to be fobbed off with the word 'prima', which means 'before'. But before what exactly? Perhaps before the fall, or at least immediately after it. Soon it becomes clear that the date is the end of January 1901, when the announcement of a death marked the twentieth century's birth. On a moonlit night in the country, the distant sound of wailing and sobbing is underscored by the leaden, battering motif of the curse that introduces *Rigoletto*. A dark figure stumbles into view, perhaps crying about a recent expulsion from the innocent garden. Gradually the figure draws closer: it is a hunchbacked jester, and he is proclaiming the bad news about a god's death, not his own mishap. He shouts 'Verdi è morto!', staggers on and tumbles at the foot of a tree, where he falls asleep. In this mythical realm, with time and place still blurrily unidentified, Rigoletto might have mutated into Falstaff, who perhaps travelled from Mantua to Windsor Forest for his nocturnal tryst beneath the oak. Unrelated to anything in the rest of Bertolucci's film, the incident is a necessary point of origin, because it marks the end of one world and the start of another – a fall that is cultural and political rather than a disobedient moral lapse. 'With Verdi,' as the novelist Alberto Moravia declared in 1963, 'the greatness of Italy died out.'

Wagner was disposed of more summarily, without public displays of grief. 'The twilight of the gods,' G. K. Chesterton announced in 1923, 'was only a mood', and the world had luckily recovered from its affected gloom. In 1914 the Italian futurist F. T. Marinetti disparaged Wagner as 'the innovator of fifty years ago', and suggested leaving his mouldy cadaver to 'the bestial lusts of his devotees'. Marinetti viewed Italy as a fustily antique museum which needed to be brought up to date by mechanization and, even better, by war; Wagner's music encouraged a self-indulgence that was inconsistent with the brisk imperatives of modernity. Marinetti directed his invective at Wagner's last and most other-worldly opera: his call to arms was 'Down with the tango and *Parsifal*!', and he ridiculed high-society hostesses who 'give tea-dances and Parsifalize themselves', swaying ecstatically back and forth like the flower maidens until the world seems about to turn to jelly. Wagner's admirers adored this sense of time stalling and reality blurring; Marinetti, keen to ride ahead into the twentieth century in one of the fast cars he drove, detested it. The only way to save *Parsifal* from its pious tedium was to hurtle through it in forty minutes, an experiment that Marinetti said was about to be undertaken in a London music hall. The surest means of exorcism was laughter. In 1925 Paul Hindemith released Wagner's hermetic music from the theatre and exposed it to the open air. He impishly recomposed the overture to *Der fliegende Holländer*, imagining how it might sound if sight-read by a second-rate string quartet at seven in the morning beside a village well. The result is a sonic mess, acidly out of tune and chaotically out of time, which settles down briefly into an interpolated waltz before lurching towards a dissonant finale.

Today the anti-Wagnerian orthodoxy belabours his politics, making him remotely responsible for the Nazi policy of genocide. Early in the twentieth century, modernists who disliked Wagner concentrated on the cloying, queasy sensuality of his music. Marinetti linked the 'masturbated waltz' of the flower maidens with the Tantric deceleration of sex practised by Tristan and Isolde, who 'hold back their climax so as to excite King Marke' and experience 'love in dribbles'. The etherealized ardour of Isolde's 'Liebestod' exemplified everything about the romantic past that seemed dishonest or repellent. James Joyce disposed of it by means of a pun: in *Finnegans Wake* he used Isolde's first lulling phrase, 'Mild und leise', as the name of a character called Mildew Lisa – the Mona Lisa of a diseased decadence. Aldous Huxley accused Wagner of pandering to our 'baser emotions'. In his novel *Ape and Essence* the 'Liebestod' becomes a plea for detumescence, and Loola and Alfie copulate to 'the strains of the Good Friday music from *Parsifal*', its oozing modulations augmented by 'a rising and falling chorus of grunts and moans, of explosively shouted obscenities and long-drawn howls of agonizing delight'. Huxley's contempt for Wagner was balanced, according to Robert Craft, by his esteem for Verdi, with *Falstaff* as his particular favourite.

For the ideologues of modernism, what mattered was that the nineteenth and twentieth centuries should butt heads. In his 1913 manifesto Luigi Russolo hailed a music of the future that would consist of crude, intemperate noise. Beethoven and Wagner, Russolo said, once 'shook our nerves and hearts'. Now he preferred to listen to the cacophony of the city: rattling trams, backfiring cars, brawling crowds. A manifesto addressed to futurist musicians by Balilla Pratella in 1910 saluted the 'glorious and revolutionary era' dominated by Wagner, and regretted that Germany had descended into banality and ostentation with Richard Strauss. Except for Mascagni, Pratella snarled at all his Italian contemporaries – Puccini and Giordano with their 'rickety and vulgar operas', Tosti and Costa with their 'nauseating Neapolitan songs and sacred music'. He made no mention of Verdi, although his comments about the decline from Wagner's revolutionary glory had a parallel closer to home. A futurist could not praise a figure so outmoded, yet Verdi's sacrosanct status made it unwise to ridicule him.

The musical agenda differed depending on which country was to be propelled into the future. In 1902 the composer Nikolai Medtner described Russia as Brünnhilde asleep, waiting to be awoken by Siegfried – that is, by Wagner and the revolutionary impetus of German culture. In Spain the futurist Ramón Gómez de la Serna, who called himself Tristan, issued a proclamation in 1910 demanding 'Insurrection! Violent onslaught! Festivals with Wagner's music!' Modernism in France, however, was defined by its hostility towards Wagner, a scapegoat for Germany, the unforgiven enemy. Jean Cocteau's essays in *Le Coq et l'Arlequin*, published in 1922, prosecuted the feud between the two countries by setting the gassy profundity and nitrous violence of the north against the sensuous charm and sprightly frivolity of the south. The French, Cocteau pointed out, lacked the mental sluggishness of Germans, who were happy to be bored by Wagner. Like Marinetti, he thought that the best place to escape from this hypnotic stupor was the music hall, or perhaps a casino or cabaret where a troupe of black musicians from America played jazz while cocktails were served instead of love philtres. Cocteau derided music that had to be listened to through your hands – heard as you gripped your head, wracked by Wagnerian mental torments. Instead he wanted music that you could walk on, grounded and fit for diurnal use, like the score Erik Satie composed for Cocteau's ballet *Parade*, in which circus acrobats perform to the accompaniment of street musicians assisted by a clacking typewriter, a pistol and a wheezing siren. Even the impressionism of Debussy seemed to be Wagner diluted, thick fog refined into an aural mist. Cocteau wished, he said, to dispense with clouds, waves, aquariums, water sprites and nocturnal scents: a comprehensive disinfection of the Wagnerian atmosphere. His recommendations included the banishment of stringed instruments, which cushioned and caressed the ear and produced the enervating sensation, so dear to Wagnerites, of soaking for a long time in a warm bath or slowly drowning. All that contemporary music needed was woodwinds, brass and percussion, guaranteed to wake one up. Elsewhere he asked for 'du pain musical' – a fortuitous link to d'Annunzio's praise of Verdi, whose music nourished Italians 'come del pane'. At least this staple was digestible, producing no metabolic upsets. Cocteau winced at Wagner because he composed a music of the entrails, liable to attack your gut as well as your central nervous system.

To taunt the Germans after a war they had lost was one thing; to undermine German cultural hegemony at a time when France was a conquered province of the Third Reich was quite another. Cocteau's film *L'Éternel Retour*, released in 1943, daringly took back the myth of Tristan, which is Celtic not Teutonic, and retold the story in modern France with no help from Wagner. The music by Georges Auric is tender, discreet, never aphrodisiac; the characters – Patrice (Jean Marais) and his two Isoldes, both called Natalie, the first his uncle's wife, the second a girl from a garage whom he romances on the rebound – do not bother with operatic tantrums, and they get by without the amplifying help of an orchestra. Patrice signals to Natalie I by whistling to imitate a nightingale, and he proposes to Natalie II while fiddling with the dial of a radio, which coughs out a snatch of song, a blitz of static, then a few bars from a dance band. Despite the musical snub, Wagner might have enjoyed Cocteau's decision to replace the faithful Kurwenal with Moulouk, Patrice's devoted hound. Perhaps canine love is truer than the precarious bond between man and woman.

Wagner, who died so long ago, had to be posthumously murdered by these defamations and defilements. The polemical modernizers could ignore Verdi: as they saw it, his reputation had predeceased him. In 1897 James Huneker marked the death of Brahms, Wagner's opponent and opposite, by saluting him as 'the last of the immortals'. Verdi was still alive, but had no hope of immortality: 'not by any excess of sentiment,' sighed Huneker, 'can we dower Italy's grand old man with the title'. In 1904 another American critic, Lawrence Gilman, salvaged as much of Verdi as he could, which meant praising the last three operas because they 'derived, honourably, from Wagner' and were composed by a man who had 'suddenly seen a great light'. Although the 'unregenerate' Verdi of *Don Carlos* subsequently changed his ways, there were limits to what he could achieve. With an air of judicious impersonality, Gilman said that 'One cannot conceive, without painfully wrenching the imagination, of Verdi as the author of such a thing as the "Liebestod"…. Nor can one believe that he was in the least aware that the world and its human pageant were not all; and even had he lifted his eyes, how much, one wonders, would he have seen?' One might ask, all the same, if human existence is such an unworthy subject. One might even wonder if it is not important to look around you or inside yourself as well as to gaze upwards.

Wagner's biographer Ernest Newman referred to 'honest old Verdi' when discussing his response to Wagner's death. Old meant old-fashioned. Newman, born William Roberts, had adopted a pseudonym that declared him to be a new man belonging to the modern century, and he smiled at Verdi as a throwback to the past. Marking his centenary in 1913, Newman dismissed *Il trovatore* as the gambolling of 'an uncommonly vigorous cub', and incredulously complimented *Falstaff* by remarking that it could have been the work of a German or an Englishman. In fact Otto Nicolai, who reviled Verdi's music, had composed *Die Lustigen Weiber von Windsor* in 1849 and Vaughan Williams, who tactfully apologized for competing with Verdi, went on to compose *Sir John in Love*, first performed in 1929. The German opera has a beery jollity, the English one – which finds room for a small anthology of folk songs – is sweetly bucolic; the unique effervescence of Verdi is missing from both. In 1933, reviewing *Don Carlos* at Covent Garden, the obstinate Newman denied all over again that Verdi was a 'thoroughbred' and summed him up as a shrewd theatrical trickster not a musical dramatist. The difference, he smugly explained, was that between 'the statesman and the politician: the latter knows all the tricks of the trade, but he has neither the brains, the cultural background, nor the vision of the former'. The brains, cultural background and vision belonged implicitly to Wagner, who in his geopolitical harangues even fancied himself as a statesman.

Cocteau challenged his contemporaries to compose a music of the earth, or of the urban pavements. Verdi had already done so, although most people had forgotten; street corners remained an appropriate theatre for his best-known tunes, remote from the sealed chamber at Bayreuth. In the same year that Gilman's patronizing account of Verdi appeared in his book *Phases of Modern Music*, Alfred Noyes published a poem called 'The Barrel-Organ'. It is often taken, wrongly, to be a critique of Verdi: the lawyer Charles Tennyson, reminiscing in 1976 about his trips to Bayreuth in the first decade of the twentieth century, said that he and his Bloomsbury friends revered Wagner but sniffed at Italian opera. 'I recall,' Tennyson said, 'how an old friend of mine, Alfred Noyes, once rhymed the name of "Verdi" with the word "hurdy-gurdy" in a long-since-forgotten poem.' The rhyme, however, occurs nowhere in the poem; it would be too easy and too injurious, which is why Noyes – who also deliberately dignifies the instrument by choosing to call it a barrel-organ – avoids it. His poem begins in a yellow, sooty London afternoon:

> There's a barrel-organ carolling across a golden street
>     In the City as the sun sinks low;
> And the music's not immortal; but the world has made it sweet
>     And fulfilled it with a sunset glow.

The repertoire cranked out by the busker is predictable:

> And there *La Traviata* sighs
>     Another sadder song;
> And there *Il Trovatore* cries
>     A tale of deeper wrong.

Noyes acknowledges the incongruity of imagining a courtesan or a troubadour in this setting:

> Verdi, Verdi, when you wrote *Il Trovatore* did you dream
>     Of the City when the sun sinks low … ?

Obviously he did not, and the circumambient din – the weary feet of pedestrians and the 'dull mechanic beat' of the idling buses – suggests a milder, more muffled Anglo-Saxon version of the metropolitan noise that excited futurist composers. But the organ-grinder manages to light up the jaded eyes of the passers-by on Piccadilly:

> with a wild Italian gleam
> As *A che la morte* parodies the world's eternal theme,

and Noyes gratefully concludes that:

> Though the music's only Verdi there's a world to make it sweet.

Only Verdi? The grudging phrase is unfortunate, because Noyes's poem – rhythmically lame, and as repetitive as the barrel-organ's edited extracts – is not Verdian enough; afraid to be wild and Italian, it avoids intensity by choosing to treat Manrico's lament from the tower as a parody of our mortal dread and by imagining that Violetta wistfully sighs about the approach of death rather than protesting against it with righteous ferocity. The mistake is to assume that Verdi wants to sweeten the world, since both the operas Noyes mentions end with abrupt, disconsolate brutality.

The poem does allow this treacly memento of Verdi to alleviate the modern city's routine of toil, which is more than Wagner manages when T. S. Eliot and James Joyce cite him in *The Waste Land* and *Ulysses*. Eliot's quotations are silent, commenting on the vernacular chatter of his futile Londoners but not contributing to the life of the streets like the arias emitted by the barrel-organ. *The Waste Land* begins with one of its anonymous characters recalling a holiday beside the Starnbergsee, the lake in which Ludwig II drowned. Among assorted scraps of speech or unspoken thought, like the scrambled collective unconsciousness of Noyes's crowd in Piccadilly, the poem then quotes two snippets from *Tristan und Isolde*. One is the sailor's report about the speedy progress of Tristan's ship, which provokes Isolde's first spitting outburst, and the other is the survey of the wide, empty sea by the piping shepherd, who looks in vain for Isolde's ship and makes Tristan despair by relaying the news. Both extracts are marginal to the opera, heard as if from offstage, sung by characters disengaged from the erotic obsession of the hero and heroine; Eliot's poem about sexual desuetude has to exclude the heart of the opera, when the lovers are blissfully united. A reference to *Parsifal* is to be expected, since *The Waste Land* recycles the myth of the fisher king who, like Amfortas, reigns over a country rendered sterile by his sin. The allusion keeps its distance, not even quoting Wagner directly: an anthology of stray sounds – a pub ballad, the twittering of birds – includes a line from Paul Verlaine's poem about *Parsifal*, which wonders at the childrens' voices singing in the dome during the Grail ceremony. On the oily Thames, Eliot recalls the primal babbling of a more pristine river when he quotes the refrain of the Rhinemaidens, 'Weialala leia/Wallala leialala'. Immediately afterwards he refers to Queen Elizabeth I and Leicester sailing down the Thames in their barge; a note taken from a witness says that during their cruise they were talking 'nonsense'. Is this Eliot's verdict on the language of the *Ring*, which tries to record the liquid onomatopoeia of nature?

In Rome in 1907 Joyce twice attended performances of *The Dusk of the Gods*, as he called it, and on the first occasion watched in delight as Brünnhilde's horse 'evacuated' onstage during the immolation. He was amused by his garlicky neighbours in the gallery and their attempts to make the funeral march hummable; otherwise, as he wrote to his brother, 'nothing in the opera moved me'. Immunity to Wagner's charms was his proud proof of modernity. In *Ulysses* Stephen Dedalus woozily chants the oath of blood brotherhood from *Götterdämmerung* in Bella Cohen's brothel, then brandishes his ashplant – a cane that is his equivalent to Wotan's spear, hewn from an ash tree, and Siegfried's sword – to smash the chandelier. 'Nothung!' he cries, as the jet of gas unmelodically hisses 'Pwfungg!' Time's final flame goes out, and masonry topples to the floor as it does during Brünnhilde's immolation. But the novel is a mock-epic, and comedy frustrates Wagner's eagerness for annihilation: the world does not end.

|||||||||||||||||||

Verdi said that *Tristan* terrified him, which was a polite exaggeration. In principle he was alarmed by its innovations, in practice his stubborn independence enabled him to disregard it. Composers who came later found *Tristan* impossible to ignore. They felt it to be both an end and a beginning: its tonal irresolution freed them from classical rules, yet Wagner's score stood in their way, defying them – as their quotations from it implied – to do more than add footnotes. The notorious chord from the opera's prelude recurs in the emotionally strained final movement of Alban Berg's *Lyric Suite*, his coded confession of an extramarital love for Hannah Fuchs-Robettin, Franz Werfel's sister. Here there is no chance of recovery from dissonance and disaffection; without a climactic 'Liebestod', the suite expires in misery. Was Berg downcast about Hannah's unattainability, or about the pre-eminence of Wagner? Richard Strauss's attitude to the problem of succession was pushier. His father detested Wagner's music, grumbled when he had to play it under the composer's direction, and was outraged when he discovered the adolescent Richard studying the scores. Hans von Bülow anointed the young man as Wagner's rightful heir, but dubbed him Richard III: 'there is,' he loyally specified, 'no second'. Seizing his inheritance, Strauss inserted a scrap from *Tristan* into his showy, convoluted *Burleske* for piano and orchestra, and forced the wilting, satiated melody through some disrespectful metamorphoses. The *Tristan* chord trips up a dancing doll in 'Golliwogg's Cake-Walk' from Debussy's piano suite *Children's Corner*; luckily its power has weakened, and the pause before the jazzy antics resume is momentary. Hindemith truncates the same motif in his piano suite *In Einer Nacht*, reducing it to a random nocturnal noise: the title he gave to this tiny section claims that it transcribes the fantastic duet of two trees seen through a window. A later and even terser section of *In Einer Nacht*, entitled 'Böser Traum: Rigoletto', pounds out the Duke's promiscuous credo 'Questa o quella', then splices onto it the curse that haunts the jester. Verdi too, as Hindemith points out, can cause nightmares.

Artists of all kinds were susceptible to Wagner. Wassily Kandinsky heard *Lohengrin* in 1896 in Moscow and felt the sounds materializing as colours. The violins, basses and wind instruments visibly sketched 'wild, almost crazy lines', convincing Kandinsky that 'painting could develop such powers as music possesses'. He thought of music as the only truly abstract art, which meant that he disapproved of Wagner's illustrative motifs and sought, when he painted sounds, to catch 'spiritual vibrations'. Rather than suffusing the air with what Kandinsky called 'colour-tones', Wagner's example goaded the constructivist Vladimir Tatlin to dream up ways of climbing into the sky, as if scrambling up Jacob's ladder. Between 1915 and 1918 Tatlin worked on designs for *Der fliegende Holländer* that ignored the sea and chose to follow the thrusting vertical lines of a ship's masts and its rigging; he expected the chorus to scale those heights while singing. His ideas fed into his scheme for a Monument to the Third International in 1920. The geometrical network of wooden spars and taut ropes in the Wagner design now became a tower that would have consisted, if it had been built, of a cube, pyramid and cylinder revolving at separate speeds, with a radio transmitter at its peak to propagate the good news about Bolshevism.

Wagner, the engineer of rainbows, led Tatlin upwards and onwards. For the surrealists, he pointed back down, into the fecund mire of our fantasies. In 1930 in Luis Buñuel's *L'Age d'or* a man and a woman have the courage to act out the selections from *Tristan* that play on the scratchy soundtrack. During the opera's prelude, they lustfully wrestle in the mud, ignoring a religious ceremony in progress nearby. When they are prised apart, the man angrily imagines his female accomplice seated on a lavatory. As it flushes we see a wave crashing onto a beach and a sump of wet, dark soil quaking: the Wagnerian orgasm is not so very different from the body's other excretory spasms. At a patrician party, the man beckons the woman into the garden to the accompaniment of 'Träume', the

Wesendonck song that was a sketch for *Tristan*. Outside, the stuffier guests listen to an orchestra play the 'Liebestod', while the lovers again grapple on the ground and silently writhe through their own version of the duet from the second act. The surrealist Tristan becomes fixated on the marble foot of a statue; when he is called away, his Isolde consoles herself by licking and sucking its stiff cold toe. He returns in time for the musical climax and babbles 'My love, my love' while clutching his bloody head, which seems to have internally exploded. The woman meanwhile shrieks 'What joy to kill our children!' They have none, of course; she is merely celebrating a love that is deathly, with no ambition to engender new life. There is an epilogue to this orgy in *Abismos de Pasión*, Buñuel's Mexican film of Emily Brontë's *Wuthering Heights*. At the end Heathcliff storms into the crypt where Cathy's corpse lies waiting to decay among guttering candles and rancid lilies; shot by a rival, he bleeds his life away beside her as the 'Liebestod' gushes and ebbs. For Buñuel, Wagner's opera was either a copulation manual or a guide to the specialized vice of necrophilia.

Wagner liberated dissonance; the surrealists liberated instinct, which leads to unresolvably discordant behaviour. Between bouts of synchronized Wagnerian sex, the protagonist of *L'Age d'or* kicks a dog, slaps an old lady, knocks down a blind man and insults a Cabinet minister. What Dalí prized in Wagner was this combination of erotomania and exhibitionism. In 1939 in New York he designed a ballet called *Bacchanale*, choreographed by Léonide Massine to the Venusberg music from *Tannhäuser*. The male dancers had lobsters clinging to their tights like encrusted genitalia, and the women were fitted with globular breasts. The hero was Ludwig II, who in a series of hallucinations imagined himself playing the roles of Tannhäuser, Lohengrin and Siegfried. He slew a dragon, whose gore splashed into his eyes, making him blind and delirious rather than enabling him to decipher birdsong: surrealism prefers irrationality to understanding. *Bacchanale* was followed in 1944 by *Mad Tristan*, also choreographed by Massine, which compressed the opera into two mute scenes. After Isolde waved her scarf as a signal to Tristan, maniacal figures representing Spirits of Death danced with Spirits of Love who resembled dandelions shaking their seeds into the air. Inevitably, Thanatos prevailed over Eros: the next scene caught up with Tristan on Arnold Böcklin's Isle of the Dead, where his mummy was lowered into a vault by white, wormlike arms. Dalí opined that 'for the first time, one had the glorious opportunity of hearing Wagner without the conventional banality of sordid scenery covered over with the dust of mediocrity'. It was on this occasion that the self-publicizing *Dalí News* drummed up custom by shouting in capital letters as stentorian as those of the *Daily News* that Wagner had been killed.

The modernists left Verdi unmolested, although one of his countrymen did make use of him: in 1910 in Luigi Pirandello's novella *Leonora, Addio!*, a fat Sicilian wife called Mommina, neglected by a husband who locks her in the house while he sallies off to spend evenings at the opera, is revived when she finds in his pocket an advertisement for a local performance of *La forza del destino*. She remembers the opera well from her happier, freer youth, and she sings through it, voicing Leonora's final appeal for peace with such passion that her face turns purple with the effort. Noticing her excitement, her husband wonders whether she has a lover. He comes home early to trap her, and hears her upstairs declaiming Manrico's lines in the 'Miserere' scene from *Il trovatore*. She has even inked on a moustache of burned cork to convince herself that the impersonation is authentic. Her heart is weak, and the exertion kills her; thanks to Verdi, she dies happy. Pirandello developed the idea in his play *Tonight We Improvise*, first performed in 1930. A random company of amateurs for whom no one has written roles jostle a better-drilled cast of professionals who intermittently burst into excerpts from *Trovatore*. A gramophone plays the finale from *Ballo in maschera* or *Forza* – Pirandello expresses no preference – while a film of the action is projected onto a wall: the opera, whichever it is, represents a life that has been scripted, predetermined, whereas the characters without assigned parts are compelled to improvise, making up their existences as they muddle along. It all ends like the novella, with Mommina giving a one-woman performance of *Trovatore* in which she plays both the gypsy and the troubadour. Then, as in the novella, she drops dead. The director apologizes for this breach of theatrical etiquette, and says that it must be the fault of Mommina herself, because no text or score told her that this was how she must end. Verdi is brought back to life by one woman's desperate identification with his characters, but not for long: the play ends by announcing the death of the author.

||||||||||||||||||

Revolutions require heroes as well as villains, and the futurists had to nominate a new musician of the future to replace the worn-out sorcerer they were demoting. The choice was obvious. Marinetti rallied his followers by crying 'Down with Wagner, long live Stravinsky!' Massimo Mila went to hear *Tristan* in Turin in 1929 with his fellow student Leone Ginzburg, later an anti-fascist agitator who was killed by the Gestapo. 'After *Petrushka*,' Ginzburg declared, 'one can't listen to that music.' The young Stravinsky, however, was not indifferent to Wagner: the magic fire flickers in his *Scherzo fantastique*, first performed in 1909, although the bright blaze actually describes a swarm of bees. But there was no possibility of a royal succession, as when the crown was passed, in Bülow's phrase, from Richard I to Richard III. Stravinsky once tried on one of Wagner's berets, preserved in the collection of a Swiss philanthropist; his head disappeared into it and the rim settled on his shoulders. Sent to Bayreuth on an unbeliever's pilgrimage by Serge Diaghilev in 1912, he behaved sacrilegiously. He shifted in his creaky, uncushioned seat during *Parsifal*, and at the interval rushed out to revive himself with beer, sausages and cigarettes.

Stravinsky disliked what he called the 'progressive-evolutionary standards' of German musical history, which saw Beethoven leading inevitably to Wagner, with opera as a logical sequel to the vocal finale of the Ninth Symphony; *Tristan* was then a precondition for modern music, urging it towards atonality. 'After I became a Wagnerian,' Schoenberg admitted in 1909, 'the further development came rather fast.' Stravinsky refused to join this relay race, and signalled his detachment by rehabilitating Verdi. He was an avant-gardist in reverse, progressing backwards – as Verdi recommended when offering advice to Italian composers – by studying the past. In 1933, questioning Nietzsche's prescription of *Carmen* as an antidote to Wagner, Stravinsky suggested that a better alternative would be *Un ballo in maschera*. His enthusiasm for Verdi may have begun as an affectation: his praise for the innocuous waltz from *Traviata* was a little fulsome. But he vouched for his sincerity by juggling tour dates during the 1920s so he could make side trips to hear unfamiliar Verdi operas, and affectionate allusions to Verdi intermittently crop up in his works. Leonard Bernstein detected a reminiscence of Aida's prayer for clemency in the motto that stands for fate in *Oedipus Rex*, and in the biblical cantata *The Flood* the Devil's impenitent exit winks at the blithe impunity with which the Duke escapes retribution in *Rigoletto*. After hearing *Don Carlos* in Vienna in 1963, Stravinsky praised Verdi not Wagner as 'the true progressive'. Carlos and Posa in the duet that seals their friendship are genuine libertarians, by contrast with Siegfried and Gunther – 'fat people in horns and hides' as Stravinsky called them – who drink blood to swear their murderous oath in *Götterdämmerung*.

In his memoirs the Hollywood composer Miklós Rózsa compared the mutual avoidance of Stravinsky and Schoenberg – who lived near each other on the west side of Los Angeles but 'never met, and … despised each other's music' – to the armed truce between Verdi and Wagner. Franz Werfel's novel may have not equated Verdi with Stravinsky, but it did link Wagner and Schoenberg as Verdi's antagonists. With deft subterfuge, Werfel attributed to Verdi his own hatred of a modernity that, with 'its devil's doctrines – its angles, its cubes, its curtness, its machines, its outwards precision and inner confusion', did not exist in the 1880s, when the story is set. Verdi resists and outlives Wagner, 'the northern Lucifer', but the novel also requires him to vanquish the next German generation. In his wanderings through Venice he anachronistically encounters the avant-garde composer Fischböck, who might be Werfel's caricature of Schoenberg. Fischböck is ill and impoverished; unsure whether he is a genius or a fraud, Verdi gives him money and pretends that he has found a publisher for his hopelessly obscure scores. The subsidy does not save the young man's life and he dies soon after Wagner, with no guarantee that his work will ever be heard. Is Verdi, in a novel written to challenge the historical inevitability of modernism, ensuring that the music of the future will be stillborn? At home in Vienna, this was a dangerously recusant fantasy. In 1922 Werfel, Berg and Alma Mahler – with whom Werfel was then living – played snatches of *Traviata* and Massenet's *Manon* at the piano while feasting on asparagus, meatballs, strawberries and champagne. They were amusing themselves, happily and harmlessly slumming, but a year later, when Berg learned that Werfel was writing 'a "Verdi Novel"', he told his wife that 'our "quasi-friendship" will be shipwrecked on this book'. In these high-minded circles, to admire Verdi was sufficient cause for a rupture.

Transposing Wagner and Verdi to his own time, Werfel regarded the one as a proto-Nazi authoritarian and the other as a liberal; in the long biographical study he wrote for an edition of Verdi's letters in 1942, he referred to Verdi's life as 'a parable … pointing towards the future', by which he meant the current war. He implicated modern art in the contemporary 'chaos of values', and deplored the 'fanaticism' that had muddied the discussion of culture. Wagner was a convenient scapegoat for this befouling of the temple, just as 'the poet and farmer Giuseppe Verdi' remained for Werfel 'a very star in the murk'. The choice dramatized in his novel has a parallel in Theodor Adorno's studies of Schoenberg and Stravinsky, written during 1948 and published together in his *Philosophy of Modern Music*. An essay on 'Schoenberg and Progress' is invidiously paired with another on 'Stravinsky and Restoration'. The Jewish émigré Schoenberg, driven out of Germany by Hitler's regime, made it possible for music to advance by elaborating the twelve-tone technique; by contrast Stravinsky – so scornful of the Russian revolution, so richly remunerated while Schoenberg scraped an exiguous living from teaching – composed ballets in which time stopped and music itself reached a halt. Ideological prejudice makes Adorno's attack on Stravinsky's fascist atavism and his enjoyment of violence as nasty as Max Nordau's critique of the degenerate Wagner. Adorno leniently overlooked Stravinsky's fondness for Verdi, but in 1966 he finally pronounced judgment on this ingratiating music.

Verdi's sequences, Adorno claimed, repeated ideas without changing them, like the burblings of an idiot. They were a symptom of 'musical stupidity' and also of dishonesty, because their 'reified consciousness' sneakily covered up 'social contradictions'. Pierre Boulez simplified Adorno's verdict and repeated it in triplicate: interviewed in Indianapolis during an orchestral tour in 1972, he called Verdi 'stupid, stupid, stupid'. Elsewhere Boulez coupled Verdi with the equally trivial Offenbach, and asserted that his music consisted of 'dum de dum, nothing more'.

To give his opinion of Verdi extra authority, Adorno attributed it to Schoenberg, who in fact respected Verdi's music and did not regard it as an intellectual error to set him beside Wagner. In 1940 in an essay on music and film, Schoenberg cited *Les Vêpres siciliennes* and *Rienzi* as works about 'fighters for freedom' whose liberalism would have been censured by Hollywood; he added *Uncle Tom's Cabin* by Harriet Beecher Stowe to the list in deference to his adopted country. In his opera *Moses und Aron* Schoenberg agonized over the gap between the prophet and the publicist, the visionary who stammers as he tries to articulate complex truths and the entertainer who delights his followers with the honeyed sound of his own voice. He was debating a religious problem, but also questioning the decision that had determined his itinerary as an artist. Writing about Brahms in 1947, he brooded over the nature of great art and its need for precision and brevity. Composers should assume that their listeners will be educated, and ought to write for 'upper-class minds' – but how dense can the texture of their music afford to be? It was a lonely retrospective query from one who had chosen the vocation of Moses rather than the career of Aron. Real popularity, Schoenberg thought, was 'only attained in those rare cases where power of expression is granted to men who dwell intensely in the sphere of basic human sentiments'. His examples were Schubert, Johann Strauss and Verdi. He might have added George Gershwin, his friend, neighbour and occasional tennis partner, who once asked Schoenberg to give him lessons in composition; Schoenberg smilingly replied that, considering Gershwin's popularity and the money his music brought in, it ought to be the other way around. He was tantalized by what his arcane procedures had cost him. In 1936 he wrote a note about his first Chamber Symphony – originally performed in 1907, when despite its melodic profusion it outraged its Viennese audience – in which he analysed a few bars of 'La donna è mobile' and compared its retrograde motifs with an excerpt from his own piece. 'You will possibly agree,' he touchingly remarked about Verdi's most cheekily irrepressible aria, 'that I possibly could have written it – although with other notes'; he went on to plead that because of their common technique 'the relation between myself and Verdi is not so strange than it seems!' Robert Craft, given a glimpse of Schoenberg's studio in Los Angeles in 1951, spotted scores of *Otello* and *Falstaff*; it is more surprising and endearing to find him poring over a hit tune from *Rigoletto*.

Schoenberg's own music, like Wagner's, appealed to initiates. As a boy, Michel Leiris was struck by the way his parents distinguished between those who 'understood' Wagner and those who did not (and Leiris, puzzled and aroused by the suppurating wound of Amfortas in *Parsifal*, suspected that the secrets reserved for the understanders were sexual). But we should not undervalue music that requires no special effort of understanding. It is accessible to all because, as Schoenberg said, it deals with sentiments that everyone shares; it is, as Alberto Moravia said when he used a richly redolent and complimentary word to sum up the appeal of Verdi, 'vulgar'. Schoenberg might have insisted, as Werfel and Adorno did in their different ways, on a choice between the mountain top and the market place, between obscurantism and the common touch. Instead he saw that there was room for both in a large and profligate world with an appetite for music of every kind.

# ON THE MARCH

The critic Hermann Bahr, watching Germany mobilize in late 1914, said that the spectacle of the nation readying itself for war resembled a Wagner opera in its combination of 'ecstasy and precision'. His remark had a terrifying accuracy. Wagner's total work of art coordinated the efforts of hundreds of artists and craftsmen, all directed by a single will with the aim of trampling and exhausting the listener; music only mobilizes the air, but the result can be as stunning as ballistics. When the war took to the sky, it looked like a performance of *Die Walküre* staged in a theatre with no ceiling. The last volume of Proust's *À la Recherche du temps perdu* begins with a Zeppelin attack on Paris. Marcel's friend Robert Saint-Loup, on leave from the army, is elated by the beauty of a sky on fire, while the warning sirens seem to be playing the Ride of the Valkyries. Planes that swoop down towards targets on the ground remind him of stars dislodged and flung to earth by a god who is intent on wrecking creation. 'The Germans have to arrive,' he says, 'before you can hear Wagner in Paris.' His admiration for the enemy's pyrotechnics measures the seditious nature of art, at least for a Wagnerian: their aesthetic proclivities lead Marcel and Robert to side with the enemy.

Wagner's characters were symbolically called up for military service. Part of the defensive wall constructed in 1916–17 by the Germans in northern France – a chain of bunkers, tunnels, barbed-wire fences and machine-gun emplacements – was known as the Siegfried Line. The only armour Wagner's Siegfried needs is Brünnhilde's runes, which render his body impervious (except for his back, since she assumes he will never retreat from a foe); Germany's precautions were more systematic. Italians soon enough concluded that Attila was once more on the march. Padre Dante del Fiorentino, a monk who wrote a biography of Puccini, remembered his great-uncle saying that 'all this destruction of human life was no more than to be expected from the generation which had produced Wagner, "flagellum musicae"'. In Rome in 1916 when Toscanini concluded a concert with Siegfried's funeral march, a heckler shouted 'For the dead in Padua!', which had recently suffered a German air raid. The poet Fausto Salvatori supported the protest and declared that 'Siegfried's horn should not sound under a Latin sky in wartime.' Wagner, he said, was the deathly foe of both Greek elegance and Italy's more robust humanism, which made his work a danger to civilian morale; a ban on German music was enforced for the duration of the war.

After the war, Cocteau's colleague Auric remembered a pronouncement made by the Rosicrucian occultist who called himself Le Sar Péladan. It was Péladan's opinion that 'the man who does not admire Wagner is not civilized'. Auric wondered whether that held true in 1918: wasn't the war a display of German barbarity, fuelled in part by music? Verdi meanwhile remained synonymous with liberation. In 1917 the trench journal *Wipers Times* – slangily named after Ypres in Flanders, where it was first produced – announced a revue that would contain selections from the opera *Rigaletgo*: the Latvian city had been taken by the Germans a week before.

|||||||||||||||||||

A defeated Germany relied on the Wagnerian epic to orchestrate its revival and rearmament. In 1924 Fritz Lang directed a film version of the original Nibelungen saga in two parts, *Siegfrieds Tod* and *Kriemhilds Rache*. It was dedicated to the German people, who needed – as the scriptwriter Thea von Harbou, Lang's current wife, put it – to be re-attached to their roots. In her *Nibelungenbuch*, Harbou lamented that Germans, once 'dangerous wanderers' in the wide world, had been forced to stay meekly at home by the harsh provisions of the 1918 peace treaty. The film showed them how they could regain their strutting confidence by remembering the value of what she called 'unconditional loyalty'. She was referring to the dramatic crux of the second part, in which the warlords refuse to betray their comrade Hagen, even though he has killed Siegfried and casually slaughtered Kriemhild's child. Hagen in his turn is unconditionally loyal to the weak Gunther, and holds up his shield like a portable ceiling to shelter his king from the caved-in roof of the burning hall. The heroic cult, which values courage in the face of death and fealty to blood brothers, overrules moral scruples. Even Hagen's theft of the gold is justifiable according to his own patriotic precepts. Whereas Wagner's Hagen drowns while floundering to recover the ring, Lang's

Hagen stores the entire Nibelungen hoard in the riverbed, which is his bank vault. His aim is not to restore the treasure to its rightful source: he wants to make sure that no enemy can use the precious metals to forge weapons with which to attack the Burgundian dynasty.

After Siegfried's death, Kriemhild enters into a political marriage with Attila the Hun, called Etzel in the film. Kriemhild expects Etzel to prosecute her war against the Burgundian clan, but he does not measure up to the Attila of Friedrich Werner's play and Verdi's opera; she has to do the dirty work herself. As played by Rudolf Klein-Rogge, Etzel is a racial inferior, a cross between Asiatic idol and Red Indian chief, clad in matted skins, bedecked with amulets, a topknot sprouting from his shaved skull. While he snoozes in his tent outside the gates of Rome, his soldiers remember his threat to turn the city's churches into stables for their nags, and accuse the white woman with the plaited hair of having sapped his strength. When Kriemhild bears him a son, he drools over the baby with a soppy affection that we are expected to find unbecoming. He even refuses to slay Hagen on demand, telling his wife that he is a man of the desert for whom the laws of hospitality are sacred. Like Lady Macbeth when her husband cites a similar prohibition, she reacts with scorn. The only honour code she respects is Teutonic: the beliefs of bestial nomads do not count. When Etzel offers to negotiate a way out for the Burgundian relatives she has locked in the burning hall, he is told that he does not understand the German soul: 'Ihr kennt die deutsche Seele nicht, Herr Etzel!'

Lang later claimed to detest Wagner, and he disowned the version of *Die Nibelungen* that was released in the United States with a soundtrack of Wagnerian motifs. In effect he dismissed the *Ring* because Wagner sentimentalizes the characters of the saga, introducing emotional and moral crises that for Lang did not belong in this balefully primitive, bracingly contemporary world. The critic Kurt Pinthus was puzzled by the statuesque stiffness of the acting in the film, but guessed that Lang had intentionally suppressed the 'human element': humane sensitivity connotes feebleness, so the faces of the actors are fixed like masks, permanently grimacing to register victorious glee or vindictive contempt. Wagner's gods decline slowly, but Lang's *Nibelungen* is godless from the first, and the place of Wotan, tragically ruined by his equivocations, is taken by the glowering Hagen, who inherits the god's iconic trademarks – a patch over his missing eye, a helmet flaunting eagle wings. The film's Siegfried needs no drugged drink to corrupt him. Bustling into the court at Worms, he is a boastful thug, only too eager to conquer Brunhild. For her part, she can do without the protection of the magic fire: an athletic Amazon, she wrestles with Gunther and ties up his hands – a detail from the saga that was treasured by Leopold von Sacher-Masoch, who refers to it in 1870 in his novel *Venus in Furs*. Wagner's characters indulge in no such kinky play. In the opera, Brünnhilde righteously upbraids Siegfried for disgracing her, but Lang's Brunhild lies about being raped and cackles with witchy delight when her deception succeeds. After Siegfried's death she diverges from the Wagnerian prototype by remorsefully committing suicide, unredeemed and unenlightened; in the film's second part she is replaced by the fiendish Kriemhild, who lures the Burgundians to Etzel's court and organizes a massacre during their celebration of the summer solstice. The moment Wagner's Brünnhilde sees Siegfried's corpse she makes amends by lighting the pyre to purge Siegfried's errors and her own. In the film, Kriemhild torches the hall to avenge Siegfried by killing those trapped inside, who happen to be her kinsmen. She then stands back to gloat as they are cremated alive. Lang shared in her incendiary glee: he used a derelict factory in Spandau as the set for the hall, and personally fired an arrow tipped with magnesium to ignite it. Immovably vindictive, Kriemhild uses Siegfried's sword to kill Hagen and then, satiated, drops dead.

At the end of her *Nibelungenbuch*, Harbou compared the hall to the temple of a carnivorous god who feeds on the corpses lying about. The image is a harbinger of the dragon-mouthed engine that gobbles up workers in *Metropolis*, the next film she wrote for Lang; it also points towards the gas ovens of Auschwitz. Joseph Goebbels praised *Siegfrieds Tod*, though the Nazis forbade the re-release of *Kriemhilds Rache*, perhaps because its finale was too close to their practice of industrialized murder. After he resumed his career in Hollywood, Lang attached a more acceptably left-wing meaning to *Die Nibelungen*. In 1968 he repudiated Harbou's dedication and argued that the film was about the decadence of the Burgundian ruling class, trampled by troglodytic Huns. He quoted the end of the saga with its warning of 'der Nibelungen Not', and said that now, in a year of student uprisings, this meant 'des Kapitalismus Not', the downfall of capitalism. It was a cunning but specious Shavian reinterpretation. The truth is that Lang's *Nibelungen* makes Wagner's *Ring* look squeamishly humane.

During the 1920s the *Bayreuther Festspielführer*, a manual for visitors to the festival, described Wagner as 'ein Führer zu nationalem Sozialismus', a guide who conducted Germany into the national socialist future. In 1933, which auspiciously doubled as the fiftieth anniversary of Wagner's death, the Third Reich was inaugurated in Berlin with a performance of *Die Meistersinger* conducted by Wilhelm Furtwängler. Near the end, when the moment came to sing 'Wach'auf', the chorus ignored Hans Sachs and addressed its acclaim to Hitler, who as Chancellor presided in what was once the royal box and took responsibility for a German Renaissance like that proclaimed in the opera. Later when a new production of *Meistersinger* was commissioned to open the annual party rally in Nuremberg, Hitler tinkered with the designs and fussed about the lighting. This was no trivial hobby: toying with theatrical models was a smaller-scale rehearsal for the exercise of political power, which, as he told his architect Albert Speer, involved 'bringing the masses illusions'. At his alpine eyrie above Salzburg, Hitler sometimes listened to recordings of the prelude to *Lohengrin* as he fantasized about dominion over the world that stretched below, and productions of this opera became adjuncts of his foreign policy. He wanted to send the Bayreuth staging to Covent Garden as a coronation present for Edward VIII in 1936, but gave up on the idea when the dilettantish playboy begged to be excused from attending because opera bored him. *Lohengrin* was performed in Berlin in 1938 to mark a state visit by the Hungarian Regent Horthy, even though it begins with the king's loud request to be delivered from the menace of rabid Hungary.

Decisions about the proper interpretation of Wagner were handed down from on high. After conferring with Goebbels, Hitler agreed that the flower maidens who tempt Parsifal could in theory dance naked at Bayreuth. The purpose was not titillation: they wanted to show off the athleticism of the Teutonic super-race. Hardliners questioned the politically incorrect Christianity of *Parsifal*, and Hitler – like Wagner promising to found a new religion – announced that, once he had won the war, he intended to publish governmental guidelines for staging the opera. But such ideological debates were marginal; what mattered to Hitler was Wagner's power of mood-enhancement, not any ideas he might have been propounding. His collection of gramophone records was like a private pharmacy, with potions to arouse or relax him available on demand, and Ernst Hanfstaengl, a pianist who had studied with one of Liszt's pupils, often gave supplementary live performances. The first of these private recitals took place in the hall of Hitler's scruffy Munich apartment, where Hanfstaengl played a tinny-sounding upright piano to calm him after a day spent in court as a witness in a political trial. A Bach fugue failed to do the trick, but the *Meistersinger* prelude was more effective. It worked, however, as a stimulant not a sedative: Hitler paced to and fro, arms extended as if he were conducting, and whistled his own instrumental line as Hanfstaengl pounded the keyboard. Released from the Landsberg prison in 1924, Hitler requested the 'Liebestod' from the pianist to mark his homecoming and gurgled with delight as he heard it. A decade later in Berlin, Hanfstaengl was more than once summoned at midnight to the Chancellery to play the same piece, which for Hitler was a kind of lullaby.

Hitler's harangues were Wagner arias without the benefit of music, deploying tags from the operas and usually finishing, as Hanfstaengl noted, with his own hoarse equivalent to 'the blare of Wagner's trombones'. He liked to say 'I have only one love, and that is Germany', which paraphrased Rienzi's claim to be married to Rome, and he asked for the opera's overture to be played at party functions to underline his fancied resemblance to the tribune. His mythopoeic presumption was contagious. During rehearsals for *Die Walküre* in Berlin in 1934, the portly Hermann Goering, officially in charge of the opera company, waddled onstage to show the singer playing Wotan how to hold a spear. In 1945 when Hitler retreated to his Berlin bunker, he took along a set of Wagner's autograph scores presented to him on his fiftieth birthday in 1939 by a consortium of German industrialists – an offering of thanks for the profits they had made from the war. He refused to hand the manuscripts over to Wieland Wagner for safe-keeping: perhaps he needed to consult *Götterdämmerung* as he ordered Germans to leave nothing but a scorched earth for the invaders. Appropriately enough, Furtwängler led the Berlin Philharmonic in a performance of the immolation scene as the city burned.

This appropriation did not go uncontested. In a lecture delivered in Munich in 1933 to mark the fiftieth anniversary of Wagner's death, Thomas Mann provocatively enlisted him as an anti-fascist, a 'Kultur-Bolshevist' who built his Bayreuth theatre for 'a classless society'; the public response was so barbed that Mann prudently crossed the frontier into Switzerland. In fact the Bolsheviks disapproved of Wagner, disliking his concentration on heroes rather than the anonymous multitude that ought to be the agent of social change. When Lenin placed a wreath at the monument to the victims of the 1917 revolution, a brass band of five hundred played Siegfried's funeral march: the numbers neutralized Wagner's offence against communal ethics. In 1924 at the Mariinsky Theatre in Leningrad, *Rienzi* was re-entitled *Babeuf,* honouring a Jacobin agitator who called himself a tribune of the people and adopted the given name of Gracchus in homage to the party of land reformers in classical Rome. The communists saw Babeuf, who was guillotined in 1797, as a martyred precursor; thanks to some opportunistic rewriting, Wagner's isolated hero became a collectivizing populist.

When he directed *Die Walküre* at the Bolshoi Theatre in Moscow in late 1940, Sergei Eisenstein answered the official objection to Wagner's individualism by merging characters with the groups from which they derived their power. Hunding travelled with a horde of shaggy thugs, and Fricka had a troop of golden-fleeced ovine mutants, emasculated men who upheld her version of the moral order and deputized for the sheep that supposedly draw her chariot.

Despite this tacit compliance with Soviet doctrine, what interested Eisenstein was Wagner's primitivism, not his progressiveness. He saw *Die Walküre* as folklore, the relic of a superstitious culture still kept alive by rustic Russian legends. Hence the magical animation of the scenery in his staging. The leaves on the tree in Hunding's hut shivered and flushed: this was the world-ash, which split open to disgorge Wotan. Mountains reared and bucked during Siegmund's fight with Hunding, as if the earth were heaving in parturition, and thunderclouds solidified to carry Wotan in pursuit of the disobedient Brünnhilde. Wagner's music of transition here did more than track the emotional changes within characters; Eisenstein's moving scenery showed a world still in transition between animism and a later, secular culture that chased the gods out of nature and treated rivers, rocks and trees as the raw materials of a mercenary economy.

The Bolshoi presented *Die Walküre* to solemnize the non-aggression pact signed between Stalin and Hitler a year before. Then in June 1941 the Wehrmacht invaded Russia, and the staging was hurriedly scrapped. Theatrical productions are ephemeral, like the cordial agreements between dictators.

|||||||||||||||||||

Whereas Wagner offered a pretext for the bigotry of the Third Reich and, at the end, for its doomed nihilism, Verdi served as the music of the opposition. Ernest Newman's querulous review of *Don Carlos* at Covent Garden was written between Hitler's appointment as Chancellor in January 1933 and the establishment of a one-party state in July. In it he remarked, a little incredulously, that Verdi was currently more popular in Germany than Wagner; he did not pause to wonder why. In the same year the conductor Gianandrea Gavazzeni, marking the fiftieth anniversary of Wagner's death, announced an end to 'il binomio Wagner-Verdi', the adversary pairing that honoured music drama and snubbed melodrama. The impetus came, Gavazzeni said, from Wagner's own country, where there was a new appreciation for the spontaneity of Italian music. The change began as an aesthetic preference but gradually hardened into a matter of political conscience. In 1923 Kurt Weill grumbled to Busoni about a mannered, unidiomatic performance of *Aida* in Berlin conducted by Erich Kleiber, who tried to 'simulate the presence of Italian theatre blood simply by exercising arbitrary tempo fluctuations'. In an aside Weill moaned that Bruno Walter was now 'letting all the Bayreuth demi-gods and full-gods parade around'; he knew that these potentates were no friends to ordinary humanity. Weill had more cheerful news to report from Bologna the following year, where he wrote to Busoni while 'sitting in a café with an orchestra playing *Traviata*, and they're all singing along'. This was music for social use, to be consumed with the café's food and drink, and it seemed truly democratic because the patrons knew the words as well as the tunes.

Toscanini did not assume that Verdi belonged exclusively to Italians, and travelled to Dresden to hear Fritz Busch conduct *La forza del destino*, staged in Werfel's translation as *Die Macht des Schicksals*. In Italy the opera had a reputation for incoherence, and was also thought to bring bad luck to those who performed it; the superstition was confirmed when the soprano cast as Leonora fell ill, and Toscanini had to hear Strauss's *Die Ägyptische Helena* instead. On the advice of the composer Berthold Goldschmidt, the director Carl Ebert opened his tenure at the Städtische Oper in Berlin in 1931 with Verdi's *Macbeth*, not the more customary *Fidelio* or *Meistersinger*. Ebert's son Peter remembered a disturbingly expressionistic production, all mist and gauze, with the witches invisible behind white voodoo masks; the occultism of the work suited the contemporary politics of terror. Ebert next invited Busch to conduct his production of *Un ballo in maschera*. This opera too matched the uneasy social mood, with a threatened leader consulting a fortune-teller who tells him that he will be assassinated by one of his own ministers. Busch and Ebert made plans for a Verdi cycle, which was called off after the Nazis attacked them for engaging Jewish artists. When Busch balked at the national repertory imposed by the regime, Goering reminded him that he could be made to comply. Busch retaliated with a threat of his own. 'A compulsory performance of *Tannhäuser* conducted by me,' he said, 'would be no pleasure to you. You have never in your life heard anything that would be so stinkingly boring.' He was given a last chance to demonstrate his tractability when Toscanini – engaged in 1930 and 1931 at Bayreuth, where he was the festival's first non-German conductor – refused on principle to return in 1933, despite a letter from Hitler importuning 'the great maestro of the friendly Italian nation'. Busch was asked to replace him, which would have guaranteed his rehabilitation. During a walk in the Tiergarten, his wife encouraged him not to relent by quoting Falstaff's monologue about honour. Falstaff is hardly an example of conscientious objection, and he would have thought Busch's moral courage foolhardy, but her allusion to the opera recognized that it was composed in praise of life not Wagnerian death. Busch and Ebert chose to emigrate, implicitly following Falstaff's advice about self-preservation.

Werfel made a case for Verdi's 'prophetic socialism', based on the small welfare state he established at Sant'Agata; he is described in the novel as 'an elder brother of Tolstoy', who also grieved over the misery of his peasants. This radical reading pervades the performing versions of the three operas that Werfel prepared for the German stage after completing the novel – *La forza del destino* in 1925, *Simon Boccanegra* in 1928, *Don Carlos* in 1932. These were adaptations rather than mere translations, altering the motives of characters and in one case even rearranging the dramatic structure to make subtly dissident political points.

In *Die Macht des Schicksals* Werfel – himself eventually forced into exile by the racial policy of the Nazis – underlines the persecution of Alvaro. Leonora's father categorizes the Inca as a foreigner, 'den Fremden', but her brother Carlo has a range of uglier and more abusive epithets for which there are no equivalents in Piave's libretto. He calls Alvaro a bastard with shameful, ignoble blood in his veins, sneers at him as 'der Mestize', a half-caste, and at the monastery, before slapping his face to provoke a duel, he derides him as a 'Mischling', a word that became crucial to the Third Reich's Aryan laws, institutionalized in the Mischling Test that fussed over percentages of Jewish blood. After Carlo summarizes the plot for the benefit of his fellow travellers at the inn, Piave's chorus merely give thanks for a tale well told; Werfel has them compliment him as 'ein Hidalgo', whose unrelenting hatred for the mongrelized enemy counts as a national glory: 'Nur ein Spanier allein/Geht so unbeugsam vor'. Alvaro fights back in his retrospective aria at Velletri. In the Italian libretto he says only that his father sought to free their native land. Werfel has him directly accuse the imperialists while incidentally pointing out that cultures deemed to be subordinate have their own notions of ethnic purity and their own cherished heritage: 'Mein grosser Vater was der letzte Erbe/des reinen Inkablutes./Die heil'ge Heimat wollte er erlösen/ Von Europas elender Tyrannei'. In Italian, the camp-follower Preziosilla can be excused as a Risorgimento militant, stoking a legitimate hatred against the Germans. Her delight in the beauty of war was an embarrassment for Werfel, who evasively treated the patriotic struggle as a combat in defence of freedom. Whereas Piave's Preziosilla is a bloodthirsty bully, in German she regrets that war has to be the last resort of liberal pacifists. She encourages recruitment in order to preserve 'der Brüder heil'ge Freiheit', and makes this slogan crucial to her battle hymn: 'Der mutig für Freiheit sich schlagen kann.../Der Kriege um die Freiheit lebe hoch!' The chorus that in Italian shouts 'Viva!' here cries 'Freiheit!', which is hardly an exact translation.

At the end of Werfel's *Forza*, religion is deprived of its certainty. When Leonora dies, the Padre Guardiano tells Alvaro she has risen to God: 'Salita a Dio!' The best Werfel's character can offer is an assurance that the soul survives, though perhaps for only as long as we remember and mourn: his line is 'Die Seele lebt!' Werfel here adjusted the opera to modern disbelief by using a euphemism like those with which Verdi's librettists placated the censors. Before the renamed

*Giovanna d'Arco* was performed in Rome, papal watchdogs insisted that the word 'Dio' must be changed to the non-doctrinal 'Cielo'. In the nineteenth century it was blasphemous to invoke the deity onstage; in the twentieth century, to do so seemed quaint or foolish.

*Simon Boccanegra* allowed Werfel the chance for an even timelier reflection on social strains. He sharpened the sense of class conflict: in their duet Adorno and Fiesco vilify the knavish pretender Boccanegra while upholding the privileges of their own 'Herrenblut'. Boccanegra is no man of the people, and wrinkles his lip when he hears the noise of insurrection. In the scene added by Boito during the revision, he opens the doors of the council chamber and lets the chaotic mob charge in. 'Ecco le plebe!' he snarls, using the snobbish Roman word for underlings or plebeians. Werfel gives him a more modish noun: his greeting now is 'So ist die Masse!!' The idea of the mass – replacing what nineteenth-century novelists saw as the crowd – was a sociological novelty, recognizing that the economic disaster had levelled the hierarchy of bourgeois society, leaving a demoralized pulp that was ready to be manipulated by demagogues; analysing fascism in the late 1940s, Siegfried Kracauer said that Hitler used 'the mass as ornament' when staging his rallies at Nuremberg.

Werfel's Boccanegra makes no mention of Rienzi as a sponsor of unification, perhaps because Bulwer-Lytton's hero had been co-opted by Wagner. A German audience could not be expected to understand local references so that, instead of attempting to make peace between Adria and Liguria, Boccanegra asks 'Sind wir nicht alle/Kinder eines Vaterlandes?' Werfel evidently found the Italian Boccanegra a sentimental optimist, over-reliant on emollient melody to subdue the quarrelsome factions. In the Weimar Republic, with its hard-edged realism, less palatable truths had to be uttered. Whereas Boito's Boccanegra makes an appeal to the nurturing, maternal Italian landscape and sings about its sprouting olive trees, Werfel's character says that love pervades nature while man remains cold, cruel, egotistical. The appeal for peace is now not his idea; it has to be introduced by Amelia. Werfel saves his moral awakening for the next scene, when he pardons Adorno and announces a Utopian project that involves embracing his enemies. Verdi's hero was at best humanized by loss, humbled by mortality. Werfel's Boccanegra advances beyond personal tragedy and attains a rare and perhaps improbable public grandeur. 'Ich baue eine neue Welt,' he says: like a true revolutionary – though of the left, not the right – he intends to reconstruct the world, universalizing what he calls his 'Friedenswerk', the work of peace. Patching up family quarrels between Italian provinces is a trivial matter; the armistice he calls for will be international. Even more startlingly, he undergoes a deathbed conversion to republicanism. Instead of monarchically passing on his crown to Adorno, who is now his son-in-law, he restores sovereignty to the people. Here was Werfel's prescription for the political future in Germany, which in 1933 took a different course.

Werfel's reinterpretation of *Don Carlos* – prepared in collaboration with Lothar Wallerstein, a fellow Czech who migrated to Vienna, then sought refuge in America after the Nazis annexed Austria – rescinds the liberal hope with which his *Boccanegra* concludes. The opera begins as a comfortless flashback for Carlos, who is first seen in Madrid, dreamily reading in front of a tapestry showing the park at Fontainebleau. He recalls his happiness there, before his father Philipp II took Elisabeth for himself; the reverie fades and Carlos begs for sleep to relieve him of his misery. Rather than chanting offstage, the monks are then seen in the chapel where the supposedly dead Kaiser Karl V presides over his own funeral and places his regalia in his coffin – a pantomime that acts out what Philipp II later imagines when he foresees his own entombment. The interpolated scene reveals the deathliness of power, which mortifies those who possess it as well as rounding up their subjects for extermination. When fires are lit under the heretics at the auto-da-fé, Spain's theocracy alarmingly anticipates the sadism of the Nazis, with their necrotic icons – a crucifix twisted into a swastika, a skull as the emblem of the enforcers – and their use of meat hooks as instruments of martyrdom. Werfel and Wallerstein direct that smoke should mercifully obliterate the scene as a seraphic voice sings about the soul's flight – a dying hallucination of those whose religious credulity has cost them their lives, or history's eventual apology to the victims of persecution? This version of the opera ends as brutally as Schiller's original play. Philipp II drags Elisabeth off to an undefined punishment; no god in a machine saves Carlos, who kills himself and is removed on his bier while his grandfather watches, posthumously as it were.

The Verdi revival had a postscript after the war in New York. Rudolf Bing left Vienna in 1934 and followed Busch to Glyndebourne; in 1950 when he took over as general manager at the Metropolitan Opera, Bing decided to make *Don Carlos* his first new production. It was regarded, he reported, as 'an extremely adventurous choice' by those who did not know that 'during the late 1920s in Central Europe we had learned how to do these later Verdi operas'. The decision made manifest the new manager's artistic and political inclinations. Having given Verdi priority, Bing sidelined Wagner until the late 1950s, when the availability of Birgit Nilsson prompted him to revive *Tristan* and the *Ring*.

Busch, Ebert and Werfel could not protect Verdi from conscription by the other side. In Italy, productions of *Aida* implicitly made propaganda for

Mussolini's swashbuckling in Africa, with Radamès as a staunch blackshirt and Amonasro identified with Haile Selassie. Hitler applauded *Aida* when the tenor Beniamino Gigli sang it in Berlin in 1937, and during his weeks at the Wolf's Lair in Eastern Prussia in 1942, where he spent his sleepless nights ordering his exhausted aides to put on gramophone records, he often called for '*Aida*, last act' – significantly the account of a warrior's death, which ends with his suffocation in a bunker-like crypt. Hans Castorp listens to this act during a gramophone recital at his alpine sanatorium in Thomas Mann's *Der Zauberberg*. Mann does not name the opera and Castorp can't understand the Italian words, but the emotion of the final scene – a sense of light-headed hopelessness, as Mann defines it – is instantly comprehensible, and its lyricism is so seductive that the author feels compelled to underline the 'vulgar horror of actual fact' by speculating about decomposition in the airtight vault.

Mussolini was never sure whether to be nationalistically proud of Verdi or embarrassed by him. Although his first public speech was an oration delivered as a schoolboy after the death of the beloved 'Swan of Busseto', he preferred Wagner to Verdi, and one of the party pieces he played on his violin was a transcription of Wolfram's aria addressed to the evening star in *Tannhäuser*. He may have intended a slight to Verdi in 1931 when he disparaged the cult of Caruso as a relic of 'the old Italy', that mellifluous backwater where the trains did not run on time. In 1934 he had the chance to be proprietorial about Wagner: Hitler visited Italy to plot the annexation of Austria, and Hanfstaengl suggested that Mussolini – who met his guest at the Venice airport before they conferred at Stra, near Padua – should take him to the Palazzo Vendramin, where Wagner died. But there was no time for sentimental detours; nor did the two despots manage an amicable discussion. Afterwards Mussolini dredged up the racial clichés used by Verdi during the Franco-Prussian War: he said that the Germans were still 'the barbarians of Tacitus', and called National Socialism 'the revolt of the old Roman tribes of the primitive forests against the Latin civilization of Rome'. After concluding an alliance with the Third Reich, he turned deferential. He taught himself German so he could read Hitler's missives without a translator's help, and in 1944, after Nazi parachutists rescued him from his alpine prison, he tested his proficiency by translating an Italian translation of *Die Walküre* back into German to check on its fidelity.

Mussolini had less interest than Hitler in controlling the arts, and thought his job was to keep an eye on builders, engineers and factory workers, not to police the output of writers, painters and stage directors. His followers, however, requisitioned Verdi for use in a propaganda war. The 1941 pictorial volume *Verdi nelle immagini*, edited by the biographer Carlo Gatti, told chthonic half-truths about Verdi's peasant stock and his faith in the country's grandeur. Gatti described his Paris excursion for *Don Carlos* militaristically, awarding Verdi a doubtful victory because he supposedly forced the French to recognize that his own work represented 'l'opera latina per eccellenza'. Those who did not revere Verdi were branded as agents of an insidious international conspiracy. In 1937 a fascist newspaper published a scurrilous attack on the composer Alfredo Casella by his colleague Francesco Santoliquido. Casella lived in Paris, and could therefore be attacked as a deracinated cosmopolitan. Santoliquido imagined him returning to Italy as a missionary for 'the brand-new international Jewish musical church', with orders 'to stab the execrated Giuseppe Verdi pitilessly, to destroy *romanticism, lyricism, feeling* (all horrible prerogatives of the Italian Catholic soul), and to inoculate us instead with *cerebralism, materialism* and *cynicism*'. The accusation of cultural treason, so vexing to Verdi when critics claimed he had fallen under Wagner's influence, was now also made against Toscanini. In Bologna in 1931 the journalist Leo Longanesi struck him for refusing to perform the fascist anthem at a concert; after the assault, Longanesi railed that Toscanini had 'picked up the crumbs of Wagnerism' and had come to believe that his baton was 'Wotan's sword' – though Wotan's implement of rule is of course a spear.

There was a predictable fuss when Toscanini included some Wagner excerpts in a concert in Turin soon after the start of the Second World War. As strict about ethics as about tempi, he saw no reason to assume that Hitler had retroactively incriminated Wagner. He also did his best to prevent Verdi from being used as incidental music for official pomp. Mussolini asked him to conduct the La Scala production of *Falstaff* in Rome during the state visit of George V in 1923; Toscanini pleaded illness. Abroad, he was less of a purist, and he later used Verdi to reproach or taunt the Third Reich. In 1934 in Vienna he conducted the *Requiem* in memory of Chancellor Dollfuss, who had been murdered by the Nazis, and in 1935, after spurning Bayreuth, he performed *Falstaff* in Salzburg – almost an act of incitement, since Hitler's Bavarian power base lay a few miles off across the border. The festival had previously avoided Italian comic opera, which was thought to lack high seriousness; Toscanini insisted on *Falstaff*, which for him was the epitome of Latin genius, combining gaiety and warmth with cool-headed technical virtuosity. In 1937 he teasingly added *Die Meistersinger*, for which Bayreuth wanted him, to his Salzburg repertory. Even-handed as he was, he could not help making a choice between Verdi and Wagner, but for aesthetic not political reasons. He admired Wagner's elaborate musical depiction of dusk in Nuremberg, but Verdi, as Toscanini said to Adriano Lualdi, imparted as much information about nightfall in Windsor in just three notes.

In 1943 NBC in New York broadcast three Toscanini concerts, interspersed with requests for listeners to 'back the attack' by buying war bonds and stamps. One of these transmissions, on July 25, included a short-wave radio interview with the commander of American naval forces in Europe; the musical proceedings, which consisted of extracts from five Verdi operas, were interrupted by the announcement of Mussolini's resignation. The previous year Werfel said that he hoped 'Va, pensiero' would be heard again 'as a hymn of Thanksgiving when the present oppression and foreign rule in Italy are overthrown'. Instead the broadcast programme resumed with the third act of *Rigoletto*, a grimly uncelebratory nocturne. The war was not yet won, so rejoicing had to be postponed. At Madison Square Garden in May 1944, Toscanini conducted a benefit concert for the Red Cross. The last act of *Rigoletto* was again on the programme, along with the *Inno delle nazioni*, included at the request of the United States government. To the anthems anthologized by Boito, Toscanini attached snippets of 'The Star-Spangled Banner' and a French version of the Russian 'Internationale', so that more of the countries contributing to the war against Germany could be represented. He also added an adjective to the tenor's salute to Italy: 'oh patria mia' became 'oh patria mia tradita', denying the fascists a monopoly of patriotism. The concert maintained his customary equilibrium between cultures by including four orchestral episodes from Wagner's operas, although the Ride of the Valkyries was illustrated in the programme with a photograph of an Allied bomber squadron. Clearly the Teutonic warrior maidens on their flying horses would be outgunned by fighter planes that spat ammunition rather than shrilly yodelling. Wagner, so unscrupulously exploited by Hitler, could also be a weapon aimed against him.

The Third Reich's victims made the bravest yet most tragically ineffectual use of Verdi in the Czech concentration camp at Terezín, where the Prague composer Raphael Schächter trained a group of his fellow internees to give fifteen performances of the *Requiem*. This was both their ineffectual plea for salvation and their means of damning the Nazis, whom they imagined suffering the righteous punishment of heaven. Josef Bor's novel *The Terezín Requiem*, published in 1963, recreates the circumstances of those concerts. Bor's Schächter decides on Verdi because he assumes that the Nazis will not permit Jews to tamper with sacred music by Bach, Handel or Mozart, although another prisoner – once a music critic, now a broken-spirited scavenger – disapproves of his choice because the *Requiem* is so unJewish: it has a Catholic faith in restitution after death, whereas Jews, like Protestants, put their trust in the possibility of 'a better life here on earth'. But Verdi's 'elemental ferocity', unleashed by the brass, the kettledrums and the howling chorus, suits Schächter's purpose, which is to conjure up for the listening gauleiters a judgment day when Germany will be overrun and retributively burned by the Red Army. Like Werfel making Preziosilla an enthusiast for 'Freiheit', Schächter interprets the concluding cries of the 'Libera me' as a demand not a plea, an angry insistence on 'Liberty, liberty'. He even edits the finale, eliminating the last whispered diminuendo: his *Requiem* ends in that thundering challenge, delivered fortissimo. His aim may be political, but he is too fine a musician not to appreciate the Italianate beauty of the work, and one of his tenor soloists – they occasionally have to be replaced during the long rehearsals, as they fall ill and die or are hauled off for execution – is a young man who once belonged to the Vienna Boys' Choir but escaped to Italy after the Anschluss, only to be captured in Milan and sent home. He sings the 'Ingemisco' with a plangency and passion that makes him 'a messenger from another world, from Italy, the land of sun and of song'; the Gestapo then silences his voice by putting him to death. Schächter himself is cast by his colleagues as a standard-bearer, and instead of describing deliverance by the Archangel Michael in the 'Offertorio' the soprano at one of the rehearsals alters the text and sings the praises of another archangel, the conductor's namesake. The *Requiem* was performed at Terezín during 1942, after which Schächter and the musicians were transported to Auschwitz for extermination; Bor, however, changes the date to 1944, when the war was almost over, to give the Jews a better chance of prevailing or at least surviving. But history is immitigable: the outcome, after the irate echoes of the *Requiem* have died away, remains the same.

In prison at Spandau after the war, Albert Speer and his fellow internees Rudolf Hess and Baldur von Schirach were allowed twenty hours of music on records, consisting mostly of German symphonies and forty minutes of excerpts from operas by Verdi. Their aural diet was strictly policed. In 1960 they obtained permission weeks in advance to hear a recording of *Don Giovanni*. When the day came, a Russian official objected that an opera about love was inconsistent with their routine of penance, and they had to make do with Beethoven's Ninth Symphony. Wagner was banned, although by 1964 Speer was able to listen surreptitiously to *Parsifal* on his transistor radio. At Christmas that year a group of sympathizers arrived with gifts for Speer and his colleagues, which they were not allowed to deliver. Undeterred, the visitors played a tape before being sent away. A friendly guard reported the incident, and Speer recorded it in his diary: the tape, he wrote, began with 'the "Prisoners' Chorus" from Verdi's *Nabucco*', followed by some carols and a nationalistic sermon. His description contains a telling slip. The chorus of political prisoners is actually from Beethoven's *Fidelio*; 'Va, pensiero' is sung by Hebrew slaves, comparable to the gangs of labourers from the camp at Sachsenhausen who were worked to death making the bricks Speer needed to construct Germania, Hitler's elephantine capital. Thanks to Verdi's liberating anthem, the anti-Semitic war criminals were able to enjoy a little seasonal self-pity.

||||||||||||||||||

In 1965 Yukio Mishima wrote, directed and acted in a film of his short story 'Patriotism', which describes in surgical detail the self-disembowelling of a young lieutenant whose comrades have attempted to stage a military coup. It would be dishonourable for the lieutenant to attack the plotters, as he expects he will be ordered to do; he therefore slices open his stomach. Mishima here rehearsed for his own militarized suicide five years later, after his quixotic challenge to Japan's secular government failed. The film is silent: the lieutenant and his young wife communicate by exchanging glances and, when the agonizingly elaborate operation begins, decorum forbids him to groan or her to cry out as she kneels beside him. The emotion they cannot express is relegated to the soundtrack, for which Mishima used a compressed orchestral version of *Tristan und Isolde*. He even gave the film a Wagnerian subtitle, calling it *Patriotism, or The Rite of Love and Death*.

The allusion to Isolde's transfiguration is deliberate, but Mishima was being either vague or inaccurate when he said that the entire score consisted of what he called 'the song "Liebestod"'. We hear half an hour of orchestral extracts from the opera – the drinking of the potion when the lieutenant and his wife agree on their double suicide, the love duet when he kills himself as she admiringly watches, the 'Liebestod' only in the final scene when she pads through the puddled blood on the floor to die beside him. The recording Mishima used was an old favourite from his personal collection, the scratched vinyl grooves worn down by addictive listening. He gave no details about it, except to say that it was a performance from 1936, the same year in which mutineers from the Tokyo barracks murdered the politicians who wanted to cut the military budget. In fact the recording was Leopold Stokowski's *Symphonic Synthesis* of the opera, dating from 1932. Stokowski eliminated the drama's conflicts and its depressive lulls, leaving only climaxes; in the absence of singers, the passions are impersonal. Wagner's characters are sensitized by song, whereas Mishima strove for an inhuman anaesthesia. With the shiny brim of his military cap tugged low on his forehead, the lieutenant seems to have no eyes; stripped to a loincloth, he hides behind the cultivated physique that for Mishima was an armature of muscle. His wife repairs her makeup so that she can die with her impervious white mask intact. By contrast with their robotic demeanour – his obedience to the warrior's code, her duty of compliance – Tristan and Isolde are free agents, vexingly inconsistent, forgivably dishonest about their motives, liable to make choices that are dramatically thrilling because unexpected and inexplicable.

In the opera it is Kurwenal not Tristan who behaves heroically by loyally dying beside his master, and whatever happens during Isolde's final outpouring – death, orgasm, or a transcendent lift-off like that of Titian's Madonna in *The Assumption of the Virgin* – it does not require her to drive a dagger into her throat and choke on her own blood. Mishima misrepresented Wagner by making the music underscore images that are obscenely cruel. A pig's reeking entrails, stored in formalin, spill from the lieutenant's taut stomach when he hacks it open; he retches, foams at the mouth, and twitches as he tries to aim the sword at his neck. Meanwhile the orchestra, sweetened by extra strings, swoons in an excess of pleasure. The music that accompanies Tristan's delirium or the removal of his bandages, omitted by Stokowski, might have been more apt, but it would not have served Mishima's desire to beautify self-destruction and to uphold what he calls in the story 'the complete and unassailable morality' of seppuku. Recordings make Wagner mobile, exportable, promiscuously ready – especially when attached to images – to extenuate or glorify actions and ideas that have no source in the operas. *Patriotism* is more than politics aestheticized, which was Walter Benjamin's definition of fascism: it is politics eroticized, given an additional perversity by its collusion with music.

# After the War, Before the Revolution

In 1920 Paul Rosenfeld staked an American claim to Wagner. His music, Rosenfeld argued, belonged in a continent that had pristine woods for Siegfried to explore and plutocratic Valhallas fit for occupancy by Wotan and his privileged family. The towers of Manhattan were as arrogant as Wagner's 'commanding blasts, his upsweeping marching violins, his pompous and majestic orchestra', and the bridges that spanned the city's circumambient rivers 'shadowed forth his proud processionals, his resonant gold, his tumultuous syncopations and blazing brass and cymbals and volcanically inundating melody'. The *Ring* matched the country's 'vastness, its madly affluent wealth and multiform power and transcontinental span, its loud, grandiose promise'. Accordingly the production of the tetralogy designed by Lee Simonson for the Metropolitan Opera in 1948 was nicknamed 'the Hudson Valley *Ring*' because its vistas were so local: a torrential river between palisaded cliffs like those on the New Jersey banks, forests of conifers, angular escarpments. Simonson's Valhalla resembled Columbia-Presbyterian Medical Center on Washington Heights, and the rock he designed for the Valkyries was copied from a slab of granite in Fort Tryon Park. In addition, skyscrapers acquired legs on the Met stage. In 1936 the critic Deems Taylor joked that the sopranos who sang Brünnhilde for the company usually presented her as 'a sort of walking Empire State Building'.

This sublime materialism corresponds to the mood of Thea Kronborg when she first hears Wagner's music in Willa Cather's *The Song of the Lark*. She has lived in Chicago for months without acquiring any 'city consciousness': the surging crowds and soaring towers do not thrill her – although, since she is an operatic soprano in the making, she lingers in front of jewellers' windows and covets the tiaras, necklaces and earrings. Finally she attends a symphony concert on a biting April afternoon. The programme begins with Dvořák's *New World* Symphony, which evokes the high plains and flat prairies of her home further west. The orchestral finale of *Das Rheingold* follows, with the gods marching across the rainbow bridge as the Rhinemaidens complain below. All Thea knows is that the opera is 'about the strife between gods and men', but she is stirred by the 'troubled music', its dignity so insidiously undercut by mockery and lamentation. She has stumbled upon her vocation, and when she leaves the concert hall Wagner seems to have set Chicago to music: the gale from Lake Michigan, the infuriated sunset, the 'brutality and power' of the life that gushes through the streets like the Rhine. A young man propositions her, and Wagner has even prepared her for this. She measures herself against the city's aggressive might, as the theory of the sublime requires her to do; she dares the din of the streetcars or of Wagner's brass to batter or drown her. 'She would live for it, work for it, die for it; but she was going to have it, time after time, height after height…. She would have it, what the trumpets were singing!' 'It' is power, symbolized by high notes and by the privileged view from high buildings.

Her decadent colleagues in Europe – the libidinous sopranos described by George Moore, Huneker or Gertrude Atherton – are corrupted by Wagner's music; in the Midwest, Thea is emboldened by it, her ambition sharpened. Before long she sings Woglinde in Germany, profiting from the urban pantheism of that afternoon in Chicago: 'she simply *was* the idea of the Rhine music,' says Gustav Mahler, who conducts the performance. A few years later she appears as Elsa in *Lohengrin* at the Met, and makes the opera's conclusion match her breezy American optimism. Her Elsa does not crumple when Lohengrin departs; as an admirer puts it, Thea 'gives the distinct impression that she was just beginning'. Ahead lie Isolde and Brünnhilde, and these roles, when she undertakes them, absorb all of her tough, hardy experience on the peaks of Colorado and in the canyons of Arizona, among the man-made mountains of Chicago and the jostling mob in its streets. She is to be a collective work of art, like America itself. An old friend donates a spear to the prospective Valkyrie, glad to contribute to the amalgam. It takes a great many people to make one Brünnhilde, he says: Thea contains multitudes.

The wood engraver Lynd Ward heard the same rowdy hubris in Wagner's music. His designs for *The Story of Siegfried*, published in 1931, used the skyscrapers of New York as a scenic backdrop for the *Ring*. Valhalla, its spiky Gothic lantern emitting an electrical sunrise that slices through thunderclouds, might be the Woolworth Building in lower Manhattan; the Valkyries ride up to it on aerodynamic steeds like the winged horses that used to romp above petrol stations. Ward was a Nietzschean whose graphic novels *Gods' Man* and *Now That The Gods Are Dead* dramatized America's heroic assault on an untenanted heaven. His Siegfried raises a sword that is not horizontally aimed at enemies; it jabs the air vertically, like the masts at the pinnacles of the Chrysler or Empire State Buildings. Behind him a jagged radial sunrise announces a new age, with a semicircle of piercing beams like the columns of anti-aircraft lights that formed a colonnade after dark on the Zeppelin field in Nuremberg where the Nazis held their rallies.

For Rosenfeld, Siegfried's flashing sword and Wotan's spear were 'images of grandeur and empire … commanding the planet'. They posed no particular threat: as technological tools, they advertised 'the new body acquired by man' in industrial America. Twenty years later, that fantasy of imperial grandeur could no longer pretend to be innocently unpolitical. On the first day of 1940, from his new home in New York, Auden looked back on the disasters of the previous decade in his poem *New Year Letter*. He accounted for fascism in a psychological allegory: Nietzschean self-assertion had plunged headlong into a morass of negation, worshipping 'The Not, the Never, and the Night', in love with the idea of self-extinction. There was no need to be more explicit about the calamity because:

> The genius of the loud Steam Age,
> Loud WAGNER, put it on the stage.

The 'mental hero' of the day, as for Nordau half a century earlier, is Tristan or Amfortas, both of whom take a 'sensual pleasure' in sickness. The male weakling:

> roars for death or mother,
> Synonymous with one another;
> And Woman, passive as in dreams,
> Redeems, redeems, redeems, redeems.

The reiterated verb is a brilliantly Wagnerian joke, which precisely defines the function of the heroines and the obsessiveness of their motifs. The doubly loud Wagner also deserves his megaphonic capitals: Auden identifies him with the industrial era and the superhuman reserves of power and energy it unleashed, to the detriment of unaided, amplified individuals. But the couplets impose a clipped simplification. Was Hitler a mother's boy, and was he really as death-devoted as Tristan and Amfortas? Like Jewish financiers or artists in the Third Reich, Auden's Wagner is an expiatory beast, made to assume responsibility for the misdeeds of others or for a crisis that was too complex and all-pervasive to be anyone's fault.

In America after the war, Wagner remained the aural shorthand for a morbid violence and perverse fanaticism once confined to addled, self-destructive Europe. Film noir investigated the darkness that the returning soldiers found in the American city, which no longer looked as bright as Rosenfeld's 'vortex of steel and glass and gold'. Soundtracks quoted Wagner, suggesting that he represented a persistent danger. Jules Dassin's *Brute Force*, released in 1947, is set in an American prison as brutish as a Third Reich labour camp. A sadistic warder (Hume Cronyn) picks out a Jewish inmate (Sam Levene) and beats him with a rubber truncheon while the *Tannhäuser* prelude plays on a gramophone in his office. Levene is led in during the pilgrims' music, and the bludgeoning is synchronized with the feverish revelry of the Bacchanale. On his walls Cronyn has a framed reproduction of one of Michelangelo's bound, writhing slaves, along with other Arno Breker-like pin-ups; his decor identifies him as a homegrown Nazi, flourishing even after Germany's defeat. Fritz Lang's *The Blue Gardenia*, released in 1953, balances the music of two hemispheres, which only too recently were theatres of war and are now separate arenas of influence for America. The Blue Gardenia is a Polynesian restaurant in Los Angeles, where Nat King Cole performs the film's sultry theme song. Wagner evokes Europe and its secretive moral ordure. Richard Conte is a journalist who reports from a crime scene where the victim (Raymond Burr) had been listening to a recording of the 'Liebestod' when he was clubbed to death with a poker. A young woman is arrested and found guilty, despite Conte's misgivings; he is prompted to investigate further when he hears the 'Liebestod' again – incredibly enough as Muzak in the Los Angeles airport – before he flies off to witness the detonation of an H-bomb in the Pacific. The killer, he discovers, is the ageing shop assistant who sold Burr the recording; he made her pregnant, and she took up the poker when he spurned her. With the 'Liebestod' still playing, she retreats to the bathroom when the police arrive, smashes a glass and slits her wrists. It is not the act of an Isolde: the 'Liebestod' has become a 'Lustmord', the kind of grubby sex murder that fascinated Weimar Republic artists like George Grosz. But Wagner cannot be dismissed as a memento of the doomed culture in which Lang made his *Nibelungen* films. The chance association between the 'Liebestod' and the flight to Bikini Atoll gives him an ominous contemporary relevance; his music belongs wherever the end of the world is being experimentally tested.

The 'Liebestod' strikes again in *Humoresque*, where by remote control it directs a woman to commit suicide. Jean Negulesco's film, released in 1947, begins with John Garfield brooding on the terrace of his Manhattan penthouse. He is a virtuoso violinist, irritated when his friend Oscar Levant idly picks out the opening of the 'Liebestod' on the grand piano inside the apartment. He tells Levant he should know better: the music, it turns out, has caused the death of Joan Crawford, the rich alcoholic who was his patron and later his mistress. Garfield's concert repertoire includes Dvořák's *Humoresque*, but its poles, as far as the film is concerned, are two elaborate operatic fantasias based on *Carmen* and *Tristan und Isolde*, both composed by Franz Waxman. Here *Carmen* is tainted by Wagner's erotic fatality, rather than offering a healthy cure for it as Nietzsche expected. Garfield is rehearsing the fantasia onstage at Carnegie Hall when Crawford arrives to announce that her husband is willing to divorce her. He ignores her and goes on playing. His instrument has taken over the wily heroine's seductive tunes; the woman is reduced to an excluded looker-on. 'Go back to your music,' snaps Crawford during a later argument, 'I'm tired of playing second fiddle.' She later adds 'I hate music, I detest it!' Wagner, gendering the arts, said that music was a woman; this is why Crawford – emotionally ravenous, drunkenly uncontrolled – represents such a threat to Garfield the careerist. His misogynistic performance of the *Tristan* fantasia keeps music as a male preserve. Isolde's voice is silenced, supplanted by his violin, with some assistance from his best friend's piano. Crawford too is banished: he and Levant play the concert in Manhattan, while she listens on the radio in her beach house on Long Island. Garfield's mother – his moral guardian, who has warned Crawford to stay away – arrives just as the paraphrase of the love duet by the two men is reaching its climax. Her presence confirms the new balance of power, with family values and friendship in control and passion confined to music making. When Garfield and Levant hurl themselves into the 'Liebestod', the maudlin Crawford leaves the house and strides down the beach, buffeted by the wind. At this distance she cannot hear the radio, but she blocks her ears anyway: she has internalized Wagner's score. The 'Liebestod' continues as she wades into the ocean. She is merely obeying what Nietzsche called the 'physiological presupposition' of the music. Older composers expected listeners to dance, but Wagner, according to Nietzsche, wanted them to feel they were walking into the water and losing their footing. 'One must swim,' Nietzsche advised. Otherwise, as in Crawford's case, one might sink. Isolde, if allowed to sing the words that are paraphrased by the violin, asks whether the bystanders can see the metaphysical wonders she is describing – a breeze, foaming billows, breaking waves – which of course they cannot. Her imagery is illustrated as Crawford submerges; the orchestra is muffled, and the film ends with glimpses of drifting seaweed and a trail of bubbles seen from below the surface. The dangerous woman has been literally overwhelmed by the music the two men are producing.

Because Wagner was synonymous with crime, it is no surprise to find a Wagnerian soprano investigating homicide while at work. Helen Traubel, who sang Brünnhilde and Isolde at the Met after Kirsten Flagstad's return to Nazi-occupied Norway in 1941, later branched out into writing detective fiction (as well as singing at the Copacabana and essaying ragtime in a filmed biography of Sigmund Romberg). Her first literary effort was a story called 'The Ptomaine Canary', written with some help from Harold Q. Masur; in 1951 she published *The Metropolitan Opera Murders*. Both start at performances of *Die Walküre*. In the first, the soprano Brunhilde Wagner plans to abduct a group of detective novelists who have been invited to the performance. In the second, another soprano with the drabber name of Elsa Vaughn looks down, as she tells the evening's Siegmund about his imminent death, and sees the prompter doubled up in his hutch at the footlights. He slides out of sight as the act ends, poisoned. At a later matinee of *Tristan* the singer cast as Brangäne is shot through the head in her dressing room between the acts. Another colleague, a former Bayreuth tenor turned blackmailer, is praised for his 'encyclopaedic' knowledge of Wagner but rumoured to be 'a vitriolic, sadistic tyrant': evidence of infection by the music? The stout, sturdy Traubel makes much of the physique necessary for singing Wagner, and suggests that the same heft allows performers to handle the contemporary equivalent of swords and spears. Those who specialize in Italian roles are, by comparison, harmless lightweights. Elsa's ambitious pupil is briefly a suspect, but she lacks the 'physical resources' for 'a regimen of German opera', so her twittery lyric voice exculpates her.

When Elsa finds the dead body of her Brangäne, she makes good use of 'twenty years spent developing her lungs, larynx and diaphragm, fortified by countless Valkyrie war cries', and her screech enters the record books as 'the first time … a dramatic soprano hit an F above high C'. At the end she fends off an attack from the mad tenor, after which Brünnhilde's 'Hojotoho' ricochets through the apartment to announce her survival. This is America: despite the Wagnerian malaise or malediction, that bloodcurdling battle anthem has to sound like a salute to life not a paean to glorious death.

|||||||||||||||||

There were limits to Verdi's humane sympathy, imposed by theatrical decorum of his time. Although Violetta sends alms to the poor, the disadvantaged masses remain offstage, or appear only briefly to beg for food from Melitone in *Forza*. Not until verismo did operatic characters emerge from the lower depths: Sicilian peasants, shivering bohemians, a shabby troupe of travelling players, Californian miners down on their luck. Busoni disapprovingly asked Weill whether he intended to become 'the Verdi of the poor', and in 1932 Ernst Bloch detected traces of 'Jewish-Verdi' in *Die Bürgschaft*, Weill's parable about a cattle dealer and his creditors. Judaism in this context meant humanitarian concern sweetened by sentimental indulgence, as opposed to Wagner's operas which in Weill's opinion 'relinquished any representation of mankind'.

Weill's chosen allegiance was daringly unpatriotic. In 1928 in a Berlin newspaper he recalled playing Wagner to some schoolchildren. There were more notes than his fingers could reach, and no melodies to sing; the children nodded off. In an article the next year he complained again about Wagner's arrogant supermen, his megalomaniac climaxes, and the 'heavy viscous form' of his over-rich operas. He could not get away with such provocations indefinitely. In 1933 his opera *Der Silbersee* – directed by Detlef Sierck, who after emigrating made a career in Hollywood with the anglicized name of Douglas Sirk – opened in Leipzig, Wagner's birthplace. A critic in the *Völkische Beobachter* berated the city's music director for allowing this Jewish and unGerman satire to be performed only 'five days after the fiftieth anniversary of the death of Richard Wagner', which had been commemorated in Hitler's presence. Weill took note of the denunciation and wisely left the country a month later. Restarting his career abroad he relied on Verdi to boost his morale. When *A Kingdom for a Cow* flopped in London in 1935, he told Lotte Lenya that he was reading Verdi's letters as 'a consolation': they exhibited the resilience of a jobbing composer who, unlike Wagner, did not regard rejection as a grievous insult.

In 1937, less than two years after migrating to America, Weill wrote an essay on the future of opera for the periodical *Modern Music* in which he credited Verdi's influence for 'a new peak in popular opera' after the last war. Descending from Valhalla and leaving behind the fatuous tribulations of 'kings, knights and princesses', opera had redefined itself as music theatre, exemplified by Busoni's *Arlecchino*, Stravinsky's *L'Histoire du soldat* and his own *Dreigroschenoper*. It is questionable whether these jaunty, small-scale pieces – a capriccio whose characters resemble vocal marionettes, a folk tale that is spoken, acted and danced but not sung, and a pastoral displaced to the criminal underworld where beggars and pickpockets perform shop-soiled popular melodies – owe anything to Verdi; the argument was a polemical ploy, devised to snub Wagner once again and to blame him for the beefy aesthetics of the Third Reich. Weill used the kind of language best calculated to recommend Verdi in America: he equated capitalism with artistic freedom and declared that Verdi, who wrote for a market and tailored roles to fit the available talent, exemplified 'the healthiest conditions of the theatre'. Weill himself was probably happier than Verdi to accommodate venal impresarios and a fickle public. In Boston in 1943 he told an interviewer that he did not mind all-night sessions making adjustments to his scores before a Broadway opening. Unlike Wagnerian music drama, American musical comedy was 'a custom-made job', and Weill was content to do the practical work of customizing.

Weill died in 1950. Two years later, *Aida* made it to Broadway, and managed to stay there for three months. Charles Friedman, encouraged by the success of Oscar Hammerstein II's musical *Carmen Jones*, translated the opera's sung texts and created a new historical context for them: in his *My Darlin' Aida*, Memphis, Egypt became Memphis, Tennessee in 1861, the year in which the state aligned itself with the Confederacy against the Union. The show's title was the first line of 'Celeste Aida', with an omitted consonant to denote the lazy drawl of the Deep South. Friedman anticipated what many directors now do as a matter of course, transposing Verdi's opera to a time and place he found more relevant to contemporary concerns – although directors today do not bother to rewrite the texts of the works they dislocate. The palace became the Big House, a neoclassical temple beside a malarial swamp, occupied by the plantation landowner General Farrow, Friedman's pharaoh. The priests were the cloaked and hooded Knights of the White Cross, who meet in the cemetery beside what Friedman calls 'the Negro church' to discuss lynching uppity slaves. Radamès was wittily renamed Ray Demarest, a 'monkish' fellow who has spent time away in 'the shrill North' at West Point, and has been corrupted, according to the 'blooded males' of his class, by 'Yankee ideas' about racial equality. Aida remained a slave, though her privileged position in the plantation owner's household was explained by the fact that she had a white father; Friedman's Amonasro – an underground leader called Adam Brown, who leads a slave revolt with guns supplied by Lincoln's army – married her mother and treated her child as his own. There was ingenuity in this, and also an evasive cunning, since Aida's mixed blood and light skin lessen the shock of her affair with Ray Demarest. Sometimes Friedman's translations correspond so closely to Ghislanzoni's original words that they suggest a punning parody. A brash colloquialism trips up the hieratic expostulations of grand opera: the warmongering shout of 'Guerra! Guerra!' becomes 'Get 'em! Get 'em!' The setting for the triumphal scene was the levee beside the Mississippi, with the

Confederate troops returning from their victory at Bull Run in Virginia; instead of glorifying Egypt, Isis and the ruler of the delta, the chorus gloated over the region's economic riches and jeered at the enemy:

> Sing as our legions swing along!
> Sing to the King called Cotton!
> When Lincoln is forgotten
> This new and great
> Confederated State
> Still will be great and strong!

Aida's plight was no longer individual: she represented an oppressed race, sustained by its plaintive religious hope. In the opera she has only the unspecific, unnamed gods to whom she appeals in 'Numi, pietà' to set against Isis, Osiris and Fthà; Friedman touchingly strengthened her faith and enrolled her in a community of believers. He distributed the musical invocations of Verdi's unseen priestess among a chorus of slaves, who prayed around a spirit lamp in the warped wooden church while the white supremacists staged their 'morbid hocus-pocus' in the graveyard. Aida too saved up her frustration for Sunday, when she could sing her heart out in church. In addition Friedman gave a voice to the indoor servants, allowing them to express a disgruntlement not heard in Verdi: they grumbled about the money that 'keeps white folks oiled so good'. He awarded these underlings the last word after Jessica, his Amneris, sang her accustomed request for peace over the bodies of Aida and Ray Demarest, killed by the lynch mob. Then, to replace the final murmured praise of 'Immenso Fthà!' by the unseen priests and priestesses, the blacks who had gathered onstage for the funeral asked a rancorous rhetorical question: 'Why ain't we free?'

As the curtain fell, Friedman's stage direction offered a distantly optimistic answer. The sky, he directed, should be crimson, which means that dawn is near. When the campaign for civil rights got underway in the 1960s, *Aida* made a symbolic contribution to it. The definitive interpreter of the role, Leontyne Price, was a friend of Martin Luther King and Whitney Young; radicalized when the activist Medgar Evers was assassinated by a Ku Klux Klan member in her home state of Mississippi in 1963, she made donations to the cause, sang at benefit concerts, and described Aida as a luminary of what she called 'the black liberation movement'. The part, as she often remarked, was a self-portrait, for which she needed no make-up. Her Aida was a woman of stately dignity, who knelt before Amneris with unservile reluctance; the sound she made when singing about her lost homeland – as velvety as a warm dusk, soulful and grieving yet edged with righteous anger – proudly showed off the beauty of negritude. Price retired from the stage in 1985 with a last *Aida* at the Met, but did not let go of the character. In 1999, adopting the oracular role of narrator, she recorded her own version of the story, interspersed with excerpts from a performance of the opera taped in the 1970s. A spoken prelude imagined Aida's enslavement, picturing the traumatic scene that is buried in the history of all African Americans: as she slips out of her palace to play, Aida is seized by Ethiopian troops who have made a raid across the Nile, bound with ropes and chains, then carried off to Egypt. By starting the narrative earlier than Verdi does, Price exposed an iniquity the opera suppresses and put extra pressure on its reconciliatory conclusion. Her narrative mentions the frantic prayers of Amneris, who begs Isis and Osiris to overturn the sentence of death passed on Radamès. 'The gods,' she adds, 'were silent', and in the sealed vault Aida and Radamès die quietly, their passage out of life eased by Price's shimmering pianissimi. Here was the not entirely convincing answer to the last question asked by Friedman's chorus. *Aida* had undertaken to ease the friction between races in America, with death and melody as the solvents of an intractable social problem.

||||||||||||||||||

In post-war Germany, a clean musical conscience was harder to come by. Rejecting the country and its culture, the composer Hans Werner Henze moved to Italy and nominated Verdi not Wagner as the musical dramatist he most admired. In 1963, when Auden agreed to write the libretto for Henze's opera *The Bassarids*, he imposed a single strict condition: Henze first had to reacquaint himself with the legacy he spurned when he migrated south. Before he composed an opera about the worship of Dionysus – who for Nietzsche was Wagner's alter ego, the god of flaring unreason – he needed to overcome his angry intolerance. Henze obediently attended a performance of *Götterdämmerung* in Vienna, accompanied by Auden's lover and collaborator Chester Kallman to ensure that he did not bolt. Afterwards Henze admitted that the opera was 'extremely well written', but still found its 'imperialist threat' repellent and shuddered when he heard the 'disagreeably heterosexual and Aryan horn calls'. Henze only found Wagner tolerable if he could force the music to do penance. In his orchestral meditation *Tristan*, composed in 1973, the hero's madness is a reaction to the collapse of revolutionary hopes after the arrest and death of Salvador Allende and the funeral of Pablo Neruda. No voice can do justice to this dismayed fury, so it is summed up instead by an instrumental scream that, according to Henze, warps 'Isolde's deathly cry … into a shrill and metallic expression of horror'. A softly harmonizing F sharp is out of the question.

The preferred German option in the decade after 1945 was to detach music from politics. When the Bayreuth Festival was permitted to resume in 1951, Wagner's grandsons Wieland and Wolfgang had the tricky task of de-Nazifying the operas, which they did by banning the national paraphernalia that was compulsory during the Third Reich. The sets for Wieland's first *Ring* were austere and abstract, reduced to a raked disc that matched the curvature of the earth; he dressed Wotan in a vaguely Roman cloak rather than Teutonic armour. Wieland's preferred analogies for the action came from Greek myth, not the sagas: he equated Erda with Gaea, and said that Brünnhilde combined the functions of the truth-telling Pallas Athene and the rebellious Prometheus. His *Meistersinger* in 1956 ignored the regressive mystique of medieval Nuremberg. A projection on the floor sketchily suggested cobbles, but there were no crooked streets leading back into a fanciful past, no gingerbread houses, no rooted ancestral trees, only a pool of purple twilight in which the characters swam. Wieland wanted, he said, to jettison 'German sentimentality' and to stress the work's 'romantic irony' (an even more inimitably German quality, a self-consciousness that acknowledges the untruthfulness of art). He therefore replaced the meadow where the guilds disport themselves with a bank of choir stalls in which the citizens – alienated, like Brechtian characters, from the jingoism of the texts they had to mouth – dutifully sat out the embarrassing scene.

Wieland favoured singers who did not fit the Nordic prototype. His *Tannhäuser* in 1961 set the black Venus of Grace Bumbry, a pagan totem swathed in gold, against the blue-robed meridional Madonna of Victoria de los Angeles, an unstarchy Elisabeth. When Leonie Rysanek took over as Elisabeth, Wieland at first asked her to imitate a Gothic carving. Rysanek replied that she was not Gothic but baroque – restless, aflame with energy and desire, almost making love to the hall of song as she rushed around it. Wieland pretended not to be impressed by the commanding volume of Birgit Nilsson's voice, and told Antoine Goléa that what he valued was the way she overcame the usual discrepancy between Italian lyricism and German declamation. He favoured conductors who made the music speed along, rather than emphasizing its sombre weight. His *Parsifal* was conducted in 1951 by the gravely deliberate Hans Knappertsbusch; in 1965 it passed to Pierre Boulez, who lopped fifty minutes off the running time. Wieland classified Clemens Krauss as a Latin conductor – not grindingly emphatic or prone to orchestral shouts and screams, as he said to Goléa – and he praised Karl Böhm, who took over *Tristan* in 1962 and conducted a new *Ring* in 1965, for bringing a 'Mediterranean clarity of spirit' to the scores. Wieland wanted heat as well as light. He thought that dramatic truth required Isolde to be naked during the love duet, which would have been a sure way of grounding her abstruse metaphysical conversation with Tristan. In practice he had to settle for the leather dress that Nilsson's Isolde wore as a second skin, but in his Frankfurt production of *Otello* in 1965 Wieland had the tenor and soprano sing their duet in the nuptial bed: he could be more daring with Verdi than with his own august ancestor.

By way of compensation, the fascist iconography that Wieland kept out of his *Ring* productions got into *Aida*, which he directed in Berlin in 1960. Böhm conducted, with a cast of Wagnerians – Jess Thomas, Christa Ludwig, Josef Greindl among them – singing in German. The triumph took place at night, torch-lit like the Nuremberg rallies. Wieland cut the scampering festive ballet that introduces the parade of slaves: this brutal ceremony had nothing in common, he said, with the sunny C major of the *Meistersinger* finale. Radamès was loaded with a moral burden that belonged by rights to Siegfried, Germany's avenger: collusion with a foul regime, the need to be punished, a last chance of absolution. Wieland, calling the final scene in the vault 'truly *Tristan*esque', presumed that Radamès was attempting to cleanse a soul dirtied by war; he and Aida died in a glow of supernatural radiance, buoyed up by a 'spiritual passion' incomprehensible to the blatantly carnal, earthbound Amneris. As Wieland remembered it in his interview with Goléa, their last duet takes half an hour, which gives them time to etherealize. In fact they sing for only five short-breathed minutes, since all they can do is hope that unconsciousness will soon overtake them. 'Radamès knows,' Wieland said, 'that his reunion with the one he loves can only happen in death.' Mystical transports came more naturally to Wagner's grandson than the elegiac sympathy of Verdi, and his remark misses the melancholy of the opera's ending, which is a sorry waste of precious life: the one comfort of Radamès is his belief that Aida remains safe and happily ignorant of his fate, so her decision to join him in the tomb is cause for further regret.

Having first insisted on the political neutrality of Wagner's operas, Wieland eventually admitted their relevance to recent German history. After his second *Ring* production in 1965, he described Nibelheim as the first concentration camp, agreed with Goléa's comparison between Mime and Goebbels, and said that the embattled, paranoid Wotan resembled Hitler gone to ground in his bunker. But he understood that the process of updating had to continue beyond the Third Reich: Fafner, he remarked, was 'a prehistoric atom bomb'. Wieland died in 1966, and left others to carry on making reparations for the past. The film-maker Hans-Jürgen Syberberg took up the challenge, in a medium that he saw as the true artwork of the future. In 1975 he coaxed Wieland's mother Winifred, who ran the Bayreuth Festival during the Third Reich, into confessing on camera that if Hitler had walked into the room she would greet him as an old, true friend. In 1978 Syberberg's film about Hitler shows the Führer rising, his arm stiffly raised in a salute, from Wagner's tomb behind Wahnfried; later a puppet dressed as Hitler brags that 'So long as Wagner's music is not forgotten, I will be remembered.' Syberberg once commented that Germans had to be cruel to themselves if they were to watch his films, and in case they were squeamish he was prepared to contribute a little cruelty of his own. He lamented Germany's disowning of its 'creative irrationality' – a tradition that long predates both Wagner and Hitler – and believed that after the war a race of poets, philosophers and musicians settled for a cowardly imitation of its pragmatic, businesslike conquerors. This moral collapse left the country 'without a homeland', impoverished by its affluence. Syberberg planned his film of *Parsifal*, which marked the opera's centenary in 1982, as a cathartic act of recollection. Gurnemanz leads Parsifal into the Grail castle through a narrow time-tunnel hung with frayed and tattered Nazi banners. The journey involves a descent into the crypt: the temple is littered with mouldering remains, and in a cellar Titurel beds down in his coffin with a decayed swan. In this mnemonic basement, Germans are forced to confront a history that consists of unburied bodies or uprisen cadavers.

Their lost homeland turns out to be enclosed inside Wagner's head, or distributed across a calcified landscape formed by his death mask. That magnified mask constitutes the set for *Parsifal*. The white skull splits open to disclose the temple, and Klingsor's garden, like the pool from which Kundry takes water to bathe Parsifal, fits into an indentation on Wagner's pitted face. All Germans, like the opera's characters, are living inside the mind that dreamed them up. But Syberberg's Wagner is himself the creation of his culture, a marionette jerked into action by the collective unconsciousness, and the film has an additional cast of dwarfish Wagner manikins, arranged around the death mask like ornaments on a mantelpiece: Wagner writhing on a cross, parading in a velvet housecoat, hammering the eardrums of auditors, flourishing a whip. Klingsor, who wears a stormtrooper's black leather overcoat, has a collection of waxen heads – Ludwig II, Nietzsche, the bushy-bearded Marx as well as Wagner – scattered around his throne, which means that he not only awakens Kundry from her sleep but rouses these other dormant devils. After this seance, Syberberg quietens the bogeys, perhaps by relying on the German sentimentality that Wieland Wagner detested. Parsifal begins as a naïve but mettlesome young man; kissed by Kundry, he changes to a young woman. The kiss is supposed to be a venereal taint, passing on a forbidden knowledge and enabling him to share the sufferings of others. Here it has a different purpose: it disarms and feminizes Parsifal, changing the warrior into a peacemaker.

At the end of the film, the modulations in Wagner's score are accompanied by a flickery visual association of ideas. When the shrine is opened at Parsifal's request, the death mask once again splits apart. The skull of Titurel, fleshless but still crowned, now dissolves into a miniature model of the Bayreuth theatre, squeezed into a snow globe cupped in Kundry's hands; her hair is the curtain that conceals and defends the illusion. Syberberg compresses Wagner's music and his drama of quest and salvation into this glazed microcosm. Sealed there, deep-frozen by that snowfall, it can no longer spill out into our reality; it was merely the doting reverie of a man who died, as the plastery mask makes clear, a century ago.

This neatly aesthetic solution, reducing *Parsifal* to a fragile plaything, satisfied no one for long, and a later generation continues to hold Wagner accountable. In 2002 in Peter Konwitschny's Hamburg production of *Die Meistersinger*, the rioting mob ripped holes in a Gothic panorama of the city to lay bare a bombed, burned waste behind the backcloth. The Night Watchman had evidently been on patrol during a raid by the RAF, and his warning horn calls failed to prevent the blaze. Sachs sang his monologue about madness while studying an aerial view of the flattened, crumbling debris. He recovered his composure to declaim his concluding sermon about the threat of foreign adulteration and the need to treasure a holy German art – though during his peroration he was interrupted by protests from his more liberal colleagues, who actually called a halt to the performance of the opera. The argument predictably spread to the audience, with hecklers at the premiere calling Konwitschny a stooge of Erich Honecker, East Germany's overseer in the decades before the Berlin Wall fell; the conductor Ingo Metzmacher laid down his baton to listen to a dispute over which he had no control. At last a loudspeaker ordered the musicians back to the prescribed text. But there was no eruption of civic pride in the final bars, and Konwitschny dimmed the lights onstage before the curtain fell, as if pulling the plug on a celebration of which he disapproved.

Such anachronistic commentaries are now almost compulsory in German productions of Wagner. The Berlin production of *Rienzi* by Philipp Stölzl in 2010 placed the overture within quotation marks: this was the music as Hitler might have heard it, wheezing through the horn of an antique gramophone set on a desk in his alpine command post high above Berchtesgaden. As the gramophone played, Rienzi himself conducted; he then delivered a silent, gesticulating harangue to the mountains, demonstrating that the opera was a rehearsal for political action. In Hans Neuenfels's Bayreuth *Lohengrin* in 2010, an animated film of attack dogs on the prowl illustrated the king's tirade against the barbarians, with the leader of the pack collapsing into a heap of bones to disprove the proud patriotic slogan about the German empire. Neuenfels dressed the chorus members as rats because, as he explained, only genitally reprogrammed rodents would be so liable to shout the forbidden word 'Heil!' The Bayreuth production of *Parsifal* by Stefan Herheim in 2008 conducted an inquest on the century since the opera's first performance. The first Grail ceremony sent the Kaiser's troops marching off to war. Following Germany's defeat, Klingsor in the second act presided over the perverse revels of the Weimar Republic, with the flower maidens as flaunting chorines in a Berlin cabaret. Jews with bags packed on the way into exile paused to listen to Kundry's appeal to Parsifal, hoping that he would consent to rescue or redeem them. They waited too long, and were gunned down by stormtroopers. The third act began in a bomb-flattened German city, and described the painful, penitent labour of reconstruction. At last democracy was secured, following the model of the new Bayreuth: the second Grail ritual was introduced by a projected exhortation from Wieland and Wolfgang, who in 1951 described the festival as a place for peaceable debate on their green hill. The temple now changed to Norman Foster's glass-domed Reichstag, where the quarrelling deputies sorted out their differences while the German eagle, still with its talons sharpened, folded its wings over them.

Here, at least in theory, was catharsis for a nation, comparable to Leontyne Price's imagining of Aida's entrapment and transportation: horrors were purgatively re-enacted, and the hours spent in the Bayreuth auditorium counted almost as community service. But can history be revised after the event, or is it only helplessly, obsessively repeated?

|||||||||||||||||||

While Germany demonized Wagner, Italy canonized Verdi. In 1953 a hagiographic film directed by Raffaello Matarazzo presented Verdi – played by Pierre Cressoy – as a man of sorrows, Christ-like in his afflictions and in the lyrical grace that he lavished on the world, yet himself needing to be redeemed by a woman's love.

Matarazzo tightened the chronology of Verdi's early life to intensify his woes. His son dies in the midst of heedless Carnival high jinks during a performance of *Oberto*; his first wife Margherita pines in her sickbed while he attends the disastrous premiere of *Un giorno di regno*, then dies when he returns to tell her a cheery lie about the opera's reception. Gruelling moral tests follow. Verdi is reduced to poverty in an attic, denied credit by cheap restaurants. Strepponi saves him when she persuades him to set the *Nabucco* libretto; it falls from his pocket in his chilly room, and as he kneels to retrieve it he sees that it has providentially flopped open at the scene with the homesick slaves. He remains in his prayerful attitude while the music filters down from above, hummed by a seraphic choir. At the first performance an immediate ovation for 'Va, pensiero' develops into a political demonstration. Students flaunt Italian flags, aristocrats in their boxes join in the acclaim. The Austrian governor suspends the performance and calls for the composer's arrest. Strepponi again comes to the rescue. Still dressed as Abigaille – who was no friend to the downcast Israelites – she leads an encore of the chorus, with the audience, which has already memorized the words, singing along. On the way home, Verdi remembers a lowly benefactor, a chestnut seller who fed him when he was starving and refused to take his scarf as payment. He showers her with coins and wraps her in a new shawl. Having no idea who he is, she takes him for a holy fool.

Soon after Strepponi begins her affair with Verdi, she is visited by his father-in-law Barezzi who, in a non-musical reprise of the scene between Violetta and Germont, shows her a ring his dead daughter Margherita asked him to give to a woman worthy to be Verdi's second wife. He reminds Strepponi of her illegitimate offspring and her inability to have further children, and advises her to leave. When Verdi proposes marriage later that night, she refuses him, pretends that her professed love was mere play-acting, and announces that she is leaving to sing in Paris. The orchestra underlines her sacrifice by quoting Violetta's plea 'Amami, Alfredo'. Strepponi and Verdi meet again in Paris after a performance of *Rigoletto*. Again she is on a mission of mercy, raising funds to repatriate the dying Donizetti. Like Alfredo at Flora's party, Verdi indirectly denounces Strepponi during a conversation with Dumas fils, who recommends the lady of the camellias to him as a possible operatic subject. Verdi says he has no sympathy for 'women of her type'. Donizetti convinces him of his mistake, but before there can be any reconciliation Strepponi disappears again. Verdi finds a copy of the Dumas novel in her lodgings; he composes *Traviata* as a penance while searching throughout Europe for his lost one. She comes out of hiding to attend the opera's first performance in Venice, cowering in the gallery. Barezzi, now repentant like Germont, tracks her down while the soprano onstage sings 'Amami, Alfredo', brings her to Verdi, and presents her with Margherita's ring.

After this, the film reels through an uninterrupted series of successes and concludes with Verdi's consecration. As he dies, a diagonal beam – heaven's follow-spot – is trained on his hotel bed. In a voice-over he dictates his will, remembering that he was born in poverty and resolving to give all his gains back to music. The last image is his statue outside the Casa di Riposo in Milan, with d'Annunzio's tribute 'pianse ed amò per tutti' emblazoned across the screen. He wept and loved for us all: it is an obituary worthy of Christ.

Germans are troubled by Wagner because they feel disgraced by him. Italians are troubled by Verdi for a different reason: they feel unworthy of him. Hence Moravia's claim that Verdi was the last representative of a 'full-blooded, passionate, robust' Italian humanism that developed during the Renaissance, 'the age when man still saw himself as an end'. In 1946 Moravia thought there might be a chance to restore this fearless, godless sense of individual worth by disestablishing the Church and imposing socialism; in 1963, when he wrote his essay about Verdi, he acknowledged his error. Italians now aspired to membership of a conformist bourgeoisie that had never proved itself by beheading a king and was content, despite its lack of religious faith, to lick the boots of the clergy. In tracing Verdi's roots back to the Renaissance, Moravia tendentiously links him to Machiavelli, who had the same earthy acceptance of human appetite. The philandering Duke in *Rigoletto*, he claims, is a direct descendant of Cesare Borgia, Machiavelli's Duke Valentino – although in the 'degraded world' of the opera the 'ravening nobility and tigerish energy' of the politician who was exhorted by Machiavelli to unify Italy has dwindled and turned sensually selfish. Moravia might also have cited Falstaff, a Renaissance man who does his best to upset the bourgeois complacency of Windsor. But evidence is beside the point, because his essay is myth not history, an account of the country's catastrophic fall into modernity. In his novel *Il disprezzo* Moravia makes similar use of Homer as the preserver of a lively, luminous ancestral world that is complicated and distorted by contemporary neurosis. The novel's hero has written the script for a Homeric film whose German director sees the *Odyssey* as 'a dark, visceral recess', not the record of humanity's unashamed, quick-witted infancy. The director's name is Rheingold; when Jean-Luc Godard filmed the novel as *Le Mépris* he cast the owlishly monocled Fritz Lang in the role. For Moravia the Wagnerian vandals were still crossing the Alps, casting a shadow on the brilliant Mediterranean daybreak.

In 1943, when one of the earliest neo-realist films took stock of contemporary Italy – a sordid and avaricious place, grubbily unclassical and nastily unromantic – it almost inevitably began with the performance of a Verdi aria. The film was Luchino Visconti's *Ossessione*, based on *The Postman Always Rings Twice* by the opera-loving James M. Cain. The first sound to be heard, from inside a run-down bar beside a road through a dank marsh, is Germont's 'Di Provenza il mar, il suol' from *Traviata*, evoking the balmy home to which he recalls the errant Alfredo. A gruff voice bawls the melody, accompanied by an untuned piano. There is no immediate explanation: as with the jester's obituary in Bertolucci's *1900*, we are to assume that every modern Italian story is a postscript to Verdi. The singer, it transpires, is the grossly fat, sweaty owner of the bar, who is practising for an amateur contest at a café in Ancona. When the day of the event arrives he yells his way through the aria, arms flapping as he cracks the high notes, and is cheered by the patrons, who reward effort not accomplishment. He gets drunk to celebrate and, flushed with ardour, tells his young wife that it is time for them to have a child, to be called Beniamino in honour of Gigli. She and her young lover are meanwhile making plans to kill him; they do so on the drive home. Even though the aria is delivered so wretchedly by a character who lacks Germont's paternal authority, his earnest approach to it grants him a certain delicacy and nobility, or at least shows that he fancies possessing those qualities, just as the contestant who follows him – a gauche, pitiably ugly young man, who nasally mewls 'La donna è mobile' – probably dreams of himself as an irresistible seducer. Better this than listening to sugary popular songs on the radio, as the murderous wife does. The fact that these ill-favoured people sing elevates them, and it hardly matters that they have no talent.

Here Verdi's music is a forlorn summons to higher things; in Visconti's *Senso*, released in 1954, it is a call to arms that goes unheeded. The film is based on a story by Camillo Boito, Arrigo's brother, about an unhappily married Venetian aristocrat and her shaming infatuation with an Austrian officer during the occupation in 1866. As adapted by Visconti, it begins with its own sardonic version of the uprising at the premiere of *Nabucco* in Matarazzo's biographical film. The occasion is a performance of *Trovatore* at La Fenice, when during Manrico's aria about the pyre the patriots in the gallery bait the Austrian soldiers lounging in the stalls. Popular myth assumes that performances like this helped to provoke popular revolt: Cavour memorized the text of 'Di quella pira' and repeated it to himself when Austria attacked Italy. Visconti, however, dismisses the notion that the Risorgimento was a spontaneous overflow of demotic feeling, stimulated by Verdi's music. The Italians in *Senso* are dilettanti, and the true music-lovers belong to the occupying army. While the wife of the Austrian general noisily applauds, the bored Livia (Alida Valli) yawns that she has no interest in *Trovatore*. She stops listening when the fourth act begins, and instead flirts with the snakily attractive Franz Mahler (Farley Granger). From now on, the film's plot and that of the opera diverge. Verdi's Leonora sacrifices herself to rescue Manrico; Livia behaves less generously. She gives herself to Mahler, then denounces him to the army as a deserter when he replaces her with a younger mistress. Livia ironically tells the truth when she says 'I like opera, but not offstage': her conduct is weak, treacherous, even vile, and passion is no excuse, as it might be in opera.

Visconti personally made the odd decision to call the rakish gallant in Boito's story Mahler, and then – after relying on 'Di quella pira' to stir up mayhem at La Fenice – chose Bruckner's Seventh Symphony to dramatize Livia's disastrous moral choices. Having alluded to Gustav Mahler and excerpted snippets of Bruckner, why did he not make use of Wagner? A quotation from *Tristan* might have vindicated Livia, but this was an opera that Visconti treated with caution or with outright contempt, because he saw sex as a moral threat not a means of transcendence. In his film about Ludwig II, an orchestral version of the 'Liebestod' underscores the scene at Neuschwanstein when the manic king refuses to see the Austrian princess Sissi: disgusted by the prospect of marriage, he holds out against the music's insinuations. In *La caduta degli dei* – Visconti's account of the twilight of the gods, who in this case are members of an industrial clan enriched by the Third Reich – a drunken Nazi thug warbles an off-key 'Liebestod' at a male orgy, shortly before being slaughtered in bed with the young recruit he has commandeered for sex. The symphony Visconti selected for *Senso* is implicitly Wagnerian, and four Wagner tubas utter a baleful premonition of the Meister's death, which occurred while Bruckner was at work on the piece. But despite Bruckner's reverence for Wagner, he too resisted the erotic sedition of the music: his Eighth Symphony briefly recalls the cushioned, throbbing introduction to the love duet from *Tristan*, then moves aside into a slow, stately meditation that could not be less sensuous.

Rather than being voiced by a straining tenor as in the scene from *Trovatore*, the bursts of Bruckner in *Senso* are the interventions of an unseen, wordless narrator. They tally consequences, both personally and nationally, and portray Livia's lapse as a fable about the infirmity of a class and a culture. Franz is not elated when the Austrians win the battle at Custoza, lengthily documented in the film. He tells Livia that the outcome of the war is irrelevant, since they both belong to a world that has been condemned by history. After Custoza, Strepponi wrote to a friend saying that she and Verdi were in a black mood. Then a fortnight later the Prussian army trounced the Austrians at Sadowa in Bohemia. This was the battle for which d'Annunzio said that Wagner deserved to take credit, and it inadvertently contributed to the Risorgimento: Italy gained its freedom as a by-product of skirmishes beyond its borders and the diplomatic finagling of mightier powers. The disgrace of Custoza, along with the defeat at Adowa in

Ethiopia in 1896, still rankled with Mussolini, who said that Italy needed to prove its mettle by bloodily committing itself to a new war. The opening-out of Boito's story in *Senso* was calculated to remind the country of an abiding shame.

In Visconti's *Il gattopardo*, released in 1963, Verdi is co-opted by the elegantly futile ruling class. The leopard is a Sicilian prince who remains disengaged from Garibaldi's march across the island and retreats with his clan to a house in the mountains. He sees the plebiscite about unification as a tactical concession: like Livia's husband in *Senso*, he conserves inherited privileges by cannily adapting to a new order. For the ball with which the film ends, Visconti had Burt Lancaster dressed to resemble a portrait of Verdi painted in 1886 by Giovanni Boldini, whose subjects – dandies, grandees and their floridly overdressed spouses – belonged to a high society that Verdi had no ambition to join. The portrait misrepresents Verdi by making him look improbably dapper, with his shiny opera hat and his nonchalantly looped white scarf, but Boldini's image suits the impassive prince, who while walking home from the ball does not flinch when he hears distant shots as some rebels are executed. Livia at least breaks down when Mahler faces the firing squad. For the prince, an operatic display of emotion would be bad manners, and politically inadvisable as well.

At the ball, the characters dance in inconclusive circles to the sound of a forgettable waltz by Verdi, composed originally for piano and here crudely orchestrated: music is reduced to following the tergiversations of a listless leisure class. As Garibaldi advanced through Palermo in 1860, bands in the streets saluted him with excerpts from *Vêpres siciliennes*. When the prince and his family reach their refuge in the mountains, they are welcomed with some less apposite snatches of Verdi. As they parade down the main street, the local musicians treat them to a lumpish digest of the gambling scene from *Traviata*, an opera safely lacking political significance – although the song of the dancing gypsies might be a comment on these dishevelled, migratory aristocrats. When they troop into the church to express feigned gratitude for their arrival, the organ puffs out Violetta's 'Amami, Alfredo', with the band's account of the gypsy dance from Flora's party still audible outside. They sit in the pews with the dust from their journey still on them, looking like the calcified citizens of Pompeii. Suddenly 'Amami, Alfredo' – played by an organist who is an unregenerate royalist, no friend of the unifiers – sounds like the plea of a doomed class, not the outburst of a single, insecure woman.

Moravia clung to Verdi as a lost leader who might still be used to prod the enemies of the bourgeoisie into action; he can equally well be held up as a bulwark against modernity. Franco Zeffirelli planned his *Falstaff* at the Met in 1964 as a privileged glimpse of merry England, or of a merry, undemocratized

Italy – 'a rough-hewn world, of country folk in home-made clothes, everything wood, wool, sacking and stone', with a ban on the metallic sheen of contemporary decoration; in its many versions Zeffirelli's *Traviata* always fondly evoked what he called 'the flamboyant fin de siècle', lit by gas chandeliers. Although the films of Bertolucci acknowledge that Verdi's death meant a breach with the past, he knows that the operas cannot restore an imaginary paradise. Bertolucci's *Strategia del ragno*, made for television in 1970, asks whether the recent history of Italy is merely an operatic front, with politicians gesturing and posturing to cover up more squalid compromises. The spider's stratagem of the title is a plot uncovered by a young man who returns to the town near Parma where his father, an anti-fascist agitator, was shot in 1936 during a performance of *Rigoletto*. The investigation of the past happens under Verdi's auspices: as young Athos walks into town down a street named after his father, the soundtrack quotes the orchestral introduction to Odabella's ruminative aria in the second act of *Attila* – a tragic lullaby in which she scrutinizes the clouds for traces of her own dead father's visage; the tag recurs throughout the film in moments of grieving retrospection. Athos discovers that the victim and his radical cronies were originally to be the assassins. Hearing that Mussolini would be visiting the town for the opening of their opera house, they planned to shoot him during the 'Maledizione'. But the Duce changed his plans, and the older Athos – who had betrayed the plot to the fascists – agreed to be killed in his place. His death made him 'a hero people can love', a benign collective parent like Verdi, but he is a false god who betrayed his colleagues; the film wonders whether Verdi too might not be a useful stooge, legitimizing lies about the history of the nineteenth century. One of the conspirators, whose avocation is curing and tasting salami, tells young Athos that the plot against Mussolini was never more than an attempt to play at politics: he and his colleagues enjoyed skulking in the shadows and muttering like the malcontents in *Ernani* or *Ballo in maschera*. Is opera a national glory or proof that Italians, stylish but infinitely ironic, take nothing seriously?

Bertolucci's *Prima della rivoluzione* accuses Verdi of being a substitute for a promised but indefinitely delayed revolution that did not occur during the Risorgimento or during the struggle against Mussolini or during the student protests of the 1960s. The film's hero Fabrizio, named after Stendhal's protagonist in *La Chartreuse de Parme*, talks about political engagement and the possibility of a better world, then settles for a bourgeois marriage and a subscription to the opera. At the end of the film there is a jolting cut from a communist festival in a Parma park at the end of summer to the performance of Verdi's *Macbeth* that opens the city's opera season after Christmas. With its flags and its choral anthems, the opera adopts the same theatrical methods as the outdoor festival, but makes different political use of them. Surveying the theatre, the camera passes across the empty royal box: although *Macbeth* is about regicide, this society maintains a hierarchical order by treating attendance at the opera as if it were a ceremony enacted at court. There are no glimpses of what happens onstage, because the performance is merely an excuse for Parma's wealthier citizens to get their fur coats out of mothballs. Verdi's music is heard but not seen, spliced together with images on which it comments sarcastically. The opening chorus of witches, for instance, accompanies a scene in which a coven of frumpy crones is greeted by hand-kissing municipal dignitaries in the marble lobby of the Teatro Regio. Fabrizio – as indifferent as Livia during *Trovatore* – watches *Macbeth* from a box with his fiancée's family, then dodges downstairs to sever relations with an edgy, emotionally dangerous lover who happens to be his aunt. She walks him back to the box, delivering him to his chosen future of respectability. On the way she says that she hates Verdi, because he is everything she and her contemporaries are not. She means, she explains, that he is optimistic, convinced that life is worthwhile; she prefers Mozart, whom she assumes is an eighteenth-century cynic.

In 1979 in *La luna* Bertolucci at last allows Verdi to contribute more than noises off. The thin, nervy Jill Clayburgh is cast – not very plausibly – as an operatic soprano called Caterina Silveri, whose husband dies as she is about to leave New York for engagements in Italy; in his place she takes along her troublesome teenage son. Between her performances in *Trovatore* and *Ballo* and his heroin-befuddled wanderings through the Roman slums, they indulge in a groping sexual intimacy that ends when she hands him over to his true father, a schoolteacher who still lives with his own mother. They also take a gratuitous side trip to Parma, with an unscheduled stop at Sant'Agata where – since the owners of the estate would not allow Bertolucci's crew onto the premises – Caterina rhapsodizes about Verdi outside the main gate, which she treats as if it were a velvet curtain before which she is taking a bow. In a film about the problems of parentage and the difficulty of separating sexual from familial love, she tellingly describes Verdi as 'like a father to me'; unimpressed, her son remains in the car. After quarrelling on the journey, she and the boy are reconciled at a roadside inn. The owner is the gnarled, hobbling salami-taster from *Strategia del ragno*, who takes them to a private room where the last of their exploratory sessions in bed occurs. In the earlier film he sings 'Eri tu' from *Ballo*, an aria about the choice of a sacrificial victim. This time, leading the way to a chamber of shamefully private revelation, he croaks 'Condotta ell'era in ceppi' from *Trovatore*, the narrative in which Azucena describes her mother being dragged to the pyre: like a spirit-guide, he introduces a scene of maternal perversity, though the secret in this case is not infanticide but wishful incest.

During Caterina's performance in *Trovatore*, Bertolucci's camera unpicks the theatrical illusion, with glimpses of the prompter, the supplementary conductor who beats time for Manrico as he performs his serenade in the wings, and the stagehands who operate the rollers covered with plastic flaps that pretend to be a cascading waterfall. Her *Ballo* is outdoors at the Baths of Caracalla, where during a rehearsal in brutal daylight the chorus shuffles and blunders through the masked ball. Caterina's singing is meant to rise above this makeshift chaos, just as the myth of Verdi supersedes the operas. As Leonora, she sings her opening aria behind a gauze on which the stars and a moon have been painted; vocalizing, she ascends into the sky and, thanks to some unseen hydraulics, is installed among the constellations. She concludes the scene holding the hands of Manrico and Luna, who ought to be fighting a duel over her. It makes no dramatic sense, but for Bertolucci what matters is to present the Verdian soprano as a harmonizer and pacifier, like the cool, white moon. The film ends with the finale of *Ballo*. Caterina's mask is a white veil, a shroud that covers her entire head. Depersonalized by it, she sings Amelia's last lines of benediction while reaching out to the audience, folding her son and his father into a crowded embrace; her extended arm goes further, as if she wants to grab the swollen, full-bodied moon that predictably hovers overhead. Woman, as Auden said about the Wagnerian soprano, is our designated redeemer.

In Bertolucci's other films Verdi functions as a political oracle. Here he is a psychoanalyst or a father confessor, listening to the secrets of characters he might have created. 'Tutte le feste al tempio' from *Rigoletto* – Gilda's confessional reverie about a dangerous attraction to a handsome young man – plays on the soundtrack when Caterina wanders fretfully through her apartment in Rome, trying to understand her son's addiction. The sick, faltering prelude to the last act of *Traviata* follows when she tucks him, doped, into bed. On the wall of the unkempt, rackety room Caterina has a portrait of her honorary father, blown up from a nineteenth-century magazine illustration. Verdi sits in his tidier home, a score open on his knees. He does not blink when Caterina and the boy – who needs a fix and punctures his arm with a fork because he has no syringe – throw the furniture at each other; he is equally unsurprised when she cradles her son and lets him nuzzle her breast while her open hand caresses his crotch. Verdi is an all-seeing, all-accepting god, unconditional in his love, forewarned by his operas about the perversities and crimes of passion that his descendants and dependants will one day commit in his name.

# Notes on the Redefinition of Culture

The modernists declared theoretical war on classical culture: Marinetti and Cocteau disparaged the opera house and claimed to prefer the fair, the circus or the cabaret. Before long, actual hostilities broke out between high and low, polite and popular. In *A Night at the Opera*, released in 1935, the Marx Brothers run amok during a performance of *Il trovatore*, shredding the scenery, dousing the lights, and kidnapping the tenor as he sings an aria. Groucho Marx mocks the illusion from the box he shares with the humourlessly regal matron whose cheques pay for the opera season. When the bedraggled, gap-toothed Azucena begins her psychotic recitation, he asks 'How'd you like to feel the way she looks?' It is a good question: why has a sanctimoniously formal audience assembled to witness the ravings of a madwoman they would avoid on the street?

While Groucho remains outside the proscenium as a critic, Chico and Harpo take part in the action, or do their best to derail it. Their campaign of disruption starts in the pit during the brief orchestral prelude. Harpo challenges the conductor to a duel with violin bows, then slips the sheet music for 'Take Me Out to the Ball Game' between the pages of Verdi's score. When the orchestral players gallop into the song, he and Chico play catch and Groucho sells bags of peanuts to the affronted toffs: opera after all is a sport as well as an art, a contest for vocal athletes. When the curtain rises, Harpo and Chico smuggle themselves onstage. Harpo, dressed as a gypsy woman, mimics Azucena's voodoo shuddering. An apache dance, not imagined by Verdi, suddenly interrupts the scene – though the battle between the pimp with the whip and the scantily clad harlot he punishes also fits the opera's atmosphere of sexual aggression and accusation – and gives the eternally lecherous Chico a chance to help the woman out of her skirt. For once the anvil chorus is truly violent, with the brothers using frying pans to administer synchronized blows to the heads of their pursuers. The desecration is not so very different from the flagrant acting-out of *Tristan und Isolde* at the alfresco concert in *L'Age d'or*.

The ropes that control the canvas flats of painted scenery serve Harpo as a trapeze. Riding up and down, he changes the location of the action: the gypsy camp flies upwards and is replaced by a street in a modern American city, with tramcars and the parked carts of vendors – an alienation effect that looks sideways at the drab, dingy reality outside the theatre. At one point, while Manrico and Azucena are trying to concentrate on their duet, the canvas that rolls down from above displays the deck of a gunboat. Watching in horror from the wings, the impresario gasps 'A battleship in *Trovatore!*' But why not? Robert Carsen's production in 2007 on the lake at Bregenz set the opera on an offshore oil-drilling platform, with flares from the rig's chimneys scorching the night sky as if the characters were releasing their own combustible energies through those vents.

Thanks to their manic vitality, the Marx Brothers polish off *Trovatore* in about twenty minutes, which is even speedier than Marinetti's forty-minute *Parsifal* in the London music hall. It helps that they elide most of the last act, ending after the 'Miserere' scene. The crooner Allan Jones is rushed on as a substitute when the tenor goes missing, and he insists that his girlfriend, the simpering Kitty Carlisle, should sing Leonora. No one seems to have told them that Manrico is awaiting execution, and that Leonora is grieving with him as the monks sing their dirge. They treat the piece as a chirpy love duet, and – with Manrico somehow sprung from his prison in the tower – deliver a beaming encore while holding hands, awarding Verdi's most blackly pessimistic opera a happy ending.

In a newly affluent society, leisure had to be filled up with industrially manufactured spectacle; Hollywood had a use for opera singers as novelty items, practitioners of an art that seemed, if you made no attempt to understand it, amusing because absurd. In *The Big Broadcast of 1938* Kirsten Flagstad performs Brünnhilde's battle cry from *Die Walküre* in a nightclub on an Art Deco ocean liner. Bob Hope is the wisecracking master of ceremonies, and the acts with which Flagstad shares the bill include the loud-mouthed comedian Martha Raye, some Mexican guitarists, and a ballet troupe that whirls and stomps through a history of dance from the waltz to the cakewalk. Smiling placidly as she waves her spear, Flagstad is no more bizarre than any of her colleagues. Originally she was placed astride a headless rocking horse, with stagehands jogging her as she mimed to a playback; she was assured that the horse would later be given a head by the magic of cinematic superimposition. Then she was transferred to a crag among storm-battered tree trunks, although there was no explanation of who the Valkyrie is, or what her crazed spasm of hallooing means.

In the 1948 musical *Luxury Liner*, Flagstad's regular partner Lauritz Melchior – taking, as he put it, 'a vacation from Valhalla' at a time when his voice was weakening and his girth expanding – performs an extract from the Nile scene of *Aida*. Although he too is on board ship, sailing between engagements in New York and Rio de Janeiro, the floating theatre manages to produce a sphinx and a backdrop of pimply pyramids. Squeezed into a spangled gym slip, Melchior as Radamès is dressed for the beach not the desert, with a helmet like a bathing cap fitted with black flaps to conceal his white hair. His duet with Aida comes to a premature halt when she and Radamès agree to escape to happiness; cadential closure in the orchestra and satisfied applause from the audience signal that once again there is no need for a tragic conclusion. Radamès may be spared dishonour, but Melchior had to be disempowered, brought bumping down to earth. In this post-operatic career he aspired, as he said, to be 'an old girls' Sinatra', and in that capacity he performs Siegmund's aria about spring to an elderly cleaner as she dusts his cabin. Since they are both comfortably superannuated, erotic fervour is out of the question. Nor is there any hint of the sappy ferment swelling throughout nature as Wagner's orchestra disseminates the melody: Melchior chastely accompanies himself on a piano. The irrepressibly pert Jane Powell tries to impress Melchior by asking Xavier Cugat whether his nightclub band can accompany her in something from *Tristan, Tannhäuser* or *Lohengrin*. Cugat – who beats time while cupping a pet chihuahua in his spare hand – unsurprisingly shakes his head, so she makes do with a South American song about a peanut vendor. Melchior later gives an irate, unlyrical performance of Lohengrin's farewell to his swan, but only to shout down an obstreperous Russian soprano who is shrilling through a coloratura tantrum in Italian. Popular culture insisted on populism, which meant that opera singers had to consent to self-parody.

This forced democratization cast nasty aspersions on a highfalutin, snobbish art. Hollywood identified culture with crime: Nazis were tagged with quotations from Wagner, while gangsters were supposed to favour the meaty, bleeding passions of Italian verismo. Al Capone attends a performance of *I pagliacci* in Brian de Palma's *The Untouchables*, and in the third part of *The Godfather* the Corleone clan decamps to Sicily to see and vengefully conduct business during a performance of *Cavalleria rusticana*. In Billy Wilder's *Some Like It Hot*, George Raft plays a Chicago hoodlum whose musical tastes match his profession. A cop accosts him at a Mafia rally held in the name of the Friends of Italian Opera and asks where he was during the St Valentine's Day Massacre, which he masterminded. He has an answer ready: 'I was at *Rigoletto*.' The oafishly unmusical policeman wants to know Rigoletto's first name and his address, which makes Raft sneer. His thicker-witted henchman repeats the boss's alibi as best he can: he assumes Raft is referring to an Italian restaurant or perhaps a speakeasy, and says 'I was wit' you at Rigoletto's!' It is a legitimate error, perhaps a clever deduction. *Rigoletto* is obscure, socially marginal, appealing only to those with refined and specialized tastes; a joint or dive like Rigoletto's would cater to grosser, greasier, more popular cravings.

Opera first relied on courts, then on a high society that paid for culture and granted access only to those with the proper clothes and connections. In the twentieth century the finicky gradations of class gave way to a less discriminating mass, and culture sought a lower common denominator. Unless it drastically reforms, opera risks relegation to the museum, which is why Hans Neuenfels, directing *Aida* in Frankfurt in 1981, gave it back to the Egyptologists whose scholarly researches contributed to the libretto. Radamès became a doting archaeologist fetishistically infatuated by a statuette in a museum, Aida a drudge who cleaned the Cairo gallery of antiquities after hours. The king in this production was half-mummified – like *Aida* itself according to Neuenfels – in a constricting shroud. For the triumphal scene, Neuenfels shifted the location to an opera house with rows of red velvet boxes like La Scala, in which an onstage audience of impassive grandees watched a military parade that spoofed the goose-stepping marches and automaton-like salutes of the Third Reich. Popular culture expels opera from the theatre and challenges it to survive in our untuned outdoor reality. Now the Ride of the Valkyries thunders from a formation of American helicopters bombing a Vietnamese village, and 'Amami, Alfredo', also screechingly amplified, can be blasted through the open top of a limousine cruising the kerb in a seedy area of Los Angeles. In Francis Ford Coppola's *Apocalypse Now*, Wagner is reclassified as 'psy war ops', terrorizing the Vietcong and making them run for their lives. In Garry Marshall's *Pretty Woman*, Verdi softens the hearts of a ruthless entrepreneur and a business-like prostitute and encourages both to overcome their clenched, grasping emotional inhibitions. Hollywood of course adheres to the customary division between the two composers: Wagner is a terrorist, Verdi a therapist.

From flying horses to motorized birds is a logical evolutionary leap, and *Apocalypse Now* honours the mission of the Valkyries by having the mad Colonel Kilgore paint the slogan DEATH FROM ABOVE on the nose of his fire-breathing chopper. Despite his name, Kilgore is less ghoulish than Wotan: he has no interest in scooping up corpses and whirling them away to be retrained as robotic security guards, and his gunners, who squat on their helmets to protect their testicles, surely did not know that the warriors in the opera are women. The Valkyrie voices enter as the helicopters swoop low over the surf to strafe the Vietcong huts; then the music fades, silenced by explosions, the threshing of the rotor blades, the shrieks of victims, and the seething of napalm which ignites the jungle in a demonstration of Loge's magic fire. Warfare has taken over from music drama as the total work of art, simultaneously stupefying all the senses.

*Pretty Woman*, in which the central episode is a surprise trip to a performance of *La traviata*, seems at first to have humbled or even dirtied Verdi. Julia Roberts plays Vivian, a street-corner hooker on Hollywood Boulevard. The remains of a crack-addicted colleague are hauled from the garbage as the film begins; Vivian keeps her fees in a watertight package in her toilet cistern. AIDS replaces the breathy, high-strung consumption from which Violetta suffers, but Vivian has sanitary scruples: clients are asked to choose from a range of coloured condoms. Her Alfredo, Edward Lewis (Richard Gere), lacks the dewy naivety of his prototype in the opera, and is therefore less likely to be cruelly disillusioned. He is visiting Los Angeles to take over a shipbuilding company that he intends to dismember for quick profit. He and Vivian are better matched than Alfredo and Violetta: as he says, they both screw people for money, and they share a strict rule about separating sex from affection, let alone love. 'I do everything,' says Vivian during negotiations, 'but I don't kiss on the mouth.' 'Neither do I,' snaps Edward. He hires her to accompany him to a business dinner at a fancy restaurant and a schmoozing polo match, first sending her to buy a new wardrobe on Rodeo Drive. For him, the association begins as a social experiment: as long as she is expensively dressed, no one is likely to question her morals, and the success of the imposture will justify the cynicism of his corporate piracy.

Then comes the detour to the opera. Edward takes Vivian to San Francisco for the evening in a private jet. Although she has never heard of *Traviata*, she recognizes Violetta as a sister, sniffles through the performance, and at the end tells a hoity-toity woman in an adjacent box that she was so moved she almost peed her pants. The gaffe proves her to be a good, guileless child of nature. Later that night, back in the hotel in Beverly Hills, she gratefully kisses Edward on the prohibited spot and when she believes he is safely asleep she murmurs 'I love you.' He too returns from the operatic outing reformed. He decides not to undercut the shipbuilding firm and instead donates his own money to refloat the business. Vivian trudges back to her sleazy hotel when her term of employment ends, but Edward soon follows to rescue her, broadcasting 'Amami, Alfredo' from the stereo in his limousine. A mad black sage who passes by remarks – accurately but a little defensively – that it's a Hollywood fantasy: you are encouraged to daydream but dispensed from believing in the blissful outcome.

Verdi is harder-headed, and in *Traviata* second thoughts fail to avert tragedy. To qualify as a romantic comedy for distribution to the malls and metroplexes, the opera would need to end early in the second scene, before Germont arrives to disrupt the idyll. Instead the happy couple in their rural hideaway might perhaps be visited by Grenvil, Violetta's doctor, who could announce the discovery of a cure for consumption.

|||||||||||||||||||

Classics do not establish themselves automatically; it helps if there is an empire with cultural products to sell. After reading Gibbon, Wagner remarked that Rome had inadvertently spread Christianity, which 'held the disintegrating empire together', and he took this as a model for the dissemination of his own work: in 1870 he complacently announced that 'the whole German empire is only created to aid me in attaining my object'. Cosima thought it significant that the *Ring* 'coincided with Germany's victories', and Liszt too praised Wagner for 'extending the empire and the territorial rights of music' – a menacing image, even though all he meant was that the system of motifs had given music the capacity to articulate and combine ideas. But although Marx pejoratively described Wagner as the musician of the Prussian empire, Bismarck snubbed him, and the composer's empire depended on the activities of musical devotees: Angelo Neumann staged the *Ring* in Leipzig in 1878–79 and then took it on tour to half a dozen European countries and to Russia. Defending Strepponi against the censorious elders of Busseto, Verdi pointed out that it was he who had made the insignificant town famous throughout the world. But he did so without the assistance of political promoters; he deplored Italy's exploits in Africa, and did not expect the empire to make a civilizing gift of his works to the peoples it subjected. *Aida*, commissioned by the Khedive Ismail, might have been a craven symptom of Egypt's secession from Ottoman culture as it edged closer to Europe, and it is sometimes presented that way. In Nicolas Joël's Zurich production in 2006 Amneris perambulated in a bustle like Queen Victoria, a fan her only concession to the tropics, and in the temple of Isis grave-robbing archaeologists in pith helmets watched as the golden eye of Fthà was hauled up on a pulley for appraisal; a battleship with cannons poking from its metal flanks stood guard as national treasures were expropriated. This may be what was happening in the background, but Verdi cannot be numbered among the colonizing oppressors. He refused to travel to Cairo for the premiere of the opera, and reacted scornfully when he heard that the critic Filippo Filippi would be attending: he chose to ignore the event rather than make it an occasion for self-important swaggering.

Taking charge at Bayreuth, Cosima imposed standards of correctness that were strictly German, and rejected any proposal to detach the *Ring* from the country that for her was the source of its power. She contemptuously likened the abstract stage designs of Adolphe Appia to sketches sent back from an expedition to the North Pole, and was offended in 1905 when Edward Gordon Craig told her that the music evoked mental pictures of 'the wild pampas of South America' or a prairie fire in the American West. Inevitably she failed to confine the operas to their home base, or to the primeval past. The *Ring*, as Shaw pointed out in 1898, 'really demanded modern costumes, tall hats for Tarnhelms, factories for Nibelheims, villas for Valhallas'. He was equally adamant that *Il trovatore* must never be removed from its mock-medieval setting: Azucena had to be dressed in 'sequins and Zodiacal signs' and Luna had to wear a violet velvet tunic so stiff that he could not sit down, otherwise they risked being mistaken for specimens of 'common humanity'. Transpositions that would be ruinous in Verdi were mandatory in Wagner: the epic, as Shaw understood, was an allegory for the political economy of the present day and the moral compromises that held it together.

In his centenary *Ring* at Bayreuth in 1976 Patrice Chéreau finally did as Shaw suggested, appointing the Rhinemaidens as guardians of a hydroelectric dam and supplying Siegfried's forge with a steam hammer. Brünnhilde became 'une pétroleuse aristocratique' – not the sublimely self-destructive figure admired by the decadents but an upper-class arsonist, a colleague of the proletarian women who hurled bottles filled with petroleum or paraffin into cellar windows during the Paris Commune in 1871. Kasper Bech Holten's production of the *Ring* in Copenhagen in 2006 presented the tetralogy as a synopsis of the twentieth century, with each instalment set at a different time of crisis – *Das Rheingold* in the ideologically fractious 1930s, *Die Walküre* in the paranoid Cold War, *Siegfried* in the revolutionary year of 1968, and *Götterdämmerung* in the 1990s, with Hagen and his vassals as paramilitary thugs from Bosnia. Graham Vick concluded his *Ring* in Lisbon in 2009 by intimating that our world is more likely to be incinerated by hate than washed clean by love. At the beginning of Vick's *Götterdämmerung* the Norns, rather than checking on the security of the rope that anchors us to the past, industriously stuffed nondescript bundles into backpacks. The purpose of their chore became clear during the immolation scene, when a long line of scruffy students filed on, collected the backpacks, strapped them to their shoulders, then clambered up the walls of the theatre and swung their legs over the ledges of the tiered boxes. They pushed aside the audience members who sat there, made their exit through the back door, clattered along the corridors, scurried downstairs, then presumably wandered out into the unsuspecting city: the Norns had been training and equipping an army of suicide bombers, each of whom carried an explosive apocalypse on his or her back. Meanwhile, as the orchestra melodiously blathered about redemption, two spangled ballroom dancers rotated on and performed a waltz that warned us not to be deceived by the consoling music.

During Cosima's period in control at Bayreuth, the Munich critic Artur Seidl praised the festival as 'a stronghold of Germano-idealistic culture', which resisted 'Americanism or commercialism of art in every form'. Nowadays the empire that transmits culture around the world is American and unashamedly commercial, concerned with novelty and rapid turnover not with honouring and protecting a tradition or upholding ideals that were, in the case of Bayreuth, always spurious. Opera directors who harness this lumbering juggernaut with its freight of images do so to attack the empire and frustrate its plan to make the whole world a homogenized province of the United States. On the lake at Bregenz in 2009, Vick twisted *Aida* into a denunciation of George W. Bush's foreign policy. The Ethiopian prisoners wore the same costumes as internees at Guantanamo Bay, and slaves were led on leashes with their heads in bags as if they were performing in the punitive charades acted out at Abu Ghraib prison in Iraq. Aida, belonging to an underclass of economic migrants, scrubbed the floor for her abusive employers. Fragments of a blue Statue of Liberty were winched out of the water and reassembled for the triumphal scene: the embarrassing ideal of freedom had been drowned, and was only trotted out for purposes of show. At Bregenz in 2007, Robert Carsen pressed *Trovatore* to expose the greed that drives American belligerence. The opera took place on an oil-drilling platform that might have been a small state, an emirate with its own triangular fascistic flag and an armed garrison that drilled by torchlight. On an upper ledge, plutocrats and their trophy wives drank cocktails. Down below, gypsy guerrillas wriggled out of rusty pipes to congregate among dented drums on the greasy mudflats next to the fenced-off rig; armed with carbines, they briefly recaptured the citadel of black gold from the foreigners. More crassly, David Pountney's production of *La forza del destino* in Vienna in 2008 made Preziosilla a whorish Las Vegas cowgirl wrapped in Old Glory, and gave her a bomb to detonate at the end of her 'Rataplan'. It was a convenient way of blocking thought about the problems that the opera actually raises – the possibility of a just war to repel invaders, and the psychological attraction of supporting the right cause for the wrong reasons if, like Alvaro, you go into battle with the aim of throwing your life away. Verdi has been used, thanks to some even more elastic distortions, to show a wounded America being castigated for its misdeeds. At Erfurt in 2008 Johann Kresnik set *Ballo in maschera* in the concrete rubble of the World Trade Center, with a chorus of casualties crawling through the dust. 'Except for the music, this is no longer Verdi,' Kresnik proudly declared. The designs for *Attila* at the Metropolitan Opera in 2010 also invoked recent events. The Huns camped in an unEuropean jungle – 'a forest we have known', as the architects Herzog and de Meuron put it, 'from movies like *Apocalypse Now*' – although Attila emerged from among the rubbery thickets to stand astride a palimpsest of twisted girders and pulverized stone that again resembled the ruins at Ground Zero.

After making war and stealing oil, what the America depicted in these productions leaves behind is a glossy, trashy dream of affluence, which beguiled Eboli in the *Don Carlos* directed by Peter Konwitschny in Vienna in 2004. A detour was necessary to make the point: to give the princess time to fantasize about life in the suburbs, Konwitschny included the long ballet Verdi had to compose for the Opéra, which is usually cut – though this was a ballet without dancing. The henpecked Carlos trudged home from the office with his briefcase to find that Eboli, now his wife, had invited her in-laws to dinner. Philippe and Elisabeth, like everyone else in this phoney paradise, bravely pretended to be happy and relied on alcohol to keep their optimism topped up. The evening capsized into tipsy farce, with sprayed champagne from a shaken bottle, clouds of pepper that caused sneezes, and black smoke billowing out of the kitchen from the burnt food. After this mishap, Carlos ordered in an emergency supply of pizza, which was delivered by the depoliticized Rodrigue, here a slacker wearing a back-to-front baseball cap and a jacket advertising Posa's Pizzas – the emblem of an America dressed in copycat urban gear and glutted on fast food. In the *Rigoletto* directed by Doris Dörrie in Munich in 2005, this popular culture dehumanized the world. The jester, rightly startled, found himself in disoriented exile on a planet of the apes. The court at Mantua was a zoo of primates, as subhuman as Alberich's serfs in *Rheingold*, although these furry throwbacks were not economic victims: according to Dörrie, the apes represented the bestiality of a society that rewards celebrities for behaving hoggishly on reality TV, and during one of their parties they ransacked an opera house.

Katharina Wagner's *Meistersinger* in Bayreuth in 2007 concluded during just such a meretricious television talent show, with the competition between Beckmesser and Walther redefined as the clash between the avant-garde and populism. The malapropisms and sour notes in Beckmesser's garbled version of

Walther's song made it difficult and challenging, not inane; it offended the studio audience because it seemed, as Daniel Auber said of Wagner, not to be music at all. As he sang, Beckmesser busily restaged the creation of Adam and Eve, digging a naked man out of a tray of red earth and extracting one of his ribs to fashion a woman. This little pantomime – a justification of art, bravely upholding the metaphysical daring of our attempt to mimic the creator – was ingenious but messy, with much hurling of wet clay and a geyser of gore when the rib was extracted. The audience onstage responded with an ugly chorus of booing, and Beckmesser, marked as a degenerate like the artists who antagonized the Third Reich, sidled off into exile. Walther then strolled on to deliver a crowd-pleasing performance of his shamefully popular melody, while confecting a kitschy, flowery Eden around him on the stage – evidence of art's tendency to tell lucrative, emollient lies. Of course he won the prize and departed with the sponsor's cheque. Although Katharina Wagner was unfashionably defending the citadel of high culture, some incidental byplay with props hinted at her doubts about the venerable past and her own inheritance. During the convocation of the Mastersingers, the table around which they sat was laid with shaky piles of literary classics published by Rowohlt Verlag. The assembled worthies – who might have been publishing executives discussing which texts they will declare to be canonical – used the yellow paperbacks as part of their ritual greeting, kissing the little books and passing them from hand to hand. In a corner, the menial David toiled away duplicating one of the volumes on an office photocopier. So this is what the idea of the classic has come to mean: a boringly prescriptive text forced on long-suffering students. *Die Meistersinger* could be a prime example, which is why it had to be so wrenchingly reinterpreted.

Hero worship is out of fashion or politically suspect, and in our forgetful world ancestors are not automatically entitled to reverence. With boisterous familiarity, Katharina Wagner played tricks on her great-grandfather's effigy. A plaster bust of Richard Wagner stood on an upper gallery in the fusty museum that replaced the church in her production. During the street riot he descended from his plinth and – with the aid of an actor who had Wagner's head on his shoulders – performed a skittish little dance; at last he could escape from the rigor mortis to which the classics are condemned. A larger Wagner, with the Meister's floppy beret balanced on the papier-mâché head of a carnival monster, returned for the procession to the meadow, cavorting and squabbling with Nietzsche, Schiller and other German worthies. Under a velvet housecoat, he was naked except for a diaper – a reminder that ancestors are likely to be incontinent, dribbling and leaking as they totter through a second childhood. But this Wagner also showed off a pronged phallus like those worn by performers in Greek satyr plays, and used it to admonish the invisible conductor in the covered pit: even in senescence, he remained obscenely potent.

||||||||||||||||||

Culture no longer consists of 'the best that has been thought and said in the world', which is how Matthew Arnold restrictively defined it in 1869. To be truly popular, it must indiscriminately comprehend everything that is thought, said, seen, heard, eaten or worn in a world that is defined as a teeming bazaar. In this emporium Verdi and Wagner are mainly valued because they supply marketing tools: the memorability of popular tunes or the repetition of motifs encourages automatic responses, making the listener a consumer whose appetites can be triggered by musical cues.

In 1952 Theodor Adorno accused Wagner of opening the way towards a corrupt economy in which sales depend on the stimulation of fantasy. Although the *Ring* denounces capitalism, Adorno thought that Wagner's 'technicization of the work of art' made opera a machine for manufacturing desires. His phantasmagoric tableaux – the Venusberg, the burning hall, the mobile forest – parade the wonders of technology like sideshows at an industrial exhibition or 'wares on display' in the decorated window of a department store. The cravings he arouses can never be satisfied, but that dissatisfaction sustains the economic system: Adorno likened his chromatic tension to an inexhaustible line of credit, 'the negation of the negation', which reassures us that 'the full settlement of debt' will be 'indefinitely postponed'. Wagner could get away with this mental deception because his music, like a film score, relies on the lazy receptivity of the ear, which in Adorno's theory 'lags behind technology' and refuses to keep up with the effortfulness of 'the advanced-industrial era'. This is the aperture through which society indoctrinates us: Adorno startlingly describes the slogan Wotan utters as he raises his spear at the end of *Die Walküre* as an advertising jingle. The god issues a challenge, declaring the fire to be impassable; his words, according to Adorno, 'could easily be supplemented by copy in praise of a piece of equipment that would enable the cautious but resolute buyer to pass through the fire notwithstanding'. Since Proust said that Wagner's workshop was Vulcan's forge, how about imagining a suit of vulcanized fireproof rubber instead of armour?

Wagner's motifs, as Adorno aptly said, are 'allegorical': musical notes personify a sword-wielding hero or a spear-brandishing god, or represent a block of metal or a potion. When the orchestra wordlessly repeats the phrase, we obediently spell out the verbal formula that deciphers the motto, whether it is Lohengrin's ban on questions or Sieglinde's praise of fulfilment and fertility. Nowadays the allegorists are the writers of advertising copy, who erase Wagner's words and give the music a new and more lucrative significance. The Ride of the Valkyries can always whip us into a state of keen expectancy; it has therefore been used in television commercials to sell commodities of every kind, from Citroen cars to Finish detergent and Pampers diapers. The connection with automobiles is obvious enough, but it takes more ingenuity to hear a pitch for washing powder and nappies in the lashing, flicking musical phrases. Do dishwashers flush out gore and grime like the Valkyries when they repair the corpses of the heroes they gather up? Are infant bowel movements as unstoppable as the wind on which Wagner's equestrians ride? The music consents to illustrate any new plot to which it is attached. In a television advertisement for British Gas, busy engineers in blue vans – the colour of a chirpy pilot light – soar through the stratosphere to the sound of Wagner's cavalcade, on their way to reactivate boilers that have broken down in the houses of earthlings.

For a while British Airways adopted 'Va, pensiero' as its corporate theme: there is no need to pine for a lost home when you can pay to be flown there, almost at the speed of thought. The chorus that once helped a nation to cohere here ventured to do the same on a global scale, pooling emotion so as to lubricate commerce. On American television 'La donna è mobile' sings the praises of Dr Oettker's pizza, and in Europe the hymn to the Virgin and her attendant angels from *La forza del destino*, rustically rescored for a harmonica, underscores commercials for Stella Artois lager. The 'Dies Irae' from Verdi's *Requiem* recently accompanied a baffling scenario in which jerky dummies in a grey industrial dystopia found a secret entrance to a crypt where they did gym workouts, got their bodies waxed and exfoliated, conditioned their hair, and refreshed or revved up their engines with low-carb beer and genuine espresso. They then bounded home, tearing off their drab clothes as they ran. One of them broke ranks and rushed upstairs naked to unwrap a new pair of jeans. A slogan advised 'Uncomplicate your life'; the way to do so, apparently, was to buy the latest Levi 501s. Any purchase might make the world seem brighter for a while, but why did the campaign invoke Verdi's day of wrath with its hurricane of despair? Perhaps because the urge to physical self-betterment has replaced the desire for religious salvation, as we seek bodily perfection not the soul's extraction from the flesh. The advertisement sought to terrorize us into buying jeans, and Verdi's crashing drums and howling voices threaten us with perdition if we do not tone up and slim down to be worthy of them.

D'Annunzio described Verdi as a dietary necessity like bread, and bakers were quick to offer a particle of the composer for sale. Cafés in Parma still recommend a brand of biscuit that Verdi allegedly dipped in his morning coffee, and at Christmas sell quantities of the chocolate panettone that Ricordi sent to him while he was working on *Otello*. The museum of curios at Wahnfried contains a piece of so-called Grail bread scavenged from a local restaurant, along with a cake that softly sculpts Wagner's ruthless profile. We consume music, so why not make composers edible? Listening to Verdi and Wagner, we are absorbing them, celebrating an alimentary communion that pervades the body and, as Tristan says about the potion, penetrates the brain. Their motive may be profit, but the advertisers still place their trust in the charm of music – Verdi's emotional advocacy, Wagner's irresistible enchantment.

# ACTS OF REMEMBRANCE

As long as their works are looked at or listened to or performed or read, artists can do without monuments. Politicians and generals, whose contribution to the world is their deeds, need statues to prolong their power and maintain their presence in the public realm. What artists look like matters less, since we know something about how it feels to be inside their minds and can hold an intimate communion with them in a book-lined room, or a room where the fourth wall is removed to let us look into an alternative world. Even so, certain artists deserve a place outdoors, on public display in crowded squares or in a garden like the one in Venice. They may be there for the wrong reasons, since those who make decisions about monuments usually commemorate artists only if they embody or embellish national pride. But to stumble across the busts in the Giardini Pubblici makes you pause, remember the value of art, and think about individuals who have augmented our lives or helped us to feel more intensely alive. An unforthcoming, dourly withdrawn man like Verdi found within himself melodies corresponding to emotional states that were probably no part of his own experience. A more defiantly or deviously unconventional man like Wagner, often called monstrous, knew how to entice our erotic instincts and our high-pitched, deep-diving spirits out of the silence in which they hide. Music in the one case makes us aware of our humanity and of the emotions – love, hate and jealousy, happiness and grief, the fear of death – that we share with our fellows, and in the other gives a voice to the tides and firestorms and whirlwinds inside us and to our longing for release from our aching, overstretched bodies.

Genius is not easy to portray; the imagination is invisible, and creativity looks like any other manual labour. Wagner, however, dressed for the role of artist. Preparing to be photographed by Franz Hanfstaengl in Munich in 1871, he wore his customary beret and a housecoat with the quilted cuffs rolled up to show off puffy shirtsleeves; a jewelled pin fastened his silk cravat, and for another photograph from the same session he draped a shaggy pelt across his chest. Deduct the accoutrements and he could be mistaken for a hard-faced businessman, with chilling eyes and a tight, ungenerous mouth. The fancy dress at best succeeded in presenting him as an actor, given to self-transformation. For Verdi, dressing up was a kind of self-negation, one of the many kinds of camouflage on which his temperament relied. Evening clothes are a uniform, which make you indistinguishable from all the other men who wear them, and Francesco Barzaghi's marble statue of Verdi in the foyer of La Scala – the homage of the citizens of Milan, according to the inscription on its base – defines him as a member of a class, not an individual. The worthies who subscribed to pay for the tribute in 1880 wanted to see him as one of them, the first among equals. As in Boldini's top-hatted portrait, Verdi here is elegant yet disarmingly casual, with a coat slung over his arm and a sheaf of music paper rolled up in one hand. Marble ingeniously catches the texture of his combed beard and the crinkling of his sleeves and trousers, as if apologizing for the statue's stiff, posed formality, but no sculptor could ever do justice to the wariness of his eyes or to their seasoned amusement and kindness in the last photographs taken of him in 1899 and 1900.

The truest memorials of Verdi catch him off duty, his posture conveying clues to his character. In Busseto, in the square between the Teatro Verdi and Barezzi's house, he sits in a chair atop a pedestal, offending against the upright protocol of statuary. As sculpted by Luigi Secchi, he leans backwards, placing his weight on his right elbow, his left arm reaching forward. The swivelling pose saves the figure from stiffness; it also matches the position the elderly Verdi adopted when lounging in a garden chair at Sant'Agata in photographs taken in 1898. Although he straightens his back for the camera, his right shoulder pulls his body away from it and retracts his arm in an attitude that signals diffidence, retreat. The native son ensconced in Busseto looks as if he has no particular ambition to be immortal. His left hand fiddles nervously, despite the sculptor's efforts to settle and eternalize it, and he gazes off to one side almost absent-mindedly rather than staring confidently into the future. Without the chair, Verdi assumes a very similar attitude while sitting on a clump of rock on a monument in Piazza San Giovanni in Trieste. Alessandro Laforêt's sculpture was set up in 1906, on the fifth anniversary of Verdi's death; the promoters moved fast because they were using his image as a symbol of their campaign to reclaim the city from Austria. The marble figure was damaged by loyalists in 1915, then recast in bronze and ceremonially restored to its place in 1926. By that time Trieste had been handed back to Italy, with Verdi as an honorary broker of the annexation. Yet he seems to disavow the agitation that swirled around the base of his monument, and he twists even further backwards to his right than he does in Busseto, firmly planting his feet at an oblique angle and again looking over the faces of any crowd that might gather to demonstrate in his name. Wrapped in a longer, bulkier overcoat than the garment he wears in Busseto, with his knees covered, he remains stubbornly sedentary, a reluctant hero. As he said when elected a deputy, he had no talent for public speaking; oratory he left to Otello and Simon Boccanegra. Nor did he like being placed on public view.

To mark his centenary in 1913, a statue by Enrico Butti was installed outside the Casa di Riposo in Milan. Around the pedestal, an honour guard of his characters summarizes humanity's tribulations on the way from birth to death. Butti specialized in effigies of slumped grief for the patrician tombs in the Milanese cemetery where Verdi and Strepponi were at first interred, so the mournful anthology of operatic scenes suited him. But the man on the pedestal does not share the sombre mood. This time he stands rather than being seated, with his head cocked to admire the building that he called the finest of his works, and his hands are clasped beneath the bunched-up tail of his coat. It is a gesture that is temporary or even momentary, and it again upsets the decorous equilibrium of statuary, whose subjects – according to classical theory – ought to adopt a posture that can be maintained indefinitely. Verdi appears this way, holding the small of his back to steady and straighten himself, when photographed with Boito in Ricordi's garden in 1892. Butti ignored the aching weariness of the stance in the photograph, and made Verdi younger and more vigorous than he was when he supervised the building of the rest home. With the lapels of his jacket pulled back by his clasped hands and his hair brushed away from his forehead, he looks almost windswept. Though marooned on a traffic island, he might be patrolling his fields at home.

In the year of the centenary, work began in Parma on Italy's grandest homage to Verdi, on the site of the ancient Foro Boario in the forecourt of the railway station; it was not completed until 1920. The architect Lamberto Cusani designed a triumphal arch with a goddess restraining the team of lions that drew her chariot as she raised a glorifying torch. On either side of this gateway, a colonnade of smaller arches bent in a semicircle, with niches between them to house twenty-eight of Verdi's characters. The composer appeared in bronze in front of this arcade, seated brooding on a block of granite designed by the sculptor Ettore Ximenes. On the rear Ximenes carved a trilogy of political tableaux, with scenes from the Lombard League and the Sicilian Vespers, those supposed rehearsals for the Risorgimento, and a third panel shows Verdi being presented to Vittorio Emanuele in Parma. The commission, according to the official guide to Parma's celebrations of the centenary, called for a heroic image. Ximenes was required to portray Verdi as 'artista, creatore, ideatore, sacerdote': artist, creator, thinker and priest – the roles that Wagner customarily played. Since bourgeois clothes were banned, along with the umbrella or newspaper that Verdi carries in photographs, Ximenes wrapped him in a classical cloak like a bed sheet, leaving his shoulder and one of his feet bare. He is surrounded not by the worldly operatic characters who stood in the arcade but by figures like those on the sgraffito above the front door of Wahnfried: nymph-like personifications of poetry and dance, a grief-stricken symbol of tragedy, and a crowd that is a representative sample of the clamorous Italian soul. A laurel wreath – too large for a crown, almost a supplementary arch – is held above his head by two of the winged angelic flunkeys from the frieze behind him. Verdi's hands are clenched, and although he holds no pen he frowns to announce that he is, as expected, making art, creating, thinking and preaching. Rather than settling into his chair with his weight on his right elbow as at Busseto, he leans forward and uses his left elbow, placed on his knee, as a fulcrum. The commanding position is uncharacteristic, but the reason for it, and for his hangdog expression, is clear. Verdi is trying, despite being made of bronze, to wriggle away from two importunate female admirers, like the muses who pressed favours and funds on Wagner. A woman playing a mandolin nestles on one of Verdi's shoulders, while another, naked to the waist, leans her head on his arm with a besotted rapture that he tries to ignore. To be the object of their adoration embarrasses him. The role of national hero is evidently onerous; it is an advantage to be dead.

The arch and the colonnade were damaged by bombs in the 1940s and later demolished. All that remains of Parma's encyclopaedic tribute is the granite ledge and its frieze, which has been shunted away from the station to a vacant space on a lawn behind the Palazzo della Pilotta. No sign explains that it is a memorial to Verdi; African trinket-sellers crowd around it during the day, and play concerts of ethnic music after dark.

Wagner's posthumous rank was a foregone conclusion, and in 1913 his bust was installed in Valhalla, the neoclassical temple near Regensburg where Germany's cultural gods are enshrined, along with an assortment of field marshals, statesmen and merchants, plus one saint and a single victim of the Nazis. By then he had a monument all to himself in the new German capital. The memorial in Berlin's Tiergarten was an assertion of imperial pomp, underpinned by industrial prosperity: funds were provided by a manufacturer of cosmetics called Leichner, who advertised his devotion to Wagner by making his car horn squeeze out Donner's thundery motif from *Das Rheingold*. In 1901 Kaiser Wilhelm II personally sketched a design for the honorific block. On the base Wolfram von Eschenbach, with his lyre slung over his shoulder, salutes Wagner, who is not so much seated as enthroned, with one hand cupping his chin to support it as he contemplates Germany. Wolfram, clearly not at the song contest in the Wartburg, wears full armour and has his shield lying beside him; his vizored helmet might have looked odd in conjunction with Wagner's beret, so the Kaiser's scribble changed that notoriously effete bonnet into one of Napoleon's two-cornered military hats. In the event, the sculptor Gustav Eberlein avoided disagreements about dress by leaving Wagner bareheaded. One of his hands opens to pluck sounds from the air while the other rests on the head of a lion that is actually part of his carved chair. In Parma, the heraldic animals drawing the chariot of the goddess kept well away from Verdi himself; Wagner, however, has lordship over wild beasts. The broody Verdi in Parma is unlike the man himself, who never struck such Rodinesque, intellectually constipated poses. But Wagner, to whose 'sufferings and greatness' Thomas Mann paid tribute, enjoyed playing the heroic role. In 1876 the Berlin satirical journal *Ulk* published a caricature of him as Wotan, his spear reduced to a jester's wand, which is Rigoletto's implement. The wings of eagles sprout from his beret and, at his feet, jackals prepare to devour the stringy corpses delivered by the Valkyries. Apart from his headgear, this comical pretender is not so very different from the imperious effigy set up in earnest in the Tiergarten.

Debussy, writing about the Berlin memorial before its inauguration in 1903, remarked that Wagner had done little for Germany, which was now claiming him as the most illustrious of its offspring. He was right: during Wagner's lifetime, his efforts to orchestrate nationhood were unappreciated, and after his death his admirers concentrated on the swooning sensual allure of his music rather than the political project it supposedly served. Verdi, on the contrary, undoubtedly did much for Italy, which is why the entrepreneur Carlo Barsotti agitated for a monument to him in New York. Barsotti was an immigrant who founded a daily paper and a bank for Italian Americans; after these commercial achievements he planned a series of statues that aimed to raise the standing of his countrymen, who as Beniamino Gigli petulantly said 'were considered – in North America, for example – inferior even to the Chinese'. As a result of Barsotti's efforts, Columbus climbed onto a column in Columbus Circle while his fellow navigator Verrazano surveyed the harbour from a lookout in Battery

Park. A place was found for Garibaldi in Washington Square and another for Dante, sculpted by Ximenes, on Broadway at 64th Street. Verdi's statue, carved by Pasquale Civiletti, was allocated to a square – actually a triangle – that was later named after him on Broadway at 73rd Street. The inauguration took place on Columbus Day in 1906, when one of Barsotti's grandchildren jerked a cord to release a balloon that pulled back a veil coloured like the Italian flag. More than Columbus or Dante, Verdi stood to gain from Barsotti's promotional zeal. Snooty opera-goers in New York considered his music, according to Marcia Davenport, to be 'old hurdy-gurdy stuff' suited to the ethnic ghettos of the Lower East Side, so his appearance on the Upper West Side counted as a promotion. Appropriately enough, Civiletti dressed Verdi for the street. With his overcoat casually draped across his left arm, he seems ready to merge with the toilers who, as Algernon St John-Brenon commented in *Musical Quarterly* in 1916, trudged past him every day as they commuted 'from that part of the town that is consecrated to homes, to that which is devoted to struggle'. Unlike Eberlein's Wagner, Civiletti's Verdi does not abstractedly appeal to the high heavens. Nearer to the ground, his aim is to cheer the city's footsore workers as they trudge through their daily lives.

Characters outlive their creators, so Wagner in Berlin and Verdi in Parma or New York are accompanied by their dramatic progeny, who gather like offspring around a parent's deathbed. Wolfram dominates the pedestal in the Tiergarten, his diagonal arm saluting Wagner; he has removed the chain mail he wears in the Kaiser's sketch, so that the composer looks less like his commanding general. Around the corner Tannhaüser in his pilgrim's robes crawls along the ground towards absolution. To give priority to this opera emphasized Wagner's credentials as a starchy moralist (though that involved eliminating the Venusberg and forgetting that Elisabeth heretically assumes the role of redeemer). *Tristan* and *Parsifal* – respectively too sensual and spiritual for Hohenzollern tastes – were excluded from the memorial, but Brünnhilde is seen cradling the dead body of Siegfried, which is something she fails to do in *Götterdämmerung*, and on the back of the pedestal, like a shameful secret placed out of sight, a frog-faced Alberich is teased by the Rhinemaidens. In revenge he grasps the hoard of crowns and sceptres he has crafted from the stolen gold, gripping the jewel-encrusted ring between his fingers: an almost scurrilous admission – startling in this official setting – that power depends on money and property is theft. Nothing so indecorous occurred among the characters arranged along the arcade in Parma, although they were an eclectic lot. Arrigo, the high-minded patriot from *La battaglia di Legnano*, certainly deserved a place here, as did Attila, who had a horned Wagnerian helmet and a sword strapped at his groin like an emblem of potency, but it must have been odd to find Falstaff in their company. The few surviving designs for the sculpted figures – a dejected Rigoletto, a wasted Violetta shivering in her nightgown – are unheroic enough to cast doubt on the exultancy of the goddess above the arch. These are people as fallible as the rest of us, not saviours or fiends like Wagner's creations. On Broadway, Verdi stands on a column looking down on four of his characters, three of whom are transformed into civic worthies: Falstaff looks prosperously plump not grossly obese, Otello is an invincible warrior not a jealous murderer, and Aida in a ballgown does not remotely resemble a slave. Only the harassed Leonora from *La forza del destino* bears any resemblance to the actual character, but with little of the guilty misery that drives her to seek refuge in religion. St John-Brenon remarked on the 'stern commonplace' of the clothes worn by Civiletti's Verdi, and his characters too, like the New Yorkers who walk briskly past or pause on park benches without noticing them, belong to the swarming family of man, with its hectic joys and inescapable woes.

Wagner claimed to embody 'the German spirit'. The boast was put to the test during the Third Reich in proposals for a monument in Leipzig, the birthplace he quit with so little regret. Karl Ernst Lange's design placed him in a roofless temple; Wagner lay on his back staring upwards, his arms outstretched in a cosmic embrace like that of the curving colonnade in Parma. A pen in his right hand replaced the bunched fist of the figure in the Tiergarten, because Lange wanted to display 'Der Meister in der Inspiration'. Above and behind the prone Wagner, silhouetted against a sky of storm clouds in Lange's sketch, Siegfried waved his sword – a doughtier implement, perhaps, than the pen? The circular shape of the temple symbolized endlessness, as a wedding ring is supposed to do, although the armed characters standing as sentinels along the top of the curved wall were a reminder that force necessarily backs up faith. Wagner was to be positioned near the inside wall, visible through the doorways that pierced the temple. The centre of the ring was a void or vacancy, described in Lange's proposal as a symbol of that annihilating mystery to which Wagner, like many other German metaphysicians, was so attracted: it represented 'das Geheimnis selbst; der Ort … der Ur-bedanke … der Nichts'. The idea of a monument to nothingness did not please the Nazis, and the proposal that found favour was by Emil Hipp instead. Hitler laid the foundation stone in 1934, but the scheme remained incomplete and was smashed up by the marble works after the war. It was a devotional space, square not circular. Art Deco giantesses gambolled and writhed in a Parthenon frieze of operatic episodes, with special attention given to scenes of killing: Parsifal, naked and muscled like a Greek athlete, shooting down the swan, or Hagen stabbing Siegfried in the back. At one end of this paved garden of remembrance, a fountain recalled the source of the Rhine and the bubbling provenance of myth. Balancing it at the other end was a heavy rectangular monolith, an abstract equivalent of Wagner's might and his looming presence in the Third Reich. Lange's design had a conceptual hollow at its heart; Hipp's awarded pride of place to a slab of marble cut from the innards of the Untersberg, the mountain Hitler gazed at from his aquiline lair near Salzburg. Is Wagner an emptiness filled up by our fantasies, or a weight you can be crushed beneath?

While he was alive, Wagner's flesh seemed to be aspiring to the condition of stone. When Eliza Wille met him in Dresden in 1843, she said that his jutting chin looked chiselled or carved. Boito, not to be outdone by German hero-worshippers, likened Verdi to a 'bronze colossus', but the image referred to his achievements not to the man himself. Only on his deathbed, during the days after his stroke, did he settle into statuesque implacability. Keeping watch in the Milan hotel room, Boito noted that the paralysed Verdi had come to resemble the bust carved by Vincenzo Gemito in 1872. His head was bowed towards his chest as he lay in the bed, and he frowned, Boito said, as if weighing up his 'formidable adversary'. The expression was a reminder of his self-containment or inscrutability: the lowered chin and averted gaze of Gemito's bust caught Verdi thinking, and showed that it was possible to illustrate creativity without making the artist hold a pen or a sheaf of papers. As it happened, on the evening before Wagner's death Joukowsky sketched him as he sat reading. In the rapid, candid drawing he seems moribund, his hair wispy, his eyelids drooping shut, his face deeply creased, smudged by shadows that might suggest bruises or signs of decay. Wagner was turning back into vulnerable flesh as Joukowsky watched, whereas Boito imagined that Verdi's flesh had hardened into durable metal. Although Gemito later cast the bust in bronze, the original – on view at Sant'Agata – was in terracotta, which gives it an earthy veracity. Its unglazed texture is rough, rude, as Verdi defensively pretended to be. The streaks of white that dart across his furrowed brow like veins or thoughts are seams that derive from the baked soil; beneath this craggy head, the bust reverts at the shoulders to an almost muddy amorphousness, as if returning this rare individual to undifferentiated, malleable nature. It defines Verdi as a man of clay, composed of imperfections like the characters whose entreaties he might be listening to as he stares down at the floor.

The corresponding image of Wagner is a bronze head by Arno Breker, the sculptor favoured by the Nazis, in a garden below the Festspielhaus in Bayreuth. Wagner's forehead here is wrinkled, not serenely smooth like the faces of classical statues, his skin scratched and abraded by the anguish of intellection, a creative labour that demands more than the self-concentrated detachment of Gemito's Verdi. The head is ten times life-size, removed from the expendable body and poised on a marble base. Wagner boasted that 'I am celebrated for my exceptional cranium', and observers wondered how his meagre frame and stumpy legs could sustain its weight. Édouard Schuré admired his 'vast brow', which Frederick Praeger called 'Jupiter-like'. In Werfel's novel, however, Verdi expresses a different opinion of that dome of bone: when he sees Wagner at close range on the moonlit Grand Canal, he likens his head to 'the pallid and monstrous skull of a gnome'. When Boito praised Verdi's 'spherical' genius, he pretended not to understand the compliment and treated it as a reference to his Falstaffian paunch. Of course it was a comment on his universality and his egalitarian distribution of music to crusaders and cowards, termagants and virgins. Verdi released into the world a troop of characters like those on the Parma colonnade, who might have poured out of the spherical belly he joked about. Wagner's people, being aspects of himself, fought their battles inside the global mind sculpted by Breker. Seen in profile, with its hooked nose and set jaw, the head is a battering ram. Looked at from the front, it is terrifying. The eyes are ghoulish cavities, the pursed slit of a mouth leaves no vent for the cry that Wagner heard resounding throughout nature. At least the plastery death-mask in Syberberg's *Parsifal* is porous, allowing entry to the interior: every orifice is a doorway for the characters who burrow into it like worms, and the hollowed-out eyes are a wet pit, used as a baptismal font when Kundry is christened. Breker's bust allows no such penetration, and forbids any presumptuous communing with the hero. But if you stand behind it, forgetting about the blankly unempathetic eye sockets and the tight-lipped mouth, you can only marvel at what Syberberg called a 'Kopftempel', a templed head that was large enough to incubate a world.

Festival-goers at Bayreuth, clutching their drinks and their tickets, like to photograph each other standing under Wagner's bust before the trumpeters order them indoors with some bars from the opera of the day. They always look uncomfortable beneath the shelf of that bludgeoning chin. It is impossible to imagine Verdi performing such an obeisance, or expecting it from anyone else. He would have preferred to wander through the park that straggles down the hill and sit pensively on a bench beside the pond, wondering whether there were fish in it.

||||||||||||||||||

Perhaps it is wrong to expect the statues in the Giardini Pubblici to exchange glances: Verdi and Wagner were, like all true artists, unique.

When Wagner died, Strepponi shook her head about his great – meaning excessive – individuality. The conservative senator in Werfel's novel also bemoans the depravity of modern times, when genius is equated with madness, originality with egotism, and Wagner is promoted at the expense of Verdi. They are destined to be in competition or at war with each other; Werfel could not allow them to coexist. But Wagner believed that the divine plan called for the multiplication of existences and the ever-increasing refinement of individuality. Why, he once asked, did the stars separate? Surely it was because 'God loved to individualize.' Nature preferred duplication: looking at one of his daughters, Wagner unpaternally said 'What is individuality? Nothing – one sees that when one looks at such a child's face, and a whole species answers'. Art, surpassing nature, had the same aims as God, and did not balk at producing warped specimens, quirky variants, beings so idiosyncratic that we call them monsters. Reflecting on folk tales, Wagner speculated that 'the urge to individualize figures caused people to depict gods and creatures of divine origin with physical defects, Wotan with one eye, etc.'.

Such disfigurements also identify demons like Alberich and Klingsor, with whom Wagner had a special affinity. Verdi, unconcerned with gods or devils, applied the principle to human beings, who interested him if they were paradoxical or peculiar, like Rigoletto or Falstaff, Abigaille or Lady Macbeth. Wagner thought only about the physical consequences of rising above humanity, as a god gains a consort by sacrificing an eye or a sorcerer becomes all-powerful by self-mutilation. He disapproved of facial hair, and plucked his eyebrows when they got out of control; Cosima kept the hairs as souvenirs, admiring the depilated brows that showed 'the complete absence of animality in his nature'. She was wrong about that, but if he had been a better man – less erotically obsessive, less titanically selfish – he might not have been such a superlative artist, and without his duplicity, his manipulativeness and his greed, he would certainly have been a less successful one. Musing about gods and their flaws, he said that genius was inconsistent with 'regular beauty', the outer face of goodness. It was at best a half-truth. As Strepponi frequently remarked, Verdi was a great artist whose only faults were minor – sins that even priests would consider venial, like a tetchy temper. His beard screened a face that looked oddly ordinary, which is the most baffling enigma of all.

Although the busts in Venice remain immovable, we can move back and forth between them. We are obliged to do so, because Verdi and Wagner represent two sides of our nature that are usually not on speaking terms – the virtue of charity or caritas as opposed to the rage of the egotistical will, a need for human connection as opposed to the mind's proud solitude. 'Povero cor di donna!' says Rigoletto after Gilda will not be argued out of her devotion to a worthless man. The heart is poor, pitiable, wayward, yet it makes the girlish Gilda a woman; its impulses define our humanity, and they can neither be denied nor condemned. This is why Verdi's music goes to the aid of his characters, uplifting Elisabeth in *Don Carlos* or Desdemona in *Otello* when unjust accusers strike them down. Lina in *Stiffelio* expects her angry husband to absolve her and demands 'Ministro, confessatemi!' He refuses, so she ministers to herself and to us by singing: for Verdi, opera is the ministry of tears. Wagner has aims that are less altruistic, perhaps more intense. He predicted that the paroxysms of *Tristan und Isolde* would 'be bound to drive people mad', and ruthlessly added 'I cannot imagine it otherwise.' *Lohengrin*, he said, expressed a vertiginous desire to descend from the heights to the depths, or to connect rapture and despair. His harmony vacillates between these upper and lower worlds, whereas Verdian melody both voices and soothes the disquiets of those who, like the trembling soprano in his *Requiem*, inhabit the level ground between Wagner's dizzy peaks and abysmal gulfs. Verdi appeals to humanists, Wagner to mystics and also to misanthropes. Is it impossible for one person to love them both?

Music, the most mysterious and potent of the arts, pervades our daily lives and penetrates our dreams; it serves as an emotional release and a sexual incitement, a social amenity and a spiritual blessing, catering alike to the light and dark sides of our experience. At one time or another, if not simultaneously, we still need the two contradictory, complementary kinds of music that Verdi and Wagner left us.

# ILLUSTRATION CREDITS

Key: a = above; b = below; c = centre; l = left; r = right

Archivio Storico Ricordi, Milan 126, 127a
© Bayreuther Festspiele 2010, photo by
    Enrico Nawrath 281
bpk 287
By kind permission of the Carrara Verdi
    family and the Villa Sant'Agata, Busseto
    119b, 273a, 273b, 274b, 275b, 276
Gregory Dowling 113l, 113r
Collezione Gallini, Milan 116
Conservatorio 'G. Verdi', Milan 118b
© Danita Delimont/Alamy 286a
Galleria Nazionale d'Arte Moderna, Rome 114
Gaumont/TMS/The Kobal Collection 282
Guigoni e Bossi, Milan 285a
Historisches Museum der Stadt Wien 117a
International Museum of Photography at
    George Eastman House, Rochester, NY
    128l
Istituto Nazionale di Studi Verdiani, Parma
    128r

© David Keith Jones/Alamy 285b
Ernst Kreowski and Eduard Fuchs, *Richard
    Wagner in Der Karikatur* (Berlin, 1907)
    123, 275a, 278
Lebrecht Music & Arts 2r, 117b, 122a, 122b,
    274a, 279c, 280
*Verdi e l'Otello* issue of *L'Illustrazione Italiana*
    (1887) 127b
© MARKA/Alamy 286b
© mediacolor's/Alamy 288a
Musée du Louvre, Paris 120a, 277
Museo Teatrale alla Scala, Milan 284
Nationalarchiv der Richard-Wagner-
    Stiftung / Richard-Wagner-
    Gedenkstätte Bayreuth 115, 119a, 120b,
    124a, 124b, 283
New York City Parks & Recreation 288b
Raccolta Bertarelli, Milan 118a
Republic Pictures 121
Richard Wagner Museum, Lucerne 125

# AUTHOR'S ACKNOWLEDGMENTS

At Thames & Hudson I am grateful, as before, to Jamie Camplin, and to Helen Farr, Amanda Vinnicombe, Johanna Neurath, Karin Fremer, Avni Patel and Sam Wythe, as well as to Imogen Graham, who located and rounded up the illustrations. At United Agents, my thanks to Caroline Dawnay. It is a pleasure to acknowledge the help of two friends from earlier days in Oxford: Gregory Dowling photographed the busts in the Venetian garden where the idea of this book first occurred to me; and the manuscript was edited with ferocious exactitude by Richard Mason, whose own love for and knowledge of the subject made our work together a true collaboration.

# INDEX